Praise for

AN INTRODUCTION TO BIBLICAL GREEK

"John Schwandt knows how to teach Greek, and it shows in *An Introduction to Biblical Greek*. His explanations of how Greek works, his choice of examples—including many from the Greek New Testament itself—and his exercises make learning Greek as painless as possible. I have myself taught Greek for many years and am well aware of the challenges students face. Schwandt's introduction is the best there is. I highly recommend it."

Craig A. Evans
John Bisagno Distinguished Professor of Christian Origins, Houston Baptist University

"John Schwandt's *Introduction to New Testament Greek* provides a clear introduction to the language—logically ordered, clearly presented, and with useful exercises. It is an introduction that students can use to study the language on their own and which can also be effectively used in a classroom setting."

Douglas Moo
Kenneth T. Wessner Professor of New Testament, Wheaton College

"Students who master John Schwandt's *An Introduction to Biblical Greek* can expect to plunge immediately into exegesis of the New Testament, the Septuagint, and the Apostolic Fathers. Up-to-date and comprehensive on matters of pronunciation, morphology, and verbal aspect, the book boasts an outstanding advantage over many competitors in its emphasis on students' composing Greek as well as translating it. Added to the usual grammatical exercises and vocabulary lists, moreover, is the often neglected topic of Greek accents. Schwandt has set a new standard of utility and excellence."

Robert H. Gundry
Professor Emeritus and Scholar-in-Residence, Westmont College

"John Schwandt's *Introduction to Biblical Greek* provides an attractive and workable alternative to the growing list of beginning Greek grammars that make minimal demands on students at the cost of reduced comprehension of the language.

"With clear, straightforward explanations it introduces the essential details of Greek word formation, syntactical structure, and vocabulary and then reinforces student learning through translation and recognition assignments tailored to each chapter. The goal is to increase understanding while reducing rote memorization. Schwandt's grammatical and morphological explanations are linguistically competent and well-informed while maintaining the simple, non-technical style needed in an introductory text.

"This well-organized, self-contained book provides grammatical exercises as well as vocabulary lists that reinforce the basics of the language and point students toward careful, confident use of the language in exegesis. It includes Greek-to-English as well as English-to-Greek exercises along with excerpts from the NT itself for translation practice. The grammar also presents a thorough treatment of Greek accenting built into the chapters themselves rather than relegated to an appendix as is common today. I recommend this book enthusiastically!"

Buist Fanning
Senior Professor Emeritus of New Testament Studies, Dallas Theological Seminary

"No two people learn languages in exactly the same way, so there is always a need for new language textbooks. This first-year Koine Greek grammar introduces beginning students to most of the traditional topics and several newer ones, with precision and abundant exercises for translation practice, including many from the New Testament. Creatively but logically structured, it charts a sensible middle course between standard and cutting-edge forms of verbal aspect theory. Abundant charts, diagrams, and appendices provide excellent additional help."

Craig L. Blomberg
Distinguished Professor of New Testament, Denver Seminary

"I last taught an advanced course on the grammar of the Greek New Testament sixty years ago! Dr. John D. Schwandt's splendid *An Introduction to Biblical Greek* triggered my adrenaline to want to teach Greek grammar again. It has everything one wants in a textbook: accuracy, clarity, full of insights that relieve rote memory, rigor of composition, attention-getting, and being approachable. Besides that, it is backed up by the exceptional technical resources of Logos Bible Software. When the student has finished this text, they are ready to join the ranks of competent exegetes of the New Testament. May their tribe increase."

Bruce Waltke
Professor Emeritus of Biblical Studies, Regent College
Distinguished Professor Emeritus of Old Testament, Knox Theological Seminary

AN INTRODUCTION TO BIBLICAL GREEK

AN INTRODUCTION TO BIBLICAL GREEK

A Grammar with Exercises

John D. Schwandt

LEXHAM PRESS

An Introduction to Biblical Greek: A Grammar with Exercises

Lexham Press, 1313 Commercial St., Bellingham, WA 98225
LexhamPress.com

Scripture quotations in Greek are from the NA27 or from H.P.V. Nunn, *The Elements of New Testament Greek* (Cambridge: Cambridge University Press, 1923).

Print ISBN: 9781683591184
Digital ISBN: 9781683591191
Library of Congress Control Number: 2019955257

Lexham Editorial: Derek R. Brown, Abigail Stocker, David Bomar, Danielle Thevenaz, Ronald van der Bergh

Cover Design: Christine Christophersen
Cover Image: Papyrus 37, recto (Matthew 26:19–52; third-fourth century); used with the permission of the Papyrology Collection, University of Michigan Library (inventory number 1570)
Cover Background: Gregor Buir / stock.adobe.com

Contents

Abbreviations

1st	first person
2nd	second person
3rd	third person
acc.	accusative
act.	active
adj.	adjective
adv.	adverb
aor.	aorist
dat.	dative
fem.	feminine
gen.	genitive
impf.	imperfect
impv.	imperative
indic.	indicative
inf.	infinitive
lit.	literally
masc.	masculine
mid.	middle
n.	noun
neut.	neuter
nom.	nominative
NT	New Testament
opt.	optative
pass.	passive
perf.	perfect
pl.	plural
ptc.	participle
sg.	singular
subj.	subjunctive
v.	verb
voc.	vocative

Preface

An Introduction to Biblical Greek is grounded in the basic conviction that learning to read and write in the language of the New Testament is the best way to understand the meaning and intent of the New Testament.

Unfortunately, composition is often viewed as overshooting the target for learning biblical Greek in undergraduate studies and seminary. As a result, Greek composition is absent from the content and structure of many Greek grammars. Whereas most grammars a hundred years ago typically included an equal amount of composition and translation exercises, most grammars today have few, if any, composition exercises. There has also been a trend toward reducing the content of what is considered to be sufficient for a basic understanding of Greek. For example, some grammars ignore the importance of accent marks or expect students to learn only the most common Greek words in the New Testament. Such trends in Greek grammars have resulted in a pedagogical emphasis on rote memorization of forms and vocabulary.

By contrast, *An Introduction to Biblical Greek* explains the rationale, theories, and principles behind the spellings and grammatical structures found in biblical Greek. In my decades of teaching Greek I have encouraged students to master the grammatical fountainheads for the language (especially when it comes to spelling). This approach explores "why" questions when it comes to variations in spellings or parallel grammatical patterns. Readers will learn to parse words and forms (even ones not yet memorized!) and reduce the overall amount of rote memorization of Greek words.

An Introduction to Biblical Greek builds upon three basic morphological (spelling) patterns that provide the basis for the rest of the language (one pattern for noun and adjective cases and two patterns—past and non-past—for all verb forms). In terms of grammar and translation, it shows how every grammatical construction (apart from the core subject, verb, and object components of a sentence) has only two possible functions—adjectival or adverbial. This approach teaches the grammatical options possible within the original language, while also providing a quick and easy framework for considering grammatical options in translations.

As the foundation for *An Introduction to Biblical Greek*, I have used H. P. V. Nunn's well-regarded grammar *The Elements of New Testament Greek* (1913). The structure of the text, vocabulary, and exercises remain essentially the same as Nunn's original text, but I have complemented Nunn's grammatical explanations by adding my own material. As a result, I consider the present work a collaborative effort between scholars, though separated by many decades. I share Nunn's pedagogical emphasis on the logic and relationships among the elements of the Greek language. While Nunn's text was an abbreviated presentation of the foundational principles for beginning to learn Greek with minimal explanations, it presents a salutary diachronic approach with biblical Greek composition as a primary learning objective.

As a way of incorporating my teaching experience into *An Introduction to Biblical Greek*, I have expanded and modernized the approach to communicating the foundational principles of Greek as well as the relationship between English and Greek grammar. A person who wants to learn biblical Greek today has a very different understanding of English and grammar than Nunn's intended audience a hundred years ago. *An Introduction to Biblical Greek* will help the contemporary student not only learn Greek but come to a better understanding of how English grammar functions. Finally, Logos Mobile Education offers a video course as a companion to this grammar providing additional explanations and training.

In all this, my hope is that *An Introduction to Biblical Greek* will serve as an approachable and helpful introduction to the language of the New Testament for students of all kinds, but especially those who do not have access to a traditional class setting.

Dr. John D. Schwandt
President, Redemption Seminary

LESSON 1

The Alphabet

ALPHABET HISTORY

The Greek alphabet consists of twenty-four letters, many of them identical with the corresponding letters of the Latin alphabet, which we now see in the English alphabet. Both the Greek and Latin alphabets—along with the Hebrew alphabet—were derived from the Phoenician alphabet.

Uncial Script

The letters provided in the second column of the chart below are now used only as capital letters in printed Greek books, but originally these letters, called "uncial letters," were the only forms used in Greek writing. Manuscripts written exclusively with these letters, without any spaces between words, are called uncial manuscripts. All of the earliest manuscripts of the New Testament are uncials.

Minuscule Script

Around the ninth century AD another style of writing came into general use. This style used "cursive" or "running" letters, which resembled uncial letters but could be written without raising the pen from the paper. Since most of the cursive letters do not fill the entire height of a line, we refer to them as "minuscules."

This type of writing has remained in use in both manuscripts and printed books, with certain modifications. At this stage, you only need to be generally familiar with the capital (uncial) letters. The focus of this lesson is learning the shapes and sounds for the cursive (minuscule) letters. It is important to learn the order of the alphabet so you can find words in dictionaries and reference materials.

TRANSLITERATION

The transliteration column shows the typical conversion for each Greek letter into English letters—helpful information if you are seeking the Greek source of an English word. Note that two Greek letters are transliterated with the English letter *e* and two with the English letter *o*. The macron (¯) and breve (˘) marks written over these letters distinguish between the Greek letters corresponding to each of these English letters.

PRONUNCIATION SYSTEMS

English transliterations do not necessarily reflect the original Greek pronunciation. For example, η is transliterated as ē but pronounced as the "a" in "late." When reading a transliterated word in English, some people prefer to follow English pronunciation conventions; others prefer to pronounce the word as it would have sounded in Greek, according to the original Greek letters. Take care that your use of transliterations doesn't produce a mixed pronunciation system.

Over the centuries, plenty of contentious debates proposed different systems for Greek pronunciation. Today, most readers follow one of three general strategies: (1) historically reconstructed models (Koine system), (2) anglicized academic models (Erasmian system), and (3) the Modern Greek sound (Byzantine system). Variations within each of the systems makes this issue even more confusing. The pronunciation chart on the facing page reflects the way Greek generally sounded in the first century (Koine system). If you are using Logos Bible Software, you can hear any lemma[1] pronounced according to your preferred pronunciation model and listen to the differences between the systems.

1 A "lemma" refers to the first form of a word provided in a dictionary or lexicon.

Letter Name	Uncial Letter	Minuscule Letter	English Transliteration	Koine Pronunciation The Erasmian alternative is given where applicable.
Alpha	Α	α	a	Like the *a* in "father."
Bēta	Β	β	b	Like English *v*. Erasmian: Like English *b*.
Gamma	Γ	γ	g	Softer than English *g*, similar to a gargling sound. If pronounced with a front vowel sound, it is like English *y* in "yet."[1] Erasmian: Like *g* in "game."
Delta	Δ	δ	d	Like *th* in "brother." Erasmian: Like English *d*.
Epsilon	Ε	ε	ĕ	Like *e* in "met."
Zēta	Ζ	ζ	z	Like English z. Erasmian: Like *dz* in "kudzu."
Ēta	Η	η	ē	Like *ey* in "they."
Thēta	Θ	ϑ	th	Like *th* in "thin."
Iōta	Ι	ι	i	Like *ee* in "seen."[2] Erasmian: Like *ee* in "seen" or *i* in "image."
Kappa	Κ	κ	k	Like English *k*.
Lambda	Λ	λ	l	Like English *l*.
Mu	Μ	μ	m	Like English *m*.
Nu	Ν	ν	n	Like English *n*.
Xi	Ξ	ξ	x	Like *x* in "fox."
Omicron	Ο	ο	ŏ	Like *oa* in "oar." Erasmian: Like *o* in "office."
Pi	Π	π	p	Like English *p*.
Rhō	Ρ	ρ	r	Like European *r* (tongue flips against the top of the mouth).
Sigma	Σ	σ, ς	s	Like English *s*.
Tau	Τ	τ	t	Like English *t*.
Upsilon	Υ	υ	y	Like French *u* in "du."
Phi	Φ	φ	ph	Like English *ph*.
Chi	Χ	χ	ch	Like *ch* in Scotch "loch." If pronounced with a front vowel sound, it is like English *h*, but with the tongue lifted near the roof of the mouth.
Psi	Ψ	ψ	ps	Like *ps* in "lips."
Ōmega	Ω	ω	ō	Like *oa* in "oar."

1 "Front vowel sound" refers to the position of the tongue relative to the back or front of the mouth when the vowel is pronounced.

2 If a word begins with iōta followed by another vowel it is pronounced like *y*.

NOTES ON THE ALPHABET

The pronunciation example for the Greek υ is like the *u* in the French, "du," because we have no exact equivalent sound in English. Also note that when a Greek word is transliterated into English, a single υ always becomes "y" (rather than "u"); for example, "hydropathic" (from the Greek word for water, ὕδωρ) and "hypocrite" (from ὑποκριτής) both derive from Greek words with a single υ. However, when υ is part of a digraph—always as the second letter—such as ευ or ου, it is transliterated as "u" within the corresponding English digraph (e.g., "eu," "ou").

Two consonants adjust their sounds depending on what vowel sound accompanies them. Front vowel sounds (e.g., the sounds produced by ε, η, ι, υ) change the sounds of γ and χ because, as words are spoken rapidly, the tongue remains forward in the mouth of the speaker. So χ, when it is pronounced with back vowel sounds, will normally sound very similar to a throaty English *h*, with the tongue lying low and back in the mouth. When the tongue is forward to produce front vowel sounds, the tongue remains forward and lifted higher with the χ, producing an *h* sound, loosely similar to the sound of a cat hissing. The same tendency applies to γ: when pronounced with a back vowel (as in the name of the letter, γάμμα) it has a throaty sound somewhere between the English hard *g* and *y*. When it is pronounced with front vowel sounds, the tongue remains forward, and it simply sounds like English *y*. It is easier to remember the three basic front vowel sounds (*ĕ*, *ē*, French *u*) rather than the longer list of letters (and letter combinations) that produce these sounds that change the way we pronounce γ and χ.

Notice that two forms are given for the Greek letter sigma: when the letter occurs at the beginning or in the middle of a word, σ is used. When it occurs as the final letter of a word, ς is used.

PRONUNCIATION OF DIGRAPHS AND DIPHTHONGS

Digraphs and diphthongs are commonly confused. "Digraph" comes from the Greek δυ- ("two") and γραφ- ("write"). It refers to written letters that are paired to represent a particular sound. Examples of English digraphs include *ai, ea, ow, oo, ou*. The term "diphthong" comes from δυ- ("two") and φθογγ- ("sound"). It refers to vowel sounds that involve a glide or movement of the tongue that technically blends two sounds together. English diphthongs can be represented by a single character or a digraph. For example, *i* in "bite" and *a* in "late" are technically diphthongs (the tongue moves during the pronunciation). So are *ow* and *oy*. However, *ou* is a not a diphthong, though it is a digraph. Greek is not as complex as English; by the time of the New Testament, all diphthongs had reduced to simple sounds.

Regarding spelling, all vocalic digraphs—a digraph composed of two vowels—involve a semivowel (ι or υ) as the second letter. When υ follows α or ε, it is pronounced as a consonant (like English *v* if followed by a voiced letter; otherwise, like English *f*). Voiced letters include all vowels and the following consonants; β, δ, γ, λ, μ, ν, ρ.

	Koine Pronunciation	Erasmian Pronunciation
	Digraphs that use iōta	
αι	pronounced \e\	pronounced \ī\
ει	pronounced \ē\	pronounced \ā\
οι	pronounced like upsilon: \ü\	pronounced \ȯi\, as in "coin"
υι	pronounced \wē\ or \ē\ with a little bit of an \ü\ sound at the front of it	pronounced as \wē\
	Digraphs that use upsilon	
αυ	pronounced \äv\	pronounced \au̇\
ευ	pronounced \ev\	pronounced \eu̇\
ου	pronounced \ū\	pronounced \ū\

CLASSIFICATION OF CONSONANTS

While the pronunciation of Greek letters is fairly straightforward, spelling often proves challenging. Since Greek is a phonetic language, if the sound of a particular word changes, so does its spelling (by contrast, English has multiple ways that the letter "a" can be pronounced, but there is only one sound for α in Greek).

Consonant Stops

Consonants are divided into three types:

1. "Stops" are letters that are formed by the tongue shaping the air as it passes over the center of the tongue, often with a barrier or stop at the beginning of the sound.

Stops include β, π, φ, δ, τ, ϑ, γ, κ, χ; they are subdivided according to the part of the mouth used to shape the sounds. These three groups are sometimes referred to as the "square of stops":

"Labials," or letters produced by the lips (Latin *labia*): β, π, φ
"Dentals," or letters produced by the teeth (Latin *dens*): δ, τ, ϑ
"Gutturals," or letters produced in the throat (Latin *guttur*): γ, κ, χ

Sibilant Double Letters

2. "Double letters" are letters that combine the sounds of two consonants. Greek has three double letters: ψ, ζ, ξ. Each stop group has one double letter; these double letters consist of the sound of a stop and a sibilant.

SQUARE OF STOPS

		Location of Articulation		
		Labial	Dental	Guttural
Type of Stop	Voiced[1] Fricative	β	δ	γ
	Unvoiced[2] Stop	π	τ	κ
	Unvoiced Fricative[3]	φ	ϑ	χ
	Sibilant Double Letters	ψ	ζ	ξ

Non-Stops

3. The remaining letters, "non-stops," have three types:

"Liquids": λ, ρ
"Nasals": μ, ν (some grammars group nasals with liquids)
"Sibilant": σ

1 Voiced: The vocal cords are used during pronunciation.

2 Unvoiced: The sound of the letter is produced through the passage of air or movement of the mouth. The vocal cords are not involved in forming the sound.

3 Fricative: A sound that involves the friction of air passing through the mouth.

PRONUNCIATION OF CONSONANT BLENDS

The careful student may notice that the square of stops should have an additional row to provide a comprehensive set of sounds that correlates to the sounds in the English alphabet. Greek has both unvoiced stops and fricatives but has fewer voiced letters. There are no voiced stops that would correlate to English *b, d, g*. This does not mean that these sounds do not occur in Greek—only that there are not individual letters that correspond to these sounds. These sounds occur when a nasal precedes an unvoiced stop. The voiced sound of the nasal bleeds into the following stop and creates a blended voiced stop sound; it is a consequence of vocalizing these adjacent sounds quickly. This phonic phenomenon occurs within such words as πάντα (\'pän-dä\) or between words rapidly pronounced together (e.g., τὸν κύριον—\ˌton-'gü-rē-ōn\). The three consonant blends that produce voiced stops are the following: μπ (*mb*), ντ (*nd*), νκ (*ng*).

The letter γ sounds like English *n* within words like "honk" and "song" before all guttural letters (γ, κ, χ, ξ):

ἐγγίζω	ἄγκυρα	σύγχυσις	σάλπιγξ
\eŋ-'gē-zō\	\'äŋ-kü-rä\	\'süŋ-çü-sēs\	\'säl-pēŋx\

ENTIRE CONSONANT SUMMARY

				Location of Articulation			
				Labial	Dental	Guttural	Gutteral Blends
Type of Stop	Voiced Fricative			β	δ	γ	γγ
	Unvoiced Stop			π	τ	κ	γκ
	Unvoiced Fricative			φ	ϑ	χ	γχ
	Sibilant	σ/ς	Sibilant Double Letters	ψ	ζ	ξ	γξ
	Nasals	μ, ν	Nasal Blends	μπ	ντ	νκ	
	Liquids	λ, ρ					

EXERCISES

Memorization Exercises

1.1 Alphabet memorization: Practice writing out the lowercase Greek alphabet many times until you can produce it easily from memory. Make sure you say each letter's name and sound as you write it.

Transliteration Exercises

1.2 Become familiar with transliteration: Write out the Greek alphabet with the English transliteration for each letter.

Grammar Exercises

1.3(α) Learn to recognize and pronounce digraphs: Practice the sounds of the vowel digraphs as much as the alphabet. Digraphs are very common in Greek and will cause confusion unless you know them as well as the individual letters. Write out the vowel digraphs that would produce the sounds in the following English words.

1. food
2. set
3. left
4. queen
5. treat
6. keen
7. avocado (first syllable sound)
8. feud
9. soup
10. ewe
11. kiwi (second syllable sound)
12. soft
13. ever (first syllable sound)
14. tube
15. mauve

1.3(β) Learn how to pronounce γ and χ: Make two lists of the following letter groups: one with back vowels (throaty sounds of γ and χ) and the other with forward sounds. Practice pronouncing the lists.

1. γε
2. χα
3. γου
4. χαι
5. γω
6. χε
7. γυ
8. χι
9. γα
10. γευ
11. χου
12. χω
13. γη
14. γι
15. χοι

1.3(γ) Be able to distinguish δ and ϑ. Beginners often confuse the sounds of these two dentals because English represents both sounds with "th." Choose between δ or ϑ. Which one correlates to the sound of *th* in the following English words?

1. brother
2. theater
3. three
4. there
5. think
6. this
7. tithe
8. their
9. whether
10. thistle
11. thought
12. though
13. together
14. with
15. length

Reading Exercise

1.4 Practice sounding out and reading sentences from Matthew 1:1–16. You can intuit the word that means "beget" in this genealogy—so you are already reading Greek!

1 Βίβλος γενέσεως Ἰησοῦ Χριστοῦ υἱοῦ Δαυὶδ υἱοῦ Ἀβραάμ.

2 Ἀβραὰμ ἐγέννησεν τὸν Ἰσαάκ, Ἰσαὰκ δὲ ἐγέννησεν
τὸν Ἰακώβ, Ἰακὼβ δὲ ἐγέννησεν τὸν Ἰούδαν καὶ τοὺς
ἀδελφοὺς αὐτοῦ, 3 Ἰούδας δὲ ἐγέννησεν τὸν Φαρὲς καὶ
τὸν Ζάρα ἐκ τῆς Θαμάρ, Φαρὲς δὲ ἐγέννησεν τὸν Ἑσρώμ,
Ἑσρὼμ δὲ ἐγέννησεν τὸν Ἀράμ, 4 Ἀρὰμ δὲ ἐγέννησεν
τὸν Ἀμιναδάβ, Ἀμιναδὰβ δὲ ἐγέννησεν τὸν Ναασσών,
Ναασσὼν δὲ ἐγέννησεν τὸν Σαλμών, 5 Σαλμὼν δὲ
ἐγέννησεν τὸν Βόες ἐκ τῆς Ῥαχάβ, Βόες δὲ ἐγέννησεν
τὸν Ἰωβὴδ ἐκ τῆς Ῥούϑ, Ἰωβὴδ δὲ ἐγέννησεν τὸν Ἰεσσαί,
6 Ἰεσσαὶ δὲ ἐγέννησεν τὸν Δαυὶδ τὸν βασιλέα.

Δαυὶδ δὲ ἐγέννησεν τὸν Σολομῶνα ἐκ τῆς τοῦ Οὐρίου,
7 Σολομὼν δὲ ἐγέννησεν τὸν Ῥοβοάμ, Ῥοβοὰμ δὲ
ἐγέννησεν τὸν Ἀβιά, Ἀβιὰ δὲ ἐγέννησεν τὸν Ἀσάφ,

8 Ἀσὰφ δὲ ἐγέννησεν τὸν Ἰωσαφάτ, Ἰωσαφὰτ δὲ
ἐγέννησεν τὸν Ἰωράμ, Ἰωρὰμ δὲ ἐγέννησεν τὸν Ὀζίαν,
9 Ὀζίας δὲ ἐγέννησεν τὸν Ἰωαθάμ, Ἰωαθὰμ δὲ
ἐγέννησεν τὸν Ἀχάζ, Ἀχὰζ δὲ ἐγέννησεν τὸν Ἑζεκίαν,
10 Ἑζεκίας δὲ ἐγέννησεν τὸν Μανασσῆ, Μανασσῆς δὲ
ἐγέννησεν τὸν Ἀμώς, Ἀμὼς δὲ ἐγέννησεν τὸν Ἰωσίαν,
11 Ἰωσίας δὲ ἐγέννησεν τὸν Ἰεχονίαν καὶ τοὺς ἀδελφοὺς
αὐτοῦ ἐπὶ τῆς μετοικεσίας Βαβυλῶνος.

12 Μετὰ δὲ τὴν μετοικεσίαν Βαβυλῶνος Ἰεχονίας
ἐγέννησεν τὸν Σαλαθιήλ, Σαλαθιὴλ δὲ ἐγέννησεν
τὸν Ζοροβαβέλ, 13 Ζοροβαβὲλ δὲ ἐγέννησεν τὸν Ἀβιούδ,
Ἀβιοὺδ δὲ ἐγέννησεν τὸν Ἐλιακίμ, Ἐλιακὶμ δὲ ἐγέννησεν
τὸν Ἀζώρ, 14 Ἀζὼρ δὲ ἐγέννησεν τὸν Σαδώκ, Σαδὼκ δὲ
ἐγέννησεν τὸν Ἀχίμ, Ἀχὶμ δὲ ἐγέννησεν τὸν Ἐλιούδ,
15 Ἐλιοὺδ δὲ ἐγέννησεν τὸν Ἐλεάζαρ, Ἐλεάζαρ δὲ
ἐγέννησεν τὸν Ματθάν, Ματθὰν δὲ ἐγέννησεν τὸν
Ἰακώβ, 16 Ἰακὼβ δὲ ἐγέννησεν τὸν Ἰωσὴφ τὸν ἄνδρα
Μαρίας, ἐξ ἧς ἐγεννήθη Ἰησοῦς ὁ λεγόμενος Χριστός.

LESSON 2

Accent Marks, Additional Marks, and the Square of Stops

ACCENT MARKS

Aristophanes of Byzantium invented accent marks around 200 BC to teach foreigners how to correctly pronounce Greek. Ancient manuscripts did not include accent marks; in earlier ancient Greek, such marks denoted changes in pitch. By the New Testament period, a simple stress system in common speech had replaced the pitch system. Thus, our Greek New Testaments have multiple marks that perform the single function of marking stress.

Acute
Grave
Circumflex

The three accent marks in Greek are the acute (´), the grave (`), and the circumflex (˜). All three simply indicate which syllable should be stressed. Eventually, you will learn how modifications to the accenting of some words can inform the meaning. But at this point, it is only necessary to learn which syllable is stressed. The type of accent doesn't change the sound of particular vowels.

Stressing the right syllable is important. For example, read the following sentences aloud, stressing the syllables underlined. The meaning can be confusing if the words are stressed on the wrong syllables.

> Incorrect: Present the orange dessert to the one who pronounces syllables properly.

> Correct: Present the orange dessert to the one who pronounces syllables properly.

Incorrect: I object to and rebel against homogeneous methods of accenting words.

Correct: I object to and rebel against homogeneous methods of accenting words.

As these examples show, learning how to properly accent words is an important part of learning any language. The sounds and rhythms of language help us understand—and even provide windows into—what the author is saying. Sometimes we unintentionally use similar-sounding words when thinking about or even avoiding particular words. It is impossible to appreciate and understand the meanings wrapped within a language's poetic structures if you force a foreign system of accenting onto a language. Also, knowing which syllable is stressed can help you quickly identify a number of grammatical forms, such as some aorist participles (which can otherwise be tricky for beginning students).

Thankfully, stressing the right syllables in Greek is very easy. Nearly every word has a mark that shows which syllable should be stressed—and the system remains in use in our Greek New Testaments to this day. (Refer to Appendix 3 for a full treatment on how Greek accents function.)

ADDITIONAL MARKS

Punctuation

Greek punctuation in current printed texts is very similar to English: Greek uses periods, commas, and apostrophes (for elision). The most significant differences: Greek uses a mark similar to a semicolon (;) for a question mark, and the upper dot of a colon (˙) for a semicolon. Greek often uses the word ὅτι to mark both indirect and direct discourse. Quotation marks are not used.

Breathing Marks

You may notice that there is no Greek letter that corresponds to the English letter "h." However, in the high classical Greek period, prior to the New Testament, many words beginning with a vowel actually were pronounced with an initial *h* sound. To indicate this pronunciation pattern, the Greeks developed "breathing marks."

Since the Attic region used the Greek uncial H to represent a vowel, that letter could not be used to indicate the *h* sound. Instead, they marked the presence or absence of the *h* sound by modifying that letter visually to distinguish it from the letter H. Eventually, the symbol morphed into two similar symbols resembling a forward- and backward-facing apostrophe. The normal, forward-facing apostrophe—a "smooth breathing mark"—appears at the beginning of words without an initial *h* sound. The backward-facing apostrophe is called a "rough breathing mark" and designated an *h* sound at the beginning of the word. For example, ὁ was pronounced *hō*\\, and ἁ was pronounced *hä*\\, but ἀ was simply pronounced *ä*\\.

The pronunciation of rough breathing marks fell out of use prior to the life of Christ, but the rough and smooth breathing marks remained part of proper Greek spelling. The silent *h* in English—in words such as "hour," which derives from the Greek ὥρα (with its version of silent *h*)—is a similar convention. So, although you must learn breathing marks as part of spelling, neither breathing mark affects pronunciation.

A few general rules:

- Every word starting with a vowel must have a breathing mark.
- An initial upsilon (υ) always has a rough breathing mark.
- If a word begins with a digraph, the breathing mark is placed over the second vowel—for example, οὗτος, not *ὁῦτος.[1]
- An initial rhō (ρ) generally has a rough breathing mark—for example, ῥητορική ("rhetoric").

Iota Subscript

When ι is used to form a digraph with a long vowel, a small mark under the long vowel replaces the normal form for ι (i.e., ᾳ, ῃ, ῳ). This "iota subscript" is a relic of an ancient diphthong and often occurs at the end of words. It is not pronounced, but, like the breathing marks, it is part of proper written spelling.

1 For this lesson, an asterisk (*) in front of a word means it is a hypothetical form that does not occur in correct Greek.

SQUARE OF STOPS

Learning how to spell in Greek can be challenging, but the difficulty of the task is reduced by learning how the different types of letters react when placed next to another type of letter. Recall the three types of stops examined in Lesson 1—three groups sometimes described as the "square of stops." Memorizing the square of stops will help you employ the general spelling rules presented in this book.

		Location of Articulation		
		Labial	Dental	Guttural
Type of Stop	Voiced Fricative	β	δ	γ
	Unvoiced Stop	π	τ	κ
	Unvoiced Fricative	φ	ϑ	χ

Spelling rule: If two stops are placed next to each other, the first will usually change to conform to the type of the second. For example, the γ in λέγω changes to the corresponding letter type when followed by other stops (e.g., γ changes to κ in λέλεκται to correspond to the stop type of τ, and γ changes to χ in ἐλέχϑη to match the stop type of ϑ). Likewise, one would expect combinations such as ὀκτώ or ὀγδόη, but not *ὀγτώ.

The consonant blends that produce voiced stops (μπ, ντ, νκ) do not cause spelling changes and so do not have to be memorized as part of the square of stops.

ELISION

In Greek, two vowel sounds rarely appear adjacent to each other without a consonant or a glide between them. Thus, prepositions that end with a vowel will typically drop their final vowel if the following word begins with a vowel. The dropped letter—or "elision"—is marked with an apostrophe (compare, for example, κατὰ γραφάς and κατ' ἄνϑρωπον).

Following this pattern, if a word begins with a rough breathing mark (indicating an original unvoiced aspirated *h* sound), the preceding stop changes to its unvoiced fricative (or aspirate) form. Often, this happens when elision exposes a final consonant in a preposition. For example, κατά changes when followed by a vowel with a rough breathing mark (καθ᾽ ὁδόν or καθ᾽ ἡμέρα).

The list below shows common prepositions with their elided and aspirated forms. Notice that some prepositions don't change.

Preposition	Before Smooth Breathing	Before Rough Breathing
ἀπό	ἀπ᾽	ἀφ᾽
διά	δι᾽	δι᾽
κατά	κατ᾽	καθ᾽
μετά	μετ᾽	μεθ᾽
ὑπό	ὑπ᾽	ὑφ᾽
παρά	παρ᾽	παρ᾽
ἐπί	ἐπ᾽	ἐφ᾽

EXERCISES

Grammar Exercises

2.1(α) Accent mark exercises: Practice pronouncing the following words, which have English derivatives. Note which ones are stressed on a different syllable than you would expect in English.

1. ἀδελφός
2. βιβλίον
3. γένεσις
4. δαυίδ
5. ἔξοδος
6. ζηλωτής
7. ἥλιος
8. θεός
9. Ἰησοῦς
10. προφήτης

2.1(β) Elision exercises: Correct the preposition (if necessary) based on the word that follows it.

1. ἀπὸ ἔθνους
2. ἐπὶ αὐτοῖς
3. ὑπὸ διαβόλου
4. κατὰ κράτος
5. ἀπὸ τιμῆς
6. κατὰ ἰδίαν
7. διὰ αὐτὴν
8. ὑπὸ αὐτοῦ
9. κατὰ ἑκάστην ἡμέραν
10. διὰ χρόνον
11. παρὰ ἐλπίδα
12. μετὰ ὑμῶν
13. ἐπὶ λόγῳ
14. κατὰ ἐπιταγὴν
15. ἀπὸ ὑμῶν
16. κατὰ δύναμιν
17. ἀπὸ ἡμέρας
18. παρὰ ἡμῖν
19. ὑπὸ ὑμῶν
20. κατὰ ἡμέραν

2.1(γ) Square of stops exercises: For each pair of stops, change the first letter to match the type of stop of the second letter (for example, βκ changes to πκ).

1. φτ
2. γθ
3. κβ
4. θκ
5. χδ
6. βτ
7. γφ
8. κθ
9. χτ
10. τθ
11. φδ
12. δφ
13. γτ
14. πθ
15. χπ

Transliteration Exercise

2.2 Greek transliteration exercise: Write out the paragraph below in Greek letters, inserting breathing marks where necessary. For the purposes of this exercise:

- The English letter "h" at the beginning of a word denotes rough breathing.
- The vowels "e" and "o" are marked with a macron when they are long and unmarked when they are short. Take care to use the proper Greek letter for each.
- The letter "i" in parentheses denotes that ι subscript is to be written under the preceding vowel.
- Use minuscule letters, and do not concern yourself with accenting.

… en archē(i) ēn ho logos, kai ho logos ēn pros ton theon, kai theos ēn ho logos. houtos ēn en archē(i) pros ton theon. panta di autou egeneto. kai chōris autou egeneto oude hen. ho gegonen en autō(i) zōē ēn, kai hē zōē ēn to phōs tōn anthrōpōn. kai to phōs en tē(i) skotia(i) phainei, kai hē skotia auto ou katelaben. egeneto anthrōpos, apestalmenos para theou, onoma autō(i) iōanēs. houtos ēlthen eis martyrian hina martyrēsē(i) peri tou phōtos, hina pantes pisteusōsin di autou. ouk ēn ekeinos to phōs, all hina martyrēsē(i) peri tou phōtos. ēn to phōs to alēthinon, ho phōtizei panta anthrōpon, erchomenon eis ton kosmon.

LESSON 3

Present Active Indicative

The present active indicative of the verb λύω ("I release") is as follows:

Person	Greek Form	Elements	Translation
1 sg.	λύω	λύ-ω	I release, or I am releasing
2 sg.	λύεις	λύ-εις	you release, or you are releasing
3 sg.	λύει	λύ-ει	he, she, or it releases, or is releasing
1 pl.	λύομεν	λύ-ο-μεν	we release, or we are releasing
2 pl.	λύετε	λύ-ε-τε	you all release, or you all are releasing
3 pl.	λύουσι(ν)	λύ-ουσι(ν)	they release, or they are releasing

Note: The ν at the end of the third person plural (moveable ν) is generally used when the following word begins with a vowel.

Each of the Greek words given in the table above may be divided into three parts:

1. A *root*,[1] which denotes the meaning of the verb (i.e., λυ-, "release").

1 To reduce confusion over the different types of stems referenced in linguistics, this grammar uses the term "root" in a broad sense. According to the technical definition of "root," one would not see or refer to a root in actual language, since as soon as any mark is added to identify it as a part of speech, it is called a "stem" (i.e., verbal stem). Even if there is no spelling change, the taxonomy for this part of a word changes to "root-stem." Thus the technical definition of "root" bears some analogy to a Platonic form (holding essential meaning per se but never existing in practice). To help the student focus on the three distinct units of a verb and how they interact with one another in terms of spelling and meaning, this text uses the term "root" (or verbal root) instead of verbal stem or root-stem to distinguish the core part of the word from tense stem infixes. The modified verbal root used in present tenses is referred to as the present root spelling or form (rather than present stem). The author would rather equivocate with a term that won't be experienced in actual language than confuse the student with all sorts of references to "stem" that constantly occur.

2. A *stem* (seen clearly in some of the plural forms: -ο- and -ε-). In this paradigm, the stem contracts with personal endings. Stems often convey aspect (which you will learn about later).

3. An *ending* (such as -ς, -μεν, or -τε that changes with every person). In the present active tense, the stems and endings are contracted together. While it may seem trivial to distinguish stems and endings at this point, the distinction will be important as you learn more tenses. Greek only has two sets of verb endings: one for non-past tenses ("primary" endings) and one for past tenses ("secondary" endings). Since the endings remain consistent while the stems change, you will be able to understand and spell tenses more intuitively if you already know the difference between these stems and endings. At this point, you may memorize the stem-ending forms as units (-ω, -εις, -ει, -ομεν, -ετε, -ουσι).

The table of Greek and English verbs above illustrates a key difference between Greek and English—namely, that one word in Greek may require two or three words in English to express the same idea. For example, in English, the only present tense form that retains its personal ending is the third person singular (e.g., "runs") compared to forms for other persons (e.g., "run"). The English translations also have a personal pronoun (e.g., "I," "you," "they") before the verb indicating the person and number of the subject of the verb. By contrast, a Greek verb's ending indicates the person and number of the subject of the verb; personal pronouns are unnecessary unless special emphasis or disambiguation is required. English also sometimes employs auxiliary (or helping) verbs to form tenses (in this case, the present tense of the verb "to be"; e.g., "I *am* releasing"), while Greek uses a single word.

Another key difference: English has more tenses than Greek does, so one Greek tense often does the work of multiple English tenses. In the table, two English equivalents are given for each Greek form in the present tense. The first form given in English above is called the "present simple"; the second is called the "present continuous." The Greek present tense corresponds more closely in meaning to the English present continuous than to the present simple.

Another important difference between English and Greek is that English doesn't typically distinguish between second person singular and second person plural, but Greek does. In this text, we will use "you" for the second person singular, which should be translated as the singular in Greek, and "you all" for the second person plural, which should be translated as the plural in Greek.

EXERCISES

Memorization Exercises

3.1 Learn Vocabulary List 1: The words given in this and the following vocabulary lists are all words that occur frequently in the New Testament. Make a habit of mastering the words in the vocabularies as you go along—it will save you much effort later. The words given in parentheses after the English translations of the words are modern English words derived from the Greek words. They are intended as aids for memorization and may not necessarily match the meaning of the Greek word.

Translation Exercises

3.2 Translate the words below.

1. λέγει
2. λέγομεν
3. λέγουσι
4. λέγετε
5. λέγεις
6. εὑρίσκομεν
7. γράφει
8. βάλλετε
9. ἀποθνῄσκει
10. βλέπεις
11. ἐγείρουσι
12. κρίνετε
13. βάλλομεν
14. ἐσθίω
15. ἀποστέλλουσι
16. ἀκούουσι
17. λαμβάνετε
18. σῴζομεν
19. μένει
20. βάλλεις

Composition Exercises

3.3 Translate the following sentences into Greek.

1. we release
2. they release
3. you release
4. you all release
5. he releases
6. they are releasing
7. she is releasing
8. you release
9. they are dying
10. he dies
11. I throw
12. she rouses
13. we judge
14. you are remaining
15. I am throwing
16. you all judge
17. he sends
18. you are writing

19. you are eating
20. he finds
21. we are taking
22. they look
23. she hears
24. they throw
25. you all are judging

Scripture Translation Exercises

3.4 Translate the following verses from Scripture (particularly the underlined words, which should be familiar to you after completing this lesson). Unfamiliar words have been glossed in parentheses.

1. πῶς (how) ἀκούομεν; (Acts 2:8)
2. λέγουσιν αὐτῷ (to him)· ἰδοὺ (behold) ἡ μήτηρ σου (your mother) καὶ οἱ ἀδελφοί σου (and your brothers) ἔξω (outside) ζητοῦσίν (ζητῶ = I seek) σε (you) (Mark 3:32)
3. βλέπετε (as a command) οὖν πῶς (how then) ἀκούετε (Luke 8:18)
4. γράφω ὑμῖν (to you), τεκνία (children) (1 John 2:12)
5. ὁ λόγος (the word) τοῦ θεοῦ (of God) ἐν ὑμῖν (in you) μένει (1 John 2:14)
6. ἀγάπη (love) ἔξω (out) βάλλει τὸν φόβον (fear) (1 John 4:18)

LESSON 4

Vowel Length, Accentuation, and ε-Contract Verbs

VOWEL LENGTH

Vowel length refers to the duration of time a vowel was pronounced in ancient Greek. Don't confuse duration of time with a different type or quality of sound; for example, ο and ω always sounded exactly the same, but the "micro o" was pronounced more quickly than the "mega o." By the time of the writing of the New Testament, this distinction was lost, but the effects of a long and short vowel system remain to this day in Greek. Thus, it is important to learn the system. Even though it will not affect pronunciation, vowel length will have an effect on spelling and accenting.

Greek has three basic vowel types: A-type, E-type, and O-type. Each vowel type has a short form, a long form, and a digraph form. The digraphs αι and οι function independently from this system; they do not function as a lengthening or replacement for α or ο. Digraphs are always long except for αι and οι, which break this rule when they are the final letters in a word.

Two letters, υ and ι, are not technically vowels. They are semivowels (like *y* in English) and can be considered either long or short.

Short Version	Long Version	Digraph (Long) Version
α	α or η	none
ε	η	ει
ο	ω	ου

VOWEL CONTRACTION

When a stem or personal ending that begins with a vowel is added to a root that ends in a vowel, the vowels combine to form a digraph or a single long vowel. This is called "contraction."

One instance of contraction occurs when stems and personal endings are added to the many Greek verbs that have a root ending in ε:

- ε + ε contracts and yields the epsilon's digraph form, ει.
- ε + ο contracts and yields the omicron's digraph form, ου.
- When ε precedes a long vowel or a digraph, it is absorbed by the long vowel or digraph and is not represented by any visible change. (The long vowel can't lengthen any further.)

For example, the present tense of the verb φιλέω ("I love") is conjugated as follows:

Person	Contracted Form	Uncontracted[1]	Translation
1 sg.	φιλῶ	φιλέω	I love, or I am loving
2 sg.	φιλεῖς	φιλέεις	you love, or you are loving
3 sg.	φιλεῖ	φιλέει	he, she, or it loves, or is loving
1 pl.	φιλοῦμεν	φιλέομεν	we love, or we are loving
2 pl.	φιλεῖτε	φιλέετε	you all love, or you all are loving
3 pl.	φιλοῦσι	φιλέουσι	they love, or they are loving

ACCENTUATION OF VERBS

The accentuation of verbs is simple: the accent for verbs operates according to a recessive principle. Verbs are accented as close to the beginning of the word as possible. The length of the last syllable (the ultima) determines how far forward an accent can be placed on a word. If the last syllable of a verb is long (i.e., if it contains a long vowel or a digraph, with the exception of αι or οι),[2] the accent falls on the second-to-last syllable (the penult). If the last syllable of a verb is short (i.e., if it contains a short vowel), the accent falls on the

1 Uncontracted forms are not used in biblical Greek and are provided here only to explain the contractions.

2 For purposes of accentuation, when αι and οι are the final letters in a word they are considered short.

third-to-last syllable (the antepenult). This is the most forward position for an accent on any word.

All indicative verbs without a contracted vowel (see Lesson 3) will use the acute accent mark (ʹ).[1] Although in this lesson all contract verbs have a circumflex accent (˜), in Lesson 11 you will discover that contract verbs sometimes have an acute accent and sometimes a circumflex. Accent contract verbs according to the following rule: accent the verb in its uncontracted form (e.g., φιλέομεν) according to the standard rules for accenting verbs. Then contract the verb. If an accented syllable is the leading vowel in a contraction, it is marked with a circumflex. For example, φιλέομεν=φιλοῦμεν, φιλέει=φιλεῖ—but ἐφίλεε=ἐφίλει, φιλεέτω=φιλείτω.

1 An exception to this rule is if the verb only has two syllables and the penult is long. In that uncommon situation, the penult will have a circumflex.

EXERCISES

Memorization Exercise

4.1 Learn Vocabulary List 2.

Translation Exercises

4.2 Translate the following words:

1. λαλοῦμεν
2. αἰτεῖς
3. τηροῦσι
4. ποιεῖτε
5. παρακαλεῖ
6. μαρτυροῦσι
7. ζητεῖτε
8. καλῶ
9. θεωροῦμεν
10. τηρεῖς

Composition Exercises

4.3 Translate the following clauses into Greek:

1. they seek
2. he asks
3. you call
4. we bear witness
5. they speak
6. you all keep safe
7. I exhort
8. she makes
9. you behold
10. we love
11. they call
12. she asks
13. we seek
14. they bear witness
15. he beholds

Scripture Translation Exercises

4.4 Translate the following verses from Scripture:

1. εἰ οὖν (if then) Δαυὶδ καλεῖ αὐτὸν (him) κύριον (lord) . . . (Matt 22:45)
2. Τί δέ (and why) με (me) καλεῖτε· κύριε (lord) κύριε, καὶ (and) οὐ (not) ποιεῖτε ἃ (that which) λέγω; (Luke 6:46)
3. σημεῖον (a sign) ζητεῖ (Luke 11:29)
4. ὁ γὰρ πατὴρ (for the Father) φιλεῖ τὸν υἱόν (the son) (John 5:20)
5. Ἰουδαῖοι (the Jews) σημεῖα (signs) αἰτοῦσιν καὶ (and) Ἕλληνες (the Greeks) σοφίαν (wisdom) ζητοῦσιν (1 Cor 1:22)

LESSON 5

O-Stem Nouns (Second Declension)

NOUN ELEMENTS

We identify verbs by the stems and endings they use. Similarly, we identify nouns and adjectives by their case endings. Like verbs, nouns and adjectives consist of three parts: root, stem, and ending. The case system in Greek includes three types of stems: O-stems, A-stems, and consonant stems. These three types of stems combine with case endings to create three patterns, called "declensions."

Nearly all nouns in the O-stem pattern—or "second declension"—are masculine (see Lesson 7 for further discussion of gender and nouns). These nouns all have an ο/ε variable vowel for a stem before the case ending. O-stem nouns are declined as follows:

	Name of Case	Greek Example	Original Ending	English
sg.	Nominative	λόγος	ς	a word (subject)
	Vocative	λόγε	-	O word (direct address)
	Accusative	λόγον	ν	a word (object)
	Genitive	λόγου	ος (contracting to ου)	of a word
	Dative	λόγῳ	σι (changing to long stem and iota subscript)	to or for a word
pl.	Nominative	λόγοι	ι	words (subject)
	Vocative	λόγοι	ι	O words (direct address)
	Accusative	λόγους	νς (ν changing to long stem)	words (object)
	Genitive	λόγων	ων	of words
	Dative	λόγοις	ις	to or for words

NOUN CASES Cases (nominative, vocative, accusative, genitive, and dative) identify how the noun or adjective functions grammatically within a sentence.

English doesn't employ case endings except for apostrophe "s" (to indicate possession) and plural "s." Instead, English uses word order to indicate subjects and objects of sentences and prepositions to connect nouns. For example, a word that is the subject of a sentence nearly always comes before the verb, while the object of the sentence typically follows the verb; if we invert the order of the words, we invert the meaning of the sentence. In the sentence, "An angel finds a man," the word "angel" is the subject of the sentence and the word "man" the object. In the sentence, "A man finds an angel," "man" is the subject of the sentence and "angel" the object. We have inverted the order of the words, and in so doing we have also inverted the meaning of the sentence.

In Greek, the first sentence should be written:

ἄγγελος εὑρίσκει ἄνθρωπον.

ἄγγελος is the subject because it is in the nominative case (-ος stem-ending), and ἄνθρωπον is the object because it is in the accusative case (-ον stem-ending). In Greek, the meaning of the sentence is the same if we invert the order of the words (ἄνθρωπον εὑρίσκει ἄγγελος) because the case—not the order of the words—determines which word is the subject or object.

This lesson focuses on the function and forms of the nominative and accusative cases. Genitives and datives are covered in Lesson 6.[1] Vocatives express a direct address typically in the context of a command. This makes them easy to identify in context. You may find it helpful to notice the correlation between accusative forms of many English pronouns (him, them, whom) and the Greek accusative singular ending: both end with a nasal sound (English "m" and Greek ν). The original plural Greek form also had a nasal sound (-νς), but it dropped out and the stem vowel was lengthened to ου.[2]

1 Lesson 6 discusses the spelling changes of these cases in more detail.

2 Greek avoids letting a liquid or a nasal remain adjacent to a sibilant. One of the letters often drops out and a vowel is lengthened to compensate or mark the change (cf. compensatory lengthening).

NOMINATIVE AND ACCUSATIVE RULES

The basic elements of a sentence will use the nominative and accusative cases in the following ways.

1. The subject of a verb is in the nominative case.
2. The direct object of a verb is in the accusative case.
3. All verbs agree with their subject in number and person.

Nominative Subject

Before translating an English sentence into Greek, you must know which word is the subject of the verb and which (if any) is its direct object.

Since English uses word order to indicate the subject and object of the verb, you can identify the subject by putting "who?" or "what?" before the verb. In the sentence from above, "An angel finds a man," ask, "Who finds?" The answer is "an angel." "An angel" is therefore the subject of the sentence.

In the same way, you can see that "a man" is the subject of the second sentence, "A man finds an angel." This also works when the verb is passive: ask the same question about the sentence, "A man is found." Who is found? Answer: "a man." "A man" is the subject of the passive verb.

Accusative Direct Object

On the other hand, you can find the direct object by placing "whom?" or "what?" after the verb. In the case of the first sentence, ask, "An angel finds whom?" Answer: "a man." Therefore, "a man" is the object of the sentence.

Many verbs—such as the verb "I remain"—cannot have a direct object. These verbs are called "intransitive" verbs, because the action that they denote does not pass to another person or thing (from Latin *transire*, "to go over" or "to cross"). Verbs that can have a direct object are called "transitive" verbs, because the action that they denote passes to another person or thing. You can distinguish transitive and intransitive verbs in English by writing a sentence that contains an active form of a given verb and seeing whether a direct object can be put after it. For example, the sentence "I remain" cannot take a direct object (a noun, such as "happiness," would not make sense: "I remain happiness"); the action of the verb cannot be transferred to another object.

Subject-Verb Agreement

If the indicative verb is first or second person, then the only nominatives that can be used are the correlating first and second personal pronouns ("I," "we," "you," "you all"). All other nominatives will correlate to a third person verb. A third person verb does not require a nominative, as we saw in lessons 3 and 4 (e.g., μένει, "he/she/it remains"). Nominatives define who or what the third person subject is. The nominative must match the verb in number. If the verb is plural, the nominative must also be plural in number or consist of two or more nouns joined together by "and."

For example:

1. ἄνθρωπος ἐσθίει ἄρτον.
   "A man eats bread."

2. ἄνθρωποι ἐσθίουσιν ἄρτον.
   "Men eat bread."

3. ἄνθρωπος καὶ δοῦλος ἐσθίουσιν ἄρτον.
   "A man and a slave eat bread."

Since Greek doesn't have an indefinite article like English, the English indefinite article "a" does not have to be translated into Greek.

ACCENTUATION OF NON-VERBS

A different principle governs accenting for non-verbs than the recessive principle we used for verbs. For non-verbs the general principle is *retention*: make every effort to keep the accent on the same syllable that you memorize in the nominative vocabulary form.

General Accenutation Rules

- An acute accent may only be placed over the final three syllables of a word.
- A circumflex doesn't have the same range: it may only be placed over the final two syllables.

- If the final syllable of a word (the ultima) is long, the range of both accents is reduced by one position. In this situation, the acute can only be used on the final two syllables, and the circumflex is limited to the ultima. An acute on the ultima will change to a grave if the word is followed by another word or a punctuation mark. However, an enclitic (a word pronounced using the stress of the preceding word) will allow an acute to remain on the ultima of the preceding word.

Reasons for Changing the Accentuation on a Non-Verb

A word like λόγος (accented with an acute on the penult) never has a reason to change or move the accent. Even if the ultima changes to a long form (e.g., genitive case λόγου), an acute may still be placed over the penult. However, a word that has an accent placed at its earliest position (i.e., acute on the antepenult or circumflex on the penult, which is only possible with a short ultima) will have to change if its ultima is changed to a long syllable. Notice how the accent moves from the antepenult to the penult on ἄνθρωπος when the ending changes to a long syllable in the accusative plural ἀνθρώπους. A similar change occurs with δοῦλος: the long ultima in the accusative plural (as well as the genitive and dative cases)[1] does not allow a circumflex to be placed over the penult, so it changes to an acute (δούλους) to retain a stressed position on that syllable.

Non-verbs with an acute on the ultima have no reason to change the placement of the accent. However, they do change the type of their accent in the genitive and dative case forms. Notice this difference between these cases and the nominative and accusative cases. Grouping cases into these two groups will help you with accenting and spelling in the future. All nominative and accusative forms for θεός and ἀδελφός (including the accusative plural ἀδελφούς) will have acutes. All genitive and dative forms will have circumflexes (e.g., θεοῦ and ἀδελφοῦ.)[2]

1 Note that for purposes of accentuation, when αι and οι are the final letters in a word (such as in some nominative plural forms, e.g., ἄνθρωποι) they are considered short.

2 Due to the similar grammatical functions and the similar spelling/accenting traits of these two groups of cases, this grammar uses the historical approach for presenting case paradigms, with the accusative following the nominative.

EXERCISES

Memorization Exercises

5.1(α) Learn Vocabulary List 3. You must memorize the correct syllable to stress for pronunciation purposes when learning vocabulary. (Note: the stressed syllable may change in forms where the stem-ending has a long vowel.)

5.1(β) Memorize the stem and endings for O-stem words (it is not necessary to memorize the vocatives).

O-stem with Endings

	Singular	Plural
Nom.	-ος	-οι
Acc.	-ον	-ους
Gen.	-ου	-ων
Dat.	-ῳ	-οις

Grammar Exercises

5.2(α) Case identification exercises: It is essential that you be able to identify the case and number of any noun. Use abbreviations to speed up the process (e.g., "nom. pl." for nominative plural). The following list of exercises can be used as an example to help you build your own practice exercises. Translation exercises will also help you hone your case identification skills.

1. κύριος
2. ἁγιασμόν
3. ἀγρούς
4. ἄνθρωπον
5. ἀποστόλῳ
6. ἄρτου
7. διδάσκαλοι
8. δούλοις
9. δούλων
10. θεῷ
11. κυρίου
12. λόγοις
13. ὁδούς
14. οἴκους
15. σταυρῷ

5.2(β) Case composition exercises: For the following words, if the word is singular, provide the plural form. If the word is plural, provide the singular form.

1. ἄγγελος
2. ἀδελφῶν
3. ἄνθρωπος
4. ἀπόστολος
5. ἀποστόλῳ
6. ἄρτος
7. διδάσκαλοι
8. ἐρήμου
9. θανάτοις
10. θεοί
11. κυρίου
12. λόγοις
13. ὁδούς
14. οἴκοις
15. οἶκον

Translation Exercises

5.3 Translate the following sentences:

1. ἔχει ἄνθρωπος δούλους.
2. ἄγγελος λαὸν σῴζει.
3. κύριος λόγους γράφει.
4. ἐγείρεις δοῦλον.
5. ἄνθρωποι ὁδὸν εὑρίσκουσι.
6. βλέπει δοῦλος οἴκους.
7. ἄνθρωπος ἀποστέλλει ἀδελφούς.
8. λαμβάνετε οἶκον.
9. δοῦλος ἔχει κύριον.
10. εὑρίσκομεν ὁδόν.
11. τηρεῖτε νόμους.
12. ἄνθρωπος καὶ δοῦλος εὑρίσκουσιν ἀδελφούς.

Composition Exercises

5.4 Translate the following sentences into Greek. (If you want to use accenting, you must learn the non-verb accenting principles in Appendix 3):

1. A man hears an angel.
2. An angel rouses a man.
3. Slaves find a way.
4. A brother has a house.
5. Lords send slaves.
6. They are writing words.
7. You all find an angel.
8. A lord judges men.
9. We rouse slaves.
10. You keep laws.
11. A man and an angel see a way.
12. You behold death.

5.5 Translate the following verses from Scripture:

1. λέγουσιν αὐτῷ·[1] οὐκ ἔχομεν … εἰ μὴ[2] πέντε[3] ἄρτους (Matt 14:17)
2. ἐσθίουσιν τοὺς[4] ἄρτους (Mark 7:2)
3. Δαυὶδ λέγει ἐν βίβλῳ[5] ψαλμῶν·[6] εἶπεν[7] κύριος τῷ κυρίῳ μου·[8] κάθου ἐκ δεξιῶν μου[9] (Luke 20:42)
4. νόμος κρίνει ἄνθρωπον (from John 7:51)
5. κυρίῳ ἀποθνῄσκομεν (Rom 14:8)

1 αὐτῷ, "to him"
2 εἰ μὴ, "except"
3 πέντε, "five"
4 τοὺς, "the"
5 βίβλῳ, "the book"
6 Sound out the Greek word for the English derivative. Notice the case ending.
7 Replace with λέγει to translate.
8 μου, "my"
9 κάθου ἐκ δεξιῶν μου, "sit at my right hand"

LESSON 6

Definite Article, Genitive and Dative Cases, and Prepositions

DEFINITE ARTICLE

The definite article—"the" in English—is declined with the same cases as a noun. The forms used with words that are masculine in gender are as follows:

Masculine Definite Article

	Singular	Plural
Nom.	ὁ	οἱ
Acc.	τόν	τούς
Gen.	τοῦ	τῶν
Dat.	τῷ	τοῖς

Notice that all of the endings except the nominative singular are the same as the endings of ἀδελφός. Accenting is also consistent: Nominative and accusative cases either have no accent, or they have an acute (which will change to grave if followed by another word). Genitive and dative cases have a circumflex.

The definite article always matches the case, number, and gender of the noun it describes. So, for instance, the phrase "of the man" is τοῦ ἀνθρώπου in Greek; "to the men" is τοῖς ἀνθρώποις. Several words with O-stem endings are feminine (e.g., ἔρημος, "desert"; ὁδός, "way"; παρθένος, "maiden"). Since these are feminine, they must take a feminine article (see Lesson 8).

In addition to word order, the definite article can help determine which nouns are being modified by other words. Modifiers sometimes are placed between a noun and its article, which can reduce ambiguity. For example: "The man's house" might be written ὁ τοῦ ἀνθρώπου οἶκος, explicitly conveying who owns the house, even if there are many other nouns in the sentence.

Any modifier may appear between the noun it modifies and its corresponding article. This includes adjectives, participles, and even prepositional phrases. This provides a level of grammatical precision in Greek that is not available in English. For example, both of the Greek lines below can be translated, "the children of men in a boat." However, they carry different meanings due to word order:

τὰ ἐν πλοίῳ παιδία τῶν ἀνθρώπων (The children are in a boat.)

τὰ παιδία τῶν ἐν πλοίῳ ἀνθρώπων (The men are in a boat.)

Genitive and Dative Cases

The primary functions of the genitive and dative cases are connecting and relating nouns to each other. For example, we can add more information about a house by adding another noun. We can refer to a "house of God" or a "house of man" as two very different things. The words "God" and "man" must be connected to what they modify. We typically make these connections in English with prepositions (e.g., "of"), but Greek can create the same connection with genitive and dative case endings.

The genitive case usually is translated into English either with the preposition "of" or with the possessive case, formed by adding apostrophe "s" to the noun. For example: οἶκος ἀνθρώπου means "a house of a man" or "a man's house."

The dative case commonly denotes the person to or for whom something is done. It is used to express the indirect object after verbs meaning "to give," etc. For example: γράφει νόμους λαῷ ("He writes laws for a people"); παρέχει οἶκον ἀνθρώπῳ ("He gives a house to a man"). In the second sentence, οἶκον is the direct object; ἀνθρώπῳ is the "indirect" object, because it is not directly affected by the action of the verb.

Basic Grammar Functions

Most of the words that we encounter—with the exception of independent verb(s) of a sentence, coordinating conjunctions, and interjections—serve one of three roles:

1. Substantive (e.g., subject, direct object, object of preposition, indirect object)
2. Attributive: providing more information about a substantive (e.g., an adjective)
3. Adverbial: providing more information about a verb or adverb (how, why, when, or the conditions for the verb)

As we introduce parts of speech we will see how each part of speech can perform various roles. A noun can be used as a substantive (e.g., the subject in the nominative case)—and that noun may also be used as an attribute of another noun to provide more information about it (e.g., οἶκος ἀνθρώπου; the genitive describes the house, namely, that it belongs to the man). Some nouns (i.e., time words) may modify the timing of the verb. For example, καιρός refers to a season. In the genitive, it refers to the action of the verb occurring within that season. In the dative, the action of the verb occurs *at* that season (referring to the entire season). In the accusative, the action of the verb occurs for the duration or the extent of the whole season.

Particular syntactical roles for particular nouns will be presented in subsequent lessons and vocabulary. At this point, you only need to learn this three-part framework for language, to learn to categorize language in these three roles, and to know that nouns can perform all three grammatical functions.

		Function		
		Substantive	Attributive	Adverbial
Part of Speech	Noun or Pronoun	noun with various case endings		

PREPOSITIONS

Prepositional Objects

In addition to case endings, Greek also uses prepositions to connect nouns. For example, Greek can render "man of the people" by using a case ending (i.e., ἄνθρωπος τοῦ λαοῦ) or by using a preposition (i.e., ἄνθρωπος ἐκ τοῦ λαοῦ). When a preposition is used, the following noun must take the case ending required by the preposition. The meaning of the relationship between the nouns (e.g., possession, identification of a whole group, source, etc.) is determined by the range of meaning of the preposition, rather than the range of possible meanings of the case ending. The case ending merely supports the meaning of the preposition. For example, to determine the possible meanings for the relationship between the nouns in the phrase ἄνθρωπος τοῦ λαοῦ, one would look up meanings of the genitive case. To determine the possible meanings for the relationship between the nouns in the phrase ἄνθρωπος ἐκ τοῦ λαοῦ, one would look up the range of meanings for ἐκ in a lexicon.

Some prepositions—such as ἐκ and εἰς—will only precede a noun in one specific case: ἐκ always precedes a genitive noun, while εἰς always precedes a noun in the accusative case. Other prepositions can be used with more than one case to convey different relationships. For example, μετά precedes a noun in the genitive case to show association (e.g., "he came with me") but a noun in the accusative case to show subsequent sequence (e.g., "the man after me"). This case information must be memorized as part of vocabulary study for prepositions.

Prepositional Prefixes

Greek prepositions may also function adverbially. They can be prefixes to verbs (making them compound verbs) and are commonly repeated if a noun is used (e.g., ἐκβάλλω ἄνθρωπον ἐκ τοῦ οἴκου). For additional information regarding prepositions, refer to the summary treatment of the Greek prepositional system in Appendix 4.

Functions of Prepositions

The chart on the facing page shows how the various syntactical uses of prepositions and their objects (prepositional phrases) map with nouns. An articular prepositional phrase can act in place of a noun (substantive use, such as subject or object). A phrase that matches the articular status of a noun may serve as an attribute for that noun (the same function as an adjective—e.g., ὁ ἄνθρωπος ὁ ἐν οἴκῳ, "the man in the house"). Finally, a prepositional phrase may qualify the verb action (e.g., περιπατεῖ κατὰ τὴν ὁδόν, "he walks down the road").

<table>
<tr><th colspan="2"></th><th colspan="3">Function</th></tr>
<tr><th colspan="2"></th><th>Substantive</th><th>Attributive</th><th>Adverbial</th></tr>
<tr><th rowspan="6">Part of Speech</th><td>Noun or Pronoun</td><td colspan="3">noun with various case endings</td></tr>
<tr><td>Preposition</td><td>article + preposition + object</td><td>preposition + object</td><td>anarthrous preposition + object</td></tr>
<tr><td></td><td></td><td></td><td></td></tr>
<tr><td></td><td colspan="2"></td><td></td></tr>
<tr><td></td><td colspan="2"></td><td></td></tr>
<tr><td></td><td></td><td></td><td></td></tr>
</table>

Word Order for Prepositions

For a prepositional phrase to be used as a substantive (in place of a noun), it must be preceded by an article. If the prepositional phrase modifies a noun (attributive usage), it will generally match the articular status of the noun (i.e., if the noun has an article, so will the prepositional phrase). If the noun is anarthrous (without an article), the prepositional phrase typically will not have an article either. A prepositional phrase that modifies a verb (adverbial usage) must not have an article.[1]

PROCLITICS

Since ἐν and εἰς are both proclitics (a word pronounced using the stress of the subsequent word), they do not have their own accents. They are pronounced with the following word as if they were merely an additional syllable. If one proclitic follows another, the series of proclitics are be pronounced as the first syllables of the following accented word. The only time proclitics receive an accent is when they occur as the final word in a sentence or are followed by an enclitic (see Lesson 10).

1 This description regarding the presence or absence of an article only refers to articles preceding the preposition. The presence or absence of an article for the object of the preposition is governed by other factors common to nouns in general.

EXERCISES

Memorization Exercises

6.1(α) Review Vocabulary Lists 1, 2, and 3.

6.1(β) Learn the following prepositions (the two most common prepositions in the New Testament) from Vocabulary List 4 to complete the exercises.

- ἐν + dat. in, on (location where or time when)
- εἰς + acc. into, to (movement into a location)

Grammar Exercises

6.2(α) Genitive and dative case identification exercises: Note the case and number of each word, then translate the word in a way that brings out its case meaning. Use abbreviations to speed up the process (e.g., "gen. pl." for genitive plural). The following list of exercises can be used as an example to help you build your own practice exercises.

1. ἀποστόλῳ
2. ἄρτοις
3. θεοῦ
4. ἀδελφῶν
5. ἀγγέλοις
6. θανάτου
7. λόγων
8. νόμῳ
9. ἐρήμοις
10. ὁδοῦ

6.2(β) Case identification exercises (all cases):

1. οἶκον
2. νόμων
3. κυρίους
4. κόσμου
5. λαοῖς
6. οἶκος
7. ὁδοί
8. ἀποστόλοις
9. ἀνθρώπων
10. ἄρτον

6.2(γ) Accenting exercises: Correct any mistakes in accenting. Remember that the principle of non-verb accentuation is retention, so the accenting in the vocabulary must be learned along with memorizing the spelling of vocabulary prior to working through this exercise.

1. λόγος
2. κοσμοῦς
3. ἀπόστολῳ
4. ἀγγέλων
5. λαούς
6. ὅδοις
7. ἀγγέλου
8. ἀρτόν
9. κύριων
10. νόμους
11. θέου
12. κόσμον
13. ἀδέλφοις
14. οἴκοι
15. ἅποστολος

6.2(δ) Case composition exercises: For the following words, if the word is singular, provide the plural form. If the word is plural, provide the singular form.

1. ἄγγελον
2. νόμοι
3. κόσμοις
4. δούλους
5. ἐρήμῳ
6. κυρίου
7. ἀδελφῶν
8. ἄρτος
9. ἄνθρωπον
10. οἴκων

6.2(ε) Identify the function of the prepositions in the following sentences. Mark each phrase as substantive, attributive, or adverbial.

1. __________ οἱ ἄνθρωποι οἱ ἐν τῷ οἴκῳ βλέπουσι τοὺς ἀγγέλους (Are the men in the house, or is the house where they see the angels?)

2. __________ οἱ ἄνθρωποι ζήτουσιν τοὺς ἀγγέλους ἐν ταῖς ὁδοῖς. (Does the prepositional phrase describe where the men are looking or where the angels are?)
3. __________ τοὺς ἐν τῷ κόσμῳ λαμβάνουσιν τὸν νόμον.
4. __________ λαμβάνομεν τὸν νόμον εἰς τὸν κόσμον. (Does the prepositional phrase describe where the receiving occurs or the location-type of law?)

Translation Exercises

6.3 Translate the following sentences:

1. οἱ δοῦλοι ποιοῦσιν ὁδὸν τῷ κυρίῳ.
2. οἱ ἄνθρωποι ζήτουσιν τοὺς ἀγγέλους ἐν ὁδοῖς.
3. γράφει τὸν νόμον τοῦ κυρίου.[1]
4. ὁ ἀδελφὸς τοῦ δούλου βλέπει τὸν οἶκον.
5. γράφομεν τοὺς νόμους τῷ λαῷ.
6. ὁ[2] θεὸς φιλεῖ τοὺς ἀδελφούς.
7. ζητεῖτε τὸν τῶν ἀνθρώπων ἀδελφόν.
8. τηροῦσιν τὸν λόγον τοῦ θεοῦ.
9. οἱ δοῦλοι εὑρίσκουσιν τὴν ὁδὸν τοῖς κυρίοις.
10. λαμβάνομεν τὸν νόμον εἰς τὸν κόσμον.
11. λαλῶ τοὺς λόγους τῷ λαῷ, καὶ ὁ λαὸς πιστεύει.
12. ἀποστέλλετε τὸν ἄρτον λαῷ ἐν ἐρήμῳ.

Composition Exercises

6.4 Translate the following sentences into Greek:

1. The angel finds men in a desert.
2. They are writing the laws for the people.

1 The word κύριος sometimes has the definite article and sometimes does not. It is the word used in the Septuagint (the Greek version of the Old Testament, usually abbreviated LXX) to denote the sacred name Yahweh (also translated Jehovah).

2 θεός generally has the definite article in Greek, but not in English.

3. We are seeking the brothers of the slave in the house.
4. The lord's slaves are making a way.
5. The slave remains in the house.
6. You behold the house of God.[1]
7. We keep the law of the Lord.
8. They write words for the slaves.
9. We find a way into a desert for the people.
10. The man saves the slave's brother.
11. The man and the slave are making bread.
12. The brothers believe.
13. The angel writes laws for the world.
14. He sends an angel into the world.

Scripture Translation Exercises

6.5 Translate the following verses from Scripture:

1. ἑτοιμάσατε[2] τὴν ὁδὸν κυρίου (Matt 3:3)
2. παραδώσει[3] δὲ ἀδελφὸς ἀδελφὸν εἰς θάνατον (Matt 10:21)
3. ἐν τῇ ἐρήμῳ ἐστίν[4] (Matt 24:26)
4. οἱ ἀδελφοί σου[5] . . . ζητοῦσίν σε[6] (Mark 3:32)
5. οὐκ[7] ἀνθρώποις λαλεῖ ἀλλὰ[8] θεῷ (1 Cor 14:2)

1 This would be a fine place to place an article in front of your translation of "God." (This is true for a number of reasons; cf. Apollonius's canon.)

2 ἑτοιμάσατε, "prepare"

3 παραδώσει, "will deliver" (note the third singular ending).

4 ἐστίν, "he is"

5 σου, "your"

6 σε, "you"

7 οὐκ, "not"

8 ἀλλὰ, "but"

LESSON 7

O-Stem Neuter Nouns (Second Declension, Continued)

GRAMMATICAL GENDER

In English, nouns denoting men or male animals are in the masculine gender; nouns denoting women or female animals are in the feminine gender. English also retains some grammatical gender from Latin and Greek for some types of words: proper names of many states and countries, ships, other vehicles, and the church may be referred to as "she." However, most other nouns are neuter.

In Greek the rules are not as simple. Nearly all nouns denoting men and male animals are masculine and nearly all denoting women and female animals are feminine, but other nouns may be masculine, feminine, or neuter. Words for abstract concepts such as "love," "joy," and "gender," are typically feminine; the word expressing the concept "masculine" is also feminine. Grammatical gender is not necessarily related to physical gender, and grammatical gender—except when marking the gender of people and animals—doesn't contribute to word meaning. Rather, it helps organize spelling conventions for noun and adjective stems.

Feminine O-Stem Nouns

In the second declension, nearly all nouns terminating in -ος in the nominative singular are masculine. There are only a few exceptions to this: ὁδός ("way"), ἔρημος ("desert"), and παρθένος ("maiden"), all feminine, are the most common exceptions in the New Testament. All nouns terminating in -ον in the nominative singular are neuter.

Neuter O-Stem Nouns

As ἔργον is declined, note that the nominative, vocative, and accusative cases have the same ending. All neuter nouns have identical case spelling for their nominative, vocative, and accusative cases. This word demonstrates the matching forms for O-stem neuter nouns.

	ἔργον ("a work")	
	Singular	Plural
Nom.	ἔργον	ἔργα
Acc.	ἔργον	ἔργα
Gen.	ἔργου	ἔργων
Dat.	ἔργῳ	ἔργοις

The definite article that goes with neuter nouns is declined as follows:

	Neuter Definite Article	
	Singular	Plural
Nom.	τό	τά
Acc.	τό	τά
Gen.	τοῦ	τῶν
Dat.	τῷ	τοῖς

Subject-Verb Agreement Exception

If a sentence has a neuter plural subject, often the verb will be singular. This is an exception to subject-verb agreement, provided as a rule in Lesson 5. The reason for the exception is related to how we deal with collective nouns—such as "people," "orchestra," or "bunch." It can be difficult to determine (in both English and Greek) whether to use a singular or plural verb with such subjects. In Greek, a collection was a conceptual idea; thus, such nouns tended to be feminine singular (explaining the origin of the feminine-looking alpha ending—see Lesson 8—for the neuter nominative plural). The verb then agreed with the collective idea by using a singular form. By the time of Homer, the neuter nominative plural was truly a plural form able to take a plural verb. However, there was enough of a connection to the singular noun form that this now-optional rule for verb agreement persisted. For example, τὰ παιδία εὑρίσκει τὰ βιβλία ("The children find the books").

EXERCISES

Memorization Exercises

7.1(α) Learn Vocabulary List 4.

7.1(β) Compare the neuter stem-endings in this lesson to the masculine stem-endings in Lesson 5. (Notice that it is not necessary to memorize these forms as a separate paradigm; one can simply remember that neuter nominative forms are always the same as their accusative forms and the accusative plural form is a short α.)

O-stem with Neuter Endings

	Singular	Plural
Nom.	-ον	-α
Acc.	-ον	-α
Gen.	-ου	-ων
Dat.	-ῳ	-οις

Grammar Exercises

7.2(α) Case identification exercises: Include the grammatical gender of the noun in your answer. Use abbreviations to speed up the process (e.g., "neut. nom. pl." for neuter nominative plural). The following list of exercises can be used as an example to help you build your own practice exercises.

1. βιβλίον
2. δένδρων
3. ἀργύρια
4. ἀδελφοῖς
5. εὐαγγελίου
6. πλοίων
7. σαββάτῳ
8. τέκνα
9. πρόσωπον
10. σημεῖα

7.2(β) Case form exercises: Practice making masculine and neuter words plural. Convert the following words into their plural forms.

1. πλοῖον
2. νόμος
3. δαιμονίου
4. δοῦλον
5. ἔργῳ

7.2(γ) Case form exercises: Practice making masculine and neuter words singular. Convert the following words into their singular forms.

1. πρόβατα
2. ἱματίων
3. δούλους
4. δένδροις
5. ἔργα

Translation Exercises

7.3 Translate the following sentences:

1. τὰ ἐν ἐρήμῳ δένδρα τῶν ἀνθρώπων ὁ δοῦλος βλέπει.
2. ὁ κύριος ποιεῖ τὰ ἔργα τῷ κόσμῳ.
3. εὑρίσκομεν τὸ τοῦ θεοῦ ἱερόν.
4. τὰ πρόβατα θεωρεῖ τὰ δένδρα.
5. ἀκούουσι τὸ εὐαγγέλιον.
6. τηρεῖς τὰ βιβλία.
7. δαιμόνιον ἔχεις.
8. λαμβάνετε τὰ πλοῖα.
9. θεωροῦμεν τὸ πρόσωπον τοῦ κυρίου.
10. ἀποστέλλουσι εἰς τὸν κόσμον τὰ παιδία τοῦ δούλου.
11. τηροῦμεν τὰ σάββατα τοῦ κυρίου.
12. σῴζετε τὰ τέκνα.
13. τὰ παιδία ἔχει τὰ βιβλία.

Composition Exercises

7.4 Translate the following sentences into Greek:

1. They take the garments of the men into the temple.
2. We send the brother's children into the house of the Lord.
3. The angel receives the books for the people.
4. The children have the garments.
5. He beholds the face of God.
6. You have the sheep.
7. You all find the trees in a desert.
8. The Lord judges the works of men.
9. We seek the temple.
10. God works miracles (does signs) for the people.
11. The man seeks the young child.
12. The children eat the loaves in a boat.
13. You keep the money safe.

Scripture Translation Exercises

7.5 Translate the following verses from Scripture:

1. ἐγὼ ἀποστέλλω τὸν ἄγγελόν μου[1] πρὸ[2] προσώπου σου[3] (Matt 11:10)
2. οὐ βλέπεις εἰς[4] πρόσωπον ἀνθρώπων (Matt 22:16)
3. κύριός ἐστιν τοῦ σαββάτου ὁ υἱὸς[5] τοῦ ἀνθρώπου (Luke 6:5)
4. τί[6] ποιοῦμεν ὅτι[7] οὗτος[8] ὁ ἄνθρωπος πολλὰ[9] ποιεῖ σημεῖα; (John 11:47)
5. Παῦλος δοῦλος Χριστοῦ Ἰησοῦ, κλητὸς[10] ἀπόστολος ἀφωρισμένος[11] εἰς εὐαγγέλιον θεοῦ (Rom 1:1)

1 μου, "my"
2 πρὸ, "before"
3 σου, "your"
4 βλέπεις εἰς, "regard"
5 υἱὸς, "son"
6 τί, "what?"
7 ὅτι, "because"
8 οὗτος, "this"
9 πολλὰ, "many"
10 κλητὸς, "called"
11 ἀφωρισμένος, "set apart"

LESSON 8

A-Stem Feminine Nouns (First Declension)

A-STEM PATTERNS

The first declension is marked by A-type stem letters (contrasted to the O-type stems in the second declension). The A-type stem letters are α and η. Words in this declension with α as their stem letter are called "α-pattern." Those with η are called "η-pattern." All have α for their stem letter in their plural forms. The different declension stem letters do not convey different meanings. The difference is simply a spelling convention like the English convention "'i' before 'e' except after 'c.' " In the first declension, if the letter preceding the stem letter is a vowel or ρ, then the word will follow the α-pattern. If the stem letter is preceded by anything else, it will follow the η-pattern. Consult the next lesson for exceptions to these rules.[1]

Notice how the first and second declensions use the same case ending forms. The only difference is the stem letters. Also note the ι subscript in the dative singular.

	α-pattern ἡμέρα ("day")		**η-pattern ἀρχή ("beginning")**	
	Singular	Plural	Singular	Plural
Nom.	ἡμέρα	ἡμέραι	ἀρχή	ἀρχαί
Acc.	ἡμέραν	ἡμέρας	ἀρχήν	ἀρχάς
Gen.	ἡμέρας	ἡμερῶν	ἀρχῆς	ἀρχῶν
Dat.	ἡμέρᾳ	ἡμέραις	ἀρχῇ	ἀρχαῖς

1 Cf. George Curtius, *A Grammar of the Greek Language*, ed. William Smith (New York: Harper & Brothers, 1872), 39–40; James Hope Moulton, *An Introduction to the Study of New Testament Greek* (London: Charles H. Kelly, 1895), 32–33; William W. Goodwin, *A Greek Grammar, Revised and Enlarged* (Boston: Ginn and Company, 1892), 38, points 174 and 176; Herbert Weir Smyth, *A Greek Grammar for Colleges* (New York: American Book Company, 1920), §219.

Since the article doesn't have a vowel or ρ preceding the stem, it follows the η-pattern for its first declension forms. The feminine article is declined as follows:

Feminine Definite Article

	Singular	Plural
Nom.	ἡ	αἱ
Acc.	τήν	τάς
Gen.	τῆς	τῶν
Dat.	τῇ	ταῖς

The full declension of the definite article, in all three genders, is as follows:

Definite Article
ὁ, ἡ, τό ("the")

	Singular			Plural		
	Masc.	Fem.	Neut.	Masc.	Fem.	Neut.
Nom.	ὁ	ἡ	τό	οἱ	αἱ	τά
Acc.	τόν	τήν	τό	τούς	τάς	τά
Gen.	τοῦ	τῆς	τοῦ	τῶν	τῶν	τῶν
Dat.	τῷ	τῇ	τῷ	τοῖς	ταῖς	τοῖς

Rule: The definite article agrees with the noun with which it is connected in number, gender, and case.

EXERCISES

Memorization Exercises

8.1(α) Learn Vocabulary List 5.

8.1(β) Compare the A-stem endings in this lesson to the (mostly masculine) O-stem endings in Lesson 5. (Notice that the main difference is the stem vowel; the case endings are nearly identical. Be careful not to confuse a neuter plural word with a feminine nominative singular word.)

Grammar Exercises

8.2(α) Case identification exercises:

1. ἁμαρτιῶν
2. ἀρχαί
3. ἄρτους
4. κεφαλήν
5. ἀργύρια
6. γῇ
7. εἰρήνην
8. ἐντολῶν
9. δικαιοσύνης
10. ἡμέραις
11. καρδίαι
12. φωνῶν
13. ψυχάς
14. ὥρας
15. παραβολή

8.2(β) Stem pattern exercises: Supply the stem letter in the following words. Bear in mind that all first declension words have an A-stem vowel in their plural forms. Genitive plural forms are not used in this exercise since the stem vowel is not visible in that case.

1. βασιλεί_ς
2. ἀγάπ_ν
3. γραφ_ῖς
4. κόσμ_ς
5. δικαιοσύν_ι
6. ὥρ_
7. ἱμάτι_ν
8. σοφί_ν
9. παραβολ_ς (genitive singular)
10. παραβολ_ς (accusative plural)
11. πρόσωπ_ν
12. ἐπαγγελί_ς
13. ἀρχ_ς (genitive singular)
14. εἰρήν_ν
15. ἐκκλησί_ς

8.2(γ) Supply the proper article that correlates to the following words. (Note: the article may have a different stem letter than the noun has.)

1. ___ εἰρήνην
2. ___ ἐκκλησίαν
3. ___ ἐπαγγελίαις
4. ___ κεφαλῶν
5. ___ ἔρημος
6. ___ καρδίαις
7. ___ ζωῆς
8. ___ κυρίου
9. ___ γραφάς
10. ___ ὁδόν
11. ___ ἐντολῇ
12. ___ δοῦλοι
13. ___ παρθένοι
14. ___ ἡμέραν
15. ___ τέκνον

Translation Exercises

8.3 Translate the following sentences:

1. ἡ ἀγάπη μένει.
2. λαμβάνομεν τὴν[1] δικαιοσύνην.
3. παρακαλοῦσι τὴν ἐκκλησίαν.
4. ὁ κύριος κρίνει τὰς ψυχὰς τῶν[2] ἀνθρώπων.
5. βλέπετε τὴν συναγωγὴν τῶν ἀδελφῶν.
6. ζητοῦμεν τὴν βασιλείαν τοῦ θεοῦ.
7. ἔχεις τὴν[3] σοφίαν καὶ τὴν[4] χαράν.
8. τηρεῖτε τὰς ἐντολὰς τῶν ἀγγέλων.
9. τὰς γραφάς οἱ ἀδελφοὶ ἀποστέλλουσιν.

Composition Exercises

8.4 Translate the following sentences into Greek:

1. We receive the promises of God.
2. They have the Lord's commands.
3. The sins of the world remain.

1 Abstract nouns generally have a definite article before them in Greek. This also occurs for proper names (without further title information) as well as other particular situations typically covered in a second-year course on syntax. The article is not translated into English.

2 Words such as ἄνθρωπος that denote a whole class often have an article that is not translated into English.

3 Article with abstract noun.

4 Article with abstract noun.

4. You hear the voice of the Lord.
5. We bear witness to the truth.[1]
6. You all exhort the church.
7. He has righteousness, peace, and joy.
8. The brethren are writing the Scriptures.
9. The Lord keeps the souls of men.
10. You all are seeking wisdom.

Scripture Translation Exercises

8.5 Translate the following verses from Scripture:

1. ἀλήθειαν λέγω (1 Tim 2:7)
2. καὶ ὁ μένων[2] ἐν τῇ ἀγάπῃ ἐν τῷ θεῷ μένει καὶ ὁ θεὸς ἐν αὐτῷ[3] μένει (1 John 4:16)
3. ἐγένετο[4] ἡ βασιλεία τοῦ κόσμου τοῦ κυρίου ἡμῶν καὶ τοῦ χριστοῦ αὐτοῦ[5] (Rev 11:15)
4. ἐν τῷ βιβλίῳ τῆς ζωῆς (Rev 13:8)
5. ἐξουσίαν ὡς[6] βασιλεῖς[7] μίαν[8] ὥραν[9] λαμβάνουσιν μετὰ[10] τοῦ θηρίου[11] (Rev 17:12)

1 Use the dative case.
2 καὶ ὁ μένων, "and the one who remains"
3 αὐτῷ, "him"
4 ἐγένετο, "has become"
5 αὐτοῦ, "his"
6 ὡς, "as"
7 βασιλεῖς, "king" (notice the same root as βασιλεία)
8 μίαν, "one"
9 This is an example of an adverbial use of a noun. A word denoting time in the accusative case can refer to the extent of time the verb occurs.
10 μετὰ, "with"
11 θηρίου, "beast"

LESSON 9

Exceptions to First Declension Patterns

MASCULINE A-STEM NOUNS

Just as some O-stem (second declension) nouns are feminine, there are A-stem (first declension) masculine nouns that are exceptions. A-stem masculine nouns follow the stem rules presented in Lesson 8. If the letter that precedes the stem is a vowel or a ρ, the noun will be an α-pattern. If the preceding letter is not a vowel or a ρ, it will be an η-pattern. (Remember, all first declension nouns use an α in their plural forms.) These masculine nouns of the first declension differ in case endings from feminine nouns in just two forms. The masculine nominative singular is -ης or -ας (instead of -η or -α). The genitive singular form follows the second declension -ου. Masculine words of the first declension define a type of person such as a role or profession and are declined as follows:

	α-pattern **νεανίας ("young man")**		**η-pattern** **προφήτης ("prophet")**	
	Singular	Plural	Singular	Plural
Nom.	νεανίας	νεανίαι	προφήτης	προφῆται
Voc.	νεανία	νεανίαι	προφῆτα	προφῆται
Acc.	νεανίαν	νεανίας	προφήτην	προφήτας
Gen.	νεανίου	νεανιῶν	προφήτου	προφητῶν
Dat.	νεανίᾳ	νεανίαις	προφήτῃ	προφήταις

α-PATTERN FEMININE NOUNS PRECEDED BY A COMPOUND SIBILANT

There are some A-stem (first declension) nouns that in their singular forms have an α that is not preceded by a vowel or the letter ρ. These exceptions to the α-pattern in the first declension can be anticipated because they have a compound sibilant (ζ, ξ, σσ) preceding the stem vowel. They are declined as follows:

	Irregular α-pattern δόξα ("glory")	
	Singular	Plural
Nom.	δόξα	δόξαι
Acc.	δόξαν	δόξας
Gen.	δόξης	δοξῶν
Dat.	δόξῃ	δόξαις

Note that all A-stem (first declension) nouns have the same pattern of endings in the plural.

EXERCISES

Memorization Exercises

9.1 Learn Vocabulary List 6. Note: The conjunctions δέ, γάρ, and οὖν never stand as the first word of a sentence. (These types of words are called "postpositive.") The prepositions ἐν, σύν, ἀπό, ἐκ, πρό, and εἰς are always followed by a noun or pronoun in the proper case, as mentioned in the vocabulary.

Grammar Exercises

9.2 Case identification exercises: Supply the proper article that correlates to the following words. The article identifies all information about case, number, and gender.

1. βαπτιστής
2. γραφῆς
3. ἐξουσίαν
4. νεανίου
5. θαλάσσης
6. γλώσσας
7. θαλάσσῃ
8. δεσπότην
9. μαθηταῖς
10. δόξαι
11. προφήτου
12. φωναῖs
13. ἡμέραν
14. ὥραι
15. ἐξουσίᾳ

Translation Exercises

9.3 Translate the following sentences:

1. τοὺς προφήτας οὐ καλοῦσι εἰς τὴν συναγωγήν.
2. ὁ γὰρ κύριος γράφει τὰς ἐπαγγελίας ἐν ταῖς καρδίαις τῶν ἀδελφῶν.
3. παρακαλοῦσι τοὺς[1] προφήτας σὺν τοῖς[1] μαθηταῖς.
4. τὰ δὲ πλοῖα οὐ μένει ἐν τῇ θαλάσσῃ.
5. ἐν ἀρχῇ ὁ θεὸς ἀποστέλλει τοὺς προφήτας.
6. οὐχ εὑρίσκουσι τὰ τέκνα ἐν τῇ ὁδῷ.
7. οἱ μαθηταὶ μένουσιν ἐν τῇ ἐξουσίᾳ τοῦ δεσπότου.
8. ὁ νεανίας λαμβάνει τὸ ἱμάτιον ἀπὸ τῆς κεφαλῆς τοῦ παιδίου.
9. τὰ βιβλία εὑρίσκει ἡ παρθένος.

1 The article matches its noun in gender, number, and case (but may have a different stem and thus look different).

Composition Exercises

9.4 Translate the following sentences into Greek:

1. We do not see the boats on the lake.
2. The master sends the children with the slaves from the synagogue.
3. You remain before the house of the Lord.
4. The prophets exhort the brethren and the people.
5. Therefore the sin of the world remains.
6. They behold the glory of the Lord in the temple.
7. The baptist remains in the synagogue with the disciples.
8. They send the prophet from the lake with the baptist.
9. You all send the children out of the house.
10. For the church does not hear the commandments and the promises of the prophet.
11. They call the disciples to the assembly.
12. For God writes the commandments in the hearts of the disciples.
13. The young men hear the parables of the kingdom.

Scripture Translation Exercises

9.5 Translate the following verses from Scripture:

1. καὶ ὁ Ἰησοῦς μετὰ τῶν μαθητῶν αὐτοῦ[1] ἀνεχώρησεν[2] πρὸς τὴν θάλασσαν (Mark 3:7)
2. δόξα ἡλίου (1 Cor 15:41)
3. ἀποστέλλω[3] εἰς αὐτοὺς προφήτας καὶ ἀποστόλους (Luke 11:49)
4. ὁ μαθητὴς ἐκεῖνος[4] οὐκ ἀποθνῄσκει (John 21:23)
5. ἔχουσι[5] τὴν δόξαν τοῦ θεοῦ (Rev 21:11)

1 αὐτοῦ, "his"
2 ἀνεχώρησεν, "withdrew"
3 The tense is changed for this exercise.
4 ἐκεῖνος, "that"
5 The verb form is changed for this exercise.

LESSON 10

2-1-2 Pattern Adjectives and the Verb "To Be"

2-1-2 PATTERN ADJECTIVES

Adjectives, like articles, must match the gender, number, and case of the noun they modify. In order to reflect all three genders many adjectives will use both first and second declension stems. These adjectives are sometimes referred to as 2-1-2 pattern adjectives since they use the second declension for masculine forms, first declension for feminine forms, and the second declension for neuter forms. They are declined as follows:

ἀγαθός ("good")

	Singular			Plural		
	Masc.	Fem.	Neut.	Masc.	Fem.	Neut.
Nom.	ἀγαθός	ἀγαθή	ἀγαθόν	ἀγαθοί	ἀγαθαί	ἀγαθά
Voc.	ἀγαθέ[1]					
Acc.	ἀγαθόν	ἀγαθήν	ἀγαθόν	ἀγαθούς	ἀγαθάς	ἀγαθά
Gen.	ἀγαθοῦ	ἀγαθῆς	ἀγαθοῦ	ἀγαθῶν	ἀγαθῶν	ἀγαθῶν
Dat.	ἀγαθῷ	ἀγαθῇ	ἀγαθῷ	ἀγαθοῖς	ἀγαθαῖς	ἀγαθοῖς

Note that the masculine endings are the same as those of O-stem (second declension) nouns. The feminine endings are the same as those of A-stem (first declension) nouns. The neuter endings are the same as those of O-stem (second declension) nouns (having -ον for their nominative singular stem ending).

1 Unless an alternate form is provided, the vocative is the same as the nominative.

These adjectives follow the same rules governing first declension nouns. If a vowel or the letter ρ comes immediately before the endings of an adjective, the endings in the feminine are the same as those of ἡμέρα. For example:

	ἅγιος ("holy")					
	Singular			Plural		
	Masc.	Fem.	Neut.	Masc.	Fem.	Neut.
Nom.	ἅγιος	ἁγία	ἅγιον	ἅγιοι	ἅγιαι	ἅγια
Voc.	ἅγιε[1]	ἅγιον				
Acc.	ἅγιον	ἁγίαν	ἅγιον	ἁγίους	ἁγίας	ἅγια
Gen.	ἁγίου	ἁγίας	ἁγίου	ἁγίων	ἁγίων	ἁγίων
Dat.	ἁγίῳ	ἁγίᾳ	ἁγίῳ	ἁγίοις	ἁγίαις	ἁγίοις

ADJECTIVE-NOUN AGREEMENT

Rule: Adjectives agree with the noun that they qualify in number, gender, and case.

WORD ORDER AND ARTICLE USE WITH ADJECTIVES

If an article is used with an adjective, the article will always precede the adjective. When the adjective is modifying a noun, the most frequent ordering is the same as English (article, adjective, noun), ὁ ἀγαθός ἄνθρωπος. However, Greek is free to communicate the same idea just as naturally with the following: ὁ ἄνθρωπος ὁ ἀγαθός. In both cases, an article precedes the adjective. If the noun is "man," "woman," or something communicated by the adjective's gender, number, and context, the noun doesn't have to be expressed, so an adjective preceded by an article is practically equivalent to a noun. ὁ ρῶτος "the first [man]"; τὰ ἔσχατα "the last [things]"; αἱ ἀγαθαί "the good [women]"; οἱ ἅγιοι "the holy [men or people]," or "the saints." Thus, articles are used with adjectives in the same ways that they are used with prepositional phrases. An articular adjective without a matching noun will function in place of a noun (substantive usage). An adjective that matches a noun in gender, number, and case will

1 Unless an alternate form is provided, the vocative is the same as the nominative.

also match by having or not having an article (attributive usage). If the noun doesn't have an article, neither will the adjective. The adjective may take an article in two ways:

1. The adjective may be sandwiched between a noun and its article (ὁ ἄγαθος ἄνθρωπος).
2. The article may be repeated before the adjective (ὁ ἄνθρωπος ὁ ἄγαθος).

Both constructions have the same meaning.

		Function		
		Substantive	Attributive	Adverbial
Part of Speech	Noun or Pronoun	noun with various case endings		
	Preposition	article + preposition + object	preposition + object	anarthrous preposition + object
	Adjective & Adverb	article + adjective (in place of noun)	adjective	adverb

THE VERB "TO BE"

Present Forms of εἰμί

The present indicative of the verb "to be" is as follows:

	Present Indicative of εἰμί			
	Singular		Plural	
1st	εἰμί	I am	ἐσμέν	we are
2nd	εἶ	you are	ἐστέ	you all are
3rd	ἐστί(ν)[1]	he/she/it is	εἰσί(ν)	they are

1 The ν in parentheses is called a "movable ν." It must be used when this verb is followed by another word that begins with a vowel. It is also used frequently when a punctuation mark follows the verb.

Predicate Nouns and Adjectives

The verb "to be" belongs to a class of verbs called "copulative verbs" because they couple or link together two nouns or a noun and an adjective. The coupled noun or adjective is called a predicative noun or adjective, or the "complement." Since these predicative nouns or adjectives are not direct objects, they do not use the accusative case to identify their role in the sentence. Since they are a refinement or definition of the subject (e.g., that tree is an oak), they must always be in the same case as the subject of the verb—and in the case of predicative adjectives, they must agree with the subject in number and gender as well as case.

> Rule: Predicate nouns and adjectives for the verb "to be" take the same case as the subject noun.

Examples:

Subject	Verb	Predicative Noun or Adjective
The man ὁ ἄνθρωπός	is ἐστι	a prophet προφήτης
God ὁ θεός	is ἐστιν	good ἀγαθός
We –	are ἐσμὲν	slaves δοῦλοι
You all –	are ἐστὲ	just δίκαιοι
The tongue γλῶσσά	is ἐστι	evil κακή

ENCLITICS

The verb "to be" is not typically placed as the first word in a sentence. In the present tense it is a member of a small class of words called "enclitics" that lean on the preceding word[1] for their accent.[2] Thus, enclitics typically will not start a sentence or follow a punctuation mark. For this same reason, an enclitic allows an acute to remain over the ultima of a preceding word without changing to a grave.

One-syllable Enclitics

The most common enclitics only have one syllable. The only times when monosyllabic enclitics receive an accent are: 1) when they are separated from the preceding word by a punctuation mark, 2) the preceding word lost its accent due to elision, 3) the enclitic is being particularly emphasized.

The only other consequence monosyllabic enclitics have on accentuation occurs in two situations where the enclitic forces the preceding word to receive an accent. 1) A proclitic or another enclitic preceding an enclitic will receive an accent.[3] 2) A word with an accent in its most forward position (acute on the antepenult or a circumflex on the penult) that precedes an enclitic will receive a secondary accent (an acute) on its ultima.[4]

Two-syllable Enclitics

Two-syllable enclitics (including all forms of εἰμί except the second person singular form, εἶ, which isn't an enclitic) follow the same basic principles. However, if a word preceding a disyllabic enclitic has an acute on its penult, the enclitic will receive an accent. When a disyllabic enclitic must be accented, the position of the accent must be learned as part of the word's spelling. The enclitic verb εἰμί follows a retentive principle for accenting like other enclitics.

1 They are pronounced as the final syllable(s) of the preceding word

2 The second person singular form, εἶ, is not an enclitic. It always retains the circumflex.

3 This addresses the problem of not having a preceding accent to lean on.

4 This addresses the problem of having too many syllables following an accent.

Exception for ἔστι There is a particular exception for accenting one of the forms of the verb εἰμί. The third person singular form, ἐστί will be accented on its first syllable (ἔστι) in specific situations:

- when it is the first word of a sentence;
- when it follows a proclitic like οὐκ, εἰ, or ὡς;
- when it follows καί, ἀλλά, and τοῦτο;
- when it means "exists" or "is possible."[1]

By far, the most frequent occurrence of this exception is "οὐκ ἔστιν."

1 Cf. James Hope Moulton and Wilbert Francis Howard, *A Grammar of New Testament Greek: Accidence and Word-Formation* (Edinburgh: T&T Clark, 1963–), 2:54.

EXERCISES

Memorization Exercise

10.1 Learn Vocabulary List 7.

Grammar Exercises

10.2 Matching adjectives and nouns: Translate the English adjective into Greek using a form that matches the gender, number, and case of the Greek word provided. Always take note of case meanings.

1. first σημεῖον
2. last προφηταῖς
3. good ζωῆς
4. one's own νόμου
5. wicked νεανίαις
6. first θάλασσαν
7. evil δεσπότῃ
8. good μαθητοῦ
9. righteous ἔντολης
10. another φώνην

Translation Exercises

10.3 Translate the following sentences:

1. ἡ ἐκκλησία πιστή ἐστιν.
2. οἱ ἄνθρωποι προφῆταί εἰσιν.
3. ἡ βασιλεία ἐστὶ κακή.
4. ἡ ἐντολὴ τοῦ αἰωνίου θεοῦ δικαία ἐστίν.
5. λαμβάνουσι τὰ ἴδια ἱμάτια.
6. ἕτεροι ἄνθρωποι μένουσιν ἐν τῷ πρώτῳ πλοίῳ.
7. τέκνα ἀγαπητά ἐσμεν τοῦ θεοῦ.
8. ὁ πρῶτός ἐστιν ἔσχατος, καὶ ὁ ἔσχατος πρῶτος.
9. οἱ ἅγιοι τηροῦσιν τὰ ἅγια σάββατα τοῦ θεοῦ.
10. ἡ γλῶσσα πονηρά ἐστιν.
11. αἱ πισταὶ μένουσιν ἐν τῷ ἱερῷ.
12. μαθηταί ἐστε τοῦ κυρίου.
13. ἅγιος εἶ, κύριε.
14. καλοῦμεν τοὺς ἑτέρους νεανίας.

Composition Exercises

10.4 Translate the following sentences into Greek:

1. The brethren are disciples.
2. We are prophets.
3. You are good, O master.
4. The writings of the apostles are holy.
5. A different man is in the last boat.
6. We remain in the evil world.
7. He makes his own garments.
8. The man is just and good.
9. Therefore the baptist exhorts the evil men.
10. The saints remain before the house of God.
11. God keeps the souls of the saints.
12. You all exhort the disciples.

Scripture Translation Exercises

10.5 Translate the following verses from Scripture:

1. ὁ Ἰησοῦς . . . λαμβάνει[1] τοὺς δώδεκα[2] μαθητὰς κατ' ἰδίαν[3] καὶ ἐν τῇ ὁδῷ (Matt 20:17)
2. ὁ κύριος αὐτοῦ[4] λέγει αὐτῷ[5]· δοῦλε πονηρέ (Matt 18:32)
3. ὁ δὲ Ἰησοῦς λέγει[6] αὐτῷ[7]· τί[8] με λέγεις ἀγαθόν; οὐδεὶς[9] ἀγαθὸς εἰ μὴ[10] εἷς[11] ὁ θεός (Mark 10:18)
4. οὐκ ἔστιν δίκαιος οὐδὲ εἷς[12] (Rom 3:10)
5. εἶ ὁ ἅγιος τοῦ θεοῦ (John 6:69)
6. αἱ ἡμέραι πονηραί εἰσιν (Eph 5:16)
7. πιστὸς δέ ἐστιν ὁ κύριος (2 Thess 3:3)
8. οἱ γὰρ ἄρχοντες[13] οὐκ εἰσὶν φόβος[14] τῷ ἀγαθῷ ἔργῳ ἀλλὰ τῷ κακῷ (Rom 13:3)

1 The verb tense is changed for this exercise.
2 δώδεκα, "twelve" (indeclinable adjective)
3 κατ' ἰδίαν (an idiom meaning "privately")
4 αὐτοῦ, "his"
5 αὐτῷ, "to him"
6 The verb tense is changed for this exercise.
7 αὐτῷ, "to him"
8 τί, "why"
9 οὐδεὶς, "no one"
10 εἰ μὴ, "except"
11 εἷς, "one"; notice the same root in οὐδείς.
12 οὐδὲ, "not even"; εἷς, "one"; compare to the contracted form οὐδείς.
13 ἄρχοντες, "rulers"
14 φόβος, "a terror"

LESSON 11

Imperfect Active Indicative and Accentuation of Verbs

TEMPORAL ENDINGS

Greek verbs build out from their roots in both directions, adding stems and endings in front of and after the root. Greek only has two sets of verb endings: non-past endings (called "primary" endings) and past endings (called "secondary" endings). In addition to slightly modified forms at the end of the verb, the secondary endings use the letter ε, which is called the "augment," in front of the verb's root (e.g., present, λύω; imperfect, ἔλυον).

Imperfect Tense

Since the imperfect tense, like the present tense, has an incomplete aspect (i.e., the two tenses only differ in timing), the imperfect shares the root spelling and stem of the present tense. The thematic stem (the variable vowel ε/ο) as is used in the present tense reflects the unfolding nature of the present. In the past tense, this stem often denotes an unfolding action in past time, such as a continuous or repeated past action.

		Aspectual Meanings	
		Incomplete	Complete (commonly marked by a particular stem spelling)
Temporal Endings	Non-past (primary)	PRESENT (root[1] + thematic stem + primary endings)	FUTURE
	Past (secondary)	**IMPERFECT (root + thematic stem + secondary endings)**	(SIMPLE PAST)

1 The root form used in this column is called the "present root." This will be explained in Lesson 17.

As a general rule, translate the Greek imperfect with the English past continuous forms provided in the example table. However, a simple past tense (e.g., "I said," "I loved") may be sufficient in some contexts. Use the Greek imperfect to translate all the past tenses in the composition exercises until the aorist tense is learned in Lesson 18.

Person	Augment	Root[1]	Stem (ε/ο)	Past Ending	Imperfect Tense Conjugation	Translation
1 sg.	ἐ +	λυ	+ ο	+ ν	ἔλυον	I was releasing, or I used to release
2 sg.	ἐ +	λυ	+ ε	+ ς	ἔλυες	you were releasing, or you used to release
3 sg.	ἐ +	λυ	+ ε	+ (ν)	ἔλυε(ν)	he/she/it was releasing, or he/she/it used to release
1 pl.	ἐ +	λυ	+ ο	+ μεν	ἐλύομεν	we were releasing, or we used to release
2 pl.	ἐ +	λυ	+ ε	+ τε	ἐλύετε	you all were releasing, or you all used to release
3 pl.	ἐ +	λυ	+ ο	+ ν	ἔλυον	they were releasing, or they used to release

AUGMENT RULES If the verb begins with a consonant, the augment is simply placed before that consonant. If the verb begins with a vowel, that vowel lengthens instead of using the augment. (See long vowel forms in Lesson 4.)

- α lengthens to η;
- ε lengthens to η (except in the verb ἔχω, where an augment is used and then contracts with the ε in the root to form ει); and
- ι, ο, υ lengthen to ῑ, ω, ῡ.

1 Both the present and imperfect tenses often modify the true verbal root (but not for this verb). The present and imperfect form of the root can be identified within the first principal part (the lexical form) in reference works. See Lesson 18 for more details regarding principal parts.

A digraph lengthens its first vowel:

- αι becomes ῃ;
- ει becomes ῃ;
- οι becomes ῳ; and
- ευ becomes ηυ.

Examples:

Present	Imperfect
ἀκούω	ἤκουον
ἐγείρω	ἤγειρον
ὁμολογέω	ὡμολόγουν
αἰτέω	ᾔτουν
οἰκέω	ᾤκουν
εὑρίσκω	ηὕρισκον
Exception:	
ἔχω	εἶχον

Carefully note these changes—they take place at a word's beginning and so you will not be able to find them in a dictionary, since verbs generally are listed according to present tense form.

Augmentation of Compound Verbs

When a verb combines with a preposition (compare the English verbs "to outnumber," and "to undertake") the augment generally follows the prepositional prefix. In these cases, when a vowel is the final letter of a preposition, that vowel generally drops out (see "Elision" in Lesson 2.) Also, ἐκ becomes ἐξ when followed by a vowel.

Examples:

Present		Imperfect
ἀποθνῄσκω		ἀπέθνῃσκον
παρακαλέω		παρεκάλουν
ἐκβάλλω		ἐξέβαλλον
ὑπάγω		ὑπῆγον
	Exception:	
περιπατέω		περιεπάτουν

Imperfect Tense with ε-Contract Verbs

The conjugation of the imperfect active indicative of ε-contract verbs is provided below. Notice that contract verbs in the imperfect sometimes have an acute accent and sometimes a circumflex accent (˜). (Review the accent principles for verbs in Lesson 4 to understand when to use each accent mark.) Notice how the short ultimas in the secondary endings allow some forms of contract verbs to avoid the accent within a contracted syllable.

ε-Contract Verb Imperfect Tense Conjugation	Uncontracted Forms	Translation
ἐφίλουν	ἐφίλεον	I was loving or I used to love
ἐφίλεις	ἐφίλεες	you were loving or you used to love
ἐφίλει	ἐφίλεε	he/she/it was loving or he used to love
ἐφιλοῦμεν	ἐφιλέομεν	we were loving or we used to love
ἐφιλεῖτε	ἐφιλέετε	you all were loving or you all used to love
ἐφίλουν	ἐφίλεον	they were loving or they used to love

EXERCISES

Memorization Exercises

11.1(α) Learn Vocabulary List 8.

11.1(β) Review and compare primary and secondary endings. Since Greek only has two sets of temporal personal endings, learn all of the forms in both of these paradigms so you can instantly identify or produce any of them. Remember that the forms in the chart below contain contractions between the stem (ε/ο) and the endings. The actual secondary endings (excluding the augment) without the stem are -ν, -ς, -, -μεν, -τε, -ν.

	Present Active Indicative		**Imperfect Active Indicative**	
	Singular	Plural	Singular	Plural
1st	root—ω	root—ομεν	ε—root—ον	ε—root—ομεν
2nd	root—εις	root—ετε	ε—root—ες	ε—root—ετε
3rd	root—ει	root—ουσι	ε—root—ε(ν)	ε—root—ον

Grammar Exercises

11.2(α) Accent the following imperfect verbs.[1]

1. ἐξεβαλλε
2. ἐφιλουμεν
3. ἐζητουν
4. ἐδοξαζον
5. ἐκαλουν
6. ἐθεωρειτε
7. ἀπεθνῃσκες
8. ἠσθιον
9. ἐβλεπεν
10. ἐθεωρουμεν
11. ἐλαλει
12. ἐμαρτυρουν
13. ἐλαμβανον
14. ἐμενε
15. ἀπεστελλες

1 Remember to accent verbs as early on the word as possible.

11.2(β) Vocabulary identification: Write the vocabulary form (present active indicative first person singular) for each imperfect verb.

1. ἦγε
2. ἔπειθον
3. ἐκηρύσσομεν
4. ἐδόξαζον
5. ἐζητεῖτε
6. παρεκάλουν
7. ἐθεώρει
8. ἐλέγομεν
9. εἶχεν
10. ἔμενον

11.2(γ) Augment identification: Scan the following translation exercises (11.3) and mark all augments (or vowels) that were lengthened instead of augmented.

Translation Exercises

11.3 Translate the following sentences:

1. ἀπεκτείνετε τοὺς προφήτας τοῦ κυρίου.
2. ὁ θεὸς ἔπεμπε τοὺς ἀγγέλους εἰς τὸν κόσμον.
3. ἦγε[1] τοὺς μαθητὰς ἀπὸ τῆς θαλάσσης.
4. οἱ νεανίαι ἔχαιρον.
5. τὰ πρόβατα ὑπῆγον[2] ἐκ τῆς ἐρήμου.
6. ὁ βαπτιστὴς βαπτίζει τὰς παρθένους.
7. ὁ ἄγγελος ἀπέλυε τὸν ἀπόστολον.
8. οἱ μαθηταὶ ἐδόξαζον τὸν κύριον.
9. ἔφερον οἱ ἀγαθοὶ δοῦλοι τὰ πρόβατα.
10. Ἰωάννης[3] ὁ βαπτιστὴς ἔκραζε ἐν τῇ ἐρήμῳ.
11. ἐδίδασκες τὰ παιδία σὺν τοῖς δούλοις.
12. ἐκηρύσσομεν τὸ εὐαγγέλιον τῷ λαῷ.
13. ἔπειθον οὖν τοὺς ἀνθρώπους.
14. περιεπατοῦμεν ἐν τῷ ἱερῷ.
15. ἐξέβαλλες τὰ δαιμόνια.

1 If the accent falls on the second to last syllable (penult) of any word in which that syllable is long, and the last syllable is short, the accent is always circumflex.

2 The accent never goes back prior to the augment.

3 Proper names followed by a title or description often do not have an article.

Composition Exercises

11.4 Translate the following sentences into Greek:

1. They were proclaiming the gospel to the disciples.
2. The maidens were departing from the house.
3. They were dragging[1] the slave's boat to the sea.
4. The prophets used to teach the children in the houses.
5. You all glorified the Lord, O angels.
6. You were teaching the people.
7. They were driving the sheep together to the trees.
8. The child was reading the Scriptures in the temple.
9. We were departing from the lake.
10. John the Baptist did not work signs.
11. The Lord walked about in the wilderness.
12. Therefore you were persuading the people.
13. The saints were rejoicing.
14. He was casting out demons.
15. We were carrying the boat.
16. You all were releasing the slaves.

Scripture Translation Exercises

11.5 Translate the following verses from Scripture:

1. ὁ ἀγαθὸς ἄνθρωπος ἐκ τοῦ ἀγαθοῦ θησαυροῦ[2] ἐκβάλλει ἀγαθά, καὶ ὁ πονηρὸς ἄνθρωπος ἐκ τοῦ πονηροῦ θησαυροῦ ἐκβάλλει πονηρά (Matt 12:35)
2. ἐδίδασκεν αὐτοὺς ἐν τῇ συναγωγῇ αὐτῶν (Matt 13:54)
3. εἶ ὁ χριστὸς ὁ υἱὸς τοῦ θεοῦ (Matt 16:16)
4. εἰ[3] οὖν Δαυὶδ καλεῖ αὐτὸν κύριον, πῶς[4] υἱὸς αὐτοῦ ἐστιν; (Matt 22:45)
5. διδάσκεις καὶ οὐ λαμβάνεις πρόσωπον, ἀλλ'[5] ἐπ'[6] ἀληθείας τὴν ὁδὸν τοῦ θεοῦ διδάσκεις (Luke 20:21)
6. καὶ ἀνεγίνωσκεν τὸν προφήτην Ἠσαΐαν.[7] (Acts 8:28)
7. οἱ γὰρ ἄρχοντες[8] οὐκ εἰσὶν φόβος[9] τῷ ἀγαθῷ ἔργῳ ἀλλὰ τῷ κακῷ. (Rom 13:3)

1 Use ἄγω (with proper inflection, imperfect active indicative third-person plural).
2 θησαυροῦ, "treasure"
3 εἰ, "if"
4 πῶς, "how"
5 the elided form of ἀλλά
6 ἐπ', "in"
7 Ἠσαΐαν, "Isaiah"
8 ἄρχοντες, "rulers"
9 φόβος, "a terror"

LESSON 12

Imperfect of εἰμί, Demonstrative Pronouns, and αὐτός

IMPERFECT FORMS OF εἰμί

The imperfect tense of the verb "to be" uses an older set of secondary endings than those covered in Lesson 11. Alternate forms are included within parentheses since these spellings were not standardized by the New Testament period. Notice that this verb is not an enclitic in the imperfect tense and uses standard verb-accenting principles. Its forms are:

	Imperfect Indicative of εἰμί			
	Singular		Plural	
1st	ἤμην	I was	ἦμεν (ἤμεθα)	we were
2nd	ἦς (ἦσθα)	you were	ἦτε	you all were
3rd	ἦν	he/she/it was	ἦσαν	they were

DEMONSTRATIVE PRONOUNS

The demonstrative pronouns οὗτος ("this") and ἐκεῖνος ("that") are declined as follows:

	Near Demonstrative Pronoun: οὗτος ("this")					
	Singular			Plural		
	Masc.	Fem.	Neut.	Masc.	Fem.	Neut.
Nom.	οὗτος	αὕτη	τοῦτο	οὗτοι	αὗται	ταῦτα
Acc.	τοῦτον	ταύτην	τοῦτο	τούτους	ταύτας	ταῦτα
Gen.	τούτου	ταύτης	τούτου	τούτων	τούτων	τούτων
Dat.	τούτῳ	ταύτῃ	τούτῳ	τούτοις	ταύταις	τούτοις

	Far Demonstrative Pronoun: ἐκεῖνος ("that")					
	Singular			Plural		
	Masc.	Fem.	Neut.	Masc.	Fem.	Neut.
Nom.	ἐκεῖνος	ἐκείνη	ἐκεῖνο	ἐκεῖνοι	ἐκεῖναι	ἐκεῖνα
Acc.	ἐκεῖνον	ἐκείνην	ἐκεῖνο	ἐκείνους	ἐκείνας	ἐκεῖνα
Gen.	ἐκείνου	ἐκείνης	ἐκείνου	ἐκείνων	ἐκείνων	ἐκείνων
Dat.	ἐκείνῳ	ἐκείνῃ	ἐκείνῳ	ἐκείνοις	ἐκείναις	ἐκείνοις

Notice that the root forms of οὗτος vary, while the root of ἐκεῖνος remains consistent. When the stem vowel for οὗτος is an O-stem, the vowel in the root (the first syllable) is ου; when the stem vowel is an A-stem, the vowel in the root is αυ. These rules even apply to the neuter nominative and accusative plural forms. Also note that the nominative and vocative forms are the only forms of οὗτος that do not begin with a τ—in this respect, οὗτος is very similar to the definite article.

The pronouns οὗτος and ἐκεῖνος agree with the nouns they qualify in number, gender, and case, just like adjectives. When they qualify a noun, the noun always has the article. However, unlike adjectives, articles do not precede demonstrative pronouns.

Examples:

1. οὗτος ὁ ἄνθρωπος "This man"

or

2. ὁ ἄνθρωπος οὗτος "This man"

3. ἐκεῖνα τὰ πρόβατα "Those sheep"

or

4. τὰ πρόβατα ἐκεῖνα "Those sheep"

5. ἐκείνη ἡ ἐντολή "That commandment"

or

6. ἡ ἐντολὴ ἐκείνη "That commandment"

When οὗτος stands by itself without any word expressed for it to agree with, it is used substantivally and means "this man," αὕτη means "this woman," τοῦτο means "this thing," and ταῦτα means "these things." The far demonstrative pronoun, ἐκεῖνος, operates in the same way.

THE THREE USES OF αὐτός

Third Person Personal Pronoun

The third person personal pronoun (in English, "he," "she," "it") is the most common of the personal pronouns and looks very similar to some forms of οὗτος. Those forms of αὐτός are the forms of the article with αὐ prefixed before the τ.

The forms of this word are regular—they do not change their root spelling. It can be distinguished from feminine forms of οὗτος because it never begins with a τ and it is always accented on its final syllable (ultima). The forms of αὐτός are as follows:

Third Person Pronoun: αὐτός ("he, she, it, they")

	Singular			Plural		
	Masc.	Fem.	Neut.	Masc.	Fem.	Neut.
Nom.	αὐτός	αὐτή	αὐτό	αὐτοί	αὐταί	αὐτά
Acc.	αὐτόν	αὐτήν	αὐτό	αὐτούς	αὐτάς	αὐτά
Gen.	αὐτοῦ	αὐτῆς	αὐτοῦ	αὐτῶν	αὐτῶν	αὐτῶν
Dat.	αὐτῷ	αὐτῇ	αὐτῷ	αὐτοῖς	αὐταῖς	αὐτοῖς

In the New Testament, αὐτός is the most common word for "he, she, it," etc. When it has this substantive meaning, it is not used with an article.

Examples:

1. αὐτὸς γὰρ σῴζει τὸν λαόν.
   "For he saves the people."

2. ἦγον αὐτὸν εἰς τὴν θάλασσαν.
   "They were leading him to the sea."

3. ἔπεμπεν αὐτὴν ἀπὸ τοῦ ἱεροῦ.
   "He was sending her from the temple."

4. οὗτός ἐστιν ὁ δοῦλος αὐτοῦ.
   "This is his slave."

5. οὗτοί εἰσιν οἱ οἶκοι αὐτῆς.
   "These are her houses."

Intensifying Pronoun

Αὐτός can also intensify meaning when it matches the gender, number, and case of a noun or the implied subject of a verb. English uses "himself, herself, itself," to convey such intensification.[1] (E.g., He did it himself. I saw the manuscripts themselves.) In English we have an intensifying pronoun for every person, but Greek only uses this "third person" form for all persons.

Examples:

1. Jesus himself taught them.
   Ἰησοῦς αὐτὸς ἐδίδασκεν αὐτούς.

But also

2. I taught them myself.
   αὐτὸς ἐδίδασκον αὐτούς.

(In Classical Greek the nominative case of αὐτός only has this intensifying meaning and cannot be used in the sense of "he, she, it.")

Identity Pronoun "the Same"

If an article precedes αὐτός, this word order makes it clear that the referent is identical to its antecedent. We communicate this in English with "the same."

Example:

Jesus was saying the same word.

Ἰησοῦς ἔλεγεν τὸν αὐτὸν λόγον.

1 We also use these forms in English for our reflexive pronouns; do not assume that these forms are intensive on that basis (i.e., "he saw himself" vs. "he saw it, himself").

EXERCISES

Memorization Exercise

12.1 Review Vocabulary Lists 1–8.

Translation Exercises

12.2 Translate the following sentences:

1. οὗτοι οἱ ἄνθρωποι ἀπέθνῃσκον ἐν τῇ ἐρήμῳ.
2. ἐθεωροῦμεν τοὺς οἴκους αὐτῶν.
3. οὗτος οὖν ἦν μαθητὴς Ἰωάννου τοῦ βαπτιστοῦ.
4. ἦμεν γὰρ δοῦλοι τῆς ἁμαρτίας.
5. ἐκεῖνα δὲ τὰ δένδρα ἔβαλλον εἰς τὴν θάλασσαν.
6. αὗται ἔμενον ἐν τῷ πλοίῳ.
7. ὁ γὰρ θεὸς σῴζει αὐτοὺς ἀπὸ τοῦ πονηροῦ (the evil one).
8. ἦτε οὖν δεσπόται τοῦ λαοῦ.
9. οὐ γὰρ κρίνομεν ταῦτα.
10. οἱ υἱοὶ αὐτοῦ ἦσαν κακοί.
11. αὕτη γὰρ ἦν ἡ ἐντολὴ αὐτοῦ.
12. ἐκηρύσσομεν ταῦτα ἐν τῇ ἐκκλησίᾳ.
13. ἐκεῖνοι δὲ ἐξέβαλλον τὰ δαιμόνια.
14. ἐν ἐκείνῃ τῇ ἡμέρᾳ ἐδόξαζον τὴν σοφίαν τοῦ κυρίου.
15. αἱ παρθένοι συνῆγον τὰ πρόβατα αὐτῶν εἰς τὰ δένδρα.
16. ἐν ἐκείνῃ τῇ ὥρᾳ ἐχαίρομεν.
17. ὁ Ἰησοῦς αὐτὸς οὐκ ἐβάπτιζεν ἀλλὰ οἱ μαθηταὶ αὐτοῦ.
18. ἡ ζωὴ μένει ἐν αὐτοῖς.

Composition Exercises

12.3 Translate the following sentences into Greek:

1. In the beginning was the word.
2. This is the love of God.
3. For the Lord saves the souls of men from the evil one.
4. Peace and truth are in the kingdom of God.

5. They were glorifying his power and wisdom.
6. For in that day we were preaching the gospel of the kingdom in the synagogue, and casting out demons.
7. You saw her sons in the house.
8. We received them into the boat.
9. You all were in the temple in those days.
10. This is life eternal.
11. We heard the voice of the angel from the trees.
12. They were holy and beloved.
13. Their children were in the church.
14. You were reading the Scriptures to them in the synagogue.
15. The Jews used to kill his prophets.
16. The Baptist himself used to baptize his disciples.

Scripture Translation Exercises

12.4 Translate the following verses from Scripture:

1. καὶ ἐν τῇ σκοτίᾳ[1] περιπατεῖ καὶ οὐκ οἶδεν[2] ποῦ[3] ὑπάγει (1 John 2:11)
2. καὶ αὕτη ἡ ζωὴ ἐν τῷ υἱῷ αὐτοῦ ἐστιν (1 John 5:11)
3. αὐτὸς γὰρ σώσει[4] τὸν λαὸν αὐτοῦ ἀπὸ τῶν ἁμαρτιῶν αὐτῶν (Matt 1:21)
4. ἐν αὐτῇ τῇ ὥρᾳ (Luke 10:21)
5. ἐν αὐτῇ δὲ τῇ οἰκίᾳ μένετε (Luke 10:7)

1 τῇ σκοτίᾳ, "darkness"
2 οἶδεν, "he knows"
3 ποῦ, "where"
4 σώσει, the future third person singular form of σῴζω

LESSON 13

Passive Voice in the Present and Imperfect Indicative

VERB VOICE

A verb is in the active voice when its subject acts; a verb is in the passive voice when its subject is being acted upon. For example:

> Active: "I love," "I was striking."
>
> Passive: "I am loved," "I was being struck."

Note: Only transitive verbs (verbs that have direct objects) can have a passive voice. Verbs such as "I fall," "I slip," etc., do not take objects and are intransitive. These verbs can not be used in the passive voice.[1]

Passive Voice Endings

Greek, like Latin, communicates the passive voice by using special endings—not by using the auxiliary verb "to be," like in English. Since some very common verbs only use these passive endings, you will see them in nearly every Greek sentence—the passive endings are important to learn. These endings round out all of the possible variations for the two types of Greek verb endings (primary and secondary endings). Notice that the standard convention of using μ for marking first person, ς for second person, and τ for third person is more consistently represented in the passive verb endings. The passive forms also have fewer instances of contraction between stem and ending (the stem variable vowel appears more consistently). Additional tenses are produced not by adding additional endings but by swapping the variable vowel ε/ο stem (used in the present and imperfect) for other stems.

1 See Lesson 5 for more on transitive verbs.

Summary of Endings For comparison, the following chart lists the stems and endings for both primary and secondary tenses.

	Present Indicative		Imperfect Indicative	
	Active	Passive	Active	Passive
1 sg.	root + ω	root + ομαι	ἐ + root + ον	ἐ + root + ομην
2 sg.	root + εις	root + ῃ	ἐ + root + ες	ἐ + root + ου
3 sg.	root + ει	root + εται	ἐ + root + ε(ν)	ἐ + root + ετο
1 pl.	root + ομεν	root + ομεθα	ἐ + root + ομεν	ἐ + root + ομεθα
2 pl.	root + ετε	root + εσθε	ἐ + root + ετε	ἐ + root + εσθε
3 pl.	root + ουσι	root + ονται	ἐ + root + ον	ἐ + root + οντο

The passive voice of the present and imperfect indicative of λύω are given below. Notice that the imperfect passive includes the augment.

	Present Passive Indicative	
1 sg.	λύομαι	I am released or I am being released
2 sg.	λύῃ (λύει[1])	you are released or you are being released
3 sg.	λύεται	he/she/it is released or he/she/it is being released
1 pl.	λυόμεθα	we are released or we are being released
2 pl.	λύεσθε	you all are released or you all are being released
3 pl.	λύονται	they are released or they are being released

	Imperfect Passive Indicative	
1 sg.	ἐλυόμην	I was being released
2 sg.	ἐλύου	you were being released
3 sg.	ἐλύετο	he/she/it was being released
1 pl.	ἐλυόμεθα	we were being released
2 pl.	ἐλύεσθε	you all were being released
3 pl.	ἐλύοντο	they were being released

1 Less common alternate spelling.

Note: As in the case of the active voice, a simple past tense ("I was released," etc.) often sufficiently translates the imperfect.

The present and imperfect passive indicative of ε-contract verbs are conjugated as follows:

	Present Passive Indicative		
	Contracted Form	Uncontracted	Translation
1 sg.	φιλοῦμαι	φιλέομαι	I am loved or I am being loved
2 sg.	φιλῇ (φιλεῖ)	φιλέῃ (φιλέει)	you are loved or you are being loved
3 sg.	φιλεῖται	φιλέεται	he/she/it is loved or he/she/it is being loved
1 pl.	φιλούμεθα	φιλεόμεθα	we are loved or we are being loved
2 pl.	φιλεῖσθε	φιλέεσθε	you all are loved or you all are being loved
3 pl.	φιλοῦνται	φιλέονται	they are loved or they are being loved

	Imperfect Passive Indicative		
	Contracted Form	Uncontracted	Translation
1 sg.	ἐφιλούμην	ἐφιλεόμην	I was being loved
2 sg.	ἐφιλοῦ	ἐφιλέου	you were being loved
3 sg.	ἐφιλεῖτο	ἐφιλέετο	he/she/it was being loved
1 pl.	ἐφιλούμεθα	ἐφιλεόμεθα	we were being loved
2 pl.	ἐφιλεῖσθε	ἐφιλέεσθε	you all were being loved
3 pl.	ἐφιλοῦντο	ἐφιλέοντο	they were being loved

Agency and Instrument in Passive Contexts

Consider these sentences:

1. ὁ ἄγγελος λύει τὸν ἀπόστολον.
   "The angel releases the apostle."

2. ὁ ἀπόστολος λύεται ὑπὸ τοῦ ἀγγέλου.
   "The apostle is released by the angel."

Both of these sentences express the same idea, but they express it in different ways. When a sentence with a verb in the active voice is restated with a verb in the passive voice—as has been done in the sentences given above—the object of the first sentence ("the apostle") becomes the subject of the second, while the subject of the first sentence ("the angel") is introduced in English with the preposition "by."

Now consider this sentence:

3. ὁ κόσμος τηρεῖται τῇ σοφίᾳ τοῦ θεοῦ.
   "The world is kept by the wisdom of God."

Notice that the English translations of sentence 2 and 3 both use the preposition "by." In Greek, however, the sentences are different. Sentence 2 uses the preposition ὑπό followed by a genitive; sentence 3 uses a simple dative. The doer of the action in the first sentence above is a living person (i.e., "the angel"), but the thing that performs the action in the last sentence is not a living person (i.e., "wisdom").

In sentences similar to sentences 1 and 2, the doer of the action—a living person or animal—is called the "agent." In sentences similar to sentence 3, the doer of the action—which doesn't have a will—is described as the "instrument." This is a subtle but important distinction since they will be expressed differently in Greek.[1]

1 The same distinction exists in Latin, where the agent is expressed by *ab* with the ablative, and the instrument by the ablative alone.

Rules:

- The agent of the action of a passive verb is expressed by ὑπό with a genitive object.
- The instrument is expressed by the dative alone.

Active verbs may also be followed by a word denoting the instrument. For example:

4. ἀποκτείνει τὸν ἀπόστολον μαχαίρᾳ.
   "He kills the apostle with a sword."

The same verb may have both an agent and an instrument:

5. ὁ ἀπόστολος λύεται ὑπὸ τοῦ ἀγγέλου λόγῳ.
   "The apostle is released by the angel by a word."

The prepositions διά and μετά may be followed by a noun or pronoun in either the accusative or genitive case, with different meanings for each case. Please refer to Appendix 4. The preposition πρός is generally followed by an accusative case, and the preposition ὑπό by a genitive case. For the meanings of these prepositions, see the vocabulary.

EXERCISES

Memorization Exercise

13.1 Learn Vocabulary List 9.

Grammar Exercises

13.2 Convert verb voice forms: If the Greek verb is active, produce the passive form. If the Greek verb is passive, produce the active form. Keep all tense, person, and number meanings the same.

1. λύεται
2. τηρεῖς
3. ἐφιλούμην
4. ἄγουσιν
5. πείθομεν
6. ἐφερόμεθα
7. ἤγεσθε
8. συνάγει
9. ἐπείθοντο
10. κηρύσσει

Translation Exercises

13.3 Translate the following sentences:

1. ἐπέμπεσθε ὑπὸ τῶν διδασκάλων πρὸς ἕτερον ὄχλον.
2. ἐν τούτῳ τῷ τόπῳ ἐθεωροῦμεν τοῖς ὀφθαλμοῖς τὸν κύριον τῶν οὐρανῶν.
3. οὗτοι οἱ λόγοι ἐλαλοῦντο ὑπὸ τῶν ἀποστόλων πρὸς τοὺς πρεσβυτέρους.
4. εὐθὺς δὲ τὰ πρόβατα συνήγετο λίθοις ὑπὸ τῶν λῃστῶν.
5. ἀπεστελλόμεθα μετὰ τῶν προφητῶν διὰ τοῦ ὄχλου.
6. διὰ τοῦτο ἐπείθου τοῖς λόγοις τῶν κριτῶν.
7. μετὰ ταῦτα οἱ τελῶναι ἐδιδάσκοντο μετὰ τῶν νεανιῶν ὑπὸ τῶν πρεσβυτέρων.
8. οἱ υἱοὶ τοῦ οἰκοδεσπότου ἤσθιον τοὺς ἄρτους.
9. ὦ ὑποκριτά, οὐ περιπάτεις ἐν ταῖς ὁδοῖς τοῦ κυρίου.
10. ὁ θρόνος ἐποιεῖτο ὑπὸ τῶν ἐργάτων τῇ οἰκίᾳ τοῦ κυρίου ἐν Ἰερουσαλήμ.
11. οἱ ἐργάται ἀπέστελλον τοὺς καρποὺς τῆς γῆς πρὸς τοὺς οἰκοδεσπότας.

12. ὦ Ἰερουσαλήμ, οὐχ εὑρίσκῃ πιστή.
13. παρεκαλούμεθα τοῖς λόγοις τῶν μαθητῶν ἐν ἐκείνῳ τῷ χρόνῳ.
14. ἤγομεν τὰ τέκνα διὰ τοῦ ἱεροῦ.
15. μετ᾽ ἐκείνας τὰς ἡμέρας οἱ λῃσταὶ ὑπῆγον πρὸς τὴν ἔρημον.

Composition Exercises

13.4 Translate the following sentences into Greek:

1. The word of God was being preached by the apostles.
2. These fruits were sent by the head of household to the elders.
3. On this account the judges were being persuaded by the faithful teachers.
4. You were leading the people through the wilderness to Jerusalem.
5. After this they were being sought for by the crowd.
6. They were wicked in the eyes of the Lord.
7. The throne was being carried by the workmen to another place through the house.
8. Immediately the elders were walking with the prophets through Jerusalem.
9. The world was made through the Son of God.
10. O hypocrite, you do not keep the commandments of the Lord.
11. The young men were being taught by their own teachers.
12. You were not sent by the sons of the prophets.
13. Therefore, immediately after these things we used to preach the word of God to the disciples.
14. You all were being roused by the words of the head of household.

Scripture Translation Exercises

13.5 Translate the following verses from Scripture:

1. διὰ τί[1] οὐ περιπατοῦσιν οἱ μαθηταί σου[2] κατὰ τὴν παράδοσιν[3] τῶν πρεσβυτέρων (Mark 7:5)
2. καὶ φέρουσιν αὐτὸν ἐπὶ τὸν Γολγοθᾶν τόπον (Mark 15:22)
3. ἦν δὲ ὁ υἱὸς αὐτοῦ ὁ πρεσβύτερος ἐν ἀγρῷ (Luke 15:25)
4. καὶ συνάγει καρπὸν εἰς ζωὴν αἰώνιον (John 4:36)
5. καὶ κράζουσιν φωνῇ μεγάλῃ[4] (Rev 7:10)

1 διὰ τί, "why" (literally, "on account of what")
2 σου, "your"
3 τὴν παράδοσιν, "traditions" (literally, "things handed over")
4 μεγάλῃ, "great" (note the use of the dative case)

LESSON 14

Deponent Verbs, Present Imperative, and Relative Pronoun

DEPONENT VERBS

In traditional grammar, verbs that look passive but have active meanings are called "deponent" verbs because the early grammarians considered them to have "laid aside" (Latin *deponere*) a passive sense and assumed an active one. Greek actually has three voices: active, middle, and passive. The middle voice has the same forms as the passive in the present and imperfect tenses. It may be used for transitive verbs, and it is a common voice for intransitive verbs. The middle voice (fully explained in Lesson 16) is the true source for what we now call deponent verbs.

Deponent Verb Examples	
ἀποκρίνομαι	I answer
ἄρχομαι	I begin
ἔρχομαι	I go or come
δέχομαι	I receive

IMPERATIVE MOOD

Mood is part of every verb: it shows the way in which the action or state conveyed by the verb is to be regarded (e.g., whether it is to be regarded as a statement of specific fact, a command, a wish, a generalized condition, etc.). All the verb forms that you have learned so far have been in the indicative mood—the mood that generally is used for making statements or asking questions.

The imperative mood is used to express commands, exhortations, and entreaties. The forms given in this section are those for what is called the present imperative mood. Notice that the present tense stem variable vowel that was part of the present indicative remains as part of the present imperative.

	Present Active Imperative	
2 sg.	λῦε	release (commanding you)
3 sg.	λυέτω	let him/her/it release (where he/she/it is obligated)
2 pl.	λύετε	release (commanding you all)
3 pl.	λυέτωσαν	let them release (where they are obligated)

	Present Passive Imperative	
2 sg.	λύου	be released (commanding you)
3 sg.	λυέσθω	let him/her/it be released (obligating him/her/it)
2 pl.	λύεσθε	be released (commanding you all)
3 pl.	λυέσθωσαν	let them be released (obligating them)

The present imperative forms of ε-contract verbs are as follows:

	Present Active Imperative		
	Contracted Form	Uncontracted	Translation
2 sg.	φίλει	φίλεε	love (commanding you)
3 sg.	φιλείτω	φιλεέτω	let him/her/it love (obligating him/her/it)
2 pl.	φιλεῖτε	φιλέετε	love (commanding you all)
3 pl.	φιλείτωσαν	φιλεέτωσαν	let them love (obligating them)

	Present Passive Imperative		
	Contracted Form	Uncontracted	Translation
2 sg.	φιλοῦ	φιλέου	be loved (commanding you)
3 sg.	φιλείσθω	φιλεέσθω	let him/her/it be loved (obligating him/her/it)
2 pl.	φιλεῖσθε	φιλέεσθε	be loved (commanding you all)
3 pl.	φιλείσθωσαν	φιλεέσθωσαν	let them be loved (obligating them)

MEANING OF THE PRESENT IMPERATIVE

In Greek, the vocalic stem in the present and imperfect forms marks incompleteness—such as continuous action, action in progress, repeated action, or habitual action. Since the imperative mood does not use primary (non-past) indicative endings, the emphasis of the stem and endings focuses on how the action unfolds rather than action in present time. It's unfortunate that we label imperatives with this stem "present" imperatives, since timing is not being marked by the stem-endings! All imperatives occur in the present (time of the utterance) since they are speech acts. In other words, the present imperative often communicates a command or entreaty to continue to do an action or to do it repeatedly. Other times, the stem does not add any additional meaning beyond the verb root meaning. When the root meaning of the action is inherently repetitive, progressive, or stative, the present imperative may be used to match that aspectual meaning. Some examples of these types of verbs are "remain," "follow," and "reside."

Since English does not have an equivalent standard form of expression, it is not always possible to bring out this "incompleteness" in translating a present imperative. The translation examples below will attempt to express the full force of the Greek present imperative, but this subject also will be treated more fully when we study the aorist imperative. Note that a verb in the imperative mood is negated by μή, not by οὐ.

Examples of the use of the present imperative:

1. βάλλετε τοὺς λίθους.
   "Keep on throwing the stones."

2. πεμπέτωσαν ἄρτον τῷ προφήτῃ.
   "Let them keep on sending bread for the prophet."

3. τηρείτω τὰς ἐντολάς.
   "Let him continue to keep the commandments."

RELATIVE PRONOUN The relative pronoun is basically composed of the first and second declension stem and endings with a rough breathing mark. It is declined as follows:

Relative pronoun: ὅς, ἥ, ὅ ("who," "which")

	Singular			Plural		
	Masculine	Feminine	Neuter	Masculine	Feminine	Neuter
Nom.	ὅς	ἥ	ὅ	οἵ	αἵ	ἅ
Acc.	ὅν	ἥν	ὅ	οὕς	ἅς	ἅ
Gen.	οὗ	ἧς	οὗ	ὧν	ὧν	ὧν
Dat.	ᾧ	ᾗ	ᾧ	οἷς	αἷς	οἷς

Compare the accentuation of the relative pronoun with that of the article. Many of the nominative forms look very similar to nominative forms of the article. Note the difference between ὅ, the nominative and accusative singular neuter of the relative pronoun, and ὁ, the nominative singular masculine of the article. Compare also ἥ and ἡ; οἵ and οἱ; and αἵ and αἱ.

Case of Relative Pronoun The relative pronoun always refers back to some noun or pronoun, expressed or implied, in another clause, which is called its "antecedent." In Greek, relative pronouns must agree with their antecedent in number and gender, but not necessarily in case.

The case of a relative pronoun depends on the function that it performs within its own clause, which is typically called a relative clause.

Examples:

1. βλέπω τοὺς ἀνθρώπους οἳ ἔρχονται.
   "I see the men who are coming."

2. οἱ ἄνθρωποι οὓς ἀποστέλλετε ἀπέρχονται.
   "The men that you all are sending are going away."

3. αὕτη ἐστὶν ἡ γραφὴ ἣ τηρεῖται ἐν τῇ συναγωγῇ.
   "This is the writing that is kept in the synagogue."

4. αὕτη ἐστὶν ἡ γραφὴ ἣν εἶχεν ὁ ἀπόστολος.
   "This is the writing which the apostle used to have."

5. τὰ παιδία ἃ ἐδίδασκον ἀπέρχεται.
   "The children whom I was teaching are going away."

6. ὁ προφήτης οὗ ἀναγινώσκεις τὰ βιβλία ἅγιός ἐστιν.
   "The prophet whose books you are reading is holy."

7. οἱ ἄνθρωποι οἷς ποιῶ ταῦτα δοῦλοί εἰσιν.
   "The men for whom I am doing these things are slaves."

In example 1, ἀνθρώπους is in the accusative case because it is the object of the clause in which it stands, and οἵ is in the nominative case because it is the subject of the clause in which it stands. Carefully consider the cases of the relative pronouns in the other examples in the same way.

Adjectival Function of Relative Clause

Relative clauses are all adjectival clauses because they qualify and explain their antecedents, just like adjectives. Notice that authors have a number of grammatical options when they want to supply more descriptive or explanatory information about any noun in a sentence. You will learn about two more options later; based on what you have learned so far, an author could use:

- Another noun with a case ending (e.g., a possessive genitive showing who owns the noun)
- A preposition (matching the article status of the noun) with an object (e.g., the man in the house—ὁ ἄνθρωπος ὁ ἐν οἴκῳ)
- A relative clause

		Function		
		Substantive	Attributive	Adverbial
Part of Speech	Noun or Pronoun	noun with various case endings		
	Preposition	article + preposition + object	preposition + object	anarthrous preposition + object
	Adjective & Adverb	article + adjective (in place of noun)	adjective	adverb
	Relative Pronoun & Subordinating Conjunction	relative clause (relative pronoun + verb)		(conjunction + verb)

As translators, we have the same options in English—we can translate one attributive grammatical construction with a different one. Since English tends to prefer relative clauses, this happens often.

EXERCISES

Memorization Exercise

14.1 Learn Vocabulary List 10.

Grammar Exercises

14.2 Case identification: Label the case required to translate both the relative pronoun and its antecedent.

1. I saw the men whom you sent.
2. He came to save those who believe.
3. He who came before me is greater than I.
4. You know whom you serve.
5. This is my beloved son, in whom I'm well pleased.
6. They came for those who waited.
7. He who loves his brother abides in the light.
8. He was encouraged by those who prayed.
9. We trust in him by whose work we are saved.
10. We know those men whom you know.
11. That which we saw we testify to you.
12. He is greater than I, whose shoes I am not worthy to wear.

Translation Exercises

14.3 Translate the following sentences:

1. ἐπορευόμεθα πρὸς τὴν θάλασσαν μετὰ τῶν μαθητῶν.
2. ἠρνοῦντο τὸν κύριον τῆς δόξης ὃς τηρεῖ αὐτοὺς ἀπὸ τοῦ πονηροῦ.
3. ἐδέχεσθε τοὺς ἀγροὺς οὓς εἶχεν ὁ λαὸς Ἰσραήλ.
4. μὴ ἀποκρίνου τῷ δεσπότῃ.
5. ἀπήρχοντο πρὸς τὴν ἔρημον ἐν ᾗ ὁ Ἰωάννης ἐβάπτιζε.
6. ἀπεκρινόμην τοῖς ἀγγέλοις οἳ ἤρχοντο ἀπὸ τῶν πρεσβυτέρων.
7. μὴ ἐργάζεσθε τὴν ἀδικίαν.

8. οὗτος δέχεται τοὺς ἁμαρτωλοὺς οἳ ἔρχονται πρὸς αὐτὸν καὶ ἐσθίει μετ᾽ αὐτῶν.
9. ἅπτου τῶν κεφαλῶν τῶν παιδίων ἃ πέμπω.
10. οἱ δοῦλοι οὓς ἐδέχετο ἐργάζονται ἐν τοῖς ἀγροῖς.
11. ἀποστελλέτωσαν τὰ ἱμάτια ἃ λαμβάνουσιν εἰς τὸν οἶκον.
12. δεχέσθω τὸ βιβλίον ὃ γράφει ὁ ἀπόστολος.
13. διηρχόμεθα οὖν τοὺς ἀγροὺς αὐτῶν μετὰ τῶν τελωνῶν.
14. κακοὶ καὶ πονηροὶ δοῦλοι ἦτε.
15. ἀπτέσθωσαν τῶν λίθων τοῦ ἱεροῦ ὃ ᾠκοδομεῖτο τῷ κυρίῳ.

Composition Exercises

14.4 Translate the following sentences into Greek:

1. Let the love of the brethren remain in their hearts.
2. Keep the holy commandments that you receive from the teachers.
3. Do not deny the Lord of glory who saves you[1] from the evil world.
4. Let the elders whom they send receive the law for the people.
5. We were going through the fields in which the slaves were working.
6. After these things they were building a temple to the God of Israel.
7. Do not walk (pl.) in the way of sinners.
8. Let him receive the messengers who proclaim the kingdom of heaven.
9. The disciples whom John was baptizing remained in the wilderness.
10. Let them work the works of the Lord of glory.

1 ὑμᾶς

11. For the prophet receives the sinners who are sent to him and eats with them.
12. Do not answer the teacher.
13. After those days they were going away into the place in which the young men were remaining with the sheep.
14. This is the elder whose children were reading the books of the law that the prophet wrote.

Scripture Translation Exercises

14.5 Translate the following verses from Scripture:

1. δι᾽ ἃ ἔρχεται ἡ ὀργὴ[1] τοῦ θεοῦ (Col 3:6)
2. ὃς ἦν μετὰ σοῦ πέραν[2] τοῦ Ἰορδάνου, … οὗτος βαπτίζει καὶ πάντες[3] ἔρχονται πρὸς αὐτόν. (John 3:26)
3. ᾗ ὥρᾳ οὐ δοκεῖτε[4] ὁ υἱὸς τοῦ ἀνθρώπου ἔρχεται (Luke 12:40)
4. καὶ αὐτός ἐστιν ἡ κεφαλὴ τοῦ σώματος[5] τῆς ἐκκλησίας· ὅς ἐστιν ἀρχή (Col 1:18)

1 ἡ ὀργή, “wrath”
2 πέραν, “beyond,” “across”
3 πάντες, “all” (nominative plural)
4 δοκεῖτε, “you know”
5 τοῦ σώματος, “of the body”

LESSON 15

Present Infinitive, Personal Pronouns, and Possessive Adjectives

PRESENT INFINITIVE

The present infinitive forms are:

Present Active Infinitive	
λύειν	to release
φιλεῖν	to love
Present Passive Infinitive	
λύεσθαι	to be released
φιλεῖσθαι	to be loved

Function of the Infinitive

In both Greek and English, the infinitive mood is really the dative case of a verbal noun. In many of its uses, however, its dative sense is lost, and it is treated exactly as if it were an indeclinable verbal noun. Thus, the infinitive shares elements of both a verb and a noun: Like a verb, it has a subject expressed or implied, and it may have an object; it may be qualified by adverbs; and it has tense and voice. Like a noun, it may be the subject or object of another verb. The infinitive is always neuter, and the negative used with the infinitive in the New Testament is always μή.

There are four general uses of the infinitive in biblical Greek:

1. As a subject or object noun clause for particular verbs (which also occurs in English—e.g., "To live is Christ")
2. To show purpose or result (which also occurs in English—e.g., "He came to save")

3. To provide further explanation (which also occurs in English—e.g., "Having ears to hear")

4. As part of an adverbial clause with prepositions (this does not occur in English)

Since the infinitive can perform all three linguistic roles (substantive, attributive, and adverbial functions)—and it is a noun—each of these uses can be placed on the phrase and clause function table, which helps to illustrate equivalent uses for various parts of speech when it comes to providing explanatory or subordinate information within a sentence. (For another example of a phrase and clause function table, see Lesson 25.)

<table>
<tr><td colspan="2" rowspan="2"></td><th colspan="3">Function</th></tr>
<tr><th>Substantive</th><th>Attributive</th><th>Adverbial</th></tr>
<tr><th rowspan="6">Part of Speech</th><th>Noun or Pronoun</th><td colspan="3">noun with various case endings</td></tr>
<tr><th>Preposition</th><td>article + preposition + object</td><td>preposition + object</td><td>anarthrous preposition + object</td></tr>
<tr><th>Adjective & Adverb</th><td>article + adjective (in place of noun)</td><td>adjective</td><td>adverb</td></tr>
<tr><th>Relative Pronoun & Subordinating Conjunction</th><td colspan="2">relative pronoun + verb</td><td>conjunction + verb</td></tr>
<tr><th>Infinitive</th><td colspan="2">infinitive (with or without an article)</td><td>infinitive (with or without a conjunction or preposition[1])</td></tr>
<tr><th></th><td></td><td></td><td></td></tr>
</table>

This lesson focuses on the infinitive's uses in simple constructions (like those in English) without an introductory preposition or conjunction. Adverbial clauses with prepositions and clauses made more explicit with conjunctions will be covered in Lesson 32.

1 An infinitive used as an object of a preposition should really be placed as a type of object for an adverbial use of a prepositional phrase on this chart.

INFINITIVES AS SUBJECT OR OBJECT OF PARTICULAR VERBS

Infinitive Used as a Subject

The infinitive is especially common as the subject of an impersonal verb or of ἐστί. Even in this use, the infinitive may have a subject of its own. If this subject is expressed, it is put in the accusative case. For example:

1. παραβαίνειν ἀνθρώπινόν ἐστι.
   "To err is human."

2. ἔξεστι θεραπεύειν ἐν τῷ σαββάτῳ.
   "It is lawful to heal on the Sabbath."

3. ἔδει αὐτὸν διέρχεσθαι διὰ τῆς Σαμαρίας.
   "It was necessary for him to pass through Samaria."

4. καλόν ἐστιν ἡμᾶς εἶναι ὧδε.
   "It is good for us to be here."

Notice that in the English of the last three examples, the word "it" is placed first as a sort of preparatory subject; the real subject in each sentence is the infinitive noun clause (e.g., "to heal on the Sabbath"), as can be seen if the sentences are written in the following order:

To heal on the Sabbath is lawful.

To pass through Samaria was necessary for him.

To be here is good for us.

Examples 3 and 4 show that the subjects of the infinitives, αὐτόν and ἡμᾶς, are expressed in the accusative case.

Note that in example 2, English grammar demands that these words use a dative relationship. The verb ἔξεστι is, however, followed by a noun or pronoun in the dative case to express the person to whom the action is lawful. For example:

ἔξεστιν <u>ἡμῖν</u> θεραπεύειν ἐν τῷ σαββάτῳ.
"It is lawful <u>for us</u> to heal on the Sabbath."

Infinitive Used as an Object

Any verb expressing an action that naturally implies an object that is another action or state may use an infinitive as that object. Such verbs are generally the same in Greek as in English. For example:

1. βούλονται καταμένειν.
   "They wish to remain."

2. θέλομεν ἀκούειν.
   "We are willing to hear."

3. δύναμαι τοῦτο ποιεῖν.
   "I am able to do this."

4. ἄρχοντο οἰκοδομεῖν.
   "They begin to build."

After verbs meaning "to entreat," "to exhort," or "to command," an infinitive may be used as the direct object. Some of these verbs use various cases to express a secondary or indirect object. Such case meanings can be seen in actions such as "give charge to (an agent)" or "have charge over (an agent)." Although the genitive relationship for the agent of δέομαι isn't apparent in the English translation, this particular verb expects this construction. Such information for particular verbs is included in vocabulary lists and lexicons. Examples:

5. κελύει αὐτοὺς ἄγειν τὸν Παῦλον.
   "He commands them to bring Paul."

6. δέομαί σου θεραπεύειν τὸν υἱόν μου.
   "I implore you to heal my son."

7. παρήγγελλεν αὐτοῖς μὴ ὑπάγειν ἀπὸ Ἱεροσολύμων.
   "He used to charge them not to depart from Jerusalem."

If the subject of the infinitive is expressed, it is in the accusative case.

8. κελεύει τὸν Παῦλον ἄγεσθαι.
   "He commands Paul to be brought."

All infinitive noun clauses that stand as the subject or object of a verb are called "substantival" clauses.

Purpose Clauses

Since the infinitive is really the dative case of a verbal noun, it may be used not only as the verb in a substantival clause but also as the verb in an adverbial clause expressing purpose. This follows the same principle as when a noun in the dative case is used in English to express purpose. (For example: "He went to the market for corn.") And so both in Greek and English the infinitive is used to express purpose. For example:

1. ἀποστέλλει τοὺς δούλους <u>καλεῖν</u> τοὺς προφήτας.
   "He sends the slaves <u>to call</u> the prophets."

2. ὁ Ἰωάννης ἤρχετο πρὸς τὸν Ἰορδάνην <u>βαπτίζειν</u> τοὺς μαθητάς.
   "John used to go to the Jordan <u>to baptize</u> the disciples."

Result Clauses

Result clauses are very similar to purpose clauses, but they refer to the effect of an action rather than the intention behind it. An infinitive can be used to express this type of adverbial clause, as well. Sometimes, context will be your only help to determine whether the author is using the infinitive to convey purpose or result (or both). Normally, these clauses will be introduced with a conjunction such as ἵνα or ὥστε, but occasionally a simple infinitive is used.

Ἀβραὰμ ὑπήκουσεν <u>ἐξελθεῖν</u> (Heb 11:8)
"Abraham obeyed <u>with the result that he went out</u>"

Explanatory Uses of the Infinitive

Since infinitives are nouns, they can be used to qualify or define—just like appositional nouns. So, just as one can qualify a noun such as "tree" with another noun (e.g., "there is the tree, the oak"), one can qualify a noun with an infinitive (e.g., "there is the tree, the one to burn"). For example:

ἐγὼ βρῶσιν ἔχω <u>φαγεῖν</u>
"I have food <u>to eat</u>" (John 4:32)

PERSONAL PRONOUNS

The singular personal pronouns of the first and second persons have two versions for cases other than the nominative case. The more common version is the unaccented enclitic version. The other version has an accent and is used for emphasis. The forms are as follows:

	First Person			
	Singular		Plural	
Nom.	ἐγώ	I	ἡμεῖς	we
Acc.	με (ἐμέ)	me	ἡμᾶς	us
Gen.	μου (ἐμοῦ)	of me, my	ἡμῶν	of us, our
Dat.	μοι (ἐμοί)	to me	ἡμῖν	to us
	Second Person			
	Singular		Plural	
Nom.	σύ	you	ὑμεῖς	you all
Acc.	σε (σέ)	you	ὑμᾶς	you all
Gen.	σου (σοῦ)	of you, your	ὑμῶν	of you all, your
Dat.	σοι (σοί)	to you	ὑμῖν	to you all

The third person personal pronoun ("he," "she," "it") uses one consistent pattern of forms (αὐτός; see Lesson 12). Note that sometimes οὗτος and ἐκεῖνος are also used as personal pronouns. Examples:

1. οὗτός ἐστιν ἡ ὁδός, ἡ ἀλήθεια καὶ ἡ ζωή.
   "He is the way, the truth, and the life."

2. ἐκεῖνος δὲ ἐδίδασκεν ἐν τῷ ἱερῷ.
   "But he was teaching in the temple."

Another way to express a third person personal pronoun is the nominative case of the article followed by μέν and δέ. This construction is frequent in the classics but not in the New Testament.

3. ὁ δὲ ἀπέστελλεν αὐτόν.
   "But he was sending him away."

4. οἱ δὲ ὑπάγουσι εἰς τὴν ἔρημον.
   "But they depart into the wilderness."

Note that ὁ μέν followed by ὁ δέ should be translated by "One . . . another," while οἱ μέν followed by οἱ δέ should be translated "Some . . . others." For example:

5. οἱ μὲν ἔμενον, οἱ δὲ ἀπήρχοντο.
   "Some remained, but others were going away."

Since the personal ending of the verb is generally sufficient to identify the subject's person and number, the nominative case of the first and second person personal pronouns is not used except for emphasis. For example:

6. σὺ μὲν εἶ δοῦλος, ἐγὼ δὲ ἐλεύθερος.
   "You are a slave, but I am free."

POSSESSIVE ADJECTIVES

Possessive adjectives match the case, gender, and number of the word they are identifying as owned. Their roots are similar to the personal pronouns, and they are translated with English pronouns. However, they decline and function syntactically as adjectives. The forms are:

ἐμός, -ή, -όν	my or mine
σός, -ή, -όν	your or yours
ἡμέτερος, -α, -ον	our or ours
ὑμέτερος, -α, -ον	your or yours (plural)

Often, they are equivalent to the possessive use of the genitive of the personal pronoun. For example:

1. ὁ ἐμὸς κύριος, ὁ κύριός μου
   "My lord, my lord"

2. ὁ ἡμέτερος κύριος, ὁ κύριος ἡμῶν
   "Our lord, our lord"

Note that when a noun is qualified by a possessive pronoun or the genitive of a personal pronoun, it generally has an article before it.

The genitive singular and plural of αὐτός is used as the only option to translate "his," "hers," "its," and "their." There is no third person possessive adjective.

EXERCISES

Memorization Exercises

15.1 Learn Vocabulary List 11.

Grammar Exercises

15.2 Pronoun exercises: Translate the following possessive genitive pronouns and possessive adjectives.

1. τοῖς διδάσκαλοις ἡμετέροις
2. τοῖς ὀφειλέταις ἡμῶν (Matt 6:12)
3. τοὺς λίθους μου
4. αἱ ὑμέτεραι καρδίαι
5. ἡ χαρὰ ἡ ἐμή (John 3:29)
6. ἡ ὥρα μου (John 2:4)
7. ἐν τῷ νόμῳ δὲ τῷ ὑμετέρῳ
8. τὸ φῶς ὑμῶν (Matt 5:16)
9. τὸν οἶκόν σου (Matt 9:6)
10. ὁ λόγος ὁ σός

Translation Exercises

15.3 Translate the following sentences:

1. ἐβούλοντο ἀκούειν τοὺς λόγους οὓς ἐλάλει ὁ Ἰησοῦς.
2. διδάσκαλε, καλόν ἐστιν ἡμᾶς ὧδε εἶναι.
3. ἐδέοντο οὖν αὐτοῦ θεραπεύειν τοὺς υἱοὺς αὐτῶν.
4. οὗτος ἄρχεται οἰκοδομεῖν, ἀλλ' οὐ δύναται ποιεῖν τὸ ἔργον.
5. δεῖ ὑμᾶς ἀποκρίνεσθαι τοῖς πρεσβυτέροις.
6. κελεύω σε ἐξέρχεσθαι ἐκ τῆς οἰκίας.
7. ἔξεστιν ἡμῖν κηρύσσειν τὴν βασιλείαν τῶν οὐρανῶν.
8. ἔπεμπε τοὺς δούλους αὐτοῦ καλεῖν τοὺς πτωχοὺς καὶ τοὺς τυφλοὺς εἰς τὸν γάμον.
9. παρήγγελλεν αὐτοῖς ἄγειν τὸν Παῦλον.
10. ὁ γὰρ θεὸς πέμπει τὸν υἱὸν αὐτοῦ σῴζειν τὸν κόσμον.

11. παρεκάλουν αὐτοὺς οἱ προφῆται μένειν ἐν τῇ ἀληθείᾳ.
12. οὐ γὰρ θέλετε ἔρχεσθαι πρός με.
13. ὁ οὖν Ἰησοῦς ἤγετο εἰς τὴν ἔρημον πειράζεσθαι ὑπὸ τοῦ διαβόλου.
14. οἱ μαθηταὶ ἤρχοντο πρὸς τὸν Ἰορδάνην ὁμολογεῖν τὰς ἁμαρτίας αὐτῶν τῷ Ἰωάννῃ.
15. ἐκελεύομεν τοὺς ἀγγέλους πέμπεσθαι.
16. ὁ δὲ οὐκ ἤθελεν πορεύεσθαι ἐν ταῖς ὁδοῖς τοῦ κυρίου.
17. ἐγώ σε κελεύω ἐκεῖ μένειν, σὺ δὲ οὐκ ὑπακούεις.
18. οἱ μὲν ἦσαν δοῦλοι, οἱ δὲ ἐλεύθεροι.
19. παρεκαλοῦμεν τὸν λαὸν ὑπακούειν τοῖς προφήταις.

Composition Exercises

15.4 Translate the following sentences into Greek:

1. We must not deny the Lord of glory.[1]
2. They were not willing to obey the elders.
3. It is lawful for them to receive the money from the tax collectors.
4. I am a man, but you are children.
5. We wish to see the temple of the God of Israel.
6. We are sending the slaves to call the blind and the poor to the wedding.
7. It is bad for them to be there.
8. It was necessary for Jesus to pass through Samaria to proclaim the gospel to the people.
9. We commanded the prophet to be brought.
10. I implored him to heal my child, but he would not.
11. Jesus commanded them to send the blind man.
12. I am not able to exhort them to remain in Jerusalem.
13. They began to confess their sins to us.
14. Some went to their houses and others to the temple.

1 Use δεῖ.

15. We are free, but you are slaves.
16. Jesus is led into the desert to be tempted by the devil.
17. We came to John to be baptized by him in the Jordan.
18. They are not able to do this.
19. I sent the messenger to you, but he was not willing to depart.
20. We must work the works of him who sent us (use δεῖ).
21. They wish to read the books that you have.

Scripture Translation Exercises

15.5 Translate the following verses from Scripture:

1. ἔκρυψα[1] τὸ τάλαντόν σου ἐν τῇ γῇ· ἴδε[2] ἔχεις τὸ σόν. (Matt 25:25)
2. μένετε[3] ἐν τῷ λόγῳ τῷ ἐμῷ (John 8:31)
3. οὐκ ἐστὲ ἐκ τῶν προβάτων τῶν ἐμῶν (John 10:26)
4. ὁ λόγος ὁ σὸς ἀλήθειά ἐστιν (John 17:17)
5. ἔλεγεν τῷ ὄχλῳ ὅτι ἓξ[4] ἡμέραι εἰσὶν ἐν αἷς δεῖ ἐργάζεσθαι· ἐν αὐταῖς οὖν ἐρχόμενοι[5] θεραπεύεσθε καὶ μὴ τῇ ἡμέρᾳ τοῦ σαββάτου (Luke 13:4)
6. ἀποκρίνεται Ἰησοῦς· τὴν ψυχήν σου ὑπὲρ ἐμοῦ θήσεις;[6] (John 13:38)
7. οὐ δύναται δένδρον[7] ἀγαθὸν καρποὺς πονηροὺς ποιεῖν οὐδὲ δένδρον σαπρὸν[8] καρποὺς καλοὺς ποιεῖν (Matt 7:18)

1 ἔκρυψα, "I hid" (κρύπτω, cf. English "crypt")
2 ἴδε, "Look!, Behold!, Lo"
3 The verb was modified for this exercise.
4 ἕξ, "six"
5 This is a participle form of ἔρχομαι (form to be learned later). Treat it as an imperative plus καί in this context.
6 θήσεις, "will you lay down"
7 δένδρον, "tree"
8 σαπρὸν, "rotten"

LESSON 16

Future Active and Middle Indicative, and the Middle Voice

FUTURE TENSE

The future active indicative tense is generally formed by swapping out the thematic stem (ο/ε in the present and imperfect, used to communicate incomplete meaning) with σ + thematic vowel (producing a stem that communicates complete or simple meaning.) This sigmatic stem is followed by the non-past endings (the same that are used for the present active indicative).

Likewise, the future middle is generally formed by placing this sigmatic stem between the verbal root and the non-past endings, the same that are used for the present passive indicative.

The future active and middle forms of λύω ("I release") are as follows:

	Future Active Indicative		Future Middle Indicative	
1 sg.	λύσω	I will release	λύσομαι	I will release for my own benefit (or ransom)
2 sg.	λύσεις	you will release	λύσῃ	you will release for your own benefit (or ransom)
3 sg.	λύσει	he/she/it will release	λύσεται	he/she/it will release for his/her/its own benefit (or ransom)
1 pl.	λύσομεν	we will release	λυσόμεθα	we will release for our own benefit (or ransom)
2 pl.	λύσετε	you all will release	λύσεσθε	you all will release for your own benefit (or ransom)
3 pl.	λύσουσι	they will release	λύσονται	they will release for their own benefit (or ransom)

Future Active Infinitive		Future Middle Infinitive	
λύσειν	about to release	λύσεσθαι	about to release for one's own benefit (or ransom)

Note that each of the indicative forms is made up of the verbal root, the sigmatic stem (σ + ο/ε), and the appropriate primary (non-past) ending. The oldest Greek verbs marked aspect by changing root spelling. Some verbs continue this older system for many tenses even in the New Testament. For the future tense, however, all verbs mark the simple aspect of this tense by modifying the stem.

Why the Future Uses a Simple Aspect

The chart below shows how the future tense shares the same non-past endings of the present tense but uses a different stem spelling. Statements about the future refer to ideas. They aren't unfolding in real time, but rather are bounded by the limits of the thought. Since Greek only has two temporal endings (non-past and past), the future and present share a more general time frame (non-past) than you may expect. Given this constraint, the non-past incomplete tense is used for unfolding present events, and the non-past complete tense is used for ideas about the future.

		Aspectual Meanings	
		Incomplete	Complete (commonly marked by a particular stem spelling)
Temporal Endings	Non-past (primary)	PRESENT (Present Root + Thematic Stem + Primary Endings)	FUTURE (Verbal Root + Sigmatic Stem + Primary Endings)
	Past (secondary)	IMPERFECT	(SIMPLE PAST)

Sigmatic Stem Spelling

If the verb root ends in a consonant, this consonant combines with the stem σ, which is added to form the future tense (see the following examples). The square of stops will help you here—it can help you predict how sigma reacts with different groups of letters.[1]

1 See the comprehensive consonant chart in Lesson 1.

If the verb root terminates with a guttural letter (γ, κ, χ), the guttural joins with σ to form ξ. For example:

Guttural and Sigma Combinations

	Present	Future Active	Future Middle
I pursue	διώκω	διώξω	διώξομαι
I open	ἀνοίγω	ἀνοίξω	ἀνοίξομαι
I rule (act.) I begin (mid.)	ἄρχω	ἄρξω	ἄρξομαι
I have	ἔχω	ἕξω[1]	

If the verb root terminates with a labial letter (β, π, φ), the labial joins with σ to form ψ. For example:

Labial and Sigma Combinations

	Present	Future Active	Future Middle
I see	βλέπω	βλέψω	βλέψομαι
I write	γράφω	γράψω	γράψομαι
I send	πέμπω	πέμψω	πέμψομαι

If the verb root terminates with a dental letter (δ, τ, ϑ, or ζ), the final root letter is dropped before the σ of the sigmatic stem. For example:

Dental and Sigma Combinations

	Present	Future Active	Future Middle
I persuade	πείϑω	πείσω	πείσομαι

In ε-contract verbs, the ε lengthens to η before any verb stem that begins with a consonant (including the sigmatic stem used in the future tense). For example:

Contract Vowel and Sigma

	Present	Future Active	Future Middle
I ask	αἰτέω	αἰτήσω	αἰτήσομαι
I seek	ζητέω	ζητήσω	ζητήσομαι

1 Note the rough breathing mark on this form representing a different root for this verb used in this tense.

Future Forms of εἰμί

The future tense of εἰμί follows the same principles. The verbal root is εσ-. We add the sigmatic stem and middle endings. One of the repeated sigmas drops out (much like ζ drops prior to a sigma), and we have the following forms:

	Future Active of εἰμί			
	Indicative			
	Singular		Plural	
1st	ἔσομαι	I will be	ἐσόμεθα	we will be
2nd	ἔσῃ (ἔσει[1])	you will be	ἔσεσθε	you all will be
3rd	ἔσται	he/she/it will be	ἔσονται	they will be
	Infinitive			
	ἔσεσθαι			

MIDDLE VOICE

The middle voice generally denotes that the subject has a heightened role in the verbal action. For some verbs this may involve acting on oneself (such as washing or dressing), or in some way that concerns oneself. The middle λύσομαι involves the idea of ransoming rather than merely releasing. The middle λαμβάνομαι has more of the idea of laying hold of rather than merely receiving. Sometimes such differences are nearly indistinguishable from the active voice in meaning.

The middle voice meaning for a particular verb can convey something other than an extension of performing the active meaning with some special interest for the subject. This dramatically increases the range of meaning for a number of verbs. For example, the active meaning of ἅπτω is "I ignite," but the meaning for the middle voice ἅπτομαι is simply "I touch." Thus the middle voice allows for many more meanings without having to invent new roots.

1 Uncommon alternate spelling.

Middle Used as Active in Future Tenses of Some Verbs

Many verbs have no future active but only future middle forms. These future middles are deponents and have exactly the same meaning as if they were active. Note that unlike the present tense, future middle forms typically use different stems than future passive forms. The passive forms are presented in Lesson 24.

Learning the proper middle voice meaning is part of learning vocabulary. The meanings for the middle voice can be summarized as follows:

Three Types of Meaning for the Middle Voice

1. Special interest on the part of the subject
    - Reflexive meaning
    - Intensive meaning
    - For the benefit of the subject
2. Simple active meaning
    - Redundant meaning (i.e., same meaning) as the active voice
    - Deponent use, where the verb doesn't have an active form. This is common for the future tense of many verbs that have set aside their active future forms
3. An additional meaning unrelated to the verb's active meaning

EXERCISES

Memorization Exercise

16.1 Learn Vocabulary List 12.

Grammar Exercises

16.2 Consonant combination exercises:

1. δ + σ =
2. χ + σ =
3. β + σ =
4. κ + σ =
5. ζ + σ =
6. τ + σ =
7. φ + σ =
8. π + σ =
9. γ + σ =
10. ϑ + σ =

Translation Exercises

16.3 Translate the following sentences:

1. οὐκ ἀδικήσουσι τὰ τέκνα.
2. οἱ δὲ ἐνδύσονται τὰ ἱμάτια.
3. ἀνοίξει τοὺς ὀφθαλμοὺς τῶν τυφλῶν οἳ συνάγονται ἐν τῇ συναγωγῇ.
4. πείσομεν τοὺς ἐργάτας ἐργάζεσθαι ἐν τοῖς ἀγροῖς.
5. πέμψω πρὸς αὐτοὺς σοφοὺς καὶ προφήτας, ἀλλ᾽ οὐκ ἀκούσουσιν αὐτοὺς οἱ υἱοὶ Ἰσραήλ.
6. ἐκεῖνος ἔσται ἅγιος τῷ κυρίῳ.
7. ἄρξετε τῶν Ἰουδαίων οἳ κατοικοῦσι ἐκείνην τὴν γῆν.
8. προφητεύσεις τῷ λαῷ τούτῳ καὶ ὑπακούσουσί σοι.
9. διακονήσετε τοῖς ἐχθροῖς ὑμῶν ὅτι οὐκ ἠθέλετε ὑπακούειν μοι, ἀλλ᾽ ἐγὼ ἐλεήσω ὑμᾶς ἐν ἐκείνῃ τῇ ἡμέρᾳ.

10. κατοικήσομεν τοὺς ἀγροὺς τῶν ἐχθρῶν οἷς διηκονοῦμεν ὅτι οὐκ ἠκούομεν τὸν λόγον τοῦ κυρίου.
11. οἱ διάκονοι τῆς συναγωγῆς οὐ διώξουσι τοὺς λῃστὰς ἐν τῷ σαββάτῳ.
12. εὐλογείτωσαν τὴν δόξαν τοῦ θεοῦ Ἰσραήλ.
13. πέμψομεν τοὺς νεανίας κατοικεῖν τὴν γῆν.
14. οἱ πρεσβύτεροι ἕξουσι τὰ πρόβατα ἃ σῴζεται ἀπὸ τῶν ἐχθρῶν.
15. ἀρξόμεθα εὐλογεῖν τοὺς υἱοὺς τῶν προφητῶν.

Composition Exercises

16.4 Translate the following sentences into Greek:

1. I will open the books that are in the synagogue.
2. They will be just and faithful in that day, and I will bless them because they hear my voice.
3. We will behold the face of the Lord in the temple that is built in Jerusalem.
4. The Lord will have mercy upon them because they dwell in the land of their enemies, and he will lead them into their own land.
5. Jesus therefore began to send the apostles to proclaim the gospel to the house of Israel.
6. We will send the slaves to pursue the robbers.
7. Peace and truth will dwell in our land because we obey the commandments of the Lord.
8. He will speak these things to the multitudes in parables.
9. I will be first, but you will be last.
10. Do not praise the wicked, for the wicked will not dwell in our land.

Scripture Translation Exercises

16.5 Translate the following verses from Scripture:

1. διώκετε τὴν ἀγάπην (1 Cor 14:1)
2. δύνασθε γὰρ καθ᾽ ἕνα[1] πάντες[2] προφητεύειν (1 Cor 14:31)
3. μακάριοι[3] οἱ πτωχοὶ τῷ πνεύματι,[4] ὅτι αὐτῶν ἐστιν ἡ βασιλεία τῶν οὐρανῶν. (Matt 5:3)
4. ποῖον[5] οἶκον οἰκοδομήσετέ μοι, λέγει κύριος (Acts 7:49)
5. καὶ προφητεύσουσιν οἱ υἱοὶ ὑμῶν καὶ αἱ θυγατέρες[6] ὑμῶν (Acts 2:17)

1 ἕνα, "one by one"
2 πάντες, "all"
3 μακάριοι, "blessed"
4 τῷ πνεύματι, "spirit"
5 ποῖον, "what kind"
6 αἱ θυγατέρες, "daughters"

LESSON 17

Verb Root Forms, Reflexive Pronouns, and Questions

BASIC ROOT FORMS FOR VERBS

Before verb stems were used to denote aspect (e.g., incompleteness and completeness), Greek marked incompleteness—such as the action being ongoing, repeated, habitual—by modifying the verb root. The basic original root form would mark complete (or simple) aspectual meaning. We call this original the "verbal root form." Since the modified root form marked incompleteness (found in the present and imperfect tenses), this text refers to that modified root spelling as the "present root form."

Irregular Verb Patterns

In English we can think of examples from two broad categories for irregular verbs—namely, those that minimally change the root to denote tense (e.g., "give" vs. "gave") and those that use an unrelated root (e.g., "go" vs. "went"). Greek has these same categories. This lesson examines verbs of the first type, verbs that have two different but related roots: the verbal root and the present root. The verbal root is used to produce all the tenses with the exception of the present and imperfect, while the present root is used to produce the present and imperfect tenses.

Present Root Form

Since the present indicative is used as the primary dictionary form, we tend to have the impression that it is the original and primary form of the verb. This is, however, not the case. The present root form is really a derivative of the verbal root (generally lengthened in some way.) The verbal root is the most basic part of the verb; nouns and adjectives of kindred meaning are formed from it rather than from the present root form. For example:

Lengthened Present Roots

Verbal Root	Present	Noun	Noun Translation
κηρυκ-	κηρύσσω	κῆρυξ	herald
μαθ-	μανθάνω	μαθητής	disciple
φυγ-	φεύγω	φυγή	flight

Some additional ways in which the verbal root is modified to generate the present root form are classified below.

-τ Present Root Infix

Some verbs (typically with a labial root termination) add τ to the verbal root in order to produce their present root form.

Verbal Root	Present	Future	Translation
καλυπ-	ἀποκαλύπτω	ἀποκαλύψω	I reveal
κοπ-	ἐκκόπτω	ἐκκόψω	I cut down
κρυπ-	κρύπτω	κρύψω	I hide

Softened Guttural Present Roots

Some verbs with guttural root terminations soften the gutteral to σσ to produce their present root form.

Verbal Root	Present	Future	Translation
κηρυκ-	κηρύσσω	κηρύξω	I proclaim
πραγ-	πράσσω	πράξω	I do
ταγ-	τάσσω	τάξω	I set in order
φυλακ-	φυλάσσω	φυλάξω	I guard

-ιζ Present Root Infix

The future forms of verbs with -ιζω in their present tense spellings typically use what is called an "Attic future form" for future tenses. Sometimes the ιζ is the product of ιδ within the verbal root (e.g., ἐλπιδ- forming ἐλπίζω.) Normally it is the result of an addition (an "infix") to the verbal root originally intended to show causation or some other aspect. By the time of the New Testament, the distinction between verb forms with and without this infix was greatly reduced. Nearly all that remained was a preference toward one form or the other (similar to the common English usage of "use" vs. "utilize").

Attic Future

The Attic future is one of two places where we do not see a σ in the future active tense.[1] In addition to the absence of σ, the infixed ζ also drops out (as well as the dental in verbal roots such as ἐλπιδ-.) Note that βαπτίζω and σῴζω are notable exceptions to this rule. Understanding the ιζ as a present root form infix helps explain the appearance of the iota subscript in the present root form of σῴζω. For example:

Verbal Root	Present	Future	Translation
ἐλπιδ-	ἐλπίζω	ἐλπιῶ	I hope
ἐγγύς-	ἐγγίζω	ἐγγιῶ	I draw near
καθαρ-	καθαρίζω	καθαριῶ	I cleanse
βαπτ-	βαπτίζω	βαπτίσω	I baptize
σοτ-	σῴζω	σώσω	I save

-αζ Present Root Infix

The future forms of verbs with -αζω in their present tense spellings are typically the result of using ζ or αζ as an infix to mark an incomplete aspect. This infix is often used with roots terminating with αγ (e.g., κραγ- forming κράζω) or a modification of the neuter noun form, which terminates in a dental (ὄνοματ- forming ὀνομάζω.) Since the sigmatic stem of the future tense is added to the verbal root (not the present form), it will interact with the final verbal root letter according to principles found in the square of stops. A guttural followed by σ will form ξ. A dental will drop prior to σ. (When learning Greek it is often easier to think of the ζ prior to the sigmatic stem dropping out in the future tense. This will yield the same result in spelling only coincidentally, since we technically are not adding the sigmatic stem to the present root containing the ζ.) Examples of some common -αζω verbs:

Verbal Root	Present	Future	Translation
ἀγορα-	ἀγοράζω	ἀγοράσω	I buy
δοξα-	δοξάζω	δοξάσω	I glorify
ἑτοιμα-	ἑτοιμάζω	ἑτοιμάσω	I make ready
κραγ-	κράζω	κράξω	I cry out
θαυμα-	θαυμάζω	θαυμάσομαι	I wonder
πειρα-	πειράζω	πειράσω	I try or tempt

1 The other circumstance is that of verbs with liquid roots.

REFLEXIVE PRONOUN

Reflexive pronouns are used when a pronoun refers back to the subject within the same clause. For example, in English:

Reflexive Pronoun Example	Regular Pronoun Example
I surprised myself.	He surprised me.
He saw his own shadow.	I saw his shadow.
He bought the gift for himself.	He bought the gift for her.

Since reflexive pronouns refer back to the subject of a clause, they cannot be the subject of the clause. Thus they do not occur in the nominative case. Here are the Greek reflexive pronouns. Note that the plural forms for the first and second person reflexive pronoun are identical to the masculine plural third person reflexive pronoun forms.

	First Person			
	Singular		Plural	
Nom.	-		-	
Acc.	ἐμαυτόν	(myself)	ἑαυτούς	(ourselves)
Gen.	ἐμαυτοῦ	(of myself)	ἑαυτῶν	(of ourselves)
Dat.	ἐμαυτῷ	(for myself)	ἑαυτοῖς	(for ourselves)

	Second Person			
	Singular		Plural	
Nom.	-		-	
Acc.	σεαυτόν	(yourself)	ἑαυτούς	(yourselves)
Gen.	σεαυτοῦ	(of yourself)	ἑαυτῶν	(of yourselves)
Dat.	σεαυτῷ	(for yourself)	ἑαυτοῖς	(for yourselves)

	Third Person					
	Singular			Plural		
	Masc.	Fem.	Neut.	Masc.	Fem.	Neut.
Nom.	-	-	-	-	-	-
Acc.	ἑαυτόν	ἑαυτήν	ἑαυτό	ἑαυτούς	ἑαυτάς	ἑαυτά
Gen.	ἑαυτοῦ	ἑαυτῆς	ἑαυτοῦ	ἑαυτῶν	ἑαυτῶν	ἑαυτῶν
Dat.	ἑαυτῷ	ἑαυτῇ	ἑαυτῷ	ἑαυτοῖς	ἑαυταῖς	ἑαυτοῖς

INTENSIFYING PRONOUN

As we have already seen in Lesson 12, αὐτός, αὐτή, αὐτό, means "he," "she," "it" when it stands alone but acts as an intensifier, "self," when it matches a noun or pronoun in gender, number, and case. The English convention of using the word "self" can cause confusion when learning Greek, since we also use that word in reflexive forms.

IDENTITY PRONOUN

When αὐτός is joined to and immediately follows an article, it means "the same." The article and αὐτός are always in the same number, gender, and case.

Distinguish carefully between the following examples:

1. ὁ αὐτὸς ἄνθρωπος.
   "The same man."

2. ὁ ἄνθρωπος αὐτός.
   "The man himself."

Distinguish also between this last use of αὐτός and the use of the reflexive pronoun:

3. ὁ ἄνθρωπος αὐτὸς λέγει τοῦτο.
   "The man himself says this."

4. ὁ ἄνθρωπος βάλλει ἑαυτόν εἰς τὴν θάλασσαν.
   "The man casts himself into the sea."

Sometimes words contract together. This is called crasis. For example, τὰ αὐτά contracted to ταὐτά means "the same things." (Notice the breathing mark in the middle of the contraction that distinguishes this from ταῦτα, "these things.")

QUESTIONS

Questions are expressed in Greek not by altering the order of the words in the sentence but by placing the question mark (;) at the end of the sentence. You will notice that this question mark looks like an English semicolon. The Greek colon is a single dot above the line (·). Typically questions begin with an interrogative pronoun, such as "who?," "when?," or "where?" Questions that expect either a "yes" or "no" for an answer do not begin with an interrogative. To help the reader prepare for a question, sometimes Greek will identify a question by using ἆρα as the first word of the sentence. For example:

1. ποιοῦσι τοῦτο.
   "They are doing this."
2. ἆρα ποιοῦσι τοῦτο;
   "Are they doing this?"

EXERCISES

Memorization Exercise

17.1 Learn Vocabulary List 13.

Grammar Exercises

17.2 Write the future active indicative first person singular using the following verbal roots. Notice how the future tense root spelling normally uses the verbal root (and may involve consonant contraction with σ from the future stem).

1. κραγ-
2. κρυπ-
3. φυλακ-
4. ἐκκοπ-
5. ταγ-
6. ἐλπιδ-
7. κηρυκ-
8. διδαχ-
9. ἀποκτεν-

Translation Exercises

17.3 Translate the following sentences:

1. κρύψομεν τὸ παιδίον ἐν τῇ οἰκίᾳ;
2. οὐχ ἁγιάσουσι τὰ σάββατά μου.
3. οἱ αὐτοὶ ἄγγελοι ἑτοιμάσουσιν ἑαυτοὺς πορεύεσθαι.
4. καθαρίζετε ἑαυτούς, ὑποκριταί.
5. ἀποκαλύψεις αὐτοῖς τὴν δόξαν τῆς σοφίας.
6. ἕξετε ζωὴν ἐν ἑαυτοῖς.
7. σὺ γὰρ πράξεις τὰ αὐτά.
8. Ἰησοῦς αὐτὸς ἤγγιζε τοῖς αὐτοῖς μαθηταῖς.
9. τάξουσι τοὺς αὐτοὺς ἀνθρώπους ἐν τοῖς ἀγροῖς.
10. σκανδαλίσετε τοὺς ἁγίους;
11. ἅψεται τοῦ ἱματίου τοῦ προφήτου.
12. πορεύσομαι πρὸς τὴν αὐτὴν οἰκίαν;
13. ἁγιάζετε τὰς καρδίας ὑμῶν τῇ ἀγάπῃ τῆς ἀληθείας.
14. ἀπάξουσι τοὺς λεπροὺς ἀπὸ τοῦ ἱεροῦ.
15. ἐκκόψετε τὰ δένδρα ἅ ἐστιν ἐν ἐκείνῃ τῇ γῇ.
16. θαυμάσει τὴν δόξαν τοῦ κυρίου.

Composition Exercises

17.4 Translate the following sentences into Greek:

1. You all will set the books in order in the synagogue.
2. They will hope to behold the signs of the apostles.
3. We will draw near to hear the voice of the teacher.
4. The wicked man will do wicked things.
5. Will he cleanse himself in the same lake?
6. She will make herself ready to go.
7. I will cut down the trees that are in the field.
8. We will buy the same books for our children.
9. The Lord will guard the souls of his people.
10. We will begin to sanctify our hearts.
11. The maiden will carry the loaves for the workmen.
12. They will hide themselves in the trees.
13. You all will begin to wonder at the power of the elders.
14. We will not reveal ourselves to them.
15. Are you willing to behold peace and righteousness in the kingdom of God?
16. Will we command them to read the Scriptures to the brethren?

Scripture Translation Exercises

17.5 Translate the following verses from Scripture:

1. ὅστις[1] οὐ βαστάζει τὸν σταυρὸν[2] ἑαυτοῦ καὶ ἔρχεται ὀπίσω[3] μου, οὐ δύναται εἶναί μου μαθητής (Luke 14:27)
2. καὶ ὑπὲρ[4] αὐτῶν ἐγὼ ἁγιάζω ἐμαυτόν (John 17:19)
3. πάλιν[5] ἔρχομαι καὶ παραλήμψομαι[6] ὑμᾶς πρὸς ἐμαυτόν (John 14:3)
4. καὶ τοῦτο ὁ θεὸς ὑμῖν ἀποκαλύψει (Phil 3:15)

1 ὅστις, "he who," relative pronoun (ὅς + τις)
2 σταυρὸν, "cross"
3 ὀπίσω, "after," "behind"
4 ὑπὲρ, "for the sake of" + genitive
5 πάλιν, "again"
6 The same meaning as λήμψομαι (future deponent of λαμβάνω)

LESSON 18

Sigmatic Aorist (First Aorist) and Meanings of Aspectual Stems

The simple past tense is called the aorist indicative in Greek. In English we have a number of ways to communicate the simple past tense: For some verbs, we mark it by modifying the root (e.g., "took," "gave"). For other verbs we add an "-ed" ending (e.g., "opened," "received"). Both patterns represent different ways to convey the same simple past meaning. Rarely does a verb have the option to use either pattern (such as the older English word "beseech"). Consider the following example:

SPELLING PATTERNS TO DENOTE THE SIMPLE PAST

Present	Root Change Pattern	"-ed" Ending Pattern
beseech	besought	beseeched

Greek has a very similar two-pattern structure: the sigmatic aorist (or first aorist) and the thematic aorist (or second aorist). Like English, both will convey the same meaning. Chronologically the root-changing pattern (thematic aorist or second aorist) is the older pattern. As Greek developed, many verbs changed from using a thematic aorist spelling to using a sigmatic aorist form. In biblical Greek, we find a few common verbs in the midst of this transition. These verbs may appear using either pattern (akin to what happened with "beseech" in English).

The σα stem, which directly follows the verbal root, produces consonantal changes in accordance with the square of stops, similar to those produced by the σ inserted in the future tense. Be sure to memorize the forms in the following list.

PRINCIPAL PARTS To help people learn and reference the various stems and unrelated roots that a verb can use to produce all its tenses, lexicons and dictionaries typically provide a list of the basic root and stem forms a verb uses. These are called principal parts and can be seen in the Greek to English Glossary in this book. Greek verbs have six principal parts (although some verbs are not used in every possible tense or voice variation and thus may be described as having fewer than six principal parts.) The first principal part is the present active indicative (using a present root). The second principal part is the future active indicative (typically using the verbal root and sigmatic stem. The third principal part is the aorist active indicative (showing the type of spelling pattern the verb uses for this tense.) This is a summary of all the principal parts for a verb. Each will be fully introduced in subsequent lessons.

Principal Parts for λύω

1	2	3	4	5	6
Present (all voices) Impf. (all voices)	Future Active and Middle	Aorist Active and Middle	Perfect Active and Middle	Perfect Passive	Aorist Passive Future Passive
λύω	λύσω	ἔλυσα	λέλυκα	λέλυμαι	ἐλύθην

Verbal Root	First Principal Part (present)	Second Principal Part (future)	Third Principal Part (first aorist)
διωκ-	διώκω	διώξω	ἐδίωξα
οιγ-	ἀνοίγω	ἀνοίξω	ἀνέῳξα[1]
κηρυκ-	κηρύσσω	κηρύξω	ἐκήρυξα
κραγ-	κράζω	κράξω	ἔκραξα
βλεπ-	βλέπω	βλέψω	ἔβλεψα
γραφ-	γράφω	γράψω	ἔγραψα
κρυπ-	κρύπτω	κρύψω	ἔκρυψα
πειθ-	πείθω	πείσω	ἔπεισα
ἐλπιδ-	ἐλπίζω	ἐλπιῶ	ἤλπισα
ἁγιαδ-	ἁγιάζω	ἁγιάσω	ἡγίασα
αἰτε-	αἰτέω	αἰτήσω	ᾔτησα
καλε-	καλέω	καλέσω[2]	ἐκάλεσα
θελ-	θέλω[3]	θελήσω[4]	ἠθέλησα[5]

SIGMATIC AORIST

This lesson focuses only on the sigmatic aorist, which makes use of a stem marker (σ) rather than a root change. Thus the sigmatic aorist is analogous to the class of English verbs that use a regular root with a consistent -ed ending. The name "aorist" means "unbounded" or "unlimited"; the aorist tense is used to denote that the action is to be understood as a simple event, without any regard to the length of time or repetition for the action. Any such additional meaning, if present, would derive from the verb's meaning. The aorist is unbounded

1 This verb has a double augment (lengthens the initial vowel and adds an *epsilon*). This also occurs with ὁράω. Cf. James Hope Moulton, *An Introduction to the Study of New Testament Greek* (London: Kelly, 1895), 109.

2 καλέω is exceptional. It does not lengthen its contract vowel before sigmatic stems. Its root metathesizes the α and λ in the remaining tenses, reducing its root form to κλη for those tenses (perfect and aorist passive).

3 Impf. ἤθελον

4 The intervocalic σ produced by the sigmatic stem in the future and aorist forms of this verb remained and caused the preceding ε (which was inserted to separate the liquid and σ) to lengthen like a contract verb's root vowel prior to a consonant stem.

5 "The augment with ἠ is found in later Attic (since 300 BC) in the verbs μέλλω, δύναμαι, βούλομαι, probably by analogy of ἤ-θελον, where ἠ- was a preposition (Lat. ē, Skt. ā). Of these forms ἠβουλ. never occurs in NT." James Hope Moulton and Wilbert Francis Howard, *A Grammar of New Testament Greek: Accidence and Word-Formation* (Edinburgh: T&T Clark, 1963–), 2:188.

(unmarked), or simple. The present and imperfect tenses, on the other hand, communicate additional aspects for the action, such as continuous or repeated aspects. At this stage, translate the aorist indicative with the English simple past and the imperfect with the English continuous past, or imperfect. For example:

imperfect	ἔλυον	"I was releasing" or "I used to release"
aorist	ἔλυσα	"I released"

The sigmatic aorist is formed with three parts. The core of the word is the verbal root (regular, without modification) followed by a sigmatic stem (σα). Either secondary or nonindicative endings connect to the stem. Notice how the indicative forms basically use the same secondary endings (including augment) as the imperfect. The sigmatic aorist forms of the verb λύω are as follows:

First Aorist Active

	Indicative		Imperative	
1 sg.	ἔλυσα	I released		
2 sg.	ἔλυσας	you released	λῦσον	release (commanding you)
3 sg.	ἔλυσε(ν)	he/she/it released	λυσάτω	let him/her/it release (obligating him/her/it)
1 pl.	ἐλύσαμεν	we released		
2 pl.	ἐλύσατε	you all released	λύσατε	release (commanding you all)
3 pl.	ἔλυσαν	they released	λυσάτωσαν	let them release (obligating them)

Infinitive	
λῦσαι	to release

As in the future, σ is inserted at the front of the stem between the verb root and the endings. The characteristic vowel of this stem is α.

MEANINGS OF ASPECTUAL STEMS

There are two elements involved in verb tense: time and aspect. This is true in English as well. For example, the difference between the following past tenses is not time (they all occurred in the past) but aspect: I ran, I was running, I have run.

Incomplete Aspectual Meaning

Greek has two sets of temporal endings: primary and secondary endings. We have seen that the present and future tenses share the same primary (non-past) endings but differ in stem spelling. The present (and imperfect) use a variable vowel (ε/ο) that conveys an incomplete aspect (e.g., continuation, repetition, attempt, merely beginning, habit). Thus, a primary ending combined with an incomplete stem refers to the ever-unfolding present time (present tense). The future tense is also non-past in time but simple in aspect since the future is a complete thought or idea. Thus, the future tense uses a simple verb stem (σ + ε/ο).

Construction of Tenses

Just as the present and future non-past tenses share the same endings but differ in aspectual stem forms, the imperfect and first aorist past tenses will basically share the same endings but use different aspectual stem forms. The imperfect tense uses the variable vowel stem to refer to the incomplete aspect of its tense. The first aorist uses a stem (σα) similar to the future (σ + ε/ο) to refer to its simple aspect.

		Aspectual Meanings	
		Incomplete	Complete (commonly marked by a particular stem spelling)
Temporal Endings	Non-past (primary)	PRESENT Present Root + ε/ο+ Primary Endings	FUTURE Verbal Root + σ(ε/ο) + Primary Endings
	Past (secondary)	IMPERFECT Present Root + ε/ο+ Secondary Endings	AORIST (Sigmatic aorist—first aorist) Complete aspect marked with stem spelling; Verbal Root[1] + σα + Secondary Endings

1 This tense uses a stem to mark aspect; often the present root is the same as the verbal root for verbs that have first aorist forms.

Complete Aspectual Meaning

Simple (or complete) aspect meanings include an array of meanings that diametrically correspond to incomplete aspect meanings. Examples of corresponding aspectual meanings:

Incomplete Aspect Meanings	Simple (or Complete) Aspect Meanings
continuous	instantaneous
repeated (iterative)	simply completed once[1]
attempt (conative)	result
merely beginning (inchoative)	having started (inceptive)
habitual	simple

Word meaning and context help identify intended aspectual meaning. This list is merely to provide an overview of the aspectual system to help the student guard against the oversimplification of aspectual meaning not uncommon in commentaries and popular exegesis.

Meaning of the Aorist Imperative

The aorist imperative has no augment because it is not regarded as a past tense. The difference in meaning between it and the present imperative is that while the present imperative may denote a command or entreaty to continue performing an action or do it habitually, the aorist imperative denotes a command or entreaty simply to perform an action without any regard to its continuance or frequency. If the verb indicates an activity or a state, the present imperative would be more appropriate without necessarily implying an additional continuous or incomplete meaning.

This difference of meaning is well seen in the parallel versions of a petition in the Lord's Prayer given in two of the Gospels. The verb used in Luke is the present imperative of the verb δίδωμι ("I give"), an irregular verb explained in Lesson 32; the verb used in Matthew is the aorist imperative of the same verb.

1 Though not necessarily once for all time.

τὸν ἄρτον ἡμῶν τὸν ἐπιούσιον δίδου ἡμῖν τὸ καθ᾽ ἡμέραν.
"Give us [keep on giving us] day by day our daily bread." (Luke 11:3)

τὸν ἄρτον ἡμῶν τὸν ἐπιούσιον δὸς ἡμῖν σήμερον.
"Give to us this day our daily bread." (Matt 6:11)

The present imperative denotes a continuous or repeated act of giving and is probably used here simply to align with the meaning of the adverbial constructions translated "day by day" and "daily" rather than mark or bring out a special aspect of the verb. Luke's choice of the present imperative is natural in this context.

The aorist imperative doesn't refer in a significant way to how that giving is carried out. The two adverbs bring out the "daily" repeated aspect of action. Although Matthew is not aligning his verb stem choice with the meaning of the context, as Luke did, he is still making a very natural choice for this particular verb, "give." The aorist stem is a choice that can be expected as a natural match for the simple performative nature of the action, "give." The action of giving is a simple action (not an activity or state). In addition, prayers often make use of the aorist imperative as a polite way of petitioning. Although this example doesn't make a significant exegetical difference, it does help us better understand the authors' interest, focus, and posture.

Aorist Infinitive

The aorist infinitive differs in meaning from the present infinitive in the same way as the aorist imperative differs in meaning from the present imperative.

Its use typically aligns with performative verb root meanings or grammatical constructions that are simple in nature (are complete in their performance). It is most commonly used to convey that the action is simply happening without any regard to its continuance or frequency. However, when it is used in contexts that would surprise the reader, it may convey aspectual meaning such as resultative, inceptive, and instantaneous.

Present Infinitive

Likewise, the present root form (and thematic stem) is often selected to match nonperformative verb meanings (e.g., verbs meaning hold, live, maintain, frequent) or contextual constructions (e.g., begin to . . .). Sometimes the author cuts against the grain of verb meaning and construction meaning to bring out an incomplete nuance not otherwise expected. This use of the present infinitive denotes that the action is to be regarded as one of the incomplete aspect meanings such as continuous or repeated.

The aorist infinitive is used more frequently than the present infinitive in Greek; at this point, you should always use it unless there is some good reason to the contrary.

It is *not* confined to expressing action in past time, like the Latin perfect infinitive, and therefore it has no augment.

Examples:

1. γράφειν τὰ αὐτὰ καλόν ἐστιν ὑμῖν. (present infinitive)
   "To keep on writing the same things is good for you"

2. ἐλπίζω γράψαι ὑμῖν ταχέως. (aorist infinitive)
   "I hope to write to you soon"

EXERCISES

Memorization Exercise

18.1 Review Vocabulary Lists 9–13.

Grammar Exercises

18.2 Verbal root identification: Write the verbal roots for the following verbs.

1. ἐκαλέσαμεν
2. ᾔτησας
3. ἀνοίξεις
4. βλέπειν
5. κρυψάτωσαν
6. ἠλπίσατε
7. γράψαι
8. κηρύξουσι
9. ἐλπιοῦμεν

Translation Exercises

18.3 Translate the following sentences:

1. ἐδίωξαν τοὺς λῃστὰς οἳ ἀπῆγον τὰ πρόβατα.
2. οἱ δὲ λεπροὶ ἐπίστευσαν[1] τῷ λόγῳ τοῦ Ἰησοῦ.
3. ἔπεμψας τοὺς τελώνας ἀγοράσαι τὰ ἱμάτια.
4. σῶσον τὸ ἀργύριον ἀπὸ τῶν λῃστῶν.
5. σῷζω τὸν λαόν σου ἀπὸ τοῦ πονηροῦ.
6. ταξάτωσαν τὰ βιβλία ἐν τῷ ἱερῷ.
7. μετὰ ταῦτα ἐπείσαμεν αὐτοὺς κρύψαι τὰ παιδία.
8. ἐκαθαρίσαμεν ἑαυτοὺς ἐν τῷ ποταμῷ.
9. ὁ διδάσκαλος αὐτὸς ἐθαύμασε τὴν σοφίαν τῶν μαθητῶν.
10. ἐπορεύετο διὰ τῆς γῆς ἔκκοψαι τὰ δένδρα.
11. διὰ τοῦτο οὐ δεῖ σκανδαλίζειν τοὺς πιστούς.
12. βάστασον τὸ πλοῖον ἀπὸ τῆς θαλάσσης.
13. ἁγιάσατε ἑαυτούς, ἐγγίζει γὰρ ἡ ἡμέρα τοῦ κυρίου.

1 πιστεύω is often followed by a dative.

14. ἐκέλευσεν τὸν λεπρὸν ὁ προφήτης καθαρίσαι ἑαυτὸν ἐν τῷ Ἰορδάνῃ ποταμῷ.
15. ἡ φωνὴ τοῦ Ἰωάννου ἔκραξε ἐν τῇ ἐρήμῳ ἑτοιμάσατε τὴν ὁδὸν τῷ κυρίῳ.
16. ἐτηρήσαμεν τὰς ἐντολὰς ἃς ἠκούομεν ἀπὸ τῶν ἁγίων ἀποστόλων.
17. καλόν ἐστιν ἡμᾶς πράσσειν τὴν δικαιοσύνην.
18. ἐδέοντο[1] αὐτοῦ μὴ πρᾶξαι ἑαυτῷ κακόν.
19. μετὰ τοῦτο οὖν ἀνέῳξεν τοὺς ὀφθαλμοὺς τοῦ τυφλοῦ.
20. ἐλπίζεις θεωρεῖν τὴν δόξαν τῶν ἀγγέλων.
21. ἡ εἰρήνη κατοικείτω τὰς καρδίας ὑμῶν.
22. ταῦτα γὰρ ἠθέλησαν βλέψαι οἱ ἄγγελοι.

Composition Exercises

18.4 Translate the following sentences into Greek:

1. They baptized the tax collectors in the river.
2. You were going through the land to behold the houses and the people.
3. Hide the stones in the field.
4. Do not continue to offend the brethren.[2]
5. Let them set the men in order.
6. You revealed the commandments and promises to the church.
7. Will we begin to read the books?
8. Cleanse your hearts, all you sinners, and confess your sins to the church.
9. Is it lawful to heal on the Sabbath?
10. Save your people, O Lord, from the wickedness of this world.
11. Make ready, therefore, to hide yourselves and your children in Jerusalem.

1 This verb does not contract with O-stems.

2 Use the present imperative.

12. Let love and righteousness dwell in your hearts.
13. He commanded me to write these things in a book.
14. It is good for them to keep on reading the same things.
15. After this I will reveal my power to the children of Israel.
16. He wished to call the tax collectors to the wedding.

Scripture Translation Exercises

18.5 Translate the following verses from Scripture:

1. οἱ πρεσβύτεροι ἔπεισαν τοὺς ὄχλους (Matt 27:20)
2. ἐξ Αἰγύπτου[1] ἐκάλεσα τὸν υἱόν μου. (Matt 2:15)
3. καὶ τὰ ἔθνη[2] ἐδέξαντο τὸν λόγον τοῦ θεοῦ. (Acts 11:1)
4. καὶ ἐθεράπευσεν αὐτόν, ὥστε[3] τὸν κωφὸν λαλεῖν καὶ βλέπειν. (Matt 12:22)
5. ὅσα[4] ἠκούσαμεν γενόμενα[5] εἰς τὴν Καφαρναοὺμ ποίησον καὶ ὧδε ἐν τῇ πατρίδι[6] σου. (Luke 4:23)

1 Αἰγύπτου, "Egypt"
2 τὰ ἔθνη, "gentiles"
3 ὥστε + infinitive shows result
4 ὅσα, "However so many (things) that" (neuter plural)
5 γενόμενα, "happened"
6 τῇ πατρίδι, "fatherland"

LESSON 19

Thematic Aorist (Second Aorist) and Object Clauses

THEMATIC AORIST FORMS

Another way to mark the aorist tense is by using the verbal root form (when the verb has a different present root form) with secondary endings. Because this pattern uses a thematic variable vowel after the verbal root, it is called a thematic aorist (also called second aorist). First aorist patterns have sigmatic stems, but second aorist stems use the same thematic stem as the imperfect. In the indicative, the only difference between imperfect and thematic aorist forms is that the imperfect uses the present root spelling and the thematic aorist uses the verbal root.

		Aspectual Meanings	
		Incomplete	Complete (commonly marked by a particular stem spelling)
Temporal Endings	Non-past (primary)	PRESENT Present Root + ε/ο + Primary Endings	FUTURE Verbal Root + σ (ε/ο) + Primary Endings
	Past (secondary)	IMPERFECT Present Root + Thematic Stem (ε/ο) + Secondary Endings	AORIST (Sigmatic aorist—first aorist) Complete aspect marked with stem spelling Root + σα + Secondary Endings or (Thematic aorist—second aorist) Complete aspect marked with root spelling where the verbal root is different from the present root Verbal Root + Thematic Stem (ε/ο) + Secondary Endings

Imperfect and Thematic Aorist Comparison

Both the imperfect and thematic aorist pattern use a thematic stem and secondary endings. Regarding nonindicative forms, the stems and endings of the second aorist active imperative and infinitive are the same as those of the present active imperative and infinitive.[1]

Take, for example, the verb βάλλω ("I throw"):

	Verbal Root Form βαλ- for Simple Aspect		**Present Root Form βαλλ- for Incomplete Aspect**	
	Second Aorist Indicative	Second Aorist Imperative	Imperfect Indicative	Present Imperative
1 sg.	ἔβαλον		ἔβαλλον	
2 sg.	ἔβαλες	βάλε	ἔβαλλες	βάλλε
3 sg.	ἔβαλε(ν)	βαλέτω	ἔβαλλε(ν)	βαλλέτω
1 pl.	ἐβάλομεν		ἐβάλλομεν	
2 pl.	ἐβάλετε	βάλετε	ἐβάλλετε	βάλλετε
3 pl.	ἔβαλον	βαλέτωσαν	ἔβαλλον	βαλλέτωσαν
	Second Aorist Active Infinitive		Present Active Infinitive	
	βαλεῖν[2]		βάλλειν	

1 The second aorist infinitive always has a circumflex accent on the last syllable. This is an audible way to distinguish the thematic aorist infinitive and present infinitive forms.

2 Note how the accenting differs from the present active infinitive.

Examples of Verbs with Second Aorist Forms			
Verbal Root	Second Aorist Active Indicative	Present Active Indicative	Translation
ἁμαρτ-	ἥμαρτον	ἁμαρτάνω	I sin
λαβ-	ἔλαβον	λαμβάνω	I take
μαθ-	ἔμαθον	μανθάνω	I learn
πι-	ἔπιον	πίνω	I drink
θαν-	ἀπέθανον	ἀποθνῄσκω	I die
εὑρ-	εὗρον	εὑρίσκω	I find
πεσ-	ἔπεσον	πίπτω	I fall
τεκ-	ἔτεκον	τίκτω	I bring forth
λιπ-	κατέλιπον	καταλείπω	I abandon
φυγ-	ἔφυγον	φεύγω	I flee
ἀγ-	ἤγαγον[1]	ἄγω	I lead, or drive

ATHEMATIC AORIST FORMS

There are two very common verbs in the New Testament, γινώσκω and βαίνω,[2] that follow the second aorist pattern of using the verbal root and secondary endings, but omit the thematic stem vowel. These verbs are constructed with only roots and endings (no stem). Some grammars refer to these athematic aorists as third aorists.

Verbal Root	Aorist Active Indicative	Present Active Indicative	Translation
γνο-	ἔγνων	γινώσκω	I know
βα-	ἔβην	βαίνω	I go

1 The root ἀγ- reduplicates in the aorist to form ἀγαγ-. The aorist infinitive of this word, for example, is ἀγαγεῖν. After augmentation in the aorist indicative, it becomes ἤγαγ-.

2 βαίνω is only used with prepositional prefixes in the New Testament (e.g., ἀναβαίνω).

The vowel preceding the ending (ω in ἔγνων and η in ἔβην) is the root vowel, not a stem vowel. They are conjugated as follows:

ἔγνων ("I knew")
Athematic Active Aorist

	Indicative	Imperative
1 sg.	ἔγνων	
2 sg.	ἔγνως	γνῶθι
3 sg.	ἔγνω	γνώτω
1 pl.	ἔγνωμεν	
2 pl.	ἔγνωτε	γνῶτε
3 pl.	ἔγνωσαν	γνώτωσαν
	Infinitive	
	γνῶναι	

ἔβην ("I went")
Athematic Active Aorist

	Indicative	Imperative
1 sg.	ἔβην	
2 sg.	ἔβης	βῆθι (βά)
3 sg.	ἔβη	βήτω (βάτω)
1 pl.	ἔβημεν	
2 pl.	ἔβητε	βῆτε (βᾶτε)
3 pl.	ἔβησαν	βήτωσαν (βάτωσαν)
	Infinitive	
	βῆναι	

VERBS WITH UNRELATED ROOTS

All of the examples up to this point have had roots that are different but still related for their present and aorist forms. The present root forms are extensions of the verbal root used in the aorist. There are a number of common verbs that use unrelated roots (such as "go" and "went" in English) to generate their various tenses. In grammars and dictionaries, however, they are always connected with certain present tenses of similar meaning, and they are said to be the second aorist tenses of these presents (just as we would say "went" is the unrelated past form of "go").

This is an unfortunate arrangement in many lexicons and dictionaries since we must look up the meanings of these aorists under their unrelated present tenses. It is important to learn all of the most frequently occurring verbs that use an unrelated root for one or more of their tenses.

Root	Second Aorist Indicative	Translation	Unrelated Present Root	Associated Present Verb
ἰδ-	εἶδον	I saw	ὁρα-	ὁράω
ἐπ-	εἶπον	I said	λεγ-	λέγω
σεχ-	ἔσχον	I held	ἐχ-	ἔχω
φαγ-	ἔφαγον	I ate	ἐσθι-	ἐσθίω
παθ-	ἔπαθον	I suffered	πασχ-	πάσχω
ἐλθ-	ἦλθον	I came	ἐρχ-	ἔρχομαι
ἐνεγκ-	ἤνεγκον	I carried	φερ-	φέρω

Note: The imperative of εἶδον is ἰδέ; that of εἶπον is εἰπέ; that of ἔσχον is σχές; that of ἦλθον is ἐλθέ. These are all exceptions to standard verb-accenting rules. The imperative of the other verbs is formed in the usual way.

OBJECT CLAUSES AFTER VERBS OF SAYING OR THINKING

Greek uses a similar structure to English to express object clauses after "speaking" or "thinking" verbs. In English we employ the word "that" to introduce what was spoken or thought. The Greek word ὅτι takes the place of the English "that" in these circumstances. As in English, this word is followed by a verb in the indicative mood.[1]

Examples:

λέγουσιν ὅτι ἀκούουσι τὴν φωνήν.
"They say that they hear the voice."

πιστεύομεν ὅτι ἐβλέψαμεν τὸ ἱερόν.
"We believe that we beheld the temple."

There is only a subtle difference between Greek and English for these constructions. This difference only occurs when the "speaking" or "thinking" verb is in a past tense. English keeps the tenses of each clause relative to each other (this is called the "sequence of tenses" in English and Latin). Greek retains the tense of the verb that was used by the original speaker or thinker when he uttered the words. In English we say, "The man said that he heard the voice." The words that the man effectively uttered were "I hear the voice." In Greek the present tense is retained, and we write:

ὁ ἄνθρωπος εἶπεν ὅτι <u>ἀκούει</u> τὴν φωνήν.

Again, in the sentence "The men believed that the slave was there," the thought that the men framed in their minds was "the slave is there," and consequently we translate this sentence into Greek as follows:

οἱ ἄνθρωποι ἐπίστευσαν ὅτι ὁ δοῦλός <u>ἐστιν</u> ἐκεῖ.

1 Just as the English conjunction "that" has its origins in the relative pronoun or demonstrative "that," ὅτι has its origins as the Greek neuter relative pronoun ὅ and the indefinite pronoun τι.

Examples of an original past action that is presented with an aorist in Greek, but a pluperfect in English:

εἶπεν ὅτι εἶδε τὰ πλοῖα.
"He said that he had seen the boats."

ἐνόμισαν ὅτι εἶδον ὀπτασίαν.
"They thought that they had seen a vision."

One should always consider the original words uttered, or the original thought framed, before trying to translate such sentences as these.

EXERCISES

Memorization Exercise

19.1 Learn Vocabulary List 14.

Grammar Exercises

19.2(α) Verbal root identification, part 1: Write the verbal roots for the following verbs.

1. βῆθι
2. ἦλθεν
3. ἔσχομεν
4. εἶπε
5. εἴδετε

19.2(β) Verbal root identification, part 2: There are a number of Greek verbs that use unrelated roots to produce their various tenses. Write both roots that are used to produce the present and aorist active tenses for the following verbs. Write the root used in present forms first, then the root used to produce aorist forms.

Example: ἔφαγεν: ἐσθι-, φαγ-

1. εἶδον
2. πάσχουσι
3. φέρει
4. ἐρχόμεθα

Translation Exercises

19.3 Translate the following sentences:

1. μετὰ ταῦτα ἀπέθανεν ὁ πτωχός.
2. ἔβημεν εἰς τὸ ἱερὸν ἐν ἐκείνῃ τῇ ὥρᾳ.
3. ἔμαθες ὅτι ἔρχεται ὁ κριτής.
4. ὦ κύριε, ἥμαρτον εἰς σέ.
5. εἴδομεν ὅτι ὁ τελώνης φέρει τὸ ἀργύριον ἐκ τῆς οἰκίας.
6. ἰδὲ τοὺς δεσπότας τῆς γῆς.
7. γινώσκομεν ὅτι ὁ υἱὸς τοῦ θεοῦ ἦλθεν εἰς τὸν κόσμον σῶσαι τοὺς ἁμαρτωλούς.

8. εἶπεν ὅτι πίνουσι τὸν οἶνον καὶ ἐσθίουσι τὸν ἄρτον.
9. ἠνέγκομεν τοὺς λίθους ἀπὸ τῆς θαλάσσης.
10. τὰ δένδρα ἔπεσε εἰς τὸν ἀγρόν.
11. οἱ λῃσταὶ ἔφευγον ἀπὸ τῶν νεανίων.
12. οἱ δὲ προφῆται ἔφυγον εἰς τὴν ἔρημον.
13. ἐν τούτῳ γινώσκομεν τὴν ἀγάπην τοῦ θεοῦ ὅτι ἔπεμψεν τὸν υἱὸν αὐτοῦ τὸν ἀγαπητὸν εἰς τὸν κόσμον.
14. βῆθι εἰς τοὺς ἀγροὺς καὶ λάβε τὸν καρπὸν ἀπὸ τῶν ἐργάτων.
15. ἔγνων ὅτι ὁ κύριος ἔπεμψε τὸν ἄγγελον αὐτοῦ σῶσαι με.
16. ἐλθέτω τὰ παιδία πρός με.
17. εἴπομεν ὅτι δεῖ παθεῖν αὐτοὺς πολλά.
18. εἶδον ὅτι ἠγάγομεν τὸν ὄχλον εἰς τὴν συναγωγήν.
19. ἔσχεν τὰ βιβλία τοῦ ἀδελφοῦ μου.
20. ἔγνωμεν ὅτι πολλὰ ἔμαθον οἱ μαθηταὶ ἀπὸ τῶν ἀποστόλων.

Composition Exercises

19.4 Translate the following sentences into Greek:

1. We cast ourselves into the river.
2. You all received the garments that the elders sent for the poor.
3. They fled from the face of the judges.
4. After these things, the disciples knew that they had sinned.
5. This is the stone that fell from heaven.
6. The maiden brought forth a son, and they called him Jesus.[1]
7. You all follow[2] me, not because you all saw signs, but because you all ate the loaves.
8. The Son of Man must suffer many things.

1 accusative case

2 See vocabulary list 30.

9. After these days we went to Samaria.
10. Behold the Lamb of God.
11. He said that he had learned many things from the prophet.
12. We know that we must suffer many things.
13. Because of this they left the sheep in the fields and fled.
14. He commanded the multitude to eat the bread and drink the wine that the young men were bringing.
15. The prophet who had the book died in the wilderness.
16. We saw that the slaves were carrying the boat to the lake.[1]
17. They said that the children had eaten the fruit.[2]
18. They knew that the maidens were in the house.
19. I heard that the apostles were going to Jerusalem.

Scripture Translation Exercises

19.5 Translate the following verses from Scripture:

1. ἔλεγεν τῷ ὄχλῳ ὅτι ἓξ[3] ἡμέραι εἰσὶν ἐν αἷς δεῖ ἐργάζεσθαι· ἐν αὐταῖς οὖν . . . θεραπεύεσθε καὶ μὴ τῇ ἡμέρᾳ τοῦ σαββάτου. (Luke 13:14)
2. οὐαὶ[4] τὴν γῆν καὶ τὴν θάλασσαν, ὅτι κατέβη ὁ διάβολος πρὸς ὑμᾶς (Rev 12:12)
3. ἔγνωσαν γὰρ ὅτι πρὸς αὐτοὺς τὴν παραβολὴν εἶπεν. (Mark 12:12)
4. καὶ ἤρξατο διδάσκειν αὐτοὺς ὅτι δεῖ τὸν υἱὸν τοῦ ἀνθρώπου πολλὰ παθεῖν (Mark 8:31)
5. οὐ γὰρ ἦλθον καλέσαι δικαίους ἀλλὰ ἁμαρτωλούς. (Matt 9:13)

1 Their original thought was "they are carrying."

2 Their original words were "the children ate the fruit."

3 ἕξ, "six"

4 οὐαὶ + accusative, "woe to X"

LESSON 20

Present, Future, and Aorist Active of Liquid Verbs, Temporal Clauses, and παρά

LIQUID VERBS

The future and aorist forms of verbs that have stems ending with a liquid letter (λ, ρ) or a nasal letter (μ, ν) present some peculiarities. Such verbs are commonly called "liquid verbs." This group of letters can be memorized with the mnemonic "**L**earning **M**ore **N**onsense **R**ules."

Present Forms of Liquid Verbs

Liquid verbs typically are of the class of verbs that have a modified (lengthened) present root form to mark incompleteness. The present root for liquid verbs is typically modified in two ways: (1) it has a long vowel or a diphthong if the verbal root has a short vowel, or (2) it ends with λλ if the verbal root ends in λ (except in the case of ὀφείλω).

Future Forms of Liquid Verbs

The future active and middle tenses create a problem for liquid verbs since Greek is averse to spellings where a σ follows a liquid letter. To avoid this spelling combination an ε is inserted between the verbal root and the sigmatic stem. This creates another spelling issue: a σ between two vowels (intervocalic sigma) is a weak position for the σ. So the σ drops out, leaving the vowels to contract.[1] Thus, instead of σ marking the future active and middle tenses of liquid verbs, these verbs will look like present tense forms of ε-contract verbs.

1 Cf. William Sanford LaSor, *Handbook of New Testament Greek,* 2 vols. (Grand Rapids: Eerdmans, 1973), §24.2555; Robert W. Funk. *A Beginning-Intermediate Grammar of Hellenistic Greek,* 3 vols. (Missoula, MT: Scholars Press, 1973), §376; Smyth §535; William D. Mounce, *The Morphology of Biblical Greek,* 92 (Grand Rapids: Zondervan, 1994).

Aorist Forms of Liquid Verbs

Most liquid verbs follow the first aorist pattern. However, one does not see their sigmatic stem. The σ in the stem dropped out to avoid being placed adjacent to a liquid letter. The root vowel was then lengthened to compensate for the missing σ. This lengthened root makes it look like these aorist forms are using the present root. The similarity in spelling is merely a coincidence. The distinction is clear for roots ending in λ.[1] Some grammars refer to these aorist forms as "asigmatic" because the σ has fallen away and is represented in other ways. They still are classified as first aorist forms.

Some liquid verbs have a modified present root form and can thus avoid the difficulties of placing a σ adjacent to a liquid letter. They follow the athematic aorist pattern (second aorist), using the true verbal root and a thematic stem.

Common liquid verbs that have first aorist forms:

English	Present	Verbal Root	Future	First Aorist
I announce	ἀγγέλλω	ἀγγελ-	ἀγγελῶ	ἤγγειλα
I raise or take up	αἴρω	ἀρ-	ἀρῶ	ἦρα
I kill	ἀποκτείνω	κτεν-	ἀποκτενῶ	ἀπέκτεινα
I send	ἀποστέλλω	στελ-	ἀποστελῶ	ἀπέστειλα
I rouse	ἐγείρω	ἐγερ-	ἐγερῶ	ἤγειρα
I judge	κρίνω	κριν-	κρινῶ	ἔκρινα
I remain	μένω	μεν-	μενῶ	ἔμεινα
I ought (+ inf.)	ὀφείλω	ὀφελ-	ὀφελῶ	ὤφειλα
I sow	σπείρω	σπερ-	σπερῶ	ἔσπειρα
I manifest	φαίνω	φαν-	φανοῦμαι	ἔφανα
I destroy	φθείρω	φθερ-	φθερῶ	ἔφθειρα

1 It is also very clear that μένω isn't using a present root in its aorist form since the present form doesn't have an ι. Cf. Smyth §544.

The compound forms of these verbs—such as παραγγέλλω, ἐπαίρω, ἐκβάλλω, and κατακρίνω—form their tenses in exactly the same way as the uncompounded forms provided above. The future of ἀγγέλλω is conjugated as follows: ἀγγελῶ, ἀγγελεῖς, ἀγγελεῖ, ἀγγελοῦμεν, ἀγγελεῖτε, ἀγγελοῦσι.

The first aorist nonindicative forms of liquid verbs follow the same contraction principles as the indicative. The second person plural aorist imperative is the same as the second person plural indicative, minus the augment (ἀγγείλατε). The first aorist active singular imperative stem ending is -σον. Just as in the indicative, the σ drops after the liquid letter and is represented by the lengthening of the verbal root (ἄγγειλον.) The active infinitive follows suit. The σ in -σαι drops, and the verbal root lengthens (ἀγγεῖλαι.)

There are some liquid verbs that don't follow this asigmatic pattern and use the thematic (second aorist) pattern. Common liquid verbs that have second aorist forms include:

English	Present	Verbal Root	Future	First Aorist
I die	ἀποθνῄσκω	θαν-	ἀποθανοῦμαι	ἀπέθανον
I throw	βάλλω	βαλ-	βαλῶ	ἔβαλον

TEMPORAL CLAUSES

A temporal clause explains or conditions the timing of its governing clause. Temporal clauses are introduced by ὅτε or ὡς, meaning "when," or ἕως, meaning "while" or "until." When a temporal clause refers to a definite event, its verb is in the indicative mood, just as in English. Distinguish carefully between ὅτε "when," and ὅτι "that," or "because." For example:

1. ὅτε ἦλθε πρὸς τὴν θάλασσαν εἶδε τὰ πλοῖα.
   "When he came to the sea he saw the ships."

2. ἕως ἀνέγνω τὰ βιβλία κατέμεινεν ἐν τῇ οἰκίᾳ.
   "While he read the books he remained in the house."

3. κατέμεινεν ἐν τῇ οἰκίᾳ ἕως ἦλθεν ὁ δοῦλος.
   "He remained in the house until the slave came."

THE PREPOSITION παρά

The general meaning of παρά is "beside." It is used with a noun or pronoun in the accusative, genitive, or dative case. When used with the accusative case it generally refers to some movement to the side of or motion alongside places.

Examples:

1. ὁ δὲ σπόρος ἔπεσεν παρὰ τὴν ὁδόν.
   "But the seed fell by the roadside."

2. ὁ δὲ Ἰησοῦς ἦλθεν παρὰ τὴν θάλασσαν τῆς Γαλιλαίας.
   "But Jesus went along the side of the Sea of Galilee."

When used with the genitive case it references motion from the side of persons. For example:

3. καὶ ἔγνωσαν ὅτι παρὰ σοῦ ἐξῆλθον.
   "And they knew that I came out from you."

When used with the dative it indicates rest beside and may be translated "near," "by," "with," or "at the house of." For example:

4. ἔμειναν παρ᾽ αὐτῷ τὴν ἡμέραν ἐκείνην.
   "They remained with him that day."

EXERCISES

Memorization Exercise

20.1 Learn Vocabulary List 15.

Grammar Exercises

20.2 Verbal root identification: Convert the following verbs to their corresponding first aorist forms.

1. σπείρουσι
2. ἀπαγγελεῖς
3. κατακρινεῖ
4. αἴρομεν
5. σπερεῖτε
6. φθεροῦμεν
7. μένεις
8. ἀποκτείνω
9. ἐγείρουσι
10. ἀποστέλλει

Translation Exercises

20.3 Translate the following sentences:

1. ὅτε δὲ οἱ στρατιῶται ἦλθον εἰς τὴν οἰκίαν ἀπήγγειλαν ὅτι ἀπέστειλεν αὐτοὺς ὁ[1] Κορνήλιος.
2. κατακρινοῦσι τὰς χήρας καὶ ἀποκτενοῦσι τὰ τέκνα αὐτῶν μαχαίρᾳ.
3. οὐ μενεῖτε ἐν τῷ τόπῳ τούτῳ ἀλλ᾽ ἀποθανεῖσθε ἐν τῇ γῇ τῶν ἐχθρῶν ὑμῶν.
4. οἱ ἀπόστολοι ἔσπειραν τὸν λόγον ἐν ταῖς καρδίαις τῶν μαθητῶν.
5. ἦρεν οὖν τὸν σταυρὸν καὶ ἦλθεν ὀπίσω τοῦ Ἰησοῦ.

1 Proper nouns in Greek are often preceded by the article; this article must not be translated into English. This is less common when the name is qualified by a description such as "Jesus of Galilee" Ἰησοῦς τοῦ Γαλιλαίου (cf. James Hope Moulton and Nigel Turner, *A Grammar of New Testament Greek: Syntax* [Edinburgh: T&T Clark, 1963–], 3:166).

6. ἐν ἐκείνῳ τῷ καιρῷ οἱ κριταὶ ἔκριναν τὰς φυλὰς Ἰσραήλ.
7. ἐφθείραμεν τὰς κώμας αἱ ἦσαν παρὰ τὴν θάλασσαν.
8. ἔμεινα ἐκεῖ ἕως ἀνέγνω τὸ βιβλίον.
9. ὅτε δὲ ἀπέκτεινεν ὁ Ἡρῴδης τὰ παιδία ἐν Βηθλεὲμ κατέφυγεν ὁ Ἰωσὴφ εἰς Αἴγυπτον σὺν Μαρίᾳ.
10. δύνασθε πιεῖν τὸ ποτήριον ὃ δεῖ με πιεῖν;
11. φανοῦμαι τὸ πρόσωπόν μου αὐτοῖς καὶ βλέψουσι τὴν δόξαν μου.
12. ἐμείναμεν ἐν τῷ ἱερῷ ἕως ᾠκοδόμουν οἱ ἐργάται τὸν θρόνον.
13. ὡς δὲ ἤκουσαν ταῦτα παρὰ τῆς χήρας ἔμειναν παρ᾽ αὐτῇ.
14. ὤφειλες ἀργύριον τοῖς τελώναις.
15. ὁ δὲ Ἰησοῦς εἶπεν τῷ παραλυτικῷ Ἔγειρε, ἆρον τὴν κλίνην σου καὶ ὕπαγε εἰς τὸν οἶκόν σου, ὡς δὲ ἤκουσεν ταῦτα ἦρεν τὴν κλίνην καὶ ὑπῆγεν.
16. ἀπεστείλαμεν τοὺς ἀγγέλους ἑτοιμάσαι τὴν ὁδόν.
17. ὁ προφήτης εἶπεν ὅτι πάντα δυνατά ἐστι παρὰ τῷ θεῷ.[1]
18. παρηγγείλατε αὐτοῖς μὴ φθεῖραι τὰ πλοῖα.
19. ἠθέλησας ἄγειν τὰ πρόβατα παρὰ τὰ δένδρα.
20. παρὰ τοῖς ἀνθρώποις ἀδύνατόν ἐστιν ἀλλ᾽ οὐ παρὰ τῷ θεῷ, πάντα γὰρ δυνατὰ παρὰ τῷ θεῷ.
21. καὶ τοῦτο ἠκούσαμεν παρ᾽ αὐτοῦ ὅτι δεῖ φιλεῖν τοὺς ἀδελφοὺς ἡμῶν.
22. οἱ Φαρισαῖοι ἔλεγον ὅτι ἐσθίει παρὰ ἁμαρτωλῷ.

1 παρὰ τῷ θεῷ, etc., "near God"; translate "with God" or "to God."

Composition Exercises

20.4 Translate the following sentences into Greek:

1. Send the young men to rouse the soldiers.
2. Joseph took the child and Mary and departed into Egypt.
3. They will not die in the wilderness, for the soldiers will save them.
4. I will manifest myself to my servants[1] at that time, says the Lord.
5. The Pharisees went to eat bread at the house of the prophet.[2]
6. This is impossible with men, but it is possible with God.
7. When Herod heard these words he sent his servants to destroy the children in Bethlehem with the sword.
8. They remained in the house while the paralytic took up his bed.
9. We announced that the apostle was staying[3] in the house of Cornelius.
10. Take up your cross and carry it after me.
11. You ought not to condemn these widows.
12. I will cast the sword into the lake.
13. When the disciples came to the village they sowed the word in the hearts of the people.
14. The Son of Man[4] must suffer many things.
15. I heard this from[5] the prophet who lives[6] at the house of the widow in Bethlehem.
16. Will you not slay the wicked, O Lord?
17. They wished to throw the stones beside the temple.
18. The Pharisees said that the disciples of John did not eat with tax collectors and sinners.[7]

1 Use δοῦλος.
2 Use παρά with the dative for "at the house of."
3 Use μένω.
4 Insert the article before "of Man."
5 Use παρά.
6 Use μένω.
7 Use παρά.

Scripture Translation Exercises

20.5 Translate the following verses from Scripture:

1. καὶ ἀράτω τὸν σταυρὸν αὐτοῦ καὶ ἀκολουθείτω[1] μοι (Mark 8:34)
2. καὶ τὰ σκεύη[2] αὐτοῦ ἐν τῇ οἰκίᾳ, μὴ καταβάτω ἆραι αὐτά (Luke 17:31)
3. ὅτε δὲ ἤγγισεν ὁ καιρὸς τῶν καρπῶν, ἀπέστειλεν τοὺς δούλους αὐτοῦ πρὸς τοὺς γεωργοὺς[3] λαβεῖν τοὺς καρποὺς αὐτοῦ (Matt 21:34)
4. Ἐν ἐκείνῃ τῇ ὥρᾳ εἶπεν ὁ Ἰησοῦς τοῖς ὄχλοις· ὡς ἐπὶ λῃστὴν ἐξήλθατε μετὰ μαχαιρῶν καὶ ξύλων[4] συλλαβεῖν με; (Matt 26:55)
5. ὅτε οὖν εἶδεν ὁ ὄχλος ὅτι Ἰησοῦς οὐκ ἔστιν ἐκεῖ οὐδὲ οἱ μαθηταὶ αὐτοῦ, ἐνέβησαν αὐτοὶ εἰς τὰ πλοιάρια καὶ ἦλθον εἰς Καφαρναοὺμ (John 6:24)

1 ἀκολουθέω, "I follow"
2 τὰ σκεύη, "gear," "equipment," "stuff"
3 γεωργοὺς, "farmers"
4 ξύλων, "clubs"

LESSON 21

Consonant Stem Nouns (Third Declension)

CONSONANT STEM NOUNS

The third declension is the final Greek declension, formed by adding the basic case endings to noun stems that terminate with a consonant. Since the two semivowels, ι and υ, may be used as consonants, noun stems terminating with these letters are included in this declension. Nouns in all three genders are represented within the third declension.

Third Declension Case Endings (Masculine and Feminine)

Since most case endings begin with a vowel, their spellings remain rather constant (compared to the contractions that occur with the vocalic stems of the first and second declensions). The most noticeable difference between the third declension and the other two declensions is that the ν in accusative cases will vocalize into a short α as a result of following a consonant stem. It is simply easier to pronounce a vocalic sound following a consonant than a nasal sound. For accenting principles, remember that the α is short, rather than the long α that is used in the first declension. The resulting endings of masculine or feminine nouns in the third declension are as follows:

Third Declension Endings

	Singular	Plural
Nom.	ς	ες
Acc.	α (vocalized ν)	ας (vocalized νς)
Gen.	ος	ων
Dat.	ι	σι

We add these endings to the noun stem, which can be found by taking away the ending of the genitive singular. Often the σ, which is the nominative singular ending, obscures the final consonant of the noun stem. Examples:

Nominative	Genitive	Noun Stem
νύξ	νυκτός	νυκτ-
παῖς	παιδός	παιδ-
ἄρχων	ἄρχοντος	ἀρχοντ-

A significant amount of rote memory work can be reduced if one learns the patterns of third declension nouns according to consonant type. If one understands the basics of how consonants interact with one another and basic accenting principles, nearly all of the forms below can be inferred. This lesson examines noun stems of the following types: labials, dentals, gutturals, and liquids.

Labial Noun Stem

Only the first and last forms provided in the paradigm below (nominative singular and dative plural) have a σ that will combine with terminal noun stem consonants. These forms produce ψ, which would be expected whenever a labial is followed by a σ. Labial noun stems are not common in the New Testament. This example is provided here to illustrate the basic pattern of the third declension.

LABIAL STEM

	ὁ Ἄραψ ("Arab") **Noun Stem: Ἀραβ-**	
	Singular	Plural
Nom.	Ἄραψ	Ἄραβες
Acc.	Ἄραβα	Ἄραβας
Gen.	Ἄραβος	Ἀράβων
Dat.	Ἄραβι	Ἄραψι(ν)

Dental Noun Stem

The general principle for any dental that precedes a σ is that it will drop out. No compensatory vowel lengthening is expected for these situations. One should be able to infer the forms for dental noun stems such as ἐλπίς by applying this rule when adding memorized case endings.

	DENTAL STEM ἡ ἐλπίς ("hope") Noun Stem: ἐλπιδ-		SINGLE-SYLLABLE DENTAL STEM ὁ or ἡ παῖς[1] ("child") Noun Stem: παιδ-	
	Singular	Plural	Singular	Plural
Nom.	ἐλπίς	ἐλπίδες	παῖς	παῖδες
Voc.	ἐλπί[2]		παῖ	
Acc.	ἐλπίδα	ἐλπίδας	παῖδα	παῖδας
Gen.	ἐλπίδος	ἐλπίδων	παιδός	παίδων
Dat.	ἐλπίδι	ἐλπίσι(ν)	παιδί	παισί(ν)

Guttural Noun Stem

According to the principles learned with the square of stops, a guttural will combine with σ to form ξ. One should be able to infer the forms for guttural noun stems such as φύλαξ by applying this rule when adding memorized case endings.

	GUTTURAL STEM ὁ φύλαξ ("guard") Noun Stem: φυλακ-		GUTTURAL STEM ὁ σαλπίγξ ("trumpet") Noun Stem: σαλπιγγ-		SINGLE-SYLLABLE GUTTURAL STEM ἡ νύξ[3] ("night") Noun Stem: νύκτ-	
	Singular	Plural	Singular	Plural	Singular	Plural
Nom.	φύλαξ	φύλακες	σάλπιγξ	σάλπιγγες	νύξ	νύκτες
Acc.	φύλακα	φύλακας	σάλπιγγα	σάλπιγγας	νύκτα	νύκτας
Gen.	φύλακος	φυλάκων	σάλπιγγος	σαλπίγγων	νυκτός	νυκτῶν
Dat.	φύλαξι	φύλαξι(ν)	σάλπιγγι	σάλπιγξι(ν)	νυκτί	νυξί(ν)

1 Single-syllable roots often introduce exceptions for general spelling and accenting rules. This is seen with the rather common word παῖς. One common irregularity for monosyllabic roots is that they break the retentive accent preference for nonverbs. These types of words will move their accent to the ultima for genitive and dative cases. Παῖς has a further exception in that its accent remains on the root in the genitive plural. This is a result of the earliest form of this word being disyllabic (πάϝις).

2 Unless an alternate form is provided, the vocative is the same as the nominative.

3 Even though the noun stem of νύξ terminates with a dental (νυκτ), it functions morphologically as a guttural since the dental drops and reveals the guttural. It has a monosyllabic root, so the accents will shift to the ultima for the genitive and dative forms. Another example of a monosyllabic guttural noun stem is the Greek word for goat, ὁ αἴξ. It declines as follows: αἴξ, αἶγα, αἰγός, αἰγί, αἶγες, αἶγα, αἰγῶν, αἰξί(ν).

Liquid Noun Stem Since two case endings begin with σ, the issue of σ being adjacent to a liquid letter must be addressed. Typically, in the nominative singular, the σ drops out, and the stem vowel lengthens (ποιμήν). The issue is dealt with differently in the dative plural. Here the liquid drops out without need for lengthening. The persistence of an intervocalic stem (preceded by a short vowel) helps identify the original presence of some stem consonant. Note that some noun stems (e.g., αἰών, σωτήρ, and μήν) have an original long vowel (seen in the genitive singular form). Such long vowels can show no further lengthening in the nominative singular. Stems ending in a liquid letter:

LIQUID STEM

	ὁ ποιμήν ("shepherd") Noun Stem: ποιμεν-		ὁ ἡγεμών ("leader") Noun Stem: ἡγεμον-		ὁ αἰών ("age") Noun Stem: αἰων-		ὁ σωτήρ ("savior") Noun Stem: σωτηρ-	
	Singular	Plural	Singular	Plural	Singular	Plural	Singular	Plural
Nom.	ποιμήν	ποιμένες	ἡγεμών	ἡγεμόνες	αἰών	αἰῶνες	σωτήρ[1]	σωτῆρες
Acc.	ποιμένα	ποιμένας	ἡγεμόνα	ἡγεμόνας	αἰῶνα	αἰῶνας	σωτῆρα	σωτῆρας
Gen.	ποιμένος	ποιμένων	ἡγεμόνος	ἡγεμόνων	αἰῶνος	αἰώνων	σωτῆρος	σωτήρων
Dat.	ποιμένι	ποιμέσι(ν)	ἡγεμόνι	ἡγεμόσι(ν)	αἰῶνι	αἰῶσι	σωτῆρι	σωτῆρσι(ν)[2]

-οντ Noun Stem Many common nouns use οντ to form their noun stem. When the dental drops prior to the σ in case forms, the issue of σ being adjacent to a nasal letter must be addressed. Typically, the nominative singular will drop the σ and lengthen the stem vowel (ἄρχων), as in the pattern above. The dative plural form is handled differently than nasals without τ. A good deal of contraction occurs with neither letter persisting. The result is the stem vowel changes to ου (ἄρχουσι). This form

1 The short vowel in the vocative form of this word (σῶτερ) is an exception (not occurring in the New Testament). This noun is classified along with words such as ῥήτωρ ("orator") as belonging to liquid stems that do not change their stem vowel length. The next lesson covers liquid stems that change their stem vowel length.

2 Noun stems with ρ that don't change their stem vowel length keep the liquid preceding the σ in the dative plural. This is an exception to the rules regarding σ adjacent to a liquid.

is coincidentally identical to the third person plural present active indicative verb using the same root. Context will always distinguish these (τοῖς ἄρχουσι "for the rulers" vs. ἄρχουσι "they rule"). Nouns such as ὀδούς represent less common ways to address this issue in the nominative singular.

-οντ NOUN STEM

	ὁ ἄρχων ("ruler") Noun Stem: ἀρχοντ-		ὁ ὀδούς ("tooth") Noun Stem: ὀδοντ-	
	Singular	Plural	Singular	Plural
Nom.	ἄρχων[1]	ἄρχοντες	ὀδούς	ὀδόντες
Acc.	ἄρχοντα	ἄρχοντας	ὀδόντα	ὀδόντας
Gen.	ἄρχοντος	ἀρχόντων	ὀδόντος	ὀδόντων
Dat.	ἄρχοντι	ἄρχουσι(ν)	ὀδόντι	ὀδοῦσι(ν)

THIRD DECLENSION LEXICAL INFORMATION

Since neither the noun stem nor the gender of a third declension word can be inferred from the nominative singular form, one must learn the gender and genitive singular form when memorizing vocabulary.

The gender of nouns is generally indicated in dictionaries with the article for the noun; the article ἡ in the lexical entry for χάρις lets us know that χάρις is feminine; the article τό in the lexical entry πῦρ shows that πῦρ is neuter. Preceding the article, reference grammars and dictionaries provide the genitive singular form (especially for nouns of the third declension). Some people follow this order for memorizing vocabulary; however, for rapid and natural review you may find it easier to pronounce the article prior to the nominative form.

1 The vocative is ἄρχον.

Common Third Declension Nouns The following are some of the most common third declension nouns in the New Testament.

Nominative	Genitive	Article[1]	Translation
ἀλέκτωρ	ἀλέκτορος	ὁ	rooster
ἀμπελών	ἀμπελῶνος	ὁ	vineyard
ἄρχων	ἄρχοντος	ὁ	ruler
ἀστήρ	ἀστέρος (dat. pl. ἄστρασι)	ὁ	star
εἰκών	εἰκόνος	ἡ	image
λαμπάς	λαμπάδος	ἡ	lamp
μήν	μηνός	ὁ	month
νύξ	νυκτός	ἡ	night
παῖς	παιδός	ὁ	child
σάρξ	σαρκός	ἡ	flesh
χάρις[2]	χάριτος	ἡ	favor or grace

1 Lexicons provide the article for nouns to identify the gender of each noun.

2 Note that the accusative singular of χάρις is χάριν.

EXERCISES

Memorization Exercise

21.1 Learn Vocabulary List 16.

Translation Exercises

21.2 Translate the following sentences:

1. ἐγείρεσθε τῇ φωνῇ τῆς σάλπιγγος.
2. φυλασσέσθωσαν αἱ θύραι ὑπὸ τῶν φυλάκων.
3. ἀπέστειλαν τοὺς ποιμένας συνάγειν τὰ πρόβατα νυκτός.[1]
4. οἱ παῖδες ἦρον τὴν εἰκόνα.
5. μενοῦσι ἐν τῇ γῇ αὐτῶν εἰς τὸν αἰῶνα.[2]
6. ὅτε δὲ ἐξῆλθεν ὁ Πέτρος ἐφώνησεν ὁ ἀλέκτωρ.
7. ἔλαβες τὸν καρπὸν τοῦ ἀμπελῶνος τοῖς ποιμέσι.
8. ἐποίησα τοῦτον τὸν χιτῶνα τῷ παιδί.
9. αἱ δὲ παρθένοι ἔλαβον τὰς λαμπάδας καὶ ἐξῆλθον ἰδεῖν τὸν νυμφίον.
10. σῳζόμεθα γὰρ ἐλπίδι καὶ τῇ χάριτι τοῦ θεοῦ.
11. ἰδὲ τοὺς ἀστέρας ἐν τῷ οὐρανῷ.
12. ἐκάλουν αὐτὸν τὸν σωτῆρα τοῦ κόσμου.
13. εἰ μὴ[3] ἐσθίετε τὴν σάρκα τοῦ υἱοῦ τοῦ ἀνθρώπου οὐκ ἔχετε ζωὴν ἐν ἑαυτοῖς.
14. πέμπομαι ὑπὸ τῶν ἡγεμόνων ἀπαγγεῖλαι ὑμῖν ταῦτα.
15. ἄκουσον ἡμῶν,[4] σῶτερ[5] τοῦ Ἰσραήλ.
16. ταύτην τὴν χάριν ἔλαβον παρὰ τοῦ κυρίου.
17. μετὰ δὲ τρεῖς μῆνας οἱ ἄρχοντες εἰσῆλθον εἰς τὸ ἱερὸν νυκτός.

Composition Exercises

21.3 Translate the following sentences into Greek:

1. We destroyed the images that we saw in the temple.
2. Peter went out of the door, and immediately the rooster crowed.
3. The master sent the laborers into his vineyard.

1 νυκτός, "during night"; the genitive case is used in Greek to express the time within which something is done.
2 εἰς τὸν αἰῶνα, "until the age," a Hebrew expression generally translated "forever."
3 εἰ μή, "unless" or "except"
4 When ἀκούω refers to the person heard, that person will be in the genitive case. The message will be in the accusative case.
5 vocative of σῶτηρ

4. After three months we beheld the star in the heavens.
5. When the bridegroom came by night they took their lamps and went out to see him.
6. You all were being roused by the trumpets.
7. We announced to you all that he was the savior of the world.
8. Receive the grace of God.
9. The garments were being sent to the children by the widows.
10. The shepherds called their own sheep, and they came after them.
11. Unless we eat the flesh of the Son of man we will have no life in ourselves.
12. Here will I dwell forever, says the Lord.

Scripture Translation Exercises

21.4 Translate the following verses from Scripture:

1. λέγει αὐτοῖς· ὑπάγετε καὶ ὑμεῖς εἰς τὸν ἀμπελῶνα (Matt 20:7)
2. καὶ ἀποστελεῖ τοὺς ἀγγέλους αὐτοῦ μετὰ σάλπιγγος (Matt 24:31)
3. ἀμὴν λέγω σοι ὅτι ἐν ταύτῃ τῇ νυκτὶ πρὶν[1] ἀλέκτορα φωνῆσαι τρὶς ἀπαρνήσῃ[2] με (Matt 26:34)
4. καὶ ἐγένετο[3] ἐν τῷ ἐλθεῖν[4] αὐτὸν εἰς οἶκόν τινος[5] τῶν ἀρχόντων τῶν Φαρισαίων σαββάτῳ φαγεῖν ἄρτον (Luke 14:1)
5. εἶπεν δὲ ὁ κύριος τοῦ ἀμπελῶνος· τί ποιήσω; πέμψω τὸν υἱόν μου τὸν ἀγαπητόν[6] (Luke 20:13)
6. ἐγώ εἰμι ὁ ποιμὴν ὁ καλός. ὁ ποιμὴν ὁ καλὸς τὴν ψυχὴν αὐτοῦ τίθησιν[7] ὑπὲρ τῶν προβάτων (John 10:11)

1 πρίν + infinitive = "before" the action of the infinitive occurs (antecedent temporal clause).

2 ἀπαρνέομαι (future ἀπαρνήσομαι) same meaning as ἀρνέομαι.

3 Second aorist deponent of γίνομαι used in conjunction with an infinitive. "(The infinitive) happened." This construction historically has been translated "It came to pass." Then the infinitive was translated as an indicative subordinate clause introduced by "that."

4 ἐν + inf. shows contemporaneous time ("while" the infinitive occurred); cf. Lesson 15.

5 τινος, "a certain (man)" (genitive)

6 τὸν ἀγαπητόν, "beloved"

7 τίθησιν, "he lays down"

LESSON 22

Semivowel Stems (Third Declension Continued): Neuter and Irregular Nouns

MORE THIRD DECLENSION STEM PATTERNS

Semivowel Noun Stem

Some third declension nouns have stems ending with the semivowels ι, υ, or ευ. Such nouns decline with a notable amount of variation (ἰχθύς is the most consistent of the patterns below). Simply add the standard case endings to the noun stem to produce the proper form. Words that have stems ending in ι such as πόλις operate differently. The ι-stem is only present in two cases (singular forms of the nominative and accusative cases).[1] For all other cases the ι at the end of the stem changes to ε. There is also an ω instead of an ο used in the genitive singular. Both genitive singular and plural forms represent exceptions to accenting rules. Finally, you will notice that nominative and accusative plural forms are identical. There was a general tendency to match these forms over time. The nominative plural was formed through contraction (πόλε + ες). It was not necessary to vocalize the ν in the original accusative plural case ending since it was preceded by a vowel (ε). Thus we would have had πόλενς. The ν dropped out, being adjacent to a σ, and the vowel was lengthened to compensate for the loss (comparable to what happens in the second declension).

There are many words in Greek that have ευ stems. They belong to a larger group of words that have an upsilon digraph (i.e., -αυ, -ευ, -ου). The υ in these digraphs was a replacement for digamma, a letter

1 There is a tendency for these two case forms to be different from the rest. This occurs with the very common adjectives μέγας and πόλυς, discussed in Lesson 23.

with a "w" sound that fell out of use. The case ending patterns for words with these stems underwent many changes over time, and there are many alternate spellings, all of which have logical ties to the basic case forms. The υ (as a stand-in for digamma) often drops away (see the accusative singular form, where the υ was treated more as a consonant and caused the accusative singular case ending, ν, to vocalize). It only remains in the nominative singular and dative plural forms (the only two case endings beginning with sigma). It also follows the other semivowel patterns with an ω for the genitive singular but does not produce an exception to accenting rules. For example:

	SEMIVOWEL ι-STEM		SEMIVOWEL υ-STEM		SEMIVOWEL ευ-STEM	
	ἡ πόλις ("city") Noun Stem: πολι-		**ὁ ἰχθύς ("fish") Noun Stem: ἰχθυ-**		**ὁ βασιλεύς ("king") Noun Stem: βασιλευ-**	
	Singular	Plural	Singular	Plural	Singular	Plural
Nom.	πόλις	πόλεις	ἰχθύς	ἰχθύες	βασιλεύς	βασιλεῖς
Voc.	πόλι[1]		ἰχθύ		βασιλεῦ	
Acc.	πόλιν	πόλεις	ἰχθύν	ἰχθύας (ἰχθῦς)	βασιλέα	βασιλεῖς (βασιλέας)
Gen.	πόλεως	πόλεων	ἰχθύος	ἰχθύων	βασιλέως	βασιλέων
Dat.	πόλει	πόλεσι(ν)	ἰχθύϊ[2]	ἰχθύσι(ν)	βασιλεῖ	βασιλεῦσι(ν)

1 Unless an alternate form is provided, the vocative is the same as the nominative.

2 The mark (two dots) over the ι is a dieresis. It shows that two adjacent vowels stand as separate syllables rather than forming a diphthong.

THIRD DECLENSION NEUTER NOUNS

Third declension neuter nouns follow the same rules that govern neuter nouns of the second declension—except that there is no ending for the nominative and accusative singular cases. Greek words may only terminate with vowels and a few selected letters from the liquid and sibilant categories (ν, ρ, σ, ξ, ψ).[1] Noun stems that terminate in τ will lose their final consonant. Thus γράμματ becomes γράμμα.

Neuter Dental Noun Stem

The pattern for ματ stem neuter words is as follows:

DENTAL STEM

τὸ γράμμα ("letter")
Noun Stem: γράμματ-

	Singular	Plural
Nom.	γράμμα	γράμματα
Acc.	γράμμα	γράμματα
Gen.	γράμματος	γραμμάτων
Dat.	γράμματι	γράμμασι(ν)

Notice that as in the case of neuter nouns of the second declension, the nominative, vocative, and accusative cases have the same endings, and the nominative, vocative, and accusative plural end in α.

Neuter Sibilant Noun Stem

Neuter nouns with stems ending with ς can be particularly confusing since the exposed stem can be mistaken for a second declension nominative singular form. The final ς of the stem appears only in the nominative singular, where there is no ending added to neuter nouns of the third declension. In this case the ες is changed to ος (this type of vocalic change is called ablaut or vowel gradation; cf. English "sing," "sang," "sung"). In the other cases when the stem σ is in a weak intervocalic position, it is dropped, and the resulting adjacent two vowels contract.

1 Exceptions would be foreign transliterated names and proclitics such as οὐκ and ἐκ that are pronounced along with the following word.

Example: The stem γενες with genitive ending added becomes γενεσος; when the intervocalic σ is dropped it becomes γενεος, and then contracts to γένους. The same takes place in the other cases. The accusative plural originally was γένεσα; the σ dropped, yielding γένεα, which contracts to γένη.

SIBILANT STEM

τὸ γένος ("race")
Noun Stem: γένοσ-/γένεσ-

	Singular	Plural
Nom.	γένος	γένη
Acc.	γένος	γένη
Gen.	γένους	γενέων or γενῶν
Dat.	γένει	γένεσι(ν)

IRREGULAR THIRD DECLENSION NOUNS

There are a small number of very common irregular nouns of the third declension. They all have a short vocative form (just the noun stem) and have additional contractions in the genitive and dative singular forms. The noun stem is obscured in the nominative because the case ending ς was dropped, and the stem was lengthened to compensate. The plural forms of the genitive and dative are not contracted. To aid pronunciation the dative ε changes to α (ablaut) and then switches places with ρ. (This phenomenon is called "metathesis.") Consider the following common irregular third declension nouns.

IRREGULAR NOUNS

	ὁ πατήρ ("father")		ἡ μήτηρ ("mother")		ἡ θυγάτηρ ("daughter")	
	Singular	Plural	Singular	Plural	Singular	Plural
Nom.	πατήρ	πατέρες	μήτηρ	μητέρες	θυγάτηρ	θυγατέρες
Voc.	πάτερ[1]		μῆτερ		θυγάτερ	
Acc.	πατέρα	πατέρας	μητέρα	μητέρας	θυγατέρα	θυγατέρας
Gen.	πατρός	πατέρων	μητρός	μητέρων	θυγατρός	θυγατέρων
Dat.	πατρί	πατράσι(ν)	μητρί	μητράσι(ν)	θυγατρί	θυγατράσι(ν)

The following is the declension of ἀνήρ ("a man"). The noun stem is ανδρ. (Notice how δ changed to θ, both dentals, in ἄνθρωπος.) Having only one vowel, it is monosyllabic and follows the accenting rules for monosyllabic third declension nouns: the accent will appear one place later in the word. The dative plural has an extra vowel to aid pronunciation. The oldest forms of this word had ε instead of δ. The nominative and vocative retain a vowel from this form.

IRREGULAR MONOSYLLABIC NOUN

	ἀνήρ ("a man") Noun Stem: ἀνδρ-	
	Singular	Plural
Nom.	ἀνήρ	ἄνδρες
Voc.	ἄνερ[1]	
Acc.	ἄνδρα	ἄνδρας
Gen.	ἀνδρός	ἀνδρῶν
Dat.	ἀνδρί	ἀνδράσι(ν)

1 Unless an alternate form is provided, the vocative is the same as the nominative.

The following nouns with irregularities should also be specially noted:

	Nominative	Genitive Singular	Article	Dative Plural	Notes
knee	γόνυ	γόνατος	τό	γόνασι	Just the nominative is irregular; other cases use the stem γόνατ-
woman	γυνή (voc. γύναι)	γυναικός	ἡ	γυναιξί	Just the nominative and vocative are irregular; other cases use the stem γυναικ-
dog	κύων (voc. κύον)	κυνός	ὁ	κυσί	Add regular case endings to κύν- for other cases. Accent according to monosyllabic noun stem rules (Lesson 21).
ear	οὖς	ὠτός	τό	ὠσί	Other cases use the stem ὠτ-. Accent according to monosyllabic rules.
foot	πούς	ποδός	ὁ	ποσί	Other cases use the stem ποδ-. Accent according to monosyllabic rules.
water	ὕδωρ	ὕδατος	τό	ὕδασι	Just the nominative is irregular; other cases use the stem ὕδατ-
hand	χείρ	χειρός	ἡ	χερσί	Other cases use the stem χειρ-. Accent according to monosyllabic rules. (The actual stem of this word is χερσ-; the σ drops and the stem vowel lengthens.)

EXERCISES

Memorization Exercise

22.1 Learn Vocabulary List 17.

Grammar Exercises

22.2 Morphology exercises: Decline the following neuter words like γράμμα.

1. θέλημα, θελήματος, τό
2. αἷμα, αἵματος, τό
3. φῶς, φωτός, τό
4. πῦρ, πυρός, τό[1]
5. τέρας, τέρατος, τό
6. οὖς, ὠτός, τό

Translation Exercises

22.3 Translate the following sentences:

1. ἦλθεν ὁ Ἰωάννης εἰς τὸν Ἰορδάνην ποταμὸν καὶ ἐκήρυσσε τὸ βάπτισμα μετανοίας εἰς ἄφεσιν ἁμαρτιῶν.
2. ἴδετε πηλίκοις[2] γράμμασι ὑμῖν ἔγραψα τῇ ἐμῇ χειρί.
3. εἶπεν ὅτι οὐκ ἔστιν αὐτὸς τὸ φῶς, ἀλλ᾽ ἔρχεται μαρτυρῆσαι περὶ τοῦ φωτός.
4. οἱ ἐχθροὶ ἔφθειραν τὰς πόλεις ἡμῶν πυρί.
5. ζητεῖ ὑπὸ τῆς μητρὸς καὶ τῶν ἀδελφῶν σου.
6. οὐ δεῖ λαβεῖν τὸν ἄρτον τῶν παίδων καὶ βαλεῖν αὐτὸν τοῖς κυσίν.
7. οἱ ἄνδρες περιεπάτουν τοὺς ἀγροὺς σὺν ταῖς γυναιξὶν αὐτῶν.
8. ἐκέλευσα τοὺς ἄνδρας ἑτοιμάζειν τὴν ὁδὸν τῷ βασιλεῖ.
9. ἐγὼ μὲν βαπτίζω ὑμᾶς ὕδατι, ἐκεῖνος δὲ βαπτίσει ὑμᾶς πνεύματι ἁγίῳ καὶ πυρί.

1 This word only occurs in the singular in Greek literature.

2 πηλίκος, "how large"

10. ἔχομεν γὰρ τὴν ἄφεσιν τῶν ἁμαρτιῶν ἡμῶν διὰ τοῦ αἵματος αὐτοῦ.
11. ποιήσει σημεῖα καὶ τέρατα τῷ γένει τούτῳ.
12. οἱ παῖδες ἔλαβον τὸν ἰχθὺν ἐκ τοῦ ὕδατος.
13. ἀνοίξει τὰ ὦτα τῶν κωφῶν.
14. καὶ μετὰ ταῦτα ἦλθον οἱ μαθηταὶ αὐτοῦ καὶ ἐθαύμαζον ὅτι μετὰ γυναικὸς ἐλάλει.
15. ἔγραψα πάντα ταῦτα τῇ χειρὶ τῆς θυγατρός μου.
16. ἐγὼ γὰρ οὐκ ἦλθον ποιῆσαι τὸ θέλημά μου, ἀλλὰ τὸ θέλημα τοῦ πατρὸς ὃς ἀπέστειλέ με.
17. οἱ γραμματεῖς εἶπον ὅτι εἶδον τὴν θυγατέρα τοῦ βασιλέως.

Composition Exercises

22.4 Translate the following sentences into Greek:

1. This man did signs and wonders in the city.
2. Behold my hands and my feet.
3. You all are the light of the world.
4. The woman was wiping (ἐξέμασσε) the feet of Jesus with her hair.
5. Our fathers ate the manna (τὸ μάννα) in the wilderness.
6. He touched (ἥψατο) the ear of the deaf man with his hand.
7. The king sent this woman to bring her father from the city.
8. He was seeking his mother and his daughter.
9. The Holy Spirit will remain with them forever.
10. You say that you know the will of God.
11. The dogs were eating the fish that I took out of the water.
12. In that year my father went through your city.

13. The scribes would not receive baptism for[1] the remission of sins.
14. I read the letters that he wrote by the hand of his wife.
15. Your cities are destroyed with fire.
16. We bowed[2] our knees to the king.
17. O woman, depart in peace, for I will heal your daughter.

Scripture Translation Exercises

22.5 Translate the following verses from Scripture:

1. ὁ Ἰησοῦς εἶπεν αὐτῷ· μακάριος εἶ, Σίμων Βαριωνᾶ, ὅτι σὰρξ καὶ αἷμα οὐκ ἀπεκάλυψέν σοι ἀλλʼ ὁ πατήρ μου ὁ ἐν τοῖς οὐρανοῖς (Matt 16:17)
2. ἴδετε τὰς χεῖράς μου καὶ τοὺς πόδας μου ὅτι ἐγώ εἰμι αὐτός (Luke 24:39)
3. οὐκ ἐξ αἱμάτων οὐδὲ ἐκ θελήματος σαρκὸς οὐδὲ ἐκ θελήματος ἀνδρὸς ἀλλʼ ἐκ θεοῦ ἐγεννήθησαν[3] (John 1:13)
4. ὁ Πιλᾶτος … ἐφώνησεν τὸν Ἰησοῦν καὶ εἶπεν αὐτῷ· σὺ εἶ ὁ βασιλεὺς τῶν Ἰουδαίων; (John 18:33)
5. ἡ χάρις τοῦ κυρίου Ἰησοῦ Χριστοῦ καὶ ἡ ἀγάπη τοῦ θεοῦ καὶ ἡ κοινωνία τοῦ ἁγίου πνεύματος μετὰ πάντων ὑμῶν (2 Cor 13:14)

1 "for," εἰς
2 "we bowed," ἐκάμψαμεν
3 ἐγεννήθησαν, "they were born"

LESSON 23

Adjectives with Consonant Stems and Irregular Adjectives (Third Declension, Continued)

UNIFORM ADJECTIVES

In addition to many 2-1-2 pattern adjectives, many adjectives have consistent consonant stems for all three genders. We call this a 3-3-3 pattern since the same consonant stem (third declension) is used for each gender for the adjective. As with third declension nouns, the masculine and feminine forms are the same, and the neuter forms have no ending for the nominative and accusative singular cases as well as a short α for the plural forms of those cases.

ἀληθής FORMS

A common third declension adjective, ἀληθής ("true"), is declined as follows:

SIBILANT STEM

ἀληθής, ἀληθές ("true")
Stem: ἀληθες-

	Singular		Plural	
	Masc. and Fem.	Neut.	Masc. and Fem.	Neut.
Nom.	ἀληθής	ἀληθές	ἀληθεῖς	ἀληθῆ
Acc.	ἀληθῆ	ἀληθές	ἀληθεῖς	ἀληθῆ
Gen.	ἀληθοῦς	ἀληθοῦς	ἀληθῶν	ἀληθῶν
Dat.	ἀληθεῖ	ἀληθεῖ	ἀληθέσι(ν)	ἀληθέσι(ν)

Singular Forms

Nominative The stem of third declension adjectives can be seen in the neuter singular, since no ending is added for that case. The masculine and feminine nominative case ending adds an additional σ that drops (Greek words do not terminate with a double σ). Then the stem vowel lengthens to compensate.

Accusative The masculine and feminine accusative singular ending is a vocalized ν, which yields ἀληθέσα. Then the intervocalic σ drops. The remaining ε followed by α contracts to η (ἀληθῆ). Since the originally accented syllable was the leading vowel involved in a contraction, the acute changes to a circumflex over the second vowel of the digraph.

Genitive Similarly, the genitive singular case ending is added to the stem, yielding ἀληθέσος. The intervocalic σ drops, and ε followed by ο contracts to ου, yielding ἀληθοῦς.

Dative The same thing happens with the dative singular; the final form is the result of the addition of a case ending, causing an intervocalic σ to drop, resulting in vowels contracting.

Plural Forms

Nominative The neuter plural ending is a short α. The addition of this ending produces an intervocalic σ, ἀληθέσα, which drops. Then the remaining vowels contract. The masculine and feminine nominative plural case ending added to the noun stem yields ἀληθέσες. The intervocalic σ drops, and the two vowels (ε + ε) contract, yielding ἀληθεῖς.

Accusative The accusative plural for masculine and feminine genders follows the pattern that occurs with πολεῖς. The stem plus original case ending would be ἀληθεσνς. The σ drops prior to the ν, and the ν drops prior to the final σ. Finally, the stem vowel is lengthened, yielding ἀληθεῖς.

Genitive By the same principles, the genitive plural was produced, ἀληθέσων, yielding ἀληθῶν.

Dative

When the dative plural case ending is added to the noun stem, ἀληθέσσι, a redundant σ drops, but one σ remains, so there is no reason for compensatory lengthening in the resultant form, ἀληθέσι.

ἄφρων FORMS

The third declension adjective ἄφρων ("foolish") is less complicated, since ν does not drop out in an intervocalic position. Only the nominative singular and the dative plural have either a σ or a ν drop. It follows the same principles and is declined as follows:

LIQUID STEM

ἄφρων, ἄφρον ("foolish")
Adjective Stem: ἄφρον-

	Singular		Plural	
	Masc. and Fem.	Neut.	Masc. and Fem.	Neut.
Nom.	ἄφρων	ἄφρον	ἄφρονες	ἄφρονα
Acc.	ἄφρονα	ἄφρον	ἄφρονας	ἄφρονα
Gen.	ἄφρονος	ἄφρονος	ἀφρόνων	ἀφρόνων
Dat.	ἄφρονι	ἄφρονι	ἄφροσι(ν)	ἄφροσι(ν)

3-1-3 ADJECTIVES (VERY COMMON)

Some adjectives have consonant stems (third declension) for the masculine and neuter genders but a vocalic stem (first declension) for their feminine forms. Because of this, these types of words are classified as 3-1-3 adjectives. A very common adjective of this type is πᾶς ("all"). None of the nominative forms reveal the noun stem, πάντ-.

The masculine and neuter forms follow a pattern similar to -οντ nouns presented in Lesson 21. The neuter nominative singular form with no case ending drops the terminal τ. The stem is clearly seen in the masculine accusative singular form with the vocalized ν (turning to α) case ending. All other masculine and neuter forms should be able to be inferred given that stem and regular case endings.

The feminine forms originally used the same stem with a vocalic ending (παντια). This -τια combination had a compound sibilant sound (analogous to the English "-tion"). Thus, these feminine forms follow the pattern exemplified with δόξα in Lesson 9, and the noun stem reduced to πασ-. For example:

-ντ STEM

πᾶς, πᾶσα, πᾶν ("all")
Adjective Stem: παντ-, πασ-, παντ-

	Singular			Plural		
	Masc.	Fem.	Neut.	Masc.	Fem.	Neut.
Nom.	πᾶς	πᾶσα	πᾶν	πάντες	πᾶσαι	πάντα
Acc.	πάντα	πᾶσαν	πᾶν	πάντας	πάσας	πάντα
Gen.	παντός	πάσης	παντός	πάντων	πασῶν	πάντων
Dat.	παντί	πάσῃ	παντί	πᾶσι(ν)	πάσαις	πᾶσι(ν)

FORMS FOR "ONE"

The word for the number "one" is declined in all cases and follows a 3-1-3 adjective pattern with what looks like an unrelated stem. Smyth provides a description of the original stem: εἷς is for ἑν-ς; the stem ἑν was originally σεμ (Lat. *semel, simplex, singuli*); μία stands for σμ-ια.[1]

Be very careful to distinguish εἷς "one" (masculine) from εἰς "to" and ἕν "one" (neuter) from ἐν "in." Notice how the prepositions have smooth breathing and are proclitics (without an accent). The accenting for this word follows the normal pattern for single-syllable noun stems (presented in Lesson 21).

IRREGULAR LIQUID STEM

εἷς, μία, ἕν ("one")
Stem: ἑν-, μία-, ἑν-

	Masc.	Fem.	Neut.
Nom.	εἷς	μία	ἕν
Acc.	ἕνα	μίαν	ἕν
Gen.	ἑνός	μιᾶς	ἑνός
Dat.	ἑνί	μιᾷ	ἑνί

1 Smyth §349.

The declension of εἷς "one" also has derived words οὐδείς and μηδείς ("no one, nothing"). They are the product of a negation + δε (conjunction) + εἷς (in typical gender and case spellings). Given the singular meaning of these words, they only have singular forms.

	Compound with οὐ		
	Masc.	Fem.	Neut.
Nom.	οὐδείς	οὐδεμία	οὐδέν
Acc.	οὐδένα	οὐδεμίαν	οὐδέν
Gen.	οὐδενός	οὐδεμιᾶς	οὐδενός
Dat.	οὐδενί	οὐδεμιᾷ	οὐδενί

The negation is modified when used with nonindicative verbs.

	Compound with μη		
	Masc.	Fem.	Neut.
Nom.	μηδείς	μηδεμία	μηδέν
Acc.	μηδένα	μηδεμίαν	μηδέν
Gen.	μηδενός	μηδεμιᾶς	μηδενός
Dat.	μηδενί	μηδεμιᾷ	μηδενί

When the governing verb is indicative, οὐδείς is used; μηδείς is used when the governing verb is in the subjunctive, imperative, or infinitive mood, or a participle.

Double Negation Meanings

Compound negations such as οὐδείς and μηδείς are used to complement or reinforce (cf. 1 John 1:5) a previous negation (rather than reverse it). If a simple negation (οὐ or μή) follows another negation, each has its own independent force.[1] Examples:

1. No one told me this.	οὐδεὶς εἶπέ μοι τοῦτο.
2. They said nothing to anyone.	οὐδὲν οὐδενὶ εἶπον.
3. Do not hurt anyone.	μὴ βλάψον μηδένα.
4. I am not able to see anyone.	οὐ δύναμαι ἰδεῖν μηδένα.

IRREGULAR 2-1-2 PATTERN ADJECTIVES

Two irregular adjectives with vocalic stems occur very frequently. The stem of each of these adjectives can be derived from the noun stem seen in the feminine nominative singular case. Notice that the feminine form for both of these adjectives uses a longer stem than the other genders. Notice also in these following paradigms how each word only has four irregular forms (all singular).

μέγας, μεγάλη, μέγα ("great" or "large")

	Singular			Plural		
	Masc.	Fem.	Neut.	Masc.	Fem.	Neut.
Nom.	μέγας	μεγάλη	μέγα	μεγάλοι	μεγάλαι	μεγάλα
Acc.	μέγαν	μεγάλην	μέγα	μεγάλους	μεγάλας	μεγάλα
Gen.	μεγάλου	μεγάλης	μεγάλου	μεγάλων	μεγάλων	μεγάλων
Dat.	μεγάλῳ	μεγάλῃ	μεγάλῳ	μεγάλοις	μεγάλαις	μεγάλοις

πολύς, πολλή, πολύ ("many")

	Singular			Plural		
	Masc.	Fem.	Neut.	Masc.	Fem.	Neut.
Nom.	πολύς	πολλή	πολύ	πολλοί	πολλαί	πολλά
Acc.	πολύν	πολλήν	πολύ	πολλούς	πολλάς	πολλά
Gen.	πολλοῦ	πολλῆς	πολλοῦ	πολλῶν	πολλῶν	πολλῶν
Dat.	πολλῷ	πολλῇ	πολλῷ	πολλοῖς	πολλαῖς	πολλοῖς

1 Ernest De Witt Burton, *Syntax of the Moods and Tenses in New Testament Greek*, 3rd ed. (Edinburgh: T&T Clark, 1898), 185.

EXERCISES

Memorization Exercise

23.1 Learn Vocabulary List 18.

Translation Exercises

23.2 Translate the following sentences:

1. ἴδε ὑγιῆ ἐποίησά σε, μηκέτι ἁμάρτανε.
2. οἱ λῃσταὶ ἔφυγον εἰς τὰ ὄρη.
3. οὐδεὶς θέλει πιεῖν τὸν οἶνον τοῦτον.
4. τὸ ὄνομά μου μέγα ἔσται ἐν πᾶσι τοῖς ἔθνεσι.
5. οἱ ἱερεῖς ἦλθον νυκτὸς καὶ ἦραν τὸ σῶμα τοῦ προφήτου.
6. εἰ οὖν τὸ φῶς τὸ ἐν σοὶ σκότος ἐστίν, τὸ σκότος πόσον.[1]
7. ὦ γύναι, μεγάλη[2] σου ἡ πίστις.
8. γινώσκομεν ὅτι τὰ ῥήματα ταῦτα ἀληθῆ ἐστίν, ὅτι ἐλάλησεν αὐτὰ ὁ κύριος διὰ στόματος Δαυὶδ τοῦ προφήτου.
9. αὕτη δέ ἐστιν ἡ κρίσις ὅτι τὸ φῶς ἦλθεν εἰς τὸν κόσμον καὶ ἐφίλησαν οἱ ἄνθρωποι μᾶλλον τὸ σκότος ἢ[3] τὸ φῶς· ἦν γὰρ αὐτῶν πονηρὰ τὰ ἔργα.
10. πεμπέσθω εἷς τῶν δούλων σπείρειν τὸ σπέρμα ἐν τῷ ἀγρῷ μου.
11. συνήρχοντο δὲ πολλοὶ ἐκ τῶν κώμων καὶ ἔφερον αὐτῷ τοὺς ἀσθενεῖς καὶ ἔβαλον αυτοὺς παρὰ τοὺς πόδας αὐτοῦ, καὶ ἐδέοντο αὐτοῦ θεραπεύειν αὐτούς.
12. μηδεὶς σκανδαλιζέτω ἕνα τῶν παίδων τούτων.
13. οἱ δὲ γονεῖς αὐτοῦ οὐκ ἔγνωσαν ὅτι μένει ἐν τῇ πόλει.
14. οὐχ ἡ γραφὴ εἶπεν ὅτι ἐκ τοῦ σπέρματος Δαυίδ, καὶ ἀπὸ Βηθλεὲμ τῆς κώμης ὅπου ἦν Δαυίδ, ἔρχεται ὁ Χριστός;
15. ἐν ἐκείνῃ τῇ ὥρᾳ συνάγονται αὐτῷ πολλοὶ τῶν ἀρχιερέων οἳ λέγουσιν ὅτι οὐκ ἔσται ἀνάστασις.

1 πόσον, "how great," with an implied ἐστί
2 implied ἐστί
3 ἤ, "than"; do not confuse this form with ἡ (feminine definite article) or ἥ (feminine relative pronoun). See page 418.

Composition Exercises

23.3 Translate the following sentences into Greek:

1. You will open my mouth, O Lord, and my tongue will praise your name.
2. Didn't you sow good seed in your field?
3. Do not carry any[1] sick man to the synagogue on the Sabbath day.
4. If you want, you can (are able to) heal me.
5. I came into this world for[2] judgment.
6. One of the lepers, when he saw that he was healed, threw himself at his feet.
7. The high priests knew that this saying was true.
8. All the disciples were full of faith and of the Holy Spirit, and they healed the sick and cast out many demons.
9. None of the priests believes that there is a resurrection.
10. My parents built many houses in this city.
11. Let no one love darkness more than light.
12. When they came to the villages they preached the gospel to all the gentiles who dwelt there.
13. If I judge, my judgment is true.
14. When the disciples of John heard that he was dead, they came and took up his body.

Scripture Translation Exercises

23.4 Translate the following verses from Scripture (Matt 6:9–10):

1. Πάτερ ἡμῶν ὁ ἐν τοῖς οὐρανοῖς·
2. ἁγιασθήτω τὸ ὄνομά σου·
3. ἐλθέτω ἡ βασιλεία σου·
4. γενηθήτω[3] τὸ θέλημά σου,
5. ὡς ἐν οὐρανῷ καὶ ἐπὶ γῆς·

1 Use μηδείς.
2 Use εἰς.
3 γενηθήτω, aorist passive imperative, "let it happen"

LESSON 24

Aorist and Future Passive

AORIST PASSIVE

Regardless of whether a verb uses a sigmatic (first aorist) pattern or a thematic (second aorist) pattern for its active or middle voices, if a verb has an aorist passive form, we expect it to use ϑη for its aorist passive stem. This stem is represented in a verb's final (sixth) principal part. The indicative forms add ϑη to the verbal root (occasionally an unrelated root) and then add past personal endings (including an augment). Notice how all the endings nearly match the past (secondary) endings used in the imperfect and second aorist.[1] In addition to the ϑη stem, the only difference in this pattern is the spelling for the third person plural (but it should feel reasonable).

Nonindicative moods do not have an augment, since these moods don't reference time. The stem references some type of complete or simple aspect (as occurs with aorist active nonindicative moods). The infinitive ending used for the aorist passive has already been encountered with the verb "to be."

1 What is strange is that active forms of the secondary endings were used for this tense. Apparently, the stem identified the voice so clearly that there was not a problem.

The aorist passive conjugates as follows:

Aorist Passive Forms

	Indicative		Imperative	
1 sg.	ἐλύθην	I was released		
2 sg.	ἐλύθης	you were released	λύθητι[1]	be released
3 sg.	ἐλύθη	he/she/it was released	λυθήτω	let him/her/it be released
1 pl.	ἐλύθημεν	we were released		
2 pl.	ἐλύθητε	you all were released	λύθητε	be released (you all)
3 pl.	ἐλύθησαν	they were released	λυθήτωσαν	let them be released

Infinitive	
λυθῆναι	to be released

FUTURE PASSIVE The future passive can be intimidating to beginning students because of the number of letters involved. However, once the stem is learned, make use of previously learned roots and endings. The tense is not very common in the New Testament.

The future passive uses the same θη stem as the aorist passive, but adds an additional σ and thematic vowel (aspectually redundant). All together the stem is θησο-, to which passive primary (non-past) personal endings are attached. These are the same endings used in the present and future middle forms. Another way to think about the future passive is that it inserts θη into future middle forms. The future passive is conjugated as follows:

1 The second person singular imperative ending used with athematic stems is θι or ς. The aorist passive uses θι, but the θ reduces to τ because λύθηθι would be difficult to pronounce.

	Future Passive Forms	
	Indicative	
1 sg.	λυθήσομαι	I will be released
2 sg.	λυθήσῃ (λυθήσει)	you will be released
3 sg.	λυθήσεται	he/she/it will be released
1 pl.	λυθησόμεθα	we will be released
2 pl.	λυθήσεσθε	you (all) will be released
3 pl.	λυθήσονται	they will be released
	Infinitive	
	λυθήσεσθαι	about to be released

CONSONANT CONTRACTION

In both the aorist passive and future passive, the presence of the letter ϑ that immediately follows the verbal root causes consonantal changes according to square of stop principles. The first consonant will change to match the type of the following consonant. However, note that a dental preceding the ϑ in this stem changes to a σ. This is summarized as follows:

β, π, φ + ϑ = φϑ

δ, τ, ϑ + ϑ = σϑ

γ, κ, χ + ϑ = χϑ

In the contract verbs the short vowel is lengthened before ϑ. For example:

Present	Verbal Root	Aor. Pass.	Fut. Pass.	Notes
ἄγω	ἀγ-	ἤχθην	ἀχθήσομαι	Guttural changes to χ prior to ϑ.
πράσσω	πραγ-	ἐπράχθην	πραχθήσομαι	Guttural changes to χ prior to ϑ.
πέμπω	πεμπ-	ἐπέμφθην	πεμφθήσομαι	Labial changes to φ prior to ϑ.
πείθω	πειθ-	ἐπείσθην	πεισθήσομαι	Dental changes to σ prior to ϑ.
φιλέω	φιλε-	ἐφιλήθην	φιληθήσομαι	Contract vowel lengthens prior to a stem consonant.

Aorist Passive Stems without ϑ

Some verbs omit or drop the ϑ in the aorist passive stem (sixth principal part). Some grammars refer to this irregular stem as the second aorist passive. It bears no relation to the second aorist active. It is more of a variation on the ϑη stem than an alternative stem. It does not occur very frequently in the New Testament. One must simply memorize which verbs have this modified aorist passive stem. An example of a verb that doesn't have a ϑ in its aorist passive forms is φαίνω, conjugated here.

Aorist Passive Forms

	Indicative		Imperative	
1 sg.	ἐφάνην	I appeared		
2 sg.	ἐφάνης	you appeared	φάνηϑι[1]	appear
3 sg.	ἐφάνη	he/she/it appeared	φανήτω	let him/her/it appear
1 pl.	ἐφάνημεν	we appeared		
2 pl.	ἐφάνητε	you all appeared	φάνητε	appear (you all)
3 pl.	ἐφάνησαν	they appeared	φανήτωσαν	let them appear

Infinitive	
φανῆναι	to appear

The following are some other verbs that follow this exceptional pattern. Notice how all of their roots end in either a liquid or labial.

Exceptional Aorist Passive	Translation	Lexical Form
ἐγράφην	I was written	γράφω
ἐκρύβην	I was hidden	κρύπτω
ἐσπάρην	I was sown	σπείρω
ἐστάλην	I was sent	στέλλω
ἐστράφην	I was turned	στρέφω
ἐφϑάρην	I was destroyed	φϑείρω

1 The ϑι is the ending used for the second person singular in the aorist passive. It isn't part of the stem. The ϑι ending is able to stand because there isn't another ϑ in the stem that would typically cause this ending to reduce or simplify to τ.

The following important verbs have irregular forms[1] (altered verbal roots) for their sixth principal part (their aorist and future passive forms.)

Present Indicative	Verbal Root	Aorist Passive	Future Passive	Notes
ἀκούω	ἀκου-	ἠκούσθην	ἀκουσθήσομαι	Appearing sigma
βάλλω	βαλ-	ἐβλήθην	βληθήσομαι	Root metathesis
καλέω	καλ-	ἐκλήθην	κληθήσομαι	Root metathesis
λαμβάνω	λαβ-	ἐλήφθην	ληφθήσομαι	Lengthened root
λέγω	ἐρ- (unrelated)	ἐρρέθην, ἐρρήθην		Lengthened root
ὁράω	ὀπ- (unrelated)	ὤφθην (I was seen or I appeared)	ὀφθήσομαι (I will be seen or I will appear)	As expected
φέρω	ἐνεγκ- (unrelated)	ἠνέχθην		Compound guttural reduced

1 The unrelated roots in this section are explained in Lesson 19.

EXERCISES

Memorization Exercises

24.1 Review Vocabulary Lists 14–18.

Translation Exercises

24.2 Translate the following sentences:

1. ἤχθη ὁ Ἰησοῦς ὑπὸ τοῦ πνεύματος εἰς τὰ ὄρη πειρασθῆναι ὑπὸ τοῦ διαβόλου.
2. ὁ ἀρχιερεὺς ἐκρύβη ἐν τοῖς ὄρεσι πολλὰ ἔτη.[1]
3. τὸ ὄνομά μου κηρυχθήσεται ἐν πᾶσι τοῖς ἔθνεσι.
4. τῇ γὰρ χάριτι ἐσώθημεν διὰ θελήματος θεοῦ.
5. οἱ νεκροὶ ἐγερθήσονται ἐν ἡμέρᾳ κρίσεως τῇ φωνῇ τοῦ ἀγγέλου καὶ τῇ σάλπιγγι.
6. καὶ ὅτε ἐξεβλήθη τὸ δαιμόνιον ἐθαύμαζεν ὁ ὄχλος, ἔλεγον δὲ πολλοὶ ὅτι[2] ταῦτα τὰ τέρατα οὐκ ἐπράχθη ἐν ταῖς ἡμέραις τῶν πατέρων ἡμῶν.
7. μετὰ ταῦτα ὤφθη πᾶσι τοῖς ἀποστόλοις.
8. ἐκέλευσε τὸν ἄνδρα ἐνεχθῆναι διὰ τῆς πόλεως.
9. ἐν ἐκείνῃ τῇ ἡμέρᾳ πᾶς ὁ λαὸς κληθήσεται ἅγιος τῷ κυρίῳ.
10. αἱ γυναῖκες παρεκλήθησαν ὑπὸ τῶν ἀνδρῶν αὐτῶν.
11. ποιήσω τὰ ῥήματά μου ἀκουσθῆναι ὑπὸ τοῦ βασιλέως.
12. οὐδεὶς τῶν ἀγγέλων ἀκουσθήσεται.
13. πάντες οἱ ἰχθύες ἐβλήθησαν εἰς τὸ ὕδωρ.
14. ταῦτα ἐρρήθη διὰ στόματος Δαυίδ.
15. πεμφθήτω εἷς τῶν ἱερέων πείθειν τὸν βασιλέα.
16. ὅτε καρπὸν ἐποίησε τὸ καλὸν σπέρμα ἐφάνη καὶ τὰ ζιζάνια.[3]
17. ὦ βασιλεῦ, φιληθήσει ὑπὸ παντὸς τοῦ γένους.

1 πολλὰ ἔτη, "for many years"; the accusative case is used to express duration of time. (Cf. H. P. V. Nunn, *A Short Syntax of New Testament Greek* [Cambridge: Cambridge University Press, 1912], 18.)

2 ὅτι here is used to introduce the exact words of a speaker, functioning as English quotation marks; see Nunn, *Syntax*, 158.

3 ζιζάνια, "tares"

18. τὰ σώματα τῶν ἁγίων ἐσπάρη ἐν ἀτιμίᾳ,[1] ἐγερθήσεται δὲ ἐν δόξῃ.
19. ἐκλήθητε ἄφρονες ὑπὸ τῶν σοφῶν τοῦ αἰῶνος τούτου.

Composition Exercises

24.3 Translate the following sentences into Greek:

1. All this nation was called righteous.[2]
2. Many of these words were written in a book by the high priest.
3. The fish were taken by these boys.
4. We were sown in weakness,[3] we will be raised in power.
5. If the devil will be cast out, the crowd will wonder.
6. The good seed was carried to the fields.
7. I was sent by the king's servants to seek for you.
8. We know that this gospel will be preached to all the gentiles and that many will hear.
9. In that day many bodies of the saints arose[4] and came into the city and appeared to many.
10. We want those sheep to be driven to the hills.
11. You will be saved by faith and hope, if you will abide in them.
12. You commanded the stones to be cast into the water.
13. All these things will be done in the darkness.
14. You all have heard that it was said by our fathers, "You will not make an image of the Lord your God."
15. We were called foolish[5] by many of the rulers of the gentiles, but we know that the words that we speak are true.

1 ἐν ἀτιμίᾳ, "in dishonor"
2 neuter, agreeing with γένος (Nunn, *Syntax*, 11)
3 ἀσθένεια
4 were raised
5 "foolish," plural (Nunn, *Syntax*, 11)

Scripture Translation Exercises

24.4 Translate the following verses from Scripture:

1. πᾶν οὖν δένδρον μὴ ποιοῦν καρπὸν καλὸν ἐκκόπτεται καὶ εἰς πῦρ βάλλεται (Matt 3:10)
2. καὶ ἀπήγαγον τὸν Ἰησοῦν πρὸς τὸν ἀρχιερέα, καὶ συνέρχονται πάντες οἱ ἀρχιερεῖς καὶ οἱ πρεσβύτεροι καὶ οἱ γραμματεῖς (Mark 14:53)
3. λεπροὶ καθαρίζονται καὶ κωφοὶ ἀκούουσιν, νεκροὶ ἐγείρονται, πτωχοὶ εὐαγγελίζονται (Luke 7:22)
4. παρήγγειλεν γὰρ τῷ πνεύματι τῷ ἀκαθάρτῳ ἐξελθεῖν ἀπὸ τοῦ ἀνθρώπου (Luke 8:29)
5. πρὸ δὲ τούτων πάντων ἐπιβαλοῦσιν ἐφ'[1] ὑμᾶς τὰς χεῖρας αὐτῶν καὶ διώξουσιν (Luke 21:12)
6. ἡμῖν δὲ ἀπεκάλυψεν ὁ θεὸς διὰ τοῦ πνεύματος (1 Cor 2:10)

1 ἐφ', "on"

LESSON 25

Participles

PARTICIPLE FUNCTIONS

Participles represent the last part of speech that can produce attributive phrases, which provide more information about a noun or adverbial phrases to condition the verb action. Here is the phrase and clause function table once again for your consideration:

<table>
<tr><td colspan="2"></td><th colspan="3">Function</th></tr>
<tr><td colspan="2"></td><th>Substantive</th><th>Attributive</th><th>Adverbial</th></tr>
<tr><th rowspan="6">Part of Speech</th><th>Noun or Pronoun</th><td colspan="3">noun with various case endings</td></tr>
<tr><th>Preposition</th><td>article + preposition + object</td><td>preposition + object</td><td>anarthrous preposition + object</td></tr>
<tr><th>Adjective & Adverb</th><td>article + adjective (in place of noun)</td><td>adjective</td><td>adverb</td></tr>
<tr><th>Relative Pronoun & Subordinating Conjunction</th><td colspan="2">relative pronoun + verb</td><td>conjunction + verb</td></tr>
<tr><th>Infinitive</th><td colspan="2">infinitive (with or without an article)</td><td>infinitive (with or without a conjunction or preposition[1])</td></tr>
<tr><th>Participle</th><td>article + adjective (in place of noun)</td><td>sometimes article + adjective (matching noun)</td><td>participle (without article)</td></tr>
</table>

1 An infinitive used as an object of a preposition should really be placed as a type of object for an adverbial use of a prepositional phrase on this chart.

While English typically uses relative and adverbial clauses to provide additional information in a sentence, Greek prefers participles to elaborate on any clause. Thus they must be thoroughly understood. Often, English translations will render a Greek participle with a corresponding relative or adverbial clause using the pattern represented in this chart. Feel free to translate participles in this manner; however, the composition exercises will use English participles where a Greek participle is desired.

PARTICIPLE AS VERBAL ADJECTIVE

Notice how participles have the same syntax as adjectives in the function chart. That is because they are verbs that have been turned into adjectives by the addition of case endings (and the removal of personal endings). Thus they may be called verbal adjectives, sharing some of the characteristics both of verbs and adjectives. The main function of the participle will be to provide either additional verbal meaning relating to a noun (such as what the noun does or did) or adverbial conditioning for a verb (such as when, how, or why the verb occurred). A participle has a subject, and, if the participle was produced from a transitive verb in the active voice, it may have an object. It also has tense (used differently from an indicative verb) and voice.

When a participle provides more information about a noun mentioned within a sentence, it matches that noun in number, gender, and case. Sometimes a participle will act as a substantive adjective and not have a matching noun. In these situations, the participle will always have an article (like substantive adjectives).

ACTIVE PARTICIPLE FORMS

The active participles are declined with third declension endings for masculine and neuter genders and first declension endings for the feminine gender (3-1-3 pattern with ντ stem).[1] Consider the following examples.

	Masc.	Fem.	Neut.	Root + Stem	Translation
Pres. Act. Ptc.	λύων	λύουσα	λῦον	λυοντ-	releasing
Fut. Act. Ptc.	λύσων	λύσουσα	λῦσον	λυσοντ-	being about to release
First Aor. Act. Ptc.	λύσας	λύσασα	λῦσαν	λυσαντ-	having released
Second Aor. Act. Ptc.	βαλών	βαλοῦσα	βαλόν	βαλοντ-	having thrown
Pres. Ptc. of εἰμί	ὤν	οὖσα	ὄν	ὀντ-	being

Notice the following:

1. The future participle (which is not nearly as common as present or aorist forms, only occurring twelve times in the New Testament) uses the second principal part stem, formed from the verbal root + σο (aspectual stem) + ντ (participle stem) + case endings. For verbs that have the same spellings for the verbal root and present root form (such as λύω), the only difference between the present and future participle will be the presence of the σ before the endings.

2. Neither first or second aorist participles have augments. They do not have temporal personal endings. If they are used for temporal reasons they will merely communicate antecedent time (not objective past time) in relation to their governing verb (e.g., "having spoken, all understood," or, "having spoken all will understand").

3. First aorist active participles will continue to have the characteristic σα prior to the participle stem.

1 See Lesson 21.

4. The endings of the second aorist participle are the same as those of the present participle, but the root and the accents differ. The difference in how they sound easily distinguishes a present and second aorist participle—a good argument for committing time to becoming proficient at accenting verbs and participles.

Present Active Participle

Unfortunately, only the three nominative singular forms are learned when memorizing adjectives. Thus, 3-1-3 pattern adjectives with ντ stems don't reveal the stem. However, you can see the stem in all other masculine and neuter cases. The original ντ stem never appears in any of the feminine A-stem (first declension) forms. As εἷς and μία were produced from the same root, the feminine forms also began with the ντ stem. It was only after several contractions that the first declension ουσα stem endings were produced. The σ stands in place of a more complex sibilant sound (\tsa\ or \tza\ from τια) and thus follows δόξα with η in the genitive and dative singular forms.

Present Active Participle

	Singular			Plural		
	Masc.	Fem.	Neut.	Masc.	Fem.	Neut.
Nom.	λύων	λύουσα	λῦον	λύοντες	λύουσαι	λύοντα
Acc.	λύοντα	λύουσαν	λῦον	λύοντας	λυούσας	λύοντα
Gen.	λύοντος	λυούσης	λύοντος	λυόντων	λυουσῶν	λυόντων
Dat.	λύοντι	λυούσῃ	λύοντι	λύουσι(ν)	λυούσαις	λύουσι(ν)

Note that the masculine and neuter dative plural are the same in form as the third person plural present active indicative.

Sigmatic Aorist (First Aorist) Present Active Participle

The first aorist participle pattern is used for regular verbs that maintain the same spelling for their present root as their verbal root. Just as in the indicative mood, we add a σα stem to their verbal root. We then add the participle stem, ντ, and case endings to create the desired participle. Except for the nominative singular forms, first aorist participles will look just like present participles, with σα replacing the thematic vowel.

Sigmatic Aorist (First Aorist) Active Participle

	Singular			Plural		
	Masc.	Fem.	Neut.	Masc.	Fem.	Neut.
Nom.	λύσας	λύσασα	λῦσαν	λύσαντες	λύσασαι	λύσαντα
Acc.	λύσαντα	λύσασαν	λῦσαν	λύσαντας	λυσάσας	λύσαντα
Gen.	λύσαντος	λυσάσης	λύσαντος	λυσάντων	λυσασῶν	λυσάντων
Dat.	λύσαντι	λυσάσῃ	λύσαντι	λύσασι(ν)	λυσάσαις	λύσασι(ν)

Thematic Aorist (Second Aorist) Active Participle

Participle spelling for verbs that have thematic aorist forms will be identical to the present participle forms except for their root (which will be formed from the verbal root rather than the present root) and their accent position. So βάλλοντος is a present participle but βαλόντος is the aorist version. It should be especially clear which is which when spoken aloud.

Present Participle Forms for Contract and Irregular Verbs

The present active participles for ε-contract verbs only have three possible contractions:

1. ε + ω = ω (occurs in the masculine nominative singular)
2. ε + ου = ου (occurs in the dative plural and all feminine forms)
3. ε + ο = ου (occurs in all other cases)

The accent remains over the syllable where the ε is contracted. It will be a circumflex if the leading vowel of the pair was accented. In cases where the penult is accented, a long ultima will not allow a circumflex that far forward, so the accent is changed to an acute (e.g., feminine genitive singular). This type of contract verb is declined as follows:

Present Active Participle for ε-Contract Verb

	Singular			Plural		
	Masc.	Fem.	Neut.	Masc.	Fem.	Neut.
Nom.	φιλῶν	φιλοῦσα	φιλοῦν	φιλοῦντες	φιλοῦσαι	φιλοῦντα
Acc.	φιλοῦντα	φιλοῦσαν	φιλοῦν	φιλοῦντας	φιλούσας	φιλοῦντα
Gen.	φιλοῦντος	φιλούσης	φιλοῦντος	φιλούντων	φιλουσῶν	φιλούντων
Dat.	φιλοῦντι	φιλούσῃ	φιλοῦντι	φιλοῦσι(ν)	φιλούσαις	φιλοῦσι(ν)

The present participle of εἰμί is declined like λύων:

Present Participle of εἰμί

	Singular			Plural		
	Masc.	Fem.	Neut.	Masc.	Fem.	Neut.
Nom.	ὤν	οὖσα	ὄν	ὄντες	οὖσαι	ὄντα
Acc.	ὄντα	οὖσαν	ὄν	ὄντας	οὔσας	ὄντα
Gen.	ὄντος	οὔσης	ὄντος	ὄντων	οὐσῶν	ὄντων
Dat.	ὄντι	οὔσῃ	ὄντι	οὖσι(ν)	οὔσαις	οὖσι(ν)

MIDDLE AND PASSIVE PARTICIPLES

The present middle and passive participle is declined as a 2-1-2 pattern adjective with a different participle stem. There is no difference in accent position between the first and second aorist middle participle forms. Aorist passive participles are declined with the 3-1-3 pattern, but have a θε aspectual stem prior to the ντ participle stem. The ε in the θε stem lengthens to ει when necessary.

Pres. Mid. and Pass. Ptc.	λυόμενος, -η, -ον	ransoming (mid.), being released (pass.)
First Aorist Mid. Ptc.[1]	λυσάμενος, -η, -ον	having ransomed
Second Aorist Mid. Ptc.	βαλόμενος, -η, -ον	having thrown oneself
Aorist Pass. Ptc.	λυθείς, -θεῖσα, -θέν	something released or having been released

1 The first and second aorist middle forms are explained in Lesson 27.

The aorist passive participle is accented like the second aorist active and declines as follows:

Aorist Passive Participle

	Singular			Plural		
	Masc.	Fem.	Neut.	Masc.	Fem.	Neut.
Nom.	λυθείς	λυθεῖσα	λυθέν	λυθέντες	λυθεῖσαι	λυθέντα
Acc.	λυθέντα	λυθεῖσαν	λυθέν	λυθέντας	λυθείσας	λυθέντα
Gen.	λυθέντος	λυθείσης	λυθέντος	λυθέντων	λυθεισῶν	λυθέντων
Dat.	λυθέντι	λυθείσῃ	λυθέντι	λυθεῖσι(ν)	λυθείσαις	λυθεῖσι(ν)

Note: Participles are generally negated with μή in the New Testament.

ADJECTIVAL PARTICIPLE USAGE

Like any other adjective, when a participle is used to provide more information about a noun, it will be in an attributive position. A matching article will precede the participle (either in an article-participle-noun sequence, squeezing between the noun and its article, or having its own additional article). The only time an adjectival participle will not have an article is when the modified noun doesn't have an article. The participle preceded by an article is very common in the New Testament and will always convey an adjectival or substantive use. English style prefers that adjectival participles be translated by a clause introduced by a relative pronoun, but they may sometimes be translated by a noun. The analogous uses of these different types of phrases and clauses can been seen in the phrase and clause function table. Examples:

1. αἱ πιστεύοντες
   "those who believe," or "believers"

2. ὁ σπείρων
   "the one who sows," or "the sower"

3. οἱ πεινῶντες καὶ διψῶντες[1] τὴν δικαιοσύνην
   "they who hunger and thirst after righteousness" (Matt 5:6)

4. οὗτός ἐστιν ὁ παρὰ τὴν ὁδὸν σπαρείς
   "this is he who was sown by the wayside" (Matt 13:19)

Notice that any number of qualifying words may be inserted between the article and the participle.

ADVERBIAL PARTICIPLE USAGE

When a participle is used adverbially, it provides more information about when, why, or how the verb occurred. Participles used adverbially never have an article.

Position:[2]

- When a participle *follows* the verb, it generally provides information on how the action occurred (manner). We use English participles to convey this idea (e.g., "he came baptizing"). An adverbial participle in this postverb position may also be used to convey purpose and is typically translated with an infinitive of purpose in English (e.g., προσῆλθον αὐτῷ Φαρισαῖοι πειράζοντες αὐτόν, "Pharisees came to him to test him"). All twelve future participles in the New Testament are used to show purpose, typically after a verb of motion or sending.[3] Occasionally authors communicate the idea of purpose with other tenses.

- When a participle *precedes* the verb, it generally provides the context for the governing verb (when or why it occurred). This is equivalent to an adverbial clause modifying the governing verb. Since English prefers subordinate clauses to participles, these participles are typically translated into English by

1 For these forms, see Lesson 28.

2 "There is a meaningful distinction to be made between adverbial participles that precede the verb of the main clause and those that follow the main clause." Steven E. Runge, *Discourse Grammar of the Greek New Testament: A Practical Introduction for Teaching and Exegesis* (Bellingham, WA: Lexham Press, 2010), 249.

3 This construction is the Greek analog to the Latin supine.

a corresponding adverbial clause. The context will determine the equivalent kind of adverbial clause for the participle in question. In the New Testament, an adverbial participle is often equivalent to a temporal clause,[1] sometimes to a causal clause,[2] and less frequently to a concessive clause.[3]

Temporal Phrase

Examples with participles that are communicating a temporal relationship to another phrase or clause:

1. καὶ ἐξελθὼν εἶδεν πολὺν ὄχλον.
   "And after he came out, he saw a great multitude." (Matt 14:14)

2. καὶ ἀκούσαντες οἱ ἀρχιερεῖς καὶ οἱ Φαρισαῖοι τὰς παραβολὰς αὐτοῦ ἔγνωσαν ὅτι περὶ αὐτῶν λέγει.
   "And after the chief priests and Pharisees had heard his parables, they knew that he spoke about them." (Matt 21:45)

Generally speaking, the present participle denotes an action happening at the same time as the action of the main verb, and the aorist participle denotes action that took place before the action of the main verb.

Present Participle Example

3. ὤφθη αὐτοῖς μαχομένοις.
   "He appeared to them while they were fighting." (Acts 7:26)

Aorist Participle Example

4. καὶ νηστεύσας ἡμέρας τεσσαράκοντα καὶ τεσσαράκοντα νύκτας ὕστερον ἐπείνασεν.
   "And after he fasted forty days and forty nights he later hungered." (Matt 4:2)

1 Temporal clauses use English conjunctions such as "while" (contemporaneous), "after" (antecedent), "when" (ambiguous).

2 Causal clauses use English conjunctions such as "since" or "because." There are a number of times in the New Testament when a participle following the governing verb has causal force.

3 Concessive clauses use an English conjunction such as "although."

Causal Clause Examples with the participles communicating causation:

1. καὶ πάντες ἐφοβοῦντο αὐτόν, μὴ πιστεύοντες ὅτι ἐστὶν μαθητής.
   "And they were all afraid of him, because they did not believe that he was a disciple." (Acts 9:26)

2. ἡ δὲ εὐσέβεια πρὸς πάντα ὠφέλιμός ἐστιν, ἐπαγγελίαν ἔχουσα ζωῆς τῆς νῦν καὶ τῆς μελλούσης.
   "Godliness is profitable for everything, because it has a promise for the life that is now, as well as for that which is to come." (1 Tim 4:8)

Parallel Phrase The participle often denotes the attendant circumstances of an action and may be best translated into English by a finite verb joined to the main Greek verb with "and." Examples:

1. ἀποκριθεὶς εἶπεν . . .
   "He answered and said . . ."

2. εὐθὺς κράξας ὁ πατὴρ τοῦ παιδίου ἔλεγεν . . .
   "Immediately the father of the child cried out and said . . ." (Mark 9:24)

3. Μάρκον ἀναλαβὼν ἄγε μετὰ σεαυτοῦ.
   "Take Mark and bring him with you." (2 Tim 4:11)

Participles Expressing Manner or Means

In some cases, however, it is better to translate the Greek participle with an English participle.

Examples:

1. ἐν δὲ ταῖς ἡμέραις ἐκείναις παραγίνεται Ἰωάννης
   ὁ Βαπτιστὴς κηρύσσων ἐν τῇ ἐρήμῳ τῆς Ἰουδαίας,
   καί λέγων· μετανοεῖτε
   "In those days John the Baptist came into the wilderness of Judea preaching and saying, 'Repent' " (Matt 3:1–2)

2. καὶ ἐβαπτίζοντο ὑπ' αὐτοῦ ἐν τῷ Ἰορδάνῃ ποταμῷ
   ἐξομολογούμενοι τὰς ἁμαρτίας αὐτῶν.
   "And they were baptized by him in the river Jordan, confessing their sins." (Matt 3:6)

EXERCISES

Memorization Exercise

25.1 Learn Vocabulary List 19.

Translation Exercises

25.2 Translate the following sentences:

1. καὶ παράγων παρὰ τὴν θάλασσαν τῆς Γαλιλαίας εἶδεν Σίμωνα καὶ Ἀνδρέαν τὸν ἀδελφὸν Σίμωνος ἀμφιβάλλοντας ἐν τῇ θαλάσσῃ.
2. καὶ ἦλθεν κηρύσσων εἰς τὰς συναγωγὰς αὐτῶν καὶ δαιμόνια ἐκβάλλων.
3. πῶς δυσκόλως[1] οἱ τὰ χρήματα ἔχοντες εἰς τὴν βασιλείαν τοῦ θεοῦ εἰσελεύσονται.
4. καὶ ἦσαν οἱ φαγόντες τοὺς ἄρτους πεντακισχίλιοι[2] ἄνδρες.
5. οἱ μὲν οὖν διασπαρέντες διῆλθον εὐαγγελιζόμενοι τὸν λόγον.
6. παραγενόμενος δὲ εἰς Ἰερουσαλὴμ ἐπείραζε κολλᾶσθαι[3] τοῖς μαθηταῖς, καὶ πάντες ἐφοβοῦντο αὐτόν, μὴ πιστεύοντες ὅτι ἐστὶν μαθητής.
7. ἀκούων δὲ Ἀνανίας τοὺς λόγους τούτους πεσὼν ἐξέψυξεν.[4] καὶ ἐγένετο φόβος μέγας ἐπὶ[5] πάντας τοὺς ἀκούοντας.
8. καὶ σπαράξαν[6] αὐτὸν τὸ πνεῦμα τὸ ἀκάθαρτον καὶ φωνῆσαν φωνῇ μεγάλῃ, ἐξῆλθεν ἐξ αὐτοῦ.
9. καὶ ἦν ἐν τῇ ἐρήμῳ τεσσαράκοντα ἡμέρας καὶ τεσσαράκοντα νύκτας πειραζόμενος ὑπὸ τοῦ Σατανᾶ.
10. ὑμεῖς οὖν ἀκούσατε τὴν παραβολὴν τοῦ σπείραντος.
11. καὶ ὤφθη αὐτοῖς Μωϋσῆς καὶ Ἠλίας λαλοῦντες μετ᾽ αὐτοῦ.

1 πῶς δυσκόλως, "with what difficulty"
2 πεντακισχίλιοι, "five thousand"
3 κολλᾶσθαι, "to join himself" (see Lesson 28)
4 ἐξέψυξεν, "expired"; from ἐκψύχω
5 ἐπί, "upon"
6 σπαράξαν, first aorist participle of σπαράσσω, "to shake around"

Composition Exercises

25.3 Translate the following sentences into Greek. (*) marks when a Greek participle should be used to translate the English word.

1. Those who had preached* the word were scattered abroad.
2. And passing by the Sea of Galilee the disciples taught many people.
3. Blessed[1] are those who hear* and those who believe* the words of this book.
4. Many of the tax collectors therefore were baptized, confessing their sins.
5. But he answered* and said, "How with difficulty will you all enter into the kingdom of heaven."
6. The sower* sows the word.
7. And when he came forward* he saw a great multitude.
8. And all those who heard* kept these words in their hearts.
9. But we were afraid because we did not believe* that his words were true.
10. This is he who was sent* by the king.
11. While they were teaching* the people, they remained in the temple.
12. And having come out of the city he went to another place.
13. But the prophet cried and said,* "Behold the man who comes* after me: you all will hear him."
14. After the ruler therefore heard* this he was afraid and all who were* with him.
15. And after they had cast* (the net) into the sea they took many fish.

1 "blessed," μακάριος

16. And upon coming* to Bethlehem they tried to enter into the synagogue, but those who kept* it cast them out.
17. But while I was walking* through the fields I saw a great light from heaven and heard a voice speaking to me.
18. The prophet remained on the mountain forty days[1] and forty nights writing the words of this law.

Scripture Translation Exercises

25.4 Translate the following verses from Scripture:

1. καὶ σπαράξαν αὐτὸν τὸ πνεῦμα τὸ ἀκάθαρτον καὶ φωνῆσαν φωνῇ μεγάλῃ ἐξῆλθεν ἐξ αὐτοῦ (Mark 1:26)
2. καὶ ἐγένετο θάμβος[2] ἐπὶ πάντας καὶ συνελάλουν πρὸς ἀλλήλους[3] λέγοντες· τίς ὁ λόγος οὗτος ὅτι ἐν ἐξουσίᾳ καὶ δυνάμει ἐπιτάσσει τοῖς ἀκαθάρτοις πνεύμασιν καὶ ἐξέρχονται; (Luke 4:36)
3. πολλοὶ γὰρ τῶν ἐχόντων πνεύματα ἀκάθαρτα βοῶντα[4] φωνῇ μεγάλῃ ἐξήρχοντο, πολλοὶ δὲ παραλελυμένοι καὶ χωλοὶ ἐθεραπεύθησαν· ἐγένετο δὲ πολλὴ χαρὰ ἐν τῇ πόλει ἐκείνῃ (Acts 8:7–8)

1 "days" and "nights," use accusative case (Nunn, *Syntax*, 18)

2 θάμβος, "an amazement"

3 ἀλλήλους, "each other"

4 βοῶντα, present active participle neuter nominative plural of βοαω, "I shout"

LESSON 26

Genitive Absolute; Interrogative, Indefinite, and Relative Pronouns

GENITIVE ABSOLUTE

Sometimes an author wants to provide some background context for a sentence (an adverbial participial phrase), but the subject of the participle is not mentioned elsewhere in the sentence. This leaves the participle without a case to match. Example:

> ἐκβληθέντος τοῦ δαιμονίου ἐλάλησεν ὁ κωφός.
> "After the demon was cast out, the mute man spoke."
> (Matt 9:33)

What grammatical function is "demon" performing with respect to the governing clause ("the mute man spoke")? It isn't the subject, object, indirect object, or possessive. Since it doesn't match the case or function of a noun elsewhere within the sentence, it is called "absolute." In Greek, such nouns and their participles—"genitive absolutes"—take the genitive case.

Genitive absolute phrases are always adverbial and typically temporal; they occur at the beginning of a sentence. The genitive absolute will generally be translated by an adverbial clause in English. The context must determine whether a clause is to be temporal, causal, or concessive.

Temporal Functions Most genitive absolutes in the New Testament communicate the timing of the governing verb and will be translated as temporal clauses. Examples:

1. καὶ ἐκβληθέντος τοῦ δαιμονίου ἐλάλησεν ὁ κωφός.
   "After the demon was cast out, the mute man spoke."
   (Matt 9:33)

2. χρονίζοντος δὲ τοῦ νυμφίου ἐνύσταξαν πᾶσαι καὶ ἐκάθευδον.
   "And while the bridegroom tarried they all slumbered and slept." (Matt 25:5)

The same construction is found in Latin, but uses a case called the ablative case.[1] English also has a similar construction, though it is used rarely; in these situations, the nominative case is employed (e.g., "This done, he went home").

Exceptions Note: Although Classical Greek more closely adheres to the principle that genitive absolutes do not refer to the same person or thing as the subject or object of the sentence, there are many exceptions in the Greek New Testament where the subject of the genitive participle is mentioned within the governing clause. For example:

> καὶ ἐκπορευομένου αὐτοῦ ἐκ τοῦ ἱεροῦ λέγει αὐτῷ εἷς τῶν μαθητῶν αὐτοῦ …
> "And as he was coming out of the temple, one of his disciples said to him …" (Mark 13:1)

1 There is no ablative case in Greek.

The interrogative pronoun τίς ("who?"), τί ("what?") can take the place of either a noun or an adjective and introduce a question. The stem τίν- is seen in the genitive singular case. Thus it follows the third declension pattern for nouns with liquid stems. It declines as follows:

INTERROGATIVE PRONOUN

Interrogative Pronoun

	Singular		Plural	
	Masc. & Fem.	Neut.	Masc. & Fem.	Neut.
Nom.	τίς	τί	τίνες	τίνα
Acc.	τίνα	τί	τίνας	τίνα
Gen.	τίνος	τίνος	τίνων	τίνων
Dat.	τίνι	τίνι	τίσι(ν)	τίσι(ν)

Examples of its use:

1. τίνας ἀκούω;
   "Whom do I hear?"

2. τίνας ἀνθρώπους ἀκούω;
   "What men do I hear?"

The indefinite pronoun, τις, is generally translated by "some" or "any." It is distinguished from τίς (the interrogative) in the following ways:

INDEFINITE PRONOUN

- τις does not have an accent
- τις cannot stand as the first word in a sentence because it is an enclitic
- τις is declined in the same way as τίς, but if it must be accented, then it occurs on its ultima

Examples of its use:

1. τοῦτο λέγει τις.
   "Someone says this."

2. ἄνθρωπός τις τοῦτο λέγει.
   "A certain man says this."

RELATIVE PRONOUN

In the New Testament you will find examples of Greek words composed of two parts that both decline. There is an older grammatical form called an indefinite relative pronoun. An example of a regular relative pronoun is "who." The indefinite relative pronoun version is "whoever" or "what sort of one." In the New Testament this type of word had lost its indefinite meaning[1] and was simply used as an alternate spelling for the regular relative pronoun. This alternate spelling occurs only in the nominative case.[2] These forms are provided in parentheses as an expansion to the relative pronoun chart.

Relative Pronoun with Alternate Spelling

	Singular			Plural		
	Masc.	Fem.	Neut.	Masc.	Fem.	Neut.
Nom.	ὅς (ὅστις)	ἥ (ἥτις)	ὅ (ὅτι)	οἵ (οἵτινες)	αἵ (αἵτινες)	ἅ (ἅτινα)
Acc.	ὅν	ἥν	ὅ	οὕς	ἅς	ἅ
Gen.	οὗ	ἧς	οὗ	ὧν	ὧν	ὧν
Dat.	ᾧ	ᾗ	ᾧ	οἷς	αἷς	οἷς

1 This indefinite relative meaning is produced by using a relative pronoun followed by ἄν in the NT, or by using ἐάν.

2 And in the expression ἕως ὅτου, "until" (Matt 5:25, Luke 12:50, Luke 13:8, Luke 22:16, John 9:18).

CERTAIN PREPOSITIONS

The following prepositions present some difficulty. The meanings underlined are the most common in the New Testament.

κατά, original meaning: "down"

The preposition κατά is followed by the accusative or genitive case. When followed by an accusative it means "down along, throughout, with regard to" or "<u>according to</u>"; when followed by a genitive it means "down from" or "<u>against</u>." Examples:

1. λάβετε αὐτὸν ὑμεῖς, καὶ κατὰ τὸν νόμον ὑμῶν κρίνετε αὐτόν.
   "Take him and judge him according to your law." (John 18:31)
2. ὁ μὴ ὢν μετ᾽ ἐμοῦ κατ᾽ ἐμοῦ ἐστίν.
   "He who is not with me is against me." (Luke 11:23)

Notice the following special phrases that are an extension of the "according to" meaning of the preposition:

κατ᾽ ὄναρ, "in a dream"

κατὰ καιρόν, "in due season"

καθ᾽ ἡμέραν, "daily"

κατ᾽ ἰδίαν, "privately"

ἐπί, original meaning: "upon"

The preposition ἐπί is followed by the accusative, genitive, or dative case. It is difficult to draw any clear distinction between its meanings in these three cases; as a general rule, in the accusative it means "upon," "on," or "to," often with some idea of motion; in the genitive it means "upon," "on," or occasionally "in the time of," "in the presence of"; in the dative it means "on" or "at." Examples:

1. ἄλλα δὲ ἔπεσεν ἐπὶ τὴν γῆν τὴν καλήν.
   "And the other fell on good ground." (Matt 13:8)
2. ἄρατε τὸν ζυγόν μου ἐφ᾽ ὑμᾶς.
   "Take my yoke upon you." (Matt 11:29)

3. καὶ ἰδὼν συκῆν μίαν ἐπὶ τῆς ὁδοῦ ἦλθεν ἐπ' αὐτήν.
   "And seeing one fig tree on the road he went to it." (Matt 21:19)

4. ἐγώ σε ἐδόξασα ἐπὶ τῆς γῆς.
   "I have glorified you upon the earth." (John 17:4)

5. ἐπὶ Ἐλισαίου τοῦ προφήτου
   "In the time of Elisha the prophet" (Luke 4:27)

6. καὶ ἐθαύμαζον ἐπ' αὐτῷ.
   "And they wondered at him." (Mark 12:17)

7. γινώσκετε ὅτι ἐγγύς ἐστιν ἐπὶ θύραις.
   "Know that it is near at the doors." (Mark 13:29)

πρός, original meaning: "toward"

The preposition πρός is followed by the accusative, genitive, or dative case, but it is so rarely followed by a genitive or dative case in the New Testament that you may regard it as a preposition followed only by the accusative case. It means "toward, up to, to, with regard to" and, in certain cases, "with"; it is also used after verbs meaning "to say" where we would expect a simple dative. Examples:

1. τετάρτῃ δὲ φυλακῇ τῆς νυκτὸς ἦλθεν πρὸς αὐτοὺς περιπατῶν ἐπὶ τὴν θάλασσαν.
   "In the fourth watch of the night he went to them, walking on the sea." (Matt 14:25)

2. καὶ εἶπεν πρὸς τὸν Σίμωνα Ἰησοῦς· Μὴ φοβοῦ.
   "And Jesus said to Simon, 'Fear not.'" (Luke 5:10)

3. ὁ λόγος ἦν πρὸς τὸν θεόν.
   "The word was with God." (John 1:1)

For more information, see Appendix 4 on prepositions.

EXERCISES

Memorization Exercise

26.1 Learn Vocabulary List 20.

Translation Exercises

26.2(α) Translate the following sentences (part 1):

1. ἔτι δε λαλοῦντος τοῦ Πέτρου τὰ ῥήματα ταῦτα, ἔπεσεν τὸ πνεῦμα τὸ ἅγιον ἐπὶ πάντας τοὺς ἀκούοντας τὸν λόγον.
2. ἡ γὰρ σάρξ ἐπιθυμεῖ κατὰ τοῦ πνεύματος καὶ τὸ πνεῦμα κατὰ τῆς σαρκός.
3. ἐγγὺς δὲ οὔσης Λύδδας τῇ Ἰόππῃ, οἱ μαθηταὶ ἀκούσαντες ὅτι Πέτρος ἐστὶν ἐν αὐτῇ, ἀπέστειλαν δύο ἄνδρας πρὸς αὐτόν.
4. ὁ δὲ ἐπὶ τὰ πετρώδη[1] σπαρείς, οὗτός ἐστιν ὁ τὸν λόγον ἀκούων καὶ εὐθὺς μετὰ χαρᾶς λαμβάνων αὐτὸν.
5. ἀναχωρόντων δὲ αὐτῶν, ἰδοὺ ἄγγελος κυρίου φαίνεται κατ᾽ ὄναρ τῷ Ἰωσὴφ λέγων· παράλαβε τὸ παιδίον καὶ τὴν μητέρα αὐτοῦ, καὶ φεῦγε εἰς Αἴγυπτον.
6. ἐξεπλήσσοντο δὲ οἱ ὄχλοι ἐπὶ τῇ διδαχῇ αὐτοῦ.
7. ἀλλὰ λήμψεσθε[2] δύναμιν, ἐλθόντος τοῦ ἁγίου πνεύματος ἐφ᾽ ὑμᾶς.
8. καθ᾽ ἡμέραν δὲ προσεκαρτέρουν ὁμοθυμαδὸν[3] ἐν τῷ ἱερῷ.
9. καὶ ὄψονται τὸν υἱὸν τοῦ ἀνθρώπου ἐρχόμενον ἐπὶ τῶν νεφέλων τοῦ οὐρανοῦ.
10. τίς ἐκ τῶν δύο ἐποίησεν τὸ θέλημα τοῦ πατρός;
11. τότε προσῆλθεν αὐτῷ γυνή τις αἰτοῦσά τι παρ᾽ αὐτοῦ, ὁ δὲ εἶπεν αὐτῇ· τί θέλεις;

1 πετρώδη, “the rocky ground”
2 λήμψεσθε, future deponent of λαμβάνω
3 ὁμοθυμαδὸν, “with one accord”

26.2(β) Translate the following sentences (part 2):

1. ἐπ᾽ ἀρχιερέως Ἅννα καὶ Καιάφα ἐγένετο ῥῆμα κυρίου ἐπὶ Ἰωάννην τοῦ Ζαχαρίου ἐν τῇ ἐρήμῳ.
2. ἐπὶ ταύτῃ τῇ πέτρᾳ οἰκοδομήσω μου τὴν ἐκκλησίαν.
3. οἱ δὲ ἀρχιερεῖς καὶ τὸ συνέδριον ὅλον ἐζήτουν ψευδομαρτυρίαν[1] κατὰ τοῦ Ἰησοῦ.
4. καθ᾽ ἡμέραν ἤμην πρὸς ὑμᾶς ἐν τῷ ἱερῷ καὶ οὐκ ἐκρατήσατέ με.
5. εἶδεν ὁ Ἰησοῦς πνεῦμα θεοῦ καταβαῖνον ὡσεὶ περιστερὰν[2] ἐρχόμενον ἐπ᾽ αὐτόν.
6. καὶ θαυμάσαντες ἐπὶ τῇ ἀποκρίσει αὐτοῦ ἐσίγησαν.[3]
7. ὁ μὴ ὢν μετ᾽ ἐμοῦ κατ᾽ ἐμοῦ ἐστιν.
8. καὶ ἐσπλαγχνίσθη[4] ἐπ᾽ αὐτοῖς καὶ ἐθεράπευσέν τινας αὐτῶν.
9. ὑμεῖς κατὰ τὴν σάρκα κρίνετε, ἐγὼ δὲ κρίνω οὐδένα.
10. καὶ ἀπῆλθεν καθ᾽ ὅλην τὴν πόλιν κηρύσσων ὅσα ἐποίησεν αὐτῷ ὁ Ἰησοῦς.
11. καὶ ὥρμησεν[5] ἡ ἀγέλη[6] κατὰ τοῦ κρημνοῦ[7] εἰς τὴν θάλασσαν.
12. καὶ ἀπῆλθόν τινες τῶν σὺν ἡμῖν ἐπὶ τὸ μνημεῖον.
13. κύριε, εἰ σὺ εἶ, κέλευσόν με ἐλθεῖν πρός σε ἐπὶ τὰ ὕδατα.
14. καὶ εἰσῆλθεν κατὰ τὸ εἰωθὸς αὐτῷ[8] ἐν τῇ ἡμέρᾳ τῶν σαββάτων εἰς τὴν συναγωγήν.
15. ἐπιστάτα, δι᾽ ὅλης νυκτὸς κοπιάσαντες οὐδὲν ἐλάβομεν, ἐπὶ δὲ τῷ ῥήματί σου χαλάσω[9] τὰ δίκτυα.
16. ὁ δὲ εἶπεν πρὸς αὐτούς· ἀγωνίζεσθε[10] εἰσελθεῖν διὰ τῆς στενῆς θύρας.

1 ψευδομαρτυρίαν, "false witness"
2 ὡσεὶ περιστεράν, "like a dove"
3 ἐσίγησαν, "they became silent"
4 ἐσπλαγχνίσθη, "he was moved with compassion"
5 ὥρμησεν, "rushed"
6 ἡ ἀγέλη, "the herd"
7 τοῦ κρημνοῦ, "the cliff"
8 τὸ εἰωθὸς αὐτῷ, "his custom"
9 χαλάσω, "I will let down"
10 ἀγωνίζεσθε, "strive"

Composition Exercises

26.3 Translate the following sentences into Greek. The clauses marked * should be translated by a genitive absolute.

1. And after the disciples had entered into the boat* Jesus sent the multitudes away.
2. Then a certain man came to him and said, "What are you doing here?"
3. What power will we receive after the Holy Spirit comes upon us*?
4. The day is drawing near in which the Son of Man will come upon the clouds of heaven.
5. Take and judge these men according to your law.
6. Peter went to him, walking upon the water.
7. The disciples began to preach in the days of Caiaphas the high priest.
8. They went into the assembly on the Lord's day according to custom.
9. I was with you daily in Jerusalem.
10. The high priest therefore said to the disciples, "Who gave[1] you authority to do these things?"
11. The Pharisees will say many things against the Son of Man.
12. After the messengers of Herod had departed* the disciples told him privately all that they had done.
13. But though he sent his own son to them* they would not receive him.
14. You were astonished at his promises.
15. And after we had toiled all the night* Jesus came to us, walking on the sea.
16. And while he was holding my hand* I received power to walk.
17. Who is able to continue in these things?

1 "gave," ἔδωκεν

18. And while they were drawing near to the city* the whole multitude began to rejoice, saying, "Blessed[1] is he who comes in the name of the Lord."
19. In the days of Herod the king, Joseph went down[2] into Egypt, taking with him the child Jesus and Mary, his mother.

Scripture Translation Exercises

26.4 Translate the following verses from Scripture:

1. ἀναχωρησάντων δὲ αὐτῶν ἰδοὺ ἄγγελος κυρίου φαίνεται κατ᾽ ὄναρ[3] τῷ Ἰωσὴφ λέγων· ἐγερθεὶς παράλαβε τὸ παιδίον καὶ τὴν μητέρα αὐτοῦ καὶ φεῦγε εἰς Αἴγυπτον (Matt 2:13)
2. καὶ προσελθόντες οἱ μαθηταὶ εἶπαν αὐτῷ· διὰ τί ἐν παραβολαῖς λαλεῖς αὐτοῖς; (Matt 13:10)
3. καὶ μεθ᾽ ἡμέρας ἓξ[4] παραλαμβάνει ὁ Ἰησοῦς τὸν Πέτρον καὶ Ἰάκωβον καὶ Ἰωάννην τὸν ἀδελφὸν αὐτοῦ καὶ ἀναφέρει αὐτοὺς εἰς ὄρος ὑψηλὸν[5] κατ᾽ ἰδίαν (Matt 17:1)
4. καθ᾽ ἡμέραν ἤμην πρὸς ὑμᾶς ἐν τῷ ἱερῷ διδάσκων καὶ οὐκ ἐκρατήσατέ με (Mark 14:49)
5. ἀλλὰ λήμψεσθε δύναμιν ἐπελθόντος τοῦ ἁγίου πνεύματος ἐφ᾽ ὑμᾶς (Acts 1:8)

1 "blessed," εὐλογημένος
2 "went down," κατέβη
3 ὄναρ, "dream" (neuter accusative object of κατά)
4 ἕξ, "six"
5 ὑψηλὸν, "high"

LESSON 27

Aorist Middle and Degrees of Comparison for Adjectives and Adverbs

SIGMATIC AORIST MIDDLE FORMS

The sigmatic aorist (first aorist) middle voice uses the same sigmatic stem as the first aorist active voice. The only difference is that the past time (secondary tense) active endings are swapped out for past time (secondary tense) middle endings (the same ones used for the imperfect passive forms).

The middle and passive personal endings are as follows:

Secondary Middle Endings

	Singular	Plural
1st	-μην	-μεθα
2nd	-σο (intervocalic σ drops, and the vowels contract to ου in the imperfect)	-σθε
3rd	-το	-νται

These endings are added to verbs with sigmatic stems (first aorist forms) as follows:

Sigmatic Aorist of λύω ("I release")

	Indicative		Imperative	
1 sg.	ἐλυσάμην	I ransomed		
2 sg.	ἐλύσω[1]	you ransomed	λῦσαι	ransom
3 sg.	ἐλύσατο	he/she/it ransomed	λυσάσθω	let him/her/it ransom
1 pl.	ἐλυσάμεθα	we ransomed		
2 pl.	ἐλύσασθε	you all ransomed	λύσασθε	(a command for you all) ransom
3 pl.	ἐλύσαντο	they ransomed	λυσάσθωσαν	let them ransom
	Infinitive		**Participle**	
	λύσασθαι	to ransom	λυσάμενος, -η, -ον	having released (for one's own benefit), having ransomed

THEMATIC AORIST MIDDLE FORMS The stems and endings for middle forms of thematic aorist (second aorist) verb forms look the same as those of the imperfect passive, except that the verbal root is used instead of the present root spelling. The forms for other moods may look the same as the corresponding moods of the present passive—but again, the verbal root is used rather than the present root spelling (see Lesson 16). Thus, it is important to learn the principal parts for verbs when learning vocabulary in order to discern the verbal root (in the third principal part) from the present root spelling (in the first principal part).

1 Originally ἐλύσασο.

The thematic (second) aorist of γίνομαι "I become" is as follows:

	Thematic Aorist of γίνομαι ("I become")			
	Indicative		Imperative	
1 sg.	ἐγενόμην	I became		
2 sg.	ἐγένου	you became	γενοῦ	become or be
3 sg.	ἐγένετο	it happened	γενέσθω	let it happen or let it be
1 pl.	ἐγενόμεθα	we became		
2 pl.	ἐγένεσθε	you all became	γένεσθε	(you all) become or be
3 pl.	ἐγένοντο	they became	γενέσθωσαν	let those things happen, or let them be
	Infinitive		Participle	
	γενέσθαι	to be, to come to pass	γενόμενος, -η, -ον	being, coming to pass, happening

This word is especially common in the New Testament; it is an example of a verb that is deponent in the middle voice. The form that occurs most frequently is ἐγένετο, which has often been translated as "it came to pass."

Most of the middle forms in the New Testament are deponent and therefore are translated with an active verb in English. In some cases verbs in the middle voice denote that the subject is acting on itself, in some way that concerns itself, or is allowing something to be done to itself.[1]

1 The range of meaning for the middle voice is explained in more detail in Lesson 16.

DEGREES OF COMPARISON FOR ADJECTIVES

Adjectives come in three degrees or intensities; regular (called the positive degree), increased or greater (called the comparative degree), and maximum (called the superlative degree):

- The positive degree denotes a simple descriptive quality (e.g., "He is a tall man.")
- The comparative degree denotes a quality greater than normal or greater than what is being compared in the immediate context (e.g., "He is taller than his brother.")
- The superlative degree denotes a quality of very high or highest proportions or the greatest degree for what is being compared in the immediate context (e.g., "He is the tallest man in the town.")

The comparative and superlative degrees of comparison are expressed in Greek by adding -τερος and -τατος (respectively) to the stem of 2-1-2 pattern adjectives and to the stem of third declension adjectives ending in ες.

Note: When the regular positive adjective has a short penult, the ο preceding the comparative and superlative stems (-τερος and -τατος) is lengthened to ω. Forms in blue do not occur in the New Testament. Examples:

Regular Adjectives Degrees

Positive	Comparative	Superlative
δίκαιος "just"	δικαιότερος, -η, -ον	δικαιότατος, -η, -ον
ἰσχυρός "strong"	ἰσχυρότερος, -η, -ον	ἰσχυρότατος, -η, -ον
σοφός "wise"	σοφώτερος, -η, -ον	σοφώτατος, -η, -ον
ἀληθής "true"	ἀληθέστερος, -η, -ον	ἀληθέστατος, -η, -ον

The following adjectives form their degrees of comparison irregularly. Forms in blue do not occur in the New Testament.

Irregular Adjective Degrees

Positive	Comparative	Superlative
ἀγαθός, -ή, -όν ("good")	κρείσσων, κρεῖσσον[1] ("better")	κράτιστος, -η, -ον ("best")
κακός, -ή, -όν ("bad")	χείρων, χεῖρον or ἥσσων, ἧσσον ("worse")	χείριστος, -η, -ον ("worst")
καλός, -ή, -όν ("beautiful")	καλλίων, κάλλιον ("more beautiful")	κάλλιστος, -η, -ον ("most beautiful")
πολύς, πολλή, πολύ ("many")	πλείων, πλεῖον[2] ("more")	πλείστος, -η, -ον ("most")
μέγας, μεγάλη, μέγα ("great")	μείζων, μεῖζον ("greater")	μέγιστος, -η, -ον ("greatest")
ὀλίγος, -η, -ον ("few") or μικρός, -ά, -όν ("small")	ἐλάσσων, ἔλασσον[3] ("less")	ὀλίγιστος, -η, -ον ("fewest") ἐλάχιστος, -η, -ον ("least")

Comparative adjectives ending in -ων are declined as follows:

Comparative Adjectives with -ων

	Singular		Plural	
	Masc. & Fem.	Neut.	Masc. & Fem.	Neut.
Nom.	μείζων	μεῖζον	μείζονες	μείζονα
Acc.	μείζονα	μεῖζον	μείζονας	μείζονα
Gen.	μείζονος	μείζονος	μειζόνων	μειζόνων
Dat.	μείζονι	μείζονι	μείζοσι(ν)	μείζοσι(ν)

GENITIVE OF COMPARISON

An adjective or adverb in the comparative degree may be followed either by a noun or pronoun in the genitive case—or by ἤ ("than") followed by a noun or pronoun in the same case as the noun or pronoun with which the adjective agrees. For example, both sentences below may be translated, "He is wiser than his son":

σοφώτερός ἐστιν τοῦ υἱοῦ.

σοφώτερός ἐστιν ἢ ὁ υἱός.

1 Alternate spelling: κρείττων, κρεῖττον

2 Alternate spelling: πλέων, πλέον

3 Alternate spelling: ἐλάττων, ἔλαττον

THE DEGREES OF COMPARISON FOR ADVERBS

Positive degree adverbs are formed from adjectives by changing the ν of the genitive plural masculine to ς. (The forms in blue in the following tables are not found in the New Testament.) For example:

Adjective		Adverb	
φίλος	dear	φίλως	dearly
σοφός	wise	σοφῶς	wisely
ἀληθής	true	ἀληθῶς	truly

The comparative and superlative degrees of adverbs are the same as the neuter singular of the comparative of the adjective. The neuter plural superlative adjective is the same form as the superlative of the adverb. For example:

Regular Adverb Degrees

Positive	Comparative	Superlative
σοφῶς	σοφώτερον	σοφώτατα
ἀληθῶς	ἀληθέστερον	ἀληθέστατα

Also note the following adverb forms:

Irregular Adverb Degrees

Positive	Comparative	Superlative
εὖ ("well")	βέλτιον, κρεῖσσον ("better")	βέλτιστα ("best")
καλῶς ("well," "beautifully")	κάλλιον ("better," "more beautifully")	κάλλιστα ("best," "most beautifully")
κακῶς ("badly")	ἧσσον, ἧττον ("worse")	ἥκιστα ("worst")
μάλα ("very," "exceedingly")	μᾶλλον ("more")	μάλιστα ("most")
πολύ ("much")	πλεῖον, πλέον ("more")	πλεῖστα ("most")
ἐγγύς ("near")	ἐγγύτερον ("nearer")	ἔγγιστα ("nearest")
ταχύ ("quickly," "soon")	τάχιον ("quicker")	τάχιστα ("most quickly")

The comparative and superlative degrees of adjectives and adverbs are not common in the New Testament. The superlative degree is scarcely used at all. By the time of the New Testament, its place was taken by the comparative degree. For example:

μικρότερον ὂν πάντων τῶν σπερμάτων τῶν ἐπὶ τῆς γῆς
"being the least of all seeds that are on the earth" (Mark 4:31)

EXERCISES

Memorization Exercise

27.1 Learn Vocabulary List 21.

Translation Exercises

27.2(α) Translate the following sentences (part 1):

1. τῇ δὲ ἐπαύριον,[1] ὁδοιπορούντων ἐκείνων καὶ τῇ πόλει ἐγγιζόντων, ἀνέβη Πέτρος ἐπὶ τὸ δῶμα[2] προσεύξασθαι.
2. οὐχὶ ἡ ψυχὴ πλεῖόν ἐστι τῆς τροφῆς;
3. καὶ συνεβουλεύσαντο ἀποκτείνειν τὸν Παῦλον.
4. ὁ μείζων ἐν ὑμῖν γενέσθω ὡς ὁ νεώτερος.
5. κατελάβοντο ὅτι ἄνθρωποι ἀγράμματοι καὶ ἰδιῶται[3] εἰσίν.
6. νῦν γὰρ ἐγγύτερόν ἐστιν ἡ σωτηρία ἡμῶν ἢ ὅτε ἐπιστεύσαμεν.
7. ἀληθῶς οὗτος ὁ ἄνθρωπος υἱὸς θεοῦ ἦν.
8. καὶ ῥίψας τὰ ἀργύρια εἰς τὸν ναὸν ἀνεχώρησεν, καὶ ἀπελθὼν ἀπήγξατο.[4]
9. ὁ δὲ μικρότερος ἐν τῇ βασιλείᾳ τῶν οὐρανῶν μείζων αὐτοῦ ἐστίν.
10. νυνὶ δὲ μένει πίστις, ἐλπίς, ἀγάπη· τὰ τρία ταῦτα, μείζων δὲ τούτων ἡ ἀγάπη. (1 Cor 13:13)
11. ἔρχεται ὁ ἰσχυρότερός μου ὀπίσω μου.
12. μείζονα τούτων ὄψει.
13. καὶ νῦν τί μέλλεις; βάπτισαι, καὶ ἀπόλουσαι τὰς ἁμαρτίας σου, ἐπικαλεσάμενος τὸ ὄνομα τοῦ κυρίου.
14. πάντες οἱ πατέρες ἡμῶν εἰς τὸν Μωϋσῆν ἐβαπτίσθησαν ἐν τῇ νεφέλῃ καὶ ἐν τῇ θαλάσσῃ.

1 τῇ δὲ ἐπαύριον, "and on the next day"; ἐπαύριον is an adverb meaning "tomorrow"; τῇ agrees with ἡμέρᾳ, which is here understood implicitly.

2 τὸ δῶμα, "the housetop"

3 ἀγράμματοι καὶ ἰδιῶται, "unlettered and ignorant"

4 ἀπήγξατο, middle aorist from ἀπάγχω, "I hang"

27.2(β) Translate the following sentences (part 2):

1. οἱ δὲ μεῖζον ἔκραξαν λέγοντες· κύριε, ἐλέησον ἡμᾶς.
2. σὺ κύριε, ἀνάδειξον[1] τὸν ἄνθρωπον ὃν ἐξελέξω.
3. ἡ βασίλισσα νότου[2] ἦλθεν ἐκ τῶν περάτων[3] τῆς γῆς ἀκοῦσαι τὴν σοφίαν Σολομῶνος, καὶ ἰδοὺ πλεῖον Σολομῶνος ὧδε.
4. οὐδεὶς ἐπιβάλλει ἐπίβλημα[4] ῥάκους ἀγνάφου[5] ἐπὶ ἱματίῳ παλαιῷ. αἴρει γὰρ τὸ πλήρωμα αὐτοῦ[6] ἀπὸ τοῦ ἱματίου καὶ χεῖρον σχίσμα γίνεται.
5. ἀμὴν λέγω ὑμῖν ἐφ᾽ ὅσον[7] ἐποιήσατε ἑνὶ[8] τούτων τῶν ἀδελφῶν μου τῶν ἐλαχίστων, ἐμοὶ ἐποιήσατε.
6. καὶ γίνεται τὰ ἔσχατα τοῦ ἀνθρώπου ἐκείνου χείρονα τῶν πρώτων.
7. ἐγὼ γάρ εἰμι ὁ ἐλάχιστος τῶν ἀποστόλων.
8. εἰ οὖν οὐδὲ ἐλάχιστον δύνασθε, τί περὶ τῶν λοιπῶν μεριμνᾶτε;[9]
9. λέγω ὑμῖν μείζων ἐν γεννητοῖς[10] γυναικῶν Ἰωάννου οὐδείς ἐστιν· ὁ δὲ μικρότερος ἐν τῇ βασιλείᾳ τοῦ θεοῦ μείζων αὐτοῦ ἐστίν.
10. πειθαρχεῖν[11] δεῖ θεῷ μᾶλλον ἢ ἀνθρώποις.

1 ἀνάδειξον, "show"
2 ἡ βασίλισσα νότου, "the queen of the south"
3 ἐκ τῶν περάτων, "from the furthest parts"
4 ἐπίβλημα, "a patch," "a thing thrown over," "a covering"
5 ῥάκους ἀγνάφου, "of undressed cloth"
6 τὸ πλήρωμα αὐτοῦ, "that which fills it up"
7 ἐφ᾽ ὅσον, "inasmuch as"
8 dative of εἷς, "one"
9 μεριμνάω, "to worry" (alpha contract verbs are covered in the next lesson)
10 γεννητοῖς, "the offspring"
11 πειθαρχεῖν, "to obey," followed by a dative

Composition Exercises

27.3 Translate the following sentences into Greek:

1. And after Solomon had prayed, he departed out of the temple.
2. The younger of the sons did not want to work for[1] his father.
3. The robbers hanged themselves, for those who pursued them were more than they.
4. We called upon the name of the Lord, for he is stronger than all the kings of the earth.
5. He chose Simon, whom he named Peter.
6. Behold, love is greater than faith.
7. Why then do you all delay to go to Jerusalem, for behold, a one greater than Solomon is there?
8. It is necessary to obey the king rather than the priest.
9. They say that these days are worse than the days of our fathers.
10. You all took counsel together to slay the wisest of men.
11. He that is least will become the greatest.
12. But he cried out the more, "Behold, what things I suffer at the hands of my enemies."
13. Truly I comprehend that there is a division among them.
14. We cannot do the least of these things.
15. Inasmuch as[2] you have done this, you have done worse than all your brethren.
16. But he answered them more wisely than his father.

1 Use ὑπέρ followed by a genitive.

2 "inasmuch as," ἐφ' ὅσον

Scripture Translation Exercises

27.4 Translate the following verses from Scripture:

1. οὐκ ἔστιν μαθητὴς ὑπὲρ τὸν διδάσκαλον οὐδὲ δοῦλος ὑπὲρ τὸν κύριον αὐτοῦ (Matt 10:24)
2. τότε πορεύεται καὶ παραλαμβάνει μεθ᾽ ἑαυτοῦ ἑπτὰ ἕτερα[1] πνεύματα πονηρότερα ἑαυτοῦ καὶ εἰσελθόντα κατοικεῖ ἐκεῖ (Matt 12:45)
3. μέλλει γὰρ ὁ υἱὸς τοῦ ἀνθρώπου ἔρχεσθαι ἐν τῇ δόξῃ τοῦ πατρὸς αὐτοῦ μετὰ τῶν ἀγγέλων αὐτοῦ (Matt 16:27)
4. ὅτι τὸ μωρὸν[2] τοῦ θεοῦ σοφώτερον τῶν ἀνθρώπων ἐστὶν καὶ τὸ ἀσθενὲς τοῦ θεοῦ ἰσχυρότερον τῶν ἀνθρώπων (1 Cor 1:25)
5. ἡ γὰρ ψυχὴ πλεῖόν ἐστιν τῆς τροφῆς καὶ τὸ σῶμα τοῦ ἐνδύματος (Luke 12:23)

1 ἑπτὰ ἕτερα, "seven other"

2 μωρὸν, "foolishness"

LESSON 28

α-Contract and o-Contract Verbs

There are three vowel types, A-type, E-type, and O-type (introduced in Lesson 4). Up to this point only one contract verb type (ε-contract) has been presented. The other vowel types are represented by the less common α-contract and o-contract verbs. These are verbs with α or ο as their final root letter. These vowels will contract with stem vowels.

The rules for the contraction of the vowels in these verbs can be summarized as follows.[1]

α-CONTRACT RULES

α-contract rules:

- When α precedes an o-type vowel (ο or ω) they will contract to ω.
- When α precedes an ε-type vowel (ε or η) they will contract to α.
- When α precedes an α digraph with ι they will contract to ᾳ (ι is subscript).[2]

O-CONTRACT RULES

o-contract rules:

- When ο precedes a long vowel[3] they will contract to ω.
- When ο precedes a short vowel they will contract to ου.
- When ο precedes any digraph with ι[4] they will contract to οι.

1 For more on accenting ε-contract verbs, see Lesson 25.

2 The present active infinitive where the iota is absent is an exception. This is a result of the original iota belonging to a class called "spurious iota," a topic for advanced linguistic study (c.f. Andrew Sihler, *New Comparative Grammar of Greek and Latin* [Oxford: Oxford University Press, 2008] 72.c.4).

3 See Lesson 4 for more information on which vowels are long.

4 Whether subscript or not.

α-Contract Verb: τιμάω ("I honor")

Active Voice Synopsis

	Present Indicative	Present Imperative	Imperfect Indicative
1 sg.	τιμῶ [τιμάω]		ἐτίμων [ἐτίμαον]
2 sg.	τιμᾷς [τιμάεις]	τίμα [τίμαε]	ἐτίμας [ἐτίμαες]
3 sg.	τιμᾷ [τιμάει]	τιμάτω [τιμαέτω]	ἐτίμα [ἐτίμαε]
1 pl.	τιμῶμεν [τιμάομεν]		ἐτιμῶμεν [ἐτιμάομεν]
2 pl.	τιμᾶτε [τιμάετε]	τιμᾶτε [τιμάετε]	ἐτιμᾶτε [ἐτιμάετε]
3 pl.	τιμῶσι [τιμάουσι]	τιμάτωσαν [τιμαέτωσαν]	ἐτίμων [ἐτίμαον]
	Present Infinitive	**Present Participle**	
	τιμᾶν	Nom. τιμῶν, -ῶσα, -ῶν Acc. τιμῶντα, -ῶσαν, -ῶν	

Middle and Passive Voice Synopsis

	Present Indicative	Present Imperative	Imperfect Indicative
1 sg.	τιμῶμαι		ἐτιμώμην
2 sg.	τιμᾷ	τιμῶ	ἐτιμῶ
3 sg.	τιμᾶται	τιμάσθω	ἐτιμᾶτο
1 pl.	τιμώμεθα		ἐτιμώμεθα
2 pl.	τιμᾶσθε	τιμᾶσθε	ἐτιμᾶσθε
3 pl.	τιμῶνται	τιμάσθωσαν	ἐτιμῶντο
	Present Infinitive	**Present Participle**	
	τιμᾶσθαι	τιμώμενος, -η, -ον	

o-Contract Verb: πληρόω ("I fulfill")

Active Voice Synopsis

	Present Indicative	Present Imperative	Imperfect Indicative
1 sg.	πληρῶ [πληρόω]		ἐπλήρουν [ἐπλήροον]
2 sg.	πληροῖς [πληρόεις]	πλήρου [πλήροε]	ἐπλήρους [ἐπλήροες]
3 sg.	πληροῖ [πληρόει]	πληρούτω [πληροέτω]	ἐπλήρου [ἐπλήροε]
1 pl.	πληροῦμεν [πληρόομεν]		ἐπληροῦμεν [ἐπληρόομεν]
2 pl.	πληροῦτε [πληρόετε]	πληροῦτε [πληρόετε]	ἐπληροῦτε [ἐπληρόετε]
3 pl.	πληροῦσι(ν) [πληρόουσι(ν)]	πληρούτωσαν [πληροέτωσαν]	ἐπλήρουν [ἐπλήροον]
	Present Infinitive	**Present Participle**	
	πληροῦν	Nom. πληρῶν, -οῦσα, -οῦν Acc. πληροῦντα, -οῦσαν, -οῦν	

Middle and Passive Voice Synopsis

	Present Indicative	Present Imperative	Imperfect Indicative
1 sg.	πληροῦμαι		ἐπληρούμην
2 sg.	πληροῖ	πληροῦ	ἐπληροῦ
3 sg.	πληροῦται	πληρούσθω	ἐπληροῦτο
1 pl.	πληρούμεθα		ἐπληρούμεθα
2 pl.	πληροῦσθε	πληροῦσθε	ἐπληροῦσθε
3 pl.	πληροῦνται	πληρούσθωσαν	ἐπληροῦντο
	Present Infinitive	**Present Participle**	
	πληροῦσθαι	πληρούμενος, -η, -ον	

The verb ζάω[1] is different from other α-contract verbs, because it has a monosyllabic root (i.e., η for α in the contracted forms).

	Monosyllabic α-contract: ζάω ("I live")
	Present Active Indicative
1 sg.	ζῶ
2 sg.	ζῇς
3 sg.	ζῇ
1 pl.	ζῶμεν
2 pl.	ζῆτε
3 pl.	ζῶσι(ν)
	Present Active Infinitive
	ζῆν

Only tenses that use the present root spelling (the first principal part) have vocalic contraction. This principal part is the only one in which the aspectual stem begins with a vowel (the thematic variable vowel). The other principal parts have stems that begin with a consonant—contract verbs only use sigmatic aorist stems. Thus, the future and aorist of verbs in -αω and -οω are formed by lengthening the contract vowel of the verbal root before adding the stems. Consider these indicative examples of τιμάω and φανερόω in various tenses.

Contracting Tenses (using the first principal part)		**Other Tenses Do Not Contract** (using other principal parts)	
Present	Imperfect	Future	Aorist
Active		Active	
τιμῶ	ἐτίμων	τιμήσω	ἐτίμησα
πληρῶ	ἐπλήρουν	πληρώσω	ἐπλήρωσα
Middle & Passive		Middle	
τιμῶμαι	ἐτιμώμην	τιμήσομαι	ἐτιμησάμην
πληροῦμαι	ἐπληρούμην	πληρώσομαι	ἐπληρωσάμην
		Passive	
		τιμηθήσομαι	ἐτιμήθην
		πληρωθήσομαι	ἐπληρώθην

1 χράομαι is another monosyllabic root α-contract example.

EXERCISES

Memorization Exercise

28.1 Learn Vocabulary List 22.

Translation Exercises

28.2 Translate the following sentences:

1. ἐπυνθάνετο παρ᾽ αὐτῶν ποῦ ὁ Χριστὸς γεννᾶται.
2. θεὸς οὐκ ἔστι νεκρῶν ἀλλὰ ζώντων, πάντες γὰρ αὐτῷ ζῶσιν.
3. οὗτος ὁ λόγος οὐ φανεροῦται ἡμῖν.
4. ἔλεγον τὴν ἔξοδον αὐτοῦ ἣν ἤμελλεν[1] πληροῦν ἐν Ἰερουσαλήμ.
5. Σίμων Ἰωάννου, ἀγαπᾷς με πλέον τούτων;
6. φωνὴ βοῶντος ἐν τῇ ἐρήμῳ.
7. ἐν τῇ αὐτῇ ὥρᾳ ἠγαλλιῶντο οἱ μαθηταί.
8. ὁ γὰρ θεὸς ταπεινοῖ τοὺς ὑψοῦντας ἑαυτούς, τοὺς δὲ ταπεινοῦντας ἑαυτοὺς ὑψοῖ.
9. τότε ἐσταύρουν σὺν αὐτῷ δύο λῃστάς.
10. τί με ἐρωτᾷς περὶ τοῦ ἀγαθοῦ;
11. λέγει αὐτῷ ὁ Ἰησοῦς· πορεύου, ὁ υἱός σου ζῇ.
12. ὁ δὲ θεὸς εἴασε πάντα τὰ ἔθνη περιπατεῖν ἐν ταῖς ὁδοῖς αὐτῶν.
13. Αἰνέα,[2] ἰᾶταί σε Ἰησοῦς Χριστός.
14. οὐκ εἴα Ἰησοῦς τὰ δαιμόνια λαλεῖν.

Composition Exercises

28.3 Translate the following sentences into Greek:

1. The disciples were making manifest the things that they had heard.
2. We did not permit them to crucify the slave.
3. The king humbled those who were exalted.
4. They are inquiring whether the servant is healed.
5. Why do you all allow them to live in our city?

1 ἤμελλεν, a past tense with a double augment from μέλλω

2 Αἰνέα, "Aeneas"

6. Do you all desire to love the Lord your God, O you sons of men?
7. The voice said, "Shout," and he answered, "What will I shout?"
8. Now is fulfilled the word of the prophet.
9. When Jesus was born in Bethlehem wise men came to worship him, asking where the king of the Jews must be born.
10. God justifies the sons of men by faith and not by works.
11. And all men rejoiced greatly that the man who had the devil was healed.
12. Rejoice greatly, for your son lives.
13. Humble yourselves therefore under[1] the mighty[2] hand of God, for he will exalt you in due season.
14. I manifested your name to this people, and I will manifest it to their children.

Scripture Translation Exercises

28.4 Translate the following verses from Scripture:

1. οἱ δὲ ἐν τῷ πλοίῳ προσεκύνησαν αὐτῷ λέγοντες· ἀληθῶς θεοῦ υἱὸς εἶ. (Matt 14:33)
2. πῶς οὖν πληρωθῶσιν αἱ γραφαὶ ὅτι οὕτως δεῖ γενέσθαι; (Matt 26:54)
3. ἦσαν Μωϋσῆς καὶ Ἠλίας, οἳ ὀφθέντες ἐν δόξῃ ἔλεγον τὴν ἔξοδον αὐτοῦ, ἣν ἤμελλεν πληροῦν ἐν Ἰερουσαλήμ. (Luke 9:30–31)
4. τί ζητεῖτε τὸν ζῶντα μετὰ τῶν νεκρῶν; (Luke 24:5)
5. ἀμὴν ἀμὴν λέγω ὑμῖν ὅτι ἔρχεται ὥρα καὶ νῦν ἐστιν ὅτε οἱ νεκροὶ ἀκούσουσιν τῆς φωνῆς τοῦ υἱοῦ τοῦ θεοῦ καὶ οἱ ἀκούσαντες ζήσουσιν. (John 5:25)

1 Use ὑπό followed by an accusative.

2 "mighty," κραταιός, -ά, -όν

LESSON 29

Perfect and Pluperfect Tenses

PERFECT TENSE MEANING

The perfect tense in Greek is different from the perfect tense in Latin or English. In Latin the most common meaning of the perfect is to convey the simple past (for which Greek uses the aorist). In English the perfect tense focuses on the idea that the action has been completed, sometimes recently. We use this tense to express experiences or accomplishments (e.g., "I have climbed the mountain"). It isn't used primarily to express exact past timing, or with time references such as "yesterday." The Greek perfect is slightly different: it focuses on the resultant state of a past action. The perfect has therefore as much to do with present as with past time, since it describes the present result of a past action. The pluperfect or past perfect is the past tense of the perfect.

There is no exact equivalent to the Greek perfect in English; the English perfect formed by the auxiliary verb "have" is the nearest equivalent, but it will not always translate the resultant state of the Greek perfect. Sometimes the Greek perfect will be translated as present. For example, the perfect passive of "write" may be translated as "it has been written" or "it is written (now stands as law)." A better translation of "has fallen" may be "he is dead."

PERFECT TENSE MORPHOLOGY

The perfect is formed from the verbal root. Sometimes there is a modification such as ablaut.[1] A tense stem is added to both sides of the root. The word's first consonant is duplicated, followed by ε (called reduplication). If the first consonant is part of two blended consonants (e.g.,

1 For more on ablaut, see Lesson 22.

γράφω), only the first consonant is reduplicated (γέγραφα). There are some sounds that Greek prefers not to use in rapid succession so they will not be reduplicated. For example, unvoiced fricatives (φ, χ, ϑ) will be reduplicated with their corresponding unvoiced stop (π, κ, τ). If a root begins with a compound sibilant (ξ, ζ, ψ, στ) an initial ε with a smooth breathing mark is used.[1] This serves a different purpose from an augment (marking aspect rather than time).[2] If the verb begins with a vowel, it is lengthened. This lengthening also should not be confused with an augment (which will be added to the pluperfect, although this is often omitted in the New Testament). Examples:

Present	Perfect	Notes
ἁμαρτάνω	ἡμάρτηκα	Initial vowel lengthened in place of reduplication
στέλλω	ἔσταλκα	Compound sibilant is not reduplicated; the ε serves this purpose (it isn't an augment)
πληρόω	πεπλήρωκα	Only the first letter of a double consonant beginning with a stop is reduplicated
ψάλλω	ἔψαλκα	Compound sibilant consonant is not reduplicated; the ε serves this purpose (it isn't an augment)
φιλέω	πεφίληκα	The stop version of φ is reduplicated
ϑεάομαι	τεϑέαμαι	The stop version of ϑ is reduplicated

Following the verbal root, a consonant stem (κα) and then primary personal endings are added. In lexicons, the fourth principal part provides the root and stem spelling for the perfect active tense. Any verbal root ending with a stop consonant will undergo spelling changes consistent with square of stop principles, which don't allow adjacent stops to have different articulations. A stop followed by κ will meld with κ resulting in a voiceless fricative. However, dentals will drop prior to κ:

β, π, φ + κ = φ   γ, κ, χ + κ = χ

δ, τ, ϑ + κ = κ (dentals drop)   σσ + κ = χ

1 James Swetnam, *An Introduction to the Study of New Testament Greek*, 2nd. rev. ed. (Rome: Pontifical Biblical Institute, 1998), 140.

2 The root στα gets reduplicated with a rough breathing mark over ι or ε. This is explained in Lesson 35.

Contract vowels lengthen prior to the κ as with other consonant stems. Liquid letters either stand beside the κ or cause the κ to drop.

The conjugation for active forms of the perfect and pluperfect of λύω is as follows:

Perfect and Pluperfect Active Synopsis

	Perfect Indicative	Pluperfect Indicative
1 sg.	λέλυκα	ἐλελύκειν
2 sg.	λέλυκας	ἐλελύκεις
3 sg.	λέλυκε(ν)[1]	ἐλελύκει
1 pl.	λελύκαμεν	ἐλελύκειμεν
2 pl.	λελύκατε	ἐλελύκειτε
3 pl.	λελύκασι[2]	ἐλελύκεισαν
	Perfect Infinitive	**Perfect Participle**
	λελυκέναι	λελυκώς, λελυκυῖα, λελυκός

Perfect Active Participle Forms

	Singular			Plural		
	Masc.	Fem.	Neut.	Masc.	Fem.	Neut.
Nom.	λελυκώς	λελυκυῖα	λελυκός	λελυκότες	λελυκυῖαι	λελυκότα
Acc.	λελυκότα	λελυκυῖαν	λελυκός	λελυκότας	λελυκυίας	λελυκότα
Gen.	λελυκότος	λελυκυίας	λελυκότος	λελυκότων	λελυκυιῶν	λελυκότων
Dat.	λελυκότι	λελυκυίᾳ	λελυκότι	λελυκόσι	λελυκυίαις	λελυκόσι

1 Like in sigmatic aorist forms the third person singular uses ε instead of α, which helped reduce confusion with this form and the aorist (secondary) third person plural ending.

2 This is a primary ending, which matches stative aspect of the perfect. However, the secondary stem and ending -καν sometimes is used.

THE SECOND OR STRONG PERFECT

Some perfects are formed by adding the stem and endings directly to the root without κ. These are called strong perfects or second perfects. This way of marking the perfect tense occurs on a relatively small number of verbs, but they are very common ones. Irregular modifications to the root often occur, as well. Examples:

Present	Strong Perfect
ἀκούω	ἀκήκοα
γίνομαι	γέγονα
γράφω	γέγραφα
ἔρχομαι	ἐλήλυθα[1]
κράζω	κέκραγα
κρύπτω	κέκρυφα[2]
λείπω	λέλοιπα
πάσχω	πέπονθα
πείθω	πέποιθα

The verb λαμβάνω and the root ἐρ (used as an unrelated root for some tenses of λέγω) begin their perfect tenses with εἰ instead of a reduplication.

Present	Perfect Active	Perfect Passive
λαμβάνω	εἴληφα	εἴλημμαι
λέγω	εἴρηκα	εἴρημαι

MIDDLE AND PASSIVE VOICE

Like the present and imperfect tenses, middle and passive voices for the perfect share the same forms. They are all based off of the fifth principal part stem. This stem is composed of reduplication + root + no theme vowel + endings. Thus there will be many different types of consonant contractions produced by a root terminating in a consonant and any of the personal endings beginning with one. For this

1 From unrelated root ἐλυθ-

2 This follows standard contraction principles. The dental drops prior to κ, and then the labial and κ combine to form φ.

reason, Greek often standardizes the perfect middle and passive using the passive participle and then adding a verb of being to add grammatical information such as person, number, and mood. This is especially true with the third person plural form—λελυμένοι εἰσίν would be expected over λέλυνται. Note that the perfect passive participle expects to be accented on the penult.

Perfect and Pluperfect Middle/Passive Synopsis

	Perfect Indicative	Pluperfect Indicative
1 sg.	λέλυμαι	ἐλελύμην
2 sg.	λέλυσαι	ἐλέλυσο
3 sg.	λέλυται	ἐλέλυτο
1 pl.	λελύμεθα	ἐλελύμεθα
2 pl.	λέλυσθε	ἐλέλυσθε
3 pl.	λέλυνται	ἐλέλυντο
	Perfect Infinitive	**Perfect Participle**
	λελύσθαι	λελυμένος, -η, -ον

The perfect imperative is used very seldom[1] in the New Testament. Thus the imperative mood column is left out of the perfect verb synopsis charts.

PERFECT EXAMPLES

Examples of the perfect in the New Testament:

Perfect Indicative

1. πεπληρώκατε τὴν Ἰερουσαλὴμ τῆς διδαχῆς ὑμῶν.
   "You all have filled Jerusalem with your teaching." (Acts 5:28)

2. τὸν καλὸν ἀγῶνα ἠγώνισμαι, τὸν δρόμον τετέλεκα,
   τὴν πίστιν τετήρηκα.
   "I have fought the good fight, I have finished my course,
   I have kept the faith." (2 Tim 4:7)

1 Four occurrences with three verbs (Mark 4:39; Acts 15:29; Eph 5:5; Jas 1:19).

Pluperfect Indicative

3. τεθεμελίωτο γὰρ ἐπὶ τὴν πέτραν.
   "For it had been founded on the rock." (Matt 7:25)

Perfect Participle

4. πεπληρωμένοι πάσης τῆς γνώσεως
   "Having been filled with all knowledge" (Rom 15:14)

5. πᾶσι τοῖς ἠγαπηκόσι τὴν ἐπιφάνειαν αὐτοῦ
   "To all who love his appearing" (2 Tim 4:8)

Note that in these examples, the focus is on the resultant state from the completion of the action described, not merely that the action has terminated.

See sentence 9 in this lesson's translation exercise for a good example of the meaning of the perfect participle. Then contrast this with the meaning of the present participle of the same verb in sentence 10. Another good example is found in sentence 14, where ἐσταυρωμένον denotes a permanent quality ("one who has been crucified"). As we've already observed, it is impossible to render this meaning exactly with a simple English perfect. If the aorist participle σταυρωθείς had been used in this sentence, it would simply have denoted the historical fact that Christ was crucified.

You have now learned all tenses of the Greek verb. Greek represents these tenses with six different stems. These stems provide the basis for all the principal parts of a verb. Lexicons and dictionaries use the first person singular of the indicative mood of each of these tenses to reference these stems. You will now begin to learn all the principal parts for the verbs listed at the beginning of each exercise section.

EXERCISES

Memorization Exercises

29.1(α) Learn Vocabulary List 23.

29.1(β) Learn all of the principal parts of the following verbs. Principal parts in parentheses are alternate (or older) forms for a principal part. Principal parts in blue do not occur in the New Testament. Dashes indicate that the principal parts are not used in the New Testament or ancient Greek.

1. βάλλω, βαλῶ, ἔβαλον, βέβληκα, βέβλημαι, ἐβλήθην
2. γίνομαι (γίγνομαι), γενήσομαι, ἐγενόμην, γέγονα, γεγένημαι, ἐγενήθην
3. ἔρχομαι, ἐλεύσομαι, ἦλθον (ἦλθα), ἐλήλυθα, —, —
4. λαμβάνω, λήψομαι, ἔλαβον, εἴληφα,[1] εἴλημμαι, ἐλήφθην
5. λέγω, ἐρῶ, εἶπον, εἴρηκα, εἴρημαι, ἐρρέθην
6. ὁράω, ὄψομαι, εἶδον, ἑώρακα, ὦμμαι, ὤφθην

Translation Exercises

29.2 Translate the following sentences:

1. Ἕλληνας εἰσήγαγεν εἰς τὸ ἱερόν, καὶ κεκοίνωκεν τὸν ἅγιον τόπον.
2. πτωχὸς δέ τις ὀνόματι Λάζαρος ἐβέβλητο πρὸς τὸν πυλῶνα[2] αὐτοῦ.
3. παιδία, ἐσχάτη ὥρα ἐστίν, καὶ καθὼς ἠκούσατε ὅτι ἀντίχριστος[3] ἔρχεται καὶ νῦν ἀντίχριστοι πολλοὶ γεγόνασιν.
4. λέγει αὐτῷ ὁ Ἰησοῦς· ὅτι ἑώρακάς με πεπίστευκας; μακάριοι οἱ μὴ ἰδόντες καὶ πιστεύσαντες.
5. ὅτε δὲ γέγονα ἀνήρ, κατήργηκα[4] τὰ τοῦ νηπίου.[5]
6. καὶ ἀπελθοῦσα εἰς τὸν οἶκον αὐτῆς εὗρεν τὸ παιδίον βεβλημένον ἐπὶ τὴν κλίνην καὶ τὸ δαιμόνιον ἐξεληλυθός.

1 The λαβ root takes a double augment instead of reduplication in the perfect.
2 πυλῶνα, "door"
3 ἀντίχριστος, "antichrist"
4 κατήργηκα; perfect from καταργέω, "I bring to nothing," "I put away"
5 τὰ τοῦ νηπίου, "childish things"

7. πεπλήρωται ὁ καιρὸς καὶ ἤγγικεν ἡ βασιλεία τοῦ θεοῦ.
8. ἔρχεται πρὸς αὐτὸν Μαρία ἡ καλουμένη Μαγδαληνή, ἀφ᾽ ἧς δαιμόνια ἑπτὰ ἐξεληλύθει.
9. καὶ πολλὰ σώματα τῶν κεκοιμημένων ἁγίων ἠγέρθησαν.
10. οἱ μαθηταὶ αὐτοῦ νυκτὸς ἐλθόντες ἔκλεψαν αὐτόν, ἡμῶν κοιμωμένων.
11. Ἰουδαίους οὐδὲν ἠδίκηκα ὡς καὶ σὺ κάλλιον ἐπιγιγνώσκεις.
12. πειρασμὸς ὑμᾶς οὐκ εἴληφεν εἰ μὴ ἀνθρώπινος.[1]
13. ὁ γὰρ θεὸς εἴρηκε τοῦτο διὰ στόματος πάντων τῶν προφήτων.
14. ἡμεῖς δὲ κηρύσσομεν Χριστὸν ἐσταυρωμένον.

Composition Exercises

29.3 Translate the following sentences into Greek:

1. The days of the kingdom of heaven have been fulfilled.
2. He has not injured you all or your friends.
3. We have seen and testified that this is the prophet spoken of by Moses.
4. Then the young men were astonished, for great fear had taken hold upon them.
5. The Lord has spoken evil concerning you.
6. They have defiled the house of the Lord with dead bodies.
7. You must proclaim the things that you have seen and heard.
8. The governor asks what the slaves have done.
9. You all have suffered many things at the hands[2] of the Jews.

1 ἀνθρώπινος, "proper to a man," "such as a man can bear"

2 "at the hands," use διά + genitive

10. Then Pilate answered, saying, "What I have written, I have written."
11. But when I became king I walked in the ways of my fathers.
12. The poor and the blind are cast[1] at the doors of the rich.[2]
13. O Lord, in you have we trusted.
14. They found that the demons had gone out.
15. I have told you all the words of the kingdom, but you all did not believe me.
16. Those who have kept the faith will receive the crown[3] of life that the Lord promised to those who love him.
17. They beheld the temple filled with the glory of the Lord.

Scripture Translation Exercise

29.4 Translate the following passage from Scripture:

Ὃ ἦν ἀπ' ἀρχῆς, ὃ ἀκηκόαμεν, ὃ ἑωράκαμεν τοῖς ὀφθαλμοῖς ἡμῶν, ὃ ἐθεασάμεθα καὶ αἱ χεῖρες ἡμῶν ἐψηλάφησαν περὶ τοῦ λόγου τῆς ζωῆς—καὶ ἡ ζωὴ ἐφανερώθη, καὶ ἑωράκαμεν καὶ μαρτυροῦμεν καὶ ἀπαγγέλλομεν ὑμῖν τὴν ζωὴν τὴν αἰώνιον ἥτις ἦν πρὸς τὸν πατέρα καὶ ἐφανερώθη ἡμῖν—ὃ ἑωράκαμεν καὶ ἀκηκόαμεν, ἀπαγγέλλομεν καὶ ὑμῖν (1 John 1:1–3a)

1 "are cast"; use the perfect passive
2 "rich," πλούσιος, -α, -ον
3 "crown," στέφανος, -ου, ὁ

LESSON 30

Subjunctive Mood

INTRODUCTION TO THE SUBJUNCTIVE MOOD

Excluding participles and infinitives (which technically are not moods), there are three verb moods you need to learn to understand biblical Greek: the indicative, the imperative, and the subjunctive.[1] In distinguishing the subjunctive and the indicative, some grammars refer to the indicative as the mood for what is "real or factual" and the subjunctive as the mood for what is "unreal or hypothetical or less probable."[2] There are too many exceptions to such a description for it to be helpful. For example, ideas (not necessarily reality) can be expressed in the indicative. Even conditions that we know not to be true (contrary to fact conditions) can be phrased in the indicative. For example, both verbs in this sentence are indicative:

> εἰ δὲ ἀνάστασις νεκρῶν οὐκ ἔστιν, οὐδὲ Χριστὸς ἐγήγερται.
> "But if there is no resurrection of the dead, then Christ has not been raised" (1 Cor 15:13)

Mood in biblical Greek does not convey how real/unreal, probable/improbable, or possible/impossible a statement is. The subjunctive mood often is used when referring to future events, but that shouldn't place it in a category of something less real than the future indicative. The subjunctive in a statement about Christ's return, for example, doesn't imply that it is doubtful or somewhat less likely to occur. In the following two verses, Jesus explicitly says that he is providing

1 There is an additional mood called the optative, which had nearly ceased being used by the time of New Testament. It is covered in Lesson 37.

2 Perhaps some of this comes from the Latin name of the irrealis mood (which operates differently from Greek) or the term "subjunctive," which sounds very similar to "subjective."

facts and assurances. The subjunctives are translated with indicatives in English (underlined); all are very real, without a hint of doubt.

> And if I go and prepare a place for you, I will come again and will take you to myself, that where I am you may be also. (John 14:3 ESV)
>
> For when they rise from the dead (Mark 12:25 ESV)

The general principle behind the Greek subjunctive is that there is some part of the action that is unknown (not doubted or false) or contingent. Nearly all of its uses are in adverbial subordinate clauses—so the unknowns in the previous examples have to do with the exact timing or location. The important thing is that we will be with Christ. The heavenly street address is of little consequence, but undisclosed or contingent information warrants the use of the subjunctive. Sometimes subjunctives are used for truths that apply in all situations, since they aren't limited to a specific time. Thus, lack of specificity doesn't imply mystery or ignorance of general facts. Another example:

> If we confess our sins, he is faithful and just to forgive us our sins and to cleanse us from all unrighteousness. (1 John 1:9)

The first subjunctive verb translated in this sentence (with an English indicative, "confess") is an example of a general truth. The other two subjunctives ("forgive" and "cleanse") underlined in this translation are subjunctives used in purpose or result clauses, showing contingency on the main verb. The subordinated subjunctive (with ἵνα) is another of the many ways to construct a purpose clause. The same idea can be expressed with a future participle, an infinitive, or even ὥστε + the indicative,[1] but since this verse has a general context referring to any time, the subjunctive is the natural choice.[2]

1 See Lesson 32.

2 This is not a complete list for possible ways to construct a purpose or result clause.

SUBJUNCTIVE MORPHOLOGY

Thankfully, the forms of the subjunctive mood require no additional memory work. The mood primarily uses present and aorist stems (first, third, and sixth principal parts). In rare situations when a perfect subjunctive is used, it typically follows the perfect participle with a subjunctive form of εἰμί.

The timing of subjunctives is contextually determined. For example, the action referenced in a purpose clause typically follows the action of the governing verb. This will be true regardless of whether the subjunctive uses a present or an aorist stem. Like the imperative mood, the stem choice has nothing to do with time, only aspect. Since the various clauses that use subjunctives imply some completeness (i.e., a complete thought of a futuristic idea of purpose or result), the aorist stem is the default stem for subjunctives. Only in cases where there is an overriding idea of incompleteness—such as the meaning of a particular verb or a special intention of the author—will a subjunctive use a present stem. Regardless of stem, subjunctives always use primary (non-past) endings. Thus there is no augment for aorist subjunctives, and they are never translated with an English past tense. The endings for all subjunctives are the same as those of the present active indicative, with the exception that the vowels are lengthened and ι is subscript.

Examples of the subjunctive in all tenses and voices:

	Present Active Subjunctive	**First Aorist Active Subjunctive**	**Second Aorist Active Subjunctive**
1 sg.	λύω	λύσω	βάλω
2 sg.	λύῃς	λύσῃς	βάλῃς
3 sg.	λύῃ	λύσῃ	βάλῃ
1 pl.	λύωμεν	λύσωμεν	βάλωμεν
2 pl.	λύητε	λύσητε	βάλητε
3 pl.	λύωσι(ν)	λύσωσι(ν)	βάλωσι(ν)

	Present Middle or Passive Subjunctive	**First Aorist Middle Subjunctive**	**Second Aorist Middle Subjunctive**
1 sg.	λύωμαι	λύσωμαι	βάλωμαι
2 sg.	λύῃ	λύσῃ	βάλῃ
3 sg.	λύηται	λύσηται	βάληται
1 pl.	λυώμεθα	λυσώμεθα	βαλώμεθα
2 pl.	λύησθε	λύσησθε	βάλησθε
3 pl.	λύωνται	λύσωνται	βάλωνται

Even the aorist passive uses the same lengthened primary endings, except that there is a circumflex on the stem vowel.

	Aorist Passive Subjunctive
1 sg.	λυθῶ
2 sg.	λυθῇς
3 sg.	λυθῇ
1 pl.	λυθῶμεν
2 pl.	λυθῆτε
3 pl.	λυθῶσι(ν)

COMMON USES OF THE SUBJUNCTIVE

Purpose Clauses[1]

The Greek subjunctive is frequently employed and can be used for a number of grammatical purposes. In all of these applications, if the subjunctive is negated, it will be negated with μή. The subjunctive is used frequently to express the intention of the governing verb. Such clauses are introduced by ἵνα or ὅπως ("in order that" or "that") if affirmative, and by μή or ἵνα μή ("in order that not" or "lest") if negative. Purpose clause examples:

1. ἦλθεν ἵνα μαρτυρήσῃ περὶ τοῦ φωτός.
   "He came that he might bear witness to the light."
2. ἀπέρχονται ἵνα μὴ (or simply μὴ) ἴδωσι τὴν μαχήν.
   "They are going away that they may not see the battle (or, lest they should see the battle)."
3. μεγάλῃ τῇ φωνῇ ἔκραζε ἵνα πάντες ἀκούωσι.
   "He was crying with a loud voice that all might hear."

Prayers and Petitions

Sometimes prayers carry this intentional idea. "I pray that x" is very similar to "I want x to occur." For this reason, ἵνα + the subjunctive will commonly express the content of petitions or prayers (instead of ὅτι + indicative). Examples of prayers and petitions:

1. προσεύχεσθε, ἵνα μὴ εἰσέλθητε εἰς πειρασμόν
   "Pray that you do not enter into temptation" (Matt 26:41)
2. ἐρωτῶ σε, κυρία, . . . ἵνα ἀγαπῶμεν ἀλλήλους
   "I ask you, ma'am . . . that we love one another" (2 John 5)

Result Clauses

A result clause is very similar to a purpose clause except the focus is on the effect or result[2] of the governing verb, not necessarily the intention.

1. τίς ἥμαρτεν . . . ἵνα τυφλὸς γεννηθῇ;
   "Who sinned . . . that he should be born blind?" (John 9:2)

1 Also called "final clauses."

2 Cf. Stanley E. Porter, *Idioms of the Greek New Testament*, BLG 2 (Sheffield: JSOT Press, 1999), 235.

2. πιστός ἐστιν καὶ δίκαιος ἵνα ἀφῇ ἡμῖν τὰς ἁμαρτίας.
   "He is faithful and just, so that he might forgive our sins." (1 John 1:9)

Indefinite Relative Clauses

The subjunctive is used in all clauses introduced by a relative pronoun that does not refer to a definite person or thing—i.e., all clauses in which the word "ever" appears in English after the relative pronoun. In these clauses the word ἄν or ἐάν (a contraction of εἰ ἄν) is placed after the relative pronoun to make it more general. Nearly every time some form of ἄν is used, it will be followed by a subjunctive verb in Greek. For example:

ὃς ἂν πιστεύσῃ εἰς τὸ ὄνομα τοῦ κυρίου σωθήσεται.
"Whoever believes on the name of the Lord will be saved."

Other Indefinite Clauses

Clauses introduced by ὅταν (ὅτε ἄν) ("whenever") and ὅπου ἄν ("wherever") and referring to the future also use a subjunctive verb. Examples:

1. ὅταν ἀπέλθητε εἰσέρχεσθε εἰς τὴν πόλιν.
   "Whenever you all depart, go into the city."

2. ὅπου ἂν τὸ εὐαγγέλιον κηρύσσηται πολλοὶ ἀκούσουσι.
   "Wherever the gospel is preached, many will hear."

In clauses introduced by ἕως and generally with ἄν, the action in the subjunctive is not tied to a specific point in the day or on the calendar but is used to mark the termination of the governing verb. The action continues until whenever the subjunctive occurs. Such clauses may also be introduced by ἕως οὗ or ἕως ὅτου without ἄν. Examples:

3. ἐκεῖ μένετε ἕως ἂν ἐξέλθητε ἐκεῖθεν.
   "There remain until you all depart thence." (Mark 6:10)

4. καὶ πορεύεται ἐπὶ τὸ ἀπολωλὸς ἕως εὕρῃ αὐτό.
   "And he goes after that which is lost until he finds it." (Luke 15:4)

5. μηδενὶ εἴπητε τὸ ὅραμα ἕως οὗ ὁ υἱὸς τοῦ ἀνθρώπου ἐκ νεκρῶν ἐγερθῇ.
   "Tell the vision to no man until the Son of Man is risen from the dead." (Matt 17:9)

The Hortatory Subjunctive

The subjunctive is used in the first person plural when the speaker is exhorting others to join him in the doing of an action. For example:

ἀγαπητοί, ἀγαπῶμεν ἀλλήλους.
"Beloved, let us love one another." (1 John 4:7)

The Deliberate Subjunctive

The subjunctive is used in deliberative questions, when a person asks himself or others what he is to do. A deliberative question is a question that is answered with an imperative. For example:

τί ποιήσωμεν;
"What should we do?" (Luke 3:10)

EXERCISES

Memorization Exercises

30.1(α) Learn the principal parts for these verbs. Principal parts in blue do not occur in the New Testament. Dashes indicate that the principal parts are not used in the New Testament or ancient Greek.

1. ἄγω, ἄξω, ἤγαγον, ἀγήοχα, ἦγμαι, ἤχθην
2. ἀκούω, ἀκούσομαι, ἤκουσα, ἀκήκοα, ἤκουσμαι, ἠκούσθην
3. ἀποστέλλω, ἀποστελῶ, ἀπέστειλα, ἀπέσταλκα, ἀπέσταλμαι, ἀπεστάλην
4. δέχομαι, δέξομαι, ἐδεξάμην, —, δέδεγμαι, ἐδέχθην
5. κηρύσσω, κηρύξω, ἐκήρυξα, κεκήρυχα, κεκήρυγμαι, ἐκηρύχθην
6. κρίνω, κρινῶ, ἔκρινα, κέκρικα, κέκριμαι, ἐκρίθην

30.1(β) Learn Vocabulary List 24.

Translation Exercises

30.2 Translate the following sentences:

1. καλῶς ἀθετεῖτε τὴν ἐντολὴν τοῦ θεοῦ, ἵνα τὴν παράδοσιν ὑμῶν τηρήσητε.
2. ἄγωμεν ἀλλαχοῦ[1] εἰς τὰς ἐχομένας κωμοπόλεις,[2] ἵνα καὶ ἐκεῖ κηρύξω.
3. ὃς ἂν ἓν τῶν τοιούτων παιδίων δέξηται ἐπὶ τῷ ὀνόματί μου, ἐμὲ δέχεται· καὶ ὃς ἂν ἐμὲ δέχηται, οὐκ ἐμὲ δέχεται, ἀλλὰ τὸν ἀποστείλαντά με.
4. μὴ κρίνετε ἵνα μὴ κριθῆτε.
5. ὃς γὰρ ἂν θέλῃ τὴν ψυχὴν αὐτοῦ σῶσαι ἀπολέσει αὐτήν.
6. καὶ τοὺς ὀφθαλμοὺς αὐτῶν ἐκάμμυσαν,[3] μήποτε[4] ἴδωσιν τοῖς ὀφθαλμοῖς.
7. ὃ ἐὰν δήσῃς[5] ἐπὶ τῆς γῆς ἔσται δεδεμένον ἐν τοῖς οὐρανοῖς.

1 ἀλλαχοῦ, "elsewhere"
2 τὰς ἐχομένας κωμοπόλεις, "the next villages"
3 καμμύω, "I close"
4 μήποτε, "that ... not" (emphatic form of μή)
5 δήσῃς; from δέω

8. κύριοι, τί με δεῖ ποιεῖν ἵνα σωθῶ;
9. αὐτοῦ ἀκούσεσθε κατὰ πάντα ὅσα ἂν λαλήσῃ πρὸς ὑμᾶς.
10. λέγωμεν ἆρα·[1] ποιήσωμεν τὰ κακά, ἵνα ἔλθῃ τὰ ἀγαθά;
11. πάντοτε γὰρ τοὺς πτωχοὺς ἔχετε μεθ' ἑαυτῶν, καὶ ὅταν θέλητε δύνασθε αὐτοῖς εὖ ποιῆσαι.
12. φεῦγε εἰς Αἴγυπτον καὶ ἴσθι[2] ἐκεῖ ἕως ἂν εἴπω σοι.

Composition Exercises

30.3 Translate the following sentences into Greek:

1. The Pharisees disregarded the commandment of God that they might keep their own tradition.
2. Whatever I say to you all privately, proclaim this to all the people.
3. What should we do then? Will we continue in sin that grace may abound?[3]
4. Whenever you all see the gentiles in the holy place know that the end[4] of the age draws nigh.
5. Wherever the gospel is preached those who believe will be saved.
6. Send away the children to the wilderness that the robbers may not kill them.
7. God sent many prophets that they might teach this people.
8. Let us eat and drink, for we must depart quickly.
9. Let us go elsewhere that we may exhort the multitudes.
10. Whenever we want, we can do good to the poor.
11. Remain in the house until I call you all.
12. We have cut down all the trees that the enemy may not eat the fruit.

1 ἆρα, "then," in questions denoting surprise
2 ἴσθι, imperative second person singular from εἶναι, "to be"
3 "I abound," περισσεύω
4 "end," τέλος -ους, τό

13. I will not drink wine so that I might not cause my brother to stumble.
14. I implore you to guard my sheep until I find that which is lost.[1]
15. Whosoever wishes to be greatest among you, let him humble himself as a little child.
16. O Lord, manifest your power to us that your name may be glorified.
17. Bring the garments to me that they may be carried to the widows.

Scripture Translation Exercises

30.4 Translate the following verses from Scripture:

1. καὶ ὧδε εἰς τοῦτο ἐληλύθει ἵνα δεδεμένους αὐτοὺς ἀγάγῃ ἐπὶ τοὺς ἀρχιερεῖς; (Acts 9:21)
2. ὃς ἐὰν οὖν λύσῃ μίαν τῶν ἐντολῶν τούτων τῶν ἐλαχίστων καὶ διδάξῃ οὕτως τοὺς ἀνθρώπους, ἐλάχιστος κληθήσεται ἐν τῇ βασιλείᾳ τῶν οὐρανῶν· ὃς δ᾽ ἂν ποιήσῃ καὶ διδάξῃ, οὗτος μέγας κληθήσεται ἐν τῇ βασιλείᾳ τῶν οὐρανῶν (Matt 5:19)
3. τεκνία μου, ταῦτα γράφω ὑμῖν ἵνα μὴ ἁμάρτητε. καὶ ἐάν τις ἁμάρτῃ, παράκλητον[2] ἔχομεν πρὸς τὸν πατέρα Ἰησοῦν Χριστὸν δίκαιον (1 John 2:1)
4. καὶ αὕτη ἐστὶν ἡ ἐντολὴ αὐτοῦ, ἵνα πιστεύσωμεν τῷ ὀνόματι τοῦ υἱοῦ αὐτοῦ Ἰησοῦ Χριστοῦ (1 John 3:23)
5. ἀγαπητοί, ἀγαπῶμεν ἀλλήλους, ὅτι ἡ ἀγάπη ἐκ τοῦ θεοῦ ἐστιν, καὶ πᾶς ὁ ἀγαπῶν ἐκ τοῦ θεοῦ γεγέννηται καὶ γινώσκει τὸν θεόν (1 John 4:7)
6. ὁμοία ἐστὶν ἡ βασιλεία τῶν οὐρανῶν ζύμῃ[3] ἣν λαβοῦσα γυνὴ ἐνέκρυψεν εἰς ἀλεύρου σάτα τρία[4] ἕως οὗ ἐζυμώθη[5] ὅλον (Matt 13:33)

1 "that which is lost," τὸ ἀπολλύμενον
2 παράκλητον, "advocate," "paraclete"
3 ζύμῃ, "leaven"
4 ἀλεύρου σάτα τρία, "three measures of meal"
5 ζυμόω, "I leaven"

LESSON 31

Contract Verbs, εἰμί, and Further Uses of the Subjunctive

SUBJUNCTIVE MORPHOLOGY OF CONTRACT VERBS

Since the mark of the subjunctive mood is a lengthening of the stem vowel, and the α-contract verb pattern already has long vowels as a result of contraction, the stem of the present subjunctive will be the same as the indicative for these patterns. Thankfully, the present ε-contract verb looks slightly different in some persons of the subjunctive mood. Instead of ει and ου digraphs used in the indicative, the subjunctive will use forms of η and ω. Subjunctive forms of ο-contract verbs will only look different from the indicative where they had ου digraphs in the indicative.

	ε-Contract Verb	α-Contract Verb	ο-Contract Verb
		Present Active Subjunctive	
1 sg.	φιλῶ	τιμῶ	φανερῶ
2 sg.	φιλῇς	τιμᾷς	φανεροῖς
3 sg.	φιλῇ	τιμᾷ	φανεροῖ
1 pl.	φιλῶμεν	τιμῶμεν	φανερῶμεν
2 pl.	φιλῆτε	τιμᾶτε	φανερῶτε
3 pl.	φιλῶσι(ν)	τιμῶσι(ν)	φανερῶσι(ν)
		Present Middle/Passive Subjunctive	
1 sg.	φιλῶμαι	τιμῶμαι	φανερῶμαι
2 sg.	φιλῇ	τιμᾷ	φανεροῖ
3 sg.	φιλῆται	τιμᾶται	φανερῶται
1 pl.	φιλώμεθα	τιμώμεθα	φανερώμεθα
2 pl.	φιλῆσθε	τιμᾶσθε	φανερῶσθε
3 pl.	φιλῶνται	τιμῶνται	φανερῶνται

SUBJUNCTIVE OF εἰμί

Present Subjunctive of εἰμί	
1 sg.	ὦ
2 sg.	ᾖς
3 sg.	ᾖ
1 pl.	ὦμεν
2 pl.	ἦτε
3 pl.	ὦσι(ν)

FURTHER USES OF THE SUBJUNCTIVE

Future General Conditions

The subjunctive is used in all conditional clauses introduced by ἐάν ("if ever") when they refer to the future. For example:

> ἐὰν μὴ μετανοήσητε, πάντες ὡσαύτως ἀπολεῖσθε.
> "If you all do not repent, you all will all perish in like manner." (Luke 13:5)

Prohibitions

Prohibitions are negated commands. Positive commands (imperatives) were discussed in Lesson 14, along with the explanation of how verbal aspect functions with imperatives. Present imperatives convey or reinforce some type of incomplete aspect, whereas aorist imperatives convey or reinforce some type of simple or complete aspect. All imperatives focus on the desired state or action—basically, what the "commander" wants. Any understanding of the current state of affairs is left to either context or the realm of implications.

We might assume the same to be true for negated commands. However, negation complicates things. Does the negation merely apply to the desired action or state, or can it be read into the current state of affairs at the time of the command? Many grammars teach that a present prohibition means "Stop doing x" and an aorist prohibition means "Don't start doing x." One problem with this approach is that both of these interpretations place the focus on what the subject is currently doing rather than the prohibition itself (what they should not be doing, regardless of the current state of affairs). Also, there are far too many exceptions to hold to this rule rigidly. Finally, when the prohibition's verb stem (present or aorist) is consistent with the aspect of the implied context, it is difficult to determine whether the aspectual meaning is coming from the stem choice within the prohibition or other parts of the context.

Negated Present Imperatives

Negated present imperatives assert a prohibition of being in a certain state (regardless of whether it has begun), making an attempt, or maintaining a habit. They also may refer to discontinuing an action or activity in progress.

Mary is commanded not to be afraid in Luke 1:30. The present (incomplete) natural stem choice matches or reinforces the incomplete meaning of the stative verb "to be afraid." The context seems clear: Mary is probably fearing at the time of the command (rather than hearing a cautionary word before being frightened). So if the presumed current state is that Mary is afraid, we have to ask ourselves what exactly the negation is affecting.

Here are the options (notice the different positions of the negation in translation):

1. Do not continue being afraid (emphasis on stopping current state)
2. Be like this, not afraid (emphasis on not being a certain way)
3. Combination of the two (both the current state is negated and the new state is framed in a negative way—what not to be doing)

Since the incomplete aspect of the stem choice matches the incomplete nature of the action (fearing), it would be difficult to argue that the author is drawing special attention to his stem choice for the imperative, and adding some additional meaning beyond the contextual meaning. So option 3 would be an unlikely meaning of the negated imperative per se (although the entire context with the imperative may provide that much meaning). The use of negatives in prohibitions seems to be sufficiently flexible to allow for either options 1 or 2, so it is up to context to help us determine which idea is prominent in Luke, whether it is the stopping of the fear that is more prominent or the continuing on without fear.

Another example where a prohibition (negated present imperative) is used in the context of the action in progress is Luke 8:52 ("Weep no more"). Once again the interpreter must determine whether the negated aspect focuses on the discontinuing of the weeping or the continuing on without weeping. We also must be careful not to assume the author is drawing any special attention to the aspect of this prohibition, since the nature of weeping is an activity versus an instantaneous act or performance.[1] Translations seem divided. Many include some expressed word for stopping (NIV, NET, NLT, NASB, NCV), while others simply have Jesus focusing on how they have no cause for (and shouldn't be) weeping (ESV, GNB, KJV, NKJV, NRSV, MESSAGE).

There are plenty of examples where a negated present imperative is clearly not referring to stopping a current state of affairs but rather focuses on how to proceed in abstinence from a habit, state, or repeated activity (without comment or implication on the current state of affairs).

1. μὴ πιστεύετέ μοι.
   "Then do not believe me." (John 10:37)

2. καὶ μὴ μεθύσκεσθε οἴνῳ . . . ἀλλὰ πληροῦσθε ἐν πνεύματι.
   "Don't be drunk with wine . . . but be filled in spirit." (Eph 5:18)

3. καὶ τότε ἐάν τις ὑμῖν εἴπῃ· Ἴδε ὧδε ὁ Χριστός, Ἴδε ἐκεῖ, μὴ πιστεύετε.
   "And in that time, if anyone says to you all, 'Look, here is the Christ,' do not believe him." (Mark 13:21)

1 Activities are incomplete in aspect and can be a reason for an author to choose a present stem.

Negated Aorist Subjunctive

Greek uses μή as the negation in all prohibitions. If the author wants to have a prohibition that uses an aorist stem (conveying or reinforcing some sort of complete aspect), the aorist *subjunctive* is used instead of the aorist *imperative*. As with positive commands, the aorist stem may be used to mark the prohibition as a complete or simple thought without reference to the inception of the action.[1] One must use context, including the aspectual meaning inherent to the type of action referenced in the verb root, to determine the author's intention for choosing the prohibitory aorist subjunctive over the negated present imperative. It is difficult (and perhaps not productive) to distinguish between contexts that emphasize a specific circumstance for the prohibition and those that focus on not even starting a particular action.[2]

One of the best-known prohibitory subjunctives occurs in the Lord's Prayer (μὴ εἰσενέγκῃς ἡμᾶς εἰς πειρασμόν. "Do not lead us into temptation." Matt 6:13). I don't think the emphasis is on the negation of the very inception of the act: "Do not even begin to lead us into temptation." Given the daily focus of the prayer, I interpret this as a negation of the action as a whole, not merely the first steps. There are many other possible reasons for Matthew's choice of the aorist subjunctive over the present imperative in this verse.

- The aorist stem tends to be more polite or less presumptuous so it is preferred in prayers and petitions.
- The nature of "leading into something" is more of an instantaneous action (like entering) than an indefinitely long activity.
- Matthew also could be viewing the action as a simple whole event.[3]

1 If one were to negate the inception of an action it could be worded like "don't start doing x."

2 "It is extremely difficult to distinguish between a simple prohibition (do not do x) and the proposed DO NOT START X construction. ... The DO NOT START X conceptualization is, in a sense, a contextual motivation for a speaker to select a perfective subjunctive to express a general prohibition in the same way that the STOP DOING X usage is for specific prohibitions in the imperfective aspect." Michael Aubrey, "Greek Prohibitions," in *The Greek Verb Revisited: A Fresh Approach for Biblical Exegesis*, ed. Steven E. Runge and Christopher J. Fresch (Bellingham, WA: Lexham Press, 2016), 520.

3 "The Aorist Subjunctive forbids the action as a simple event with reference to the action as a whole or to its inception, and is most frequently used when the action has not been begun." Ernest De Witt Burton,

Other examples:

1. μὴ νομίσητε ὅτι ...

   "Don't think that ..." (Matt 5:17 and 10:34)

   It is clear that the action hasn't begun, but it is difficult to determine whether the focus is on not beginning to think or having the thought at all.

2. λάλει καὶ μὴ σιωπήσῃς.

   "Speak and don't be silent." (Acts 18:9)

   The prohibitory aorist subjunctive is often used when the action clearly isn't in progress, but may refer to the action as a whole rather than merely its starting point. This verse is a great example, since it also has a negated present imperative, μὴ φοβοῦ. "Do not be afraid."

3. ὅταν οὖν ποιῇς ἐλεημοσύνην, μὴ σαλπίσῃς ἔμπροσθέν σου

   "Whenever you give to the needy, do not blow the trumpet for yourself" (Matt 6:2)

   The aorist subjunctive probably was chosen to refer to the performance of the trumpet fanfare as a whole unit rather than referring to starting up the first blast.

Syntax of the Moods and Tenses in New Testament Greek, 3rd ed. (Edinburgh: T&T Clark, 1898), 75. Note: Burton's explanation is not tainted by Jackson's distorted work on prohibitions typically referring to stopping or not beginning actions, since Burton's work antedated Jackson's. See Daniel Wallace for a summary of the development of these theories. Daniel B. Wallace, *Greek Grammar beyond the Basics: Exegetical Syntax of the New Testament* (Grand Rapids: Zondervan, 1996), 714.

Emphatic Negation The double negative οὐ μή is used with the aorist subjunctive and occasionally with the future indicative in the sense of the future indicative with οὐ, but with more emphasis.

Examples:

1. τὸν ἐρχόμενον πρός με οὐ μὴ ἐκβάλω ἔξω.
   "He that comes to me I will in no way cast out." (John 6:37)

2. ἐὰν δέῃ με συναποθανεῖν σοι, οὐ μή σε ἀρνήσομαι.
   "If I must die with you, I will not deny you." (Mark 14:31)

Frequently however, especially in the Gospels, it is used simply as a negative future without any special emphasis.

EXERCISES

Memorization Exercises

31.1(α) Learn the principal parts of:

1. γινώσκω (γιγνώσκω), γνώσομαι, ἔγνων, ἔγνωκα, ἔγνωσμαι, ἐγνώσθην
2. ἐσθίω, φάγομαι (ἔδομαι), ἔφαγον, ἐδήδοκα, ἐδήδεμαι, —
3. θέλω (impf. ἤθελον), θελήσω, ἠθέλησα, τεθέληκα, —, ἐθελήθην
4. πίνω, πίομαι, ἔπιον, πέπωκα, —, ἐπόθην
5. πράσσω, πράξω, ἔπραξα, πέπραχα, πέπραγμαι, ἐπράχθην

31.1(β) Learn Vocabulary List 25.

Translation Exercises

31.2 Translate the following sentences:

1. κύριε, ἐὰν θέλῃς δύνασαί με καθαρίσαι.
2. ἐφώνησεν δὲ Παῦλος μεγάλῃ φωνῇ λέγων· μηδὲν πράξῃς σεαυτῷ κακόν, ἅπαντες γάρ ἐσμεν ἐνθάδε.
3. ἐὰν μὴ περισσεύσῃ ὑμῶν ἡ δικαιοσύνη πλεῖον τῶν γραμματέων καὶ φαρισαίων, οὐ μὴ εἰσέλθητε εἰς τὴν βασιλείαν τῶν οὐρανῶν.
4. μὴ οὖν μεριμνήσητε εἰς τὴν αὔριον.
5. ὃς ἂν μὴ δέξηται τὴν βασιλείαν τοῦ θεοῦ ὡς παιδίον, οὐ μὴ εἰσέλθῃ εἰς αὐτήν.
6. λέγω γὰρ ὑμῖν ὅτι οὐ μὴ φάγω αὐτὸ ἕως ὅτου πληρωθῇ ἐν τῇ βασιλείᾳ τοῦ θεοῦ.
7. ἐάν τις θέλῃ τὸ θέλημα αὐτοῦ ποιεῖν, γνώσεται περὶ τῆς διδαχῆς πότερον[1] ἐκ θεοῦ ἐστιν.
8. ὑμεῖς ἐστὲ τὸ ἅλας τῆς γῆς· ἐὰν δὲ τὸ ἅλας μωρανθῇ,[2] ἐν τίνι ἁλισθήσεται;
9. εἶπεν δὲ ὁ κύριος τῷ Παύλῳ μὴ φοβοῦ, ἀλλὰ λάλει, καὶ μὴ σιωπήσῃς.

1 πότερον, "whether"

2 μωρανθῇ, "became tasteless," "became foolish"

10. ἐὰν ἀγαπᾶτέ με, τὰς ἐντολὰς τὰς ἐμὰς τηρήσετε.
11. ἀμὴν λέγω ὑμῖν ὅτι εἰσίν τινες τῶν ὧδε ὄντων ὅτινες οὐ μὴ γεύσωνται θανάτου ἕως ἂν ἴδωσιν τὸν υἱὸν τοῦ ἀνθρώπου ἐρχόμενον ἐν τῇ βασιλείᾳ αὐτοῦ.
12. ἐὰν γὰρ ἀγαπήσητε τοὺς ἀγαπῶντας ὑμᾶς, τίνα μισθὸν ἔχετε;
13. καὶ ἐποίησεν δώδεκα ἵνα ὦσιν μετ᾽ αὐτοῦ καὶ ἵνα ἀποστέλλῃ κηρύσσειν καὶ ἔχειν ἐξουσίαν ἐκβάλλειν τὰ δαιμόνια.
14. μὴ οὖν λέγετε τί φάγωμεν; ἢ τί πίωμεν; ἢ τί περιβαλώμεθα.

Composition Exercises

31.3 Translate the following sentences into Greek:

1. If you all do good to them who do good to you, what reward do you all have?
2. Do not bring gentiles into the temple.
3. Let us not seek the things of this age, but the things of the age that is to come.[1]
4. If you all do these things you all will be loved by my father.
5. Do not be receiving the enemies of the gospel.
6. I will in no way allow you to eat bread in this place.
7. If we confess our sins he will have mercy upon us.
8. They went to the priest that they might ask him about the vision.[2]
9. And all the people were silent so that they might hear the messengers of Caesar.
10. If we love him we will keep his commandments.
11. The slaves brought me bread and fish that I might taste it.[3]
12. Sin no longer, lest a worse thing come upon you.

1 Use the present participle of ἔρχομαι.

2 "vision," ὅραμα, -ατος, τό

3 Use genitive case.

13. If these men are wicked, the Lord will destroy them and their city.
14. I will in no way manifest myself to this generation.
15. Do not carry wine to the slaves.
16. If the enemy draws near I will set the soldiers in order.
17. How will we buy bread that these may eat?
18. Let us love our parents that we may be loved by them.

Scripture Translation Exercises

31.4 Translate the following verses from Scripture:

1. καὶ ταῦτα γράφομεν ἡμεῖς, ἵνα ἡ χαρὰ ἡμῶν ᾖ πεπληρωμένη (1 John 1:4)
2. ἐὰν δὲ ἐν τῷ φωτὶ περιπατῶμεν ὡς αὐτός ἐστιν ἐν τῷ φωτί, κοινωνίαν ἔχομεν μετ᾽ ἀλλήλων καὶ τὸ αἷμα Ἰησοῦ τοῦ υἱοῦ αὐτοῦ καθαρίζει ἡμᾶς ἀπὸ πάσης ἁμαρτίας (1 John 1:7)
3. μὴ νομίσητε ὅτι ἦλθον καταλῦσαι τὸν νόμον ἢ τοὺς προφήτας· οὐκ ἦλθον καταλῦσαι ἀλλὰ πληρῶσαι (Matt 5:17)
4. καὶ μὴ εἰσενέγκῃς ἡμᾶς εἰς πειρασμόν (Matt 6:13)
5. μὴ οὖν μεριμνήσητε λέγοντες· τί φάγωμεν; ἤ· τί πίωμεν; ἤ· τί περιβαλώμεθα; (Matt 6:31)
6. ὁ ποιῶν τὴν ἁμαρτίαν ἐκ τοῦ διαβόλου ἐστίν, ὅτι ἀπ᾽ ἀρχῆς ὁ διάβολος ἁμαρτάνει. εἰς τοῦτο ἐφανερώθη ὁ υἱὸς τοῦ θεοῦ, ἵνα λύσῃ τὰ ἔργα τοῦ διαβόλου (1 John 3:8)

LESSON 32

Further Uses of the Infinitive

The infinitive is really a verbal noun and as such can be used as the subject or object of a verb.[1] Since the infinitive has verbal qualities it is able to have its own subject (in the accusative case), object, and other dependent attributive or adverbial modifiers. Its character as a noun is more apparent when articles are prefixed to it. By adding articles in different cases, it practically becomes a declinable neuter noun. Only neuter singular articles may be used with infinitives, and the various cases of the article never affect the spelling of the infinitive.

When an article precedes the infinitive—creating an "articular infinitive"—any additional modifiers such as a subject or object will generally come between the article and the infinitive and form a phrase equivalent to a noun (sometimes labeled as a noun clause).

INFINITIVE OBJECT OF PREPOSITIONS

Prepositional Purpose Phrases

The articular infinitive is frequently used in connection with a preposition. Phrases of this kind are generally best translated by an adverbial clause in English. For example, εἰς or πρός followed by the accusative articular infinitive expresses purpose:

1. καὶ παραδώσουσιν αὐτὸν τοῖς ἔθνεσιν εἰς τὸ ἐμπαῖξαι καὶ μαστιγῶσαι καὶ σταυρῶσαι.
   "And they will deliver him to the gentiles to mock and to scourge and to crucify." (Matt 20:19)

2. ἔπεμψα εἰς τὸ γνῶναι τὴν πίστιν ὑμῶν.
   "I sent that I might know your faith." (1 Thess 3:5)

1 The infinitive was introduced in Lesson 15.

3. προσέχετε δὲ τὴν δικαιοσύνην ὑμῶν μὴ ποιεῖν ἔμπροσθεν τῶν ἀνθρώπων πρὸς τὸ θεαθῆναι αὐτοῖς.
"But take heed that you all do not do your righteousness before men in order to be seen by them." (Matt 6:1)

Prepositional Causal Phrases

The preposition διά followed by an accusative articular infinitive expresses cause. For example:

καὶ διὰ τὸ μὴ ἔχειν ῥίζαν ἐξηράνθη.
"And because it had no root it withered away." (Mark 4:6)

Prepositional Temporal Phrases

The preposition ἐν followed by the dative articular infinitive expresses the time during which something takes place.

Contemporaneous Time

1. καὶ ἐν τῷ σπείρειν αὐτὸν ὃ μὲν ἔπεσεν παρὰ τὴν ὁδόν.
"And as he sowed, some fell by the wayside." (Luke 8:5)

2. ἐν δὲ τῷ καθεύδειν τοὺς ἀνθρώπους ἦλθεν αὐτοῦ ὁ ἐχθρὸς καὶ ἐπέσπειρεν ζιζάνια ἀνὰ μέσον τοῦ σίτου.
"And while men slept, his enemy came and sowed tares among the wheat." (Matt 13:25)

Antecedent Time

The preposition πρό followed by the genitive articular infinitive should be translated with "before."

οἶδεν γὰρ ὁ Πατὴρ ὑμῶν ὧν χρείαν ἔχετε πρὸ τοῦ αἰτῆσαι αὐτόν.
"For your father knows the things of which you all have need before you all ask him." (Matt 6:8)

Subsequent Time

The preposition μετά followed by the accusative articular infinitive should be translated with "after."

ἀλλὰ μετὰ τὸ ἐγερθῆναί με προάξω ὑμᾶς εἰς τὴν Γαλιλαίαν.
"But after I am raised up, I will go before you into Galilee." (Mark 14:28)

INFINITIVE WITH CONJUNCTIONS

Temporal Clauses Introduced by πρίν or πρὶν ἤ

We have been translating Greek prepositions followed by infinitives (prepositional phrases or also classified as noun clauses) with English dependent clauses (subordinated with temporal conjunctions, e.g., "after ..." or "before ..."). Greek also has temporal conjunctions, πρίν or πρὶν ἤ. Conjunctions normally require a true verb such as an indicative, imperative, or subjunctive. However the conjunctions πρίν and πρὶν ἤ can use an infinitive to convey the verbal idea within their clause. This is why we don't see an article preceding an infinitive in these constructions. Examples:

1. πρὶν ἀλέκτορα φωνῆσαι τρὶς ἀπαρνήσῃ με.
   "Before the cock crows you will deny me three times."
   (Matt 26:34)

2. κατάβηθι πρὶν ἀποθανεῖν τὸ παιδίον μου.
   "Come down before my child dies." (John 4:49)

Infinitive in Result Clauses Introduced by ὥστε

The infinitive introduced by ὥστε is often used to express the result of the action of the main verb. This is an alternative to creating a result clause by using ἵνα + a subjunctive.[1] For example:

καὶ ἰδοὺ σεισμὸς μέγας ἐγένετο ἐν τῇ θαλάσσῃ, ὥστε
τὸ πλοῖον καλύπτεσθαι ὑπὸ τῶν κυμάτων.
"And behold, there arose a great tempest in the sea so that
the boat was covered by the waves." (Matt 8:24)

INFINITIVE IN OBJECT CLAUSES AFTER VERBS OF SAYING OR THINKING

Greek has a number of ways to express object clauses. We have already seen that object clauses after verbs of saying or thinking may be expressed by a clause introduced by ὅτι with a verb in the indicative mood. After a verb of desiring (e.g., θέλω), ἵνα + subjunctive is often used to express the statement for what is desired. After verbs of seeing or perceiving, an accusative participial phrase is often used to convey

1 See Lesson 30.

the statement of what is perceived. Likewise, an infinitive with its own subject and object may be used to convey object clause information.[1]

The subject of the infinitive is put into the accusative case, unless it denotes the same person as the subject of the verb who is saying or thinking. This construction is called the "accusative and infinitive" construction. We have a similar construction in English, but it is seldom used. In English, we prefer to use the construction that corresponds to the ὅτι construction in Greek; we introduce object clauses after verbs of saying or thinking with the conjunction "that."[2]

Examples of the accusative and infinitive construction in English:

"The priests pronounced the lepers to be clean."

"We know them to be guilty."

"I perceive them to be making a mistake."

The following are examples of this construction from the New Testament.

1. λέγετε ἐν Βεελζεβοὺλ ἐκβάλλειν με τὰ δαιμόνια.
   "You all say that I cast out demons by Beelzebub." (Luke 11:18)

2. πῶς λέγουσιν τὸν Χριστὸν εἶναι Δαυὶδ υἱόν;
   "How do they say that Christ is the son of David?" (Luke 20:41)

3. οἱ Σαδδουκαῖοι οἱ λέγοντες μὴ εἶναι ἀνάστασιν
   "The Sadducees who say that there is no resurrection" (Matt 22:23)

1 Infinitives representing object clauses often are introduced by verbs of hoping, promising, swearing, and commanding. Ernest De Witt Burton, *Syntax of the Moods and Tenses in New Testament Greek*, 3rd ed. (Edinburgh: T&T Clark, 1898), 155.

2 This is called "indirect discourse" or *oratio obliqua.*

EXERCISES

Memorization Exercises

32.1(α) Learn the parts of:

1. ἀγαπάω, ἀγαπήσω, ἠγάπησα, ἠγάπηκα, ἠγάπημαι, ἠγαπήθην
2. ἀποθνῄσκω, ἀποθανοῦμαι, ἀπέθανον, ἀποτέθνηκα, —, —
3. βαίνω, βήσομαι, ἔβην, βέβηκα, —, —
4. ἔχω (impf. εἶχον), ἕξω, ἔσχον, ἔσχηκα, —, —
5. καλέω, καλέσω, ἐκάλεσα, κέκληκα, κέκλημαι, ἐκλήθην
6. πιστεύω, πιστεύσω, ἐπίστευσα, πεπίστευκα, πεπίστευμαι, ἐπιστεύθην

32.1(β) Learn Vocabulary List 26.

Translation Exercises

32.2 Translate the following sentences:

1. τὸ ἀγαπᾶν τὸν θεὸν ἐξ ὅλης καρδίας καὶ τὸ ἀγαπᾶν τὸν πλησίον ὡς ἑαυτὸν περισσότερόν ἐστι πάντων τῶν ὁλοκαυτωμάτων[1] καὶ θυσιῶν.
2. προσεῖχον δὲ οἱ ὄχλοι τοῖς λεγομένοις ὑπὸ τοῦ Φιλίππου ἐν τῷ ἀκούειν αὐτοὺς καὶ βλέπειν τὰ σημεῖα ἃ ἐποίει.
3. πρὸ γὰρ τοῦ ἐλθεῖν τινὰς ἀπὸ Ἰακώβου μετὰ τῶν ἐθνῶν συνήσθιεν ὁ Πέτρος.
4. καὶ διὰ τὸ πληθυνθῆναι τὴν ἀνομίαν ψυγήσεται[2] ἡ ἀγάπη τῶν πολλῶν.
5. μετὰ δὲ τὸ σιγῆσαι αὐτοὺς ἀπεκρίθη Ἰάκωβος.
6. τίνα λέγουσιν οἱ ἄνθρωποι εἶναι τὸν υἱὸν τοῦ ἀνθρώπου;
7. οὐκ ὀφείλομεν νομίζειν χρυσῷ ἢ ἀργύρῳ ἢ λίθῳ τὸ θεῖον[3] εἶναι ὅμοιον.

1 ὁλοκαυτωμάτων, "a whole burnt offering"

2 ψυγήσεται; future passive from ψύχω, "will grow cold"

3 τὸ θεῖον, "divine being," "divinity"

8. καὶ λιθάσαντες τὸν Παῦλον ἔσυρον ἔξω τῆς πόλεως, νομίζοντες αὐτὸν τεθνηκέναι.[1]
9. ἐὰν δὲ εἴπωμεν ἐξ ἀνθρώπων, ὁ λαὸς ἅπας καταλιθάσει ἡμᾶς, πιστεύει γὰρ Ἰωάννην προφήτην εἶναι.
10. ὁ μὲν οὖν Φῆστος ἀπεκρίθη τηρεῖσθαι τὸν Παῦλον ἐν Καισαρείᾳ, ἑαυτὸν δὲ μέλλειν ἐν τάχει[2] ἐκπορεύεσθαι.
11. καὶ ἐθαμβήθησαν ἅπαντες, ὥστε συζητεῖν αὐτοὺς λέγοντας τί ἐστι τοῦτο;
12. καὶ γνωστὸν ἐγένετο πᾶσι τοῖς κατοικοῦσιν Ἰερουσαλήμ, ὥστε κληθῆναι τὸ χωρίον ἐκεῖνο Ἀχελδαμάχ.
13. κύριε, κατάβηθι πρὶν ἀποθανεῖν τὸ παιδίον μου.
14. ἤμελλεν ἑαυτὸν ἀναιρεῖν νομίζων ἐκπεφευγέναι τοὺς δεσμίους.

Composition Exercises

32.3 Translate the following sentences into Greek, using an infinitive where possible.

1. For to love the Lord and to walk in his ways is good for the sons of men.
2. But while the elders were coming we remained in the fields.
3. The young men did not enter the temple because the priest was dead.
4. And after Paul had spoken Festus answered him.
5. Before the king saw the city, he sent three messengers to its rulers.
6. But we all were frightened, with the result that we hid among the trees.
7. All the people believe that Moses wrote these things.

1 τεθνηκέναι; perfect infinitive active from θνῄσκω, "I die"

2 ἐν τάχει, "quickly," "shortly"

8. Depart from the house before the tax collector comes.
9. But after the multitude gave heed to the apostles they did many signs among them.
10. We think that he benefited this people by teaching them to obey the king.
11. And he healed the blind man so that all men wondered.
12. The young man died before the prophet came.
13. We believe that Peter is an apostle.
14. They stoned Paul because he preached the gospel to them.
15. To love the Lord is better than gold or silver.
16. While he was coming down from the mountain he commanded his disciples to tell the vision to no man before they came to Jerusalem.
17. And now I have told you all these things before they come to pass.
18. All the Jews cried out that Paul ought not to live any longer.[1]
19. But I perceived that he was a wise and good man.
20. The people gave heed to John, for they believed that he was a prophet.

Scripture Translation Exercises

32.4 Translate the following verses from Scripture:

1. προσέχετε δὲ τὴν δικαιοσύνην ὑμῶν μὴ ποιεῖν ἔμπροσθεν τῶν ἀνθρώπων πρὸς τὸ θεαθῆναι αὐτοῖς (Matt 6:1)
2. ἀμὴν λέγω σοι ὅτι ἐν ταύτῃ τῇ νυκτὶ πρὶν ἀλέκτορα φωνῆσαι τρὶς ἀπαρνήσῃ με. λέγει αὐτῷ ὁ Πέτρος· κἂν δέῃ με σὺν σοὶ ἀποθανεῖν, οὐ μή σε ἀπαρνήσομαι (Matt 26:34–35)

1 "any longer," μηκέτι

3. Ἰησοῦς ... εἶπεν αὐτῷ· πρὸ τοῦ σε Φίλιππον φωνῆσαι ὄντα ὑπὸ τὴν συκῆν εἶδόν σε (John 1:48)
4. εἶπεν αὐτοῖς Ἰησοῦς· ἀμὴν ἀμὴν λέγω ὑμῖν, πρὶν Ἀβραὰμ γενέσθαι ἐγὼ εἰμί (John 8:58)
5. ἐπῆλθαν δὲ ἀπὸ Ἀντιοχείας καὶ Ἰκονίου Ἰουδαῖοι καὶ πείσαντες τοὺς ὄχλους καὶ λιθάσαντες τὸν Παῦλον ἔσυρον ἔξω τῆς πόλεως νομίζοντες αὐτὸν τεθνηκέναι (Acts 14:19)
6. μετὰ δὲ τὸ σιγῆσαι αὐτοὺς ἀπεκρίθη Ἰάκωβος λέγων· ἄνδρες ἀδελφοί, ἀκούσατέ μου (Acts 15:13)
7. τίνα λέγουσιν οἱ ἄνθρωποι εἶναι τὸν υἱὸν τοῦ ἀνθρώπου; (Matt 16:13)

LESSON 33

Athematic Verbs: δίδωμι

ATHEMATIC STEM

There are a small number of very common verbs that are athematic—verbs that do not have a variable vowel (thematic vowel) stem. These verbs avoid vocalic contraction since they do not have the thematic vowel. We call these verbs "athematic verbs."[1] They function as other contract verbs in their other principal parts, with a slight modification to their aorist (third principal part) stem.

Normally, the primary mark of the first principal part is the thematic variable vowel stem. This thematic vowel creates a contraction for verb roots that terminate with a vowel (typically, ε, α, or ο). In other principal parts, a stem consonant keeps the root vowel from contracting.

Notice how the six principal parts of δίδωμι only differ from regular verbs in the first and third principal parts:

1	2	3	4	5	6
δίδωμι	δώσω	ἔδωκα	δέδωκα	δέδομαι	ἐδόθην
Reduplicated and lengthened root	Expected lengthened root	κ instead of σ stem and expected lengthened root	Expected lengthened root	Nonlengthened root	Nonlengthened root

1 Many grammars refer to them as MI verbs, referring to the first person singular ending that is used.

It is especially important with these verbs to remember the distinction presented in Lesson 17 between the verbal root, used for most of the tenses, and the present root form, used only for the first principal part.

Notice that the present root form of three very common athematic verbs has reduplication but uses an ι as the vowel instead of an ε. The reduplicated σ in ἵστημι is represented by a rough breathing mark. Also note how the root vowel lengthens prior to the consonant stem.

Verbal Root	Pres. Act. Ind. 1 sg.	Translation
δο	δίδωμι	I give
θε	τίθημι	I place
στα	ἵστημι	I cause to stand

PERSONAL ENDINGS The personal endings in the present active reveal an early state of personal endings that persisted with these common verbs. Eventually (after the time of the New Testament) the endings for these verbs changed to the standard endings already covered (μι was replaced with ω for the first person singular). "Hence δίδωμι becomes δίδω (papyri) in late Greek. λέγω was originally λέγομι."[1] These personal endings were probably derived from pronoun forms (μι from με, σι from σε, and τι from το). Some of these forms can be seen in the athematic verb εἰμί. These endings then shifted into the personal ending forms for athematic verbs in the New Testament.

1 A. T. Robertson, *A Grammar of the Greek New Testament in the Light of Historical Research* (Bellingham, WA: Logos Bible Software, 2006), 335.

Personal Endings for Athematic Verbs	
1 sg.	μι
2 sg.	ς
3 sg.	σι
1 pl.	μεν
2 pl.	τε
3 pl.	ασι(ν)[1]

PRESENT AND IMPERFECT ACTIVE FORMS OF δίδωμι

As typically occurs with contract verbs, the root vowel is lengthened prior to a stem consonant. Note that this expected lengthening only occurs in singular forms. The plural forms do not lengthen or even contract in the third person plural. Note that the imperfect tense follows this same pattern but lengthens to ου instead of ω in the singular forms. The augment for the imperfect tense precedes the reduplication of the present root form. Subjunctive forms for roots ending in ο lengthen the root vowel.

Present & Imperfect Active Forms

	Present Indicative	Present Imperative	Present Subjunctive	Imperfect Indicative
1 sg.	δίδωμι		διδῶ	ἐδίδουν
2 sg.	δίδως	δίδου	διδῷς	ἐδίδους
3 sg.	δίδωσι	διδότω	διδῷ	ἐδίδου
1 pl.	δίδομεν		διδῶμεν	ἐδίδομεν
2 pl.	δίδοτε	δίδοτε	διδῶτε	ἐδίδοτε
3 pl.	διδόασι(ν)	διδόωσαν	διδῶσι(ν)	ἐδίδοσαν[2] (ἐδίδουν)[3]

Present Infinitive	Present Participle	
διδόναι	Nom.	διδούς, διδοῦσα, διδόν
	Acc.	διδόντα, διδοῦσαν, διδόν

1 The original form was νσι. We have seen ν vocalize to α before.

2 σαν is not an uncommon secondary ending.

3 This is a thematic form. This is a verb form that contains a variable vowel stem (ε/ο), which will contract with a verb root that terminates in a vowel.

PRESENT AND IMPERFECT MIDDLE/PASSIVE FORMS OF δίδωμι

The middle and passive forms for athematic verbs should be easily recognizable. There are no new personal endings, and the root vowel is consistently short except in the subjunctive, where it is expected to lengthen. Remember: there is no thematic variable vowel between the present root form and the personal endings. For this reason, these forms and the perfect passive forms show a strong similarity. Always remember that if there is the older iota type reduplication with these verbs, it must be a tense derived from the first principal part.

Present & Imperfect Middle/Passive Forms

	Present Indicative	Present Imperative	Present Subjunctive	Imperfect Indicative
1 sg.	δίδομαι		διδῶμαι	ἐδιδόμην
2 sg.	δίδοσαι	δίδοσο	διδῷ	ἐδίδοσο
3 sg.	δίδοται	διδόσθω	διδῶται	ἐδίδοτο
1 pl.	διδόμεθα		διδώμεθα	ἐδιδόμεθα
2 pl.	δίδοσθε	δίδοσθε	διδῶσθε	ἐδίδοσθε
3 pl.	δίδονται	διδόσθωσαν	διδῶνται	ἐδίδοντο

Present Infinitive	Present Participle
δίδοσθαι	διδόμενος, διδομένη, διδόμενον

AORIST ACTIVE FORMS OF δίδωμι

The thematic aorist pattern (second aorist) is constructed with the verbal root + theme vowel + secondary endings. Greek athematic verbs use this pattern without the theme vowel (verbal root + secondary endings). Some grammars call this pattern the "athematic aorist," while others call it the "third aorist pattern." You already learned the athematic aorist with the aorist forms for γινώσκω and βαίνω.[1] The surprising exception for athematic verbs is that they don't have athematic aorist forms for their active indicative forms, and thus we don't see an athematic form represented in their third principal part. These indicative forms look like sigmatic aorists that have replaced σ with κ.

1 See Lessons 19 and 20.

The subjunctive pattern looks the same as the present subjunctive but uses the verbal root (no reduplication).

Aorist Active Forms

	Indicative	Imperative	Subjunctive
1 sg.	ἔδωκα		δῶ
2 sg.	ἔδωκας	δός	δῷς
3 sg.	ἔδωκε(ν)	δότω	δῷ (δώῃ)
1 pl.	ἐδώκαμεν		δῶμεν
2 pl.	ἐδώκατε	δότε	δῶτε
3 pl.	ἔδωκαν	δότωσαν	δῶσι(ν)

Infinitive	Participle
δοῦναι	Nom. δούς, δοῦσα, δόν Acc. δόντα, δοῦσαν, δόν

AORIST MIDDLE FORMS OF δίδωμι

These verbs don't mix their patterns in their middle voice. They all follow an athematic pattern. The verbal root vowel only lengthens in the subjunctive mood.

Aorist Middle Forms

	Indicative	Imperative	Subjunctive
1 sg.	ἐδόμην		δῶμαι
2 sg.	ἔδου	δοῦ	δῷ
3 sg.	ἔδοτο	δόσθω	δῶται
1 pl.	ἐδόμεθα		δώμεθα
2 pl.	ἔδοσθε	δόσθε	δῶσθε
3 pl.	ἔδοντο	δόσθωσαν	δῶνται

Infinitive	Participle
δόσθαι	δόμενος, δομένη, δόμενον

EXERCISES

Memorization Exercises

33.1(α) Learn the parts of:

1. δίδωμι, δώσω, ἔδωκα, δέδωκα, δέδομαι, ἐδόθην
2. πίπτω, πεσοῦμαι, ἔπεσον, πέπτωκα, —, —

33.1(β) Learn Vocabulary List 27.

Translation Exercises

33.2 Translate the following sentences:

1. ὁ δὲ Ἰησοῦς ἐδίδου τὸν ἄρτον τοῖς μαθηταῖς ἵνα διδῶσιν αὐτὸν τοῖς ὄχλοις.
2. ὁ γὰρ θεὸς δίδωσι τὸ πνεῦμα τὸ ἅγιον τοῖς αἰτοῦσιν αὐτόν.
3. εἰπὲ ὑμῖν ἐν ποίᾳ ἐξουσίᾳ ταῦτα ποιεῖς, ἢ τίς ἐστιν ὁ δούς σοι τὴν ἐξουσίαν ταύτην.
4. ἀπολύετε καὶ ἀπολυθήσεσθε, δίδοτε καὶ δοθήσεται ὑμῖν.
5. καὶ διὰ τί οὐκ ἔδωκάς μου τὸ ἀργύριον ἐπὶ τράπεζαν;[1]
6. ὑμῖν δέδοται γνῶναι τὰ μυστήρια τῆς βασιλείας.
7. ἀπόδος μοι εἴ τι ὀφείλεις.
8. ὁ δὲ οὐκ ἤθελεν, ἀλλὰ ἀπελθὼν ἔβαλεν αὐτὸν εἰς φυλακὴν ἕως ἀποδῷ τὸ ὀφειλόμενον.
9. ἔξεστιν ἡμᾶς Καίσαρι φόρον[2] δοῦναι; δῶμεν ἢ μὴ δῶμεν;
10. ἐδόθη μοι πᾶσα ἐξουσία ἐν οὐρανῷ καὶ ἐπὶ γῆς.
11. ὁ πατὴρ ἀγαπᾷ τὸν υἱόν, καὶ πάντα δέδωκεν ἐν τῇ χειρὶ αὐτοῦ.
12. μακάριόν ἐστι μᾶλλον δοῦναι ἢ λαμβάνειν.
13. τίς ἡ σοφία ἡ δοθεῖσα τούτῳ;
14. εἰπέ μοι εἰ τοσούτου τὸ χωρίον ἀπέδοσθε;
15. ταῦτα πάντα σοι δώσω ἐὰν πεσὼν προσκυνήσῃς μοι.

1 ἐπὶ τράπεζαν, "to the bank"

2 φόρον, "tribute"

16. καὶ ὅταν ἄγωσιν ὑμᾶς παραδιδόντες, μὴ προμεριμνᾶτε τί λαλήσητε, ἀλλ' ὃ ἐὰν δοθῇ ὑμῖν ἐν ἐκείνῃ τῇ ὥρᾳ τοῦτο λαλεῖτε.
17. καὶ νῦν εἴρηκα ὑμῖν πρὶν γενέσθαι, ἵνα ὅταν γένηται πιστεύσητε.

Composition Exercises

33.3 Translate the following sentences into Greek:

1. I give you power over unclean spirits to cast them out.
2. This dog was given to me by my father.
3. We wish to give the gold to the high priests.
4. Do not give good things to the wicked.
5. The field was being sold to the soldiers by the tax collectors.
6. They went about giving garments to the lepers.[1]
7. I will in no way give that which is yours to the Lord.
8. You gave me water when I was thirsty.[2]
9. Let us keep the commands that have been given to us.
10. He who gives bread to the hungry[3] will in no way lose[4] his reward.
11. We were giving the money to the servants that they might give it to the widows.
12. The king has given us this city that we may live in it; let us not betray it to his enemies.
13. Sell all that you have and give to the poor.
14. If you all ask for bread, will your father give you a stone?
15. Whatever we ask will be given to us.
16. Give and it will be given to you all.

1 "those with leprosy"
2 "when (I) was thirsty," use διψάω
3 Use the proper participle form of πεινάω to translate "to the hungry."
4 This is an empahtic negation which expects the subjunctive ἀπολέσῃ ("lose").

17. This money has been given to you that you may buy the field.
18. Give us, O Lord, your grace that we may worship you in spirit and in truth.
19. What is the wisdom that is given to this man?

Scripture Translation Exercises

33.4 Translate the following verses from Scripture:

1. ὅταν δὲ παραδῶσιν ὑμᾶς, μὴ μεριμνήσητε πῶς ἢ τί λαλήσητε· δοθήσεται γὰρ ὑμῖν ἐν ἐκείνῃ τῇ ὥρᾳ τί λαλήσητε (Matt 10:19)
2. ὁ δὲ ἀποκριθεὶς εἶπεν αὐτοῖς· ὅτι ὑμῖν δέδοται γνῶναι τὰ μυστήρια τῆς βασιλείας τῶν οὐρανῶν, ἐκείνοις δὲ οὐ δέδοται (Matt 13:11)
3. εἶπεν· τί θέλετέ μοι δοῦναι, κἀγὼ ὑμῖν παραδώσω αὐτόν; (Matt 26:15)
4. εἶπεν δὲ πρὸς αὐτούς· δότε αὐτοῖς ὑμεῖς φαγεῖν. οἱ δὲ εἶπαν· οὐκ εἰσὶν ἡμῖν πλεῖον ἢ ἄρτοι πέντε[1] καὶ ἰχθύες δύο (Luke 9:13)
5. ἐγείρεσθε ἄγωμεν· ἰδοὺ ἤγγικεν ὁ παραδιδούς με (Matt 26:46)

1 πέντε, "five"

LESSON 34

Athematic Verbs: τίθημι

PRINCIPAL PARTS FOR τίθημι

Notice how the six principal parts of τίθημι operate in a similar fashion to δίδωμι:

- The verbal root is θε.
- In the first principal part, there is reduplication using the unvoiced stop form relating to θ and a lengthened root vowel.
- The second principal part uses the verbal root (θε) and then lengthens the root vowel (θη) before the consonant stem, just like a contract verb.
- The same holds true for the third principal part, where κ replaces σ for the first aorist forms in the indicative mood.
- The fifth and sixth principal parts (perfect tenses) use standard reduplication using the unvoiced stop form relating to θ.
- The root vowel is lengthened in a different way from other tenses (ει instead of η). The θη in the sixth principal part is not part of the root at all; those are the stem letters for this principal part.
- The root θ becomes a stop (τ) prior to the stem θ, and the root vowel doesn't lengthen.

1	2	3	4	5	6
τίθημι	θήσω	ἔθηκα	τέθεικα	τέθειμαι	ἐτέθην
Reduplicated and lengthened root	Expected lengthened root	κ instead of σ stem and expected lengthened root	Alternate lengthening of root	Alternate lengthening of root	Nonlengthened root changes to τε

PRESENT AND IMPERFECT ACTIVE FORMS OF τίθημι

Observe the general similarity between the endings of τίθημι and those of δίδωμι—with the exception that ε, not ο, is the root vowel. Like δίδωμι in the present and imperfect indicative, this verb only lengthens in singular forms. The plural forms do not lengthen or even contract in the third person plural. Note that the imperfect has a few forms that have progressed to contract verbs. These three forms use the thematic stem vowel, which then contracts with the root vowel. The augment for the imperfect tense precedes the reduplication of the present root form. Subjunctive forms use standard lengthened stems, like regular verbs, which replace the root vowel.

Present & Imperfect Active Forms

	Present Indicative	Present Imperative	Present Subjunctive	Imperfect Indicative
1 sg.	τίθημι		τιθῶ	ἐτίθην
2 sg.	τίθης	τίθει[1]	τιθῇς	ἐτίθεις[1]
3 sg.	τίθησι(ν)	τιθέτω	τιθῇ	ἐτίθει[1]
1 pl.	τίθεμεν		τιθῶμεν	ἐτίθεμεν
2 pl.	τίθετε	τίθετε	τιθῆτε	ἐτίθετε
3 pl.	τιθέασι(ν)	τιθέτωσαν	τιθῶσι	ἐτίθεσαν (ἐτίθουν)[1]

Present Infinitive	Present Participle
τιθέναι	Nom. τιθείς, τιθεῖσα, τιθέν Acc. τιθέντα, τιθεῖσαν, τιθέν

1 This is a thematic form. It contains a variable vowel stem (ε/ο), which contracts with a verb root that terminates in a vowel.

PRESENT AND IMPERFECT MIDDLE/PASSIVE FORMS OF τίθημι

The middle and passive forms for τίθημι follow the same predictable pattern used with δίδωμι. The root vowel is consistently short except in the subjunctive, where it is replaced with the standard subjunctive stem. One must simply remember that there is no thematic variable vowel between the present root form and the personal endings. For this reason, these forms and the perfect passive forms show a strong similarity. As with δίδωμι, the older reduplication with iota will distinguish them from the perfect.

Present & Imperfect Middle/Passive Forms

	Present Indicative	Present Imperative	Present Subjunctive	Imperfect Indicative
1 sg.	τίθεμαι		τιθῶμαι	ἐτιθέμην
2 sg.	τίθεσαι	τίθεσο	τιθῇ	ἐτίθεσο
3 sg.	τίθεται	τιθέσθω	τιθῆται	ἐτίθετο
1 pl.	τιθέμεθα		τιθώμεθα	ἐτιθέμεθα
2 pl.	τίθεσθε	τίθεσθε	τιθῆσθε	ἐτίθεσθε
3 pl.	τίθενται	τιθέσθωσαν	τιθῶνται	ἐτίθεντο

Present Infinitive	Present Participle
τίθεσθαι	τιθέμενος, τιθεμένη, τιθέμενον

AORIST ACTIVE FORMS OF τίθημι

Like δίδωμι, this athematic verb uses the athematic aorist pattern for nonindicative aorist active forms. These indicative forms look like sigmatic aorists that have replaced σ with κ. The subjunctive pattern looks the same as the present subjunctive but uses the verbal root (no reduplication).

Aorist Active Forms

	Indicative	Imperative	Subjunctive
1 sg.	ἔθηκα		θῶ
2 sg.	ἔθηκας	θές	θῇς
3 sg.	ἔθηκε(ν)	θέτω	θῇ
1 pl.	ἐθήκαμεν		θῶμεν
2 pl.	ἐθήκατε	θέτε	θῆτε
3 pl.	ἔθεκαν	θέτωσαν	θῶσι(ν)

Infinitive		Participle
θεῖναι	Nom.	θείς, θεῖσα, θέν
	Acc.	θέντα, θεῖσαν, θέν

AORIST MIDDLE FORMS OF τίθημι

Athematic verbs don't mix their patterns in their middle voice. They all follow an athematic pattern, simply using a root and ending (no stem). The verbal root vowel only lengthens in the subjunctive mood.

Aorist Middle Forms

	Indicative	Imperative	Subjunctive
1 sg.	ἐθέμην		θῶμαι
2 sg.	ἔθου	θοῦ	θῇ
3 sg.	ἔθετο	θέσθω	θῆται
1 pl.	ἐθέμεθα		θώμεθα
2 pl.	ἔθεσθε	θέσθε	θῆσθε
3 pl.	ἔθεντο	θέσθωσαν	θῶνται

Infinitive	Participle
θέσθαι	θέμενος, θεμένη, θέμενον

EXERCISES

Memorization Exercises

34.1(α) Learn the parts of:

1. αἴρω, ἀρῶ, ἦρα, ἦρκα, ἦρμαι, ἤρθην
2. τίθημι, θήσω, ἔθηκα, τέθεικα, τέθειμαι, ἐτέθην
3. φέρω, οἴσω, ἤνεγκον (ἤνεγκα), ἐνήνοχα, ἐνήνεγμαι, ἠνέχθην

34.1(β) Learn Vocabulary List 28.

Translation Exercises

34.2 Translate the following sentences:

1. οὐ καίουσιν λύχνον καὶ τιθέασιν αὐτὸν ὑπὸ τὸν μόδιον[1] ἀλλ' ἐπὶ τὴν λυχνίαν.[2]
2. και λαβὼν τὸ σῶμα ὁ Ἰωσὴφ ἔθηκεν αὐτὸ ἐν τῷ καινῷ αὐτοῦ μνημείῳ.
3. μήτι[3] ἔρχεται ὁ λύχνος ἵνα ὑπὸ τὸν μόδιον τέθῃ;
4. καὶ ὅπου ἂν εἰσεπορεύετο ἐν ταῖς ἀγοραῖς ἐτίθεσαν τοὺς ἀσθενοῦντας.
5. καὶ ἐναγκαλισάμενος[4] τὰ παιδία κατευλόγει τιθεὶς τὰς χεῖρας ἐπ' αὐτά.
6. ὁ ποιμὴν ὁ καλὸς τὴν ψυχὴν αὐτοῦ τίθησιν ὑπὲρ τῶν προβάτων.
7. ἦραν τὸν κύριον ἐκ τοῦ μνημείου, καὶ οὐκ οἴδαμεν[5] ποῦ ἔθηκαν αὐτόν.
8. οὐχ ὑμῶν ἐστι γνῶναι χρόνους ἢ καιροὺς οὓς ὁ πατὴρ ἔθετο ἐν τῇ ἰδίᾳ ἐξουσίᾳ.
9. καὶ ἔκλασεν τοὺς ἄρτους καὶ ἐδίδου τοῖς μαθηταῖς ἵνα παρατίθωσιν αὐτοῖς.
10. καὶ εἰς ἣν ἂν πόλιν εἰσέρχησθε καὶ δέχωνται ὑμᾶς, ἐσθίετε τὰ παρατιθέμενα ὑμῖν.

1 μόδιον, "a measuring vessel"
2 λυχνίαν, "a lampstand"
3 μήτι, "Doesn't, ... does it?" Expects a negative answer to the question.
4 ἐναγκαλίζομαι, "I hug"
5 οἴδαμεν, "we know"

11. καὶ ἰδοὺ ἄνδρες φέροντες ἐπὶ κλίνης ἄνθρωπον ὃς ἦν παραλυτικός, καὶ ἐζήτουν αὐτὸν εἰσενεγκεῖν καὶ θεῖναι αὐτὸν ἐνώπιον αὐτοῦ.
12. καὶ αὐτὸς ἀπεσπάσθη[1] ἀπ' αὐτῶν ὡσεὶ λίθου βολήν,[2] καὶ θεὶς τὰ γόνατα προσηύχετο.
13. κύριε, διὰ τί οὐ δύναμαί σοι ἀκολουθεῖν ἄρτι;[3] τὴν ψυχήν μου ὑπέρ σου θήσω.
14. ἔφερον τὰς τιμὰς τῶν χωρίων καὶ ἐτίθουν παρὰ τοὺς πόδας τῶν ἀποστόλων.
15. κάθου[4] ἐκ δεξιῶν μου ἕως ἂν θῶ τοὺς ἐχθρούς σου ὑποπόδιον[5] τῶν ποδῶν σου.

Composition Exercises

34.3 Translate the following sentences into Greek:

1. We placed wine and water in cups beside them.
2. We wanted to place the sick in the marketplaces.
3. And falling upon his knees he prayed to the God of heaven.
4. How will we place the lame man before his feet?
5. They used to place the books in the synagogue.
6. We will place the lamp under the measuring pot.
7. You did place me in a good land.
8. Behold, all these laid down their lives for the brethren.
9. Do not place this writing upon the cross.
10. This is the throne that was placed in the temple.
11. Place the body of the prophet in the tomb of his fathers.
12. The sword is placed in the hand of the king.
13. The apostles placed their hands upon us and blessed us.

1 ἀπεσπάσθη, "withdraw"
2 ὡσεὶ λίθου βολὴν, "about a stone's cast"
3 ἄρτι, "now," "at this moment"
4 κάθου, "sit down"
5 ὑποπόδιον, "footstool"

14. I will come down that I may place my hands upon her, and she will live.
15. The lamps will be placed in the house of the elder.
16. The nets were placed by the side of the ship.
17. The sick man was brought in on a bed and placed before him.
18. I am he who placed my hands upon your head when you were a boy.
19. You all will certainly not eat that which is set before you.
20. The bread was broken and set before them.

Scripture Translation Exercises

34.4 Translate the following verses from Scripture:

1. θήσω τὸ πνεῦμά μου ἐπ᾿ αὐτόν, καὶ κρίσιν τοῖς ἔθνεσιν ἀπαγγελεῖ (Matt 12:18)
2. καὶ παραγγέλλει τῷ ὄχλῳ ἀναπεσεῖν ἐπὶ τῆς γῆς· καὶ λαβὼν τοὺς ἑπτὰ ἄρτους εὐχαριστήσας ἔκλασεν καὶ ἐδίδου τοῖς μαθηταῖς αὐτοῦ ἵνα παρατιθῶσιν, καὶ παρέθηκαν τῷ ὄχλῳ. καὶ εἶχον ἰχθύδια[1] ὀλίγα· καὶ εὐλογήσας αὐτὰ εἶπεν καὶ ταῦτα παρατιθέναι (Mark 8:6–7)
3. ἡ δὲ Μαρία ἡ Μαγδαληνὴ καὶ Μαρία ἡ Ἰωσῆτος ἐθεώρουν ποῦ τέθειται (Mark 15:47)

1 ἰχθύδια, "(little) fish" (diminutive of ἰχθύς, -ύος, ὁ, "fish")

LESSON 35

Athematic Verbs: ἵστημι

ADDITIONAL STEM AND MEANING FOR ἵστημι

The verb ἵστημι is one of the few verbs that has both sigmatic[1] and athematic aorist patterns used in the indicative. In addition to having two patterns for aorist active forms, the patterns differ in meaning for this verb.

The present, imperfect, future, and sigmatic aorist tenses for ἵστημι are transitive and mean "I cause to stand," "I place," or similar meanings. The athematic aorist (ἔστην), perfect, and pluperfect are intransitive and refer to the self-action of standing. The only passive forms of this verb in the New Testament come from the sixth principal part and have the regular θη stem pattern. Sometimes the context will demand a true passive meaning (something stood up or placed [e.g., Matt 18:16]); more commonly it will convey a simple intransitive idea of standing: "I stand," which is the result of "having been stood up."

PRINCIPAL PARTS FOR ἵστημι

In the tenses in which there is reduplication (the present and the perfect) the first σ is represented by a rough breathing: present ἵστημι for σίστημι; perfect ἕστηκα for σέστηκα. This explains the variations in breathing marks through the various principal parts for this verb. There is a rough breathing on all the moods of the present and perfect tenses and a smooth breathing on the augmented tenses of the first and second aorist forms.

The present middle and passive don't occur in the New Testament.

1 Note that the first aorist active includes the usual σ—not κ.

1	2	3	4	5	6
ἵστημι	στήσω	ἔστησα	ἕστηκα	—	ἐστάθην
Reduplicated with rough breathing mark and lengthened root	Expected lengthened root	Expected augment and lengthened root	Rough breathing on augment and expected lengthened root	Doesn't occur in the NT	Nonlengthened root

PRESENT AND IMPERFECT ACTIVE FORMS OF ἵστημι Like other athematic verbs in the present and imperfect indicative, this verb only lengthens its root vowel in singular forms. This verb is different than other athematic present verbs in that third person plural form of this verb contracts like a regular α-contract verb. Two consecutive instances of α would be a bit much. Note that the augment for the imperfect is not visible (represented by a long ι). The secondary endings in the imperfect tense mark past time. This tense doesn't occur in the New Testament but is present in classical literature. Subjunctive forms use standard lengthened stems, like regular verbs, that replace the root vowel.

	Present & Imperfect Active Forms			
	Present Indicative	Present Imperative	Present Subjunctive	Imperfect Indicative
1 sg.	ἵστημι		ἱστῶ	ἵστην
2 sg.	ἵστης	ἵστη	ἱστῇς	ἵστης
3 sg.	ἵστησι(ν)	ἱστάτω	ἱστῇ	ἵστη
1 pl.	ἵσταμεν		ἱστῶμεν	ἵσταμεν
2 pl.	ἵστατε	ἵστατε	ἱστῆτε	ἵστατε
3 pl.	ἱστᾶσι(ν)	ἱστάτωσαν	ἱστῶσι(ν)	ἵστασαν
	Present Infinitive		Present Participle	
	Does not occur in the NT		Does not occur in the NT	

The sigmatic aorist forms of ἵστημι communicate transitive meaning—that is, "causing to stand" or "placing." They are built using the verbal root στα-, which is lengthened to στησα- with the addition of the sigmatic stem. An augment with smooth breathing is added with the indicative secondary endings. The forms for all of the moods are consistent with sigmatic aorist (first aorist) forms learned previously.

SIGMATIC AORIST ACTIVE FORMS OF ἵστημι

Sigmatic Aorist Active Forms

	Indicative	Subjunctive
1 sg.	ἔστησαν	στήσω
2 sg.	ἔστησας	στήσῃς
3 sg.	ἔστησε(ν)	στήσῃ
1 pl.	ἐστήσαμεν	στήσωμεν
2 pl.	ἐστήσατε	στήσητε
3 pl.	ἔστησαν	στήσωσι

Infinitive	Participle
στῆσαι	στήσας, στήσασα, στῆσαν

Transitive Meaning: "Cause X to Stand" or "Place X"

ATHEMATIC AORIST ACTIVE FORMS OF ἵστημι

The athematic aorist active forms of ἵστημι communicate an intransitive meaning—that is, "[simply] standing." They are built using the verbal root στα consistently using the endings learned previously. As with other athematic verbs, the subjunctive forms replace the root vowel with lengthened stem vowels. The forms look the same as the present subjunctive but use the verbal root (no reduplication).

Intransitive Meaning: "Stand"

Athematic Aorist Active Forms

	Indicative	Imperative	Subjunctive
1 sg.	ἔστην		στῶ
2 sg.	ἔστης	στῆθι	στῇς
3 sg.	ἔστη	στήτω	στῇ
1 pl.	ἔστημεν		στῶμεν
2 pl.	ἔστητε	στῆτε	στῆτε
3 pl.	ἔστησαν	στήτωσαν	στῶσι(ν)

Infinitive	Participle
στῆναι	στάς, στᾶσα, στάν

EXERCISES

Memorization Exercises

35.1(α) Learn the parts of:

1. ἀπαγγέλλω, ἀπαγγελῶ, ἀπήγγειλα, ἀπήγγελκα, ἀπήγγελμαι, ἀπηγγέλην
2. βαίνω, βήσομαι, ἔβην, βέβηκα, —, —
3. ἵστημι, στήσω, ἔστησα (ἔστην), ἕστηκα, ἕσταμαι, ἐστάθην
4. πάσχω, πείσομαι, ἔπαθον, πέπονθα, —, —
5. φαίνω, φανοῦμαι, ἔφανα, πέφηνα, πέφασμαι, ἐφάνην

35.1(β) Learn Vocabulary List 29.

Translation Exercises

35.2(α) Translate the following sentences (part 1):

1. τότε παραλαμβάνει αὐτὸν ὁ διάβολος εἰς τὴν ἁγίαν πὸλιν καὶ ἔστησεν αὐτὸν ἐπὶ τὸ πτερύγιον[1] τοῦ ἱεροῦ.
2. ταῦτα δὲ αὐτῶν λαλούντων αὐτὸς ἔστη ἐν μέσῳ αὐτῶν.
3. ἔβλεψαν σὺν αὐτοῖς ἑστῶτα τὸν ἄνθρωπον τὸν τεθεραπευμένον.
4. εἰ δὲ ὁ Σατανᾶς τὸν Σατανᾶν ἐκβάλλει, ἐφ᾽ ἑαυτὸν ἐμερίσθη· πῶς οὖν σταθήσεται ἡ βασιλεία αὐτοῦ;
5. τὰ νῦν παραγγέλλει ὁ θεὸς τοῖς ἀνθρώποις πάντας πανταχοῦ μετανοεῖν, ὅτι κατέστησεν ἡμέραν ἐν ᾗ μέλλει κρίνειν τὴν οἰκουμένην ἐν δικαιοσύνῃ.
6. ὁ Φαρισαῖος σταθεὶς ταῦτα πρὸς ἑαυτὸν προσηύχετο.
7. ὁ δὲ τελώνης μακρόθεν[2] ἑστῶς οὐκ ἤθελεν οὐδὲ τοὺς ὀφθαλμοὺς ἐπᾶραι εἰς τὸν οὐρανόν.
8. ὁ δὲ Ἰησοῦς ἐστάθη ἔμπροσθεν τοῦ ἡγεμόνος.
9. θεὶς δὲ τὰ γόνατα ἔκραξεν φωνῇ μεγάλῃ· κύριε μὴ στήσῃς αὐτοῖς ταύτην τὴν ἁμαρτίαν.

1 πτερύγιον, "pinnacle"
2 μακρόθεν, "afar off"

10. μετὰ ταῦτα ἀνέστη Ἰούδας ὁ Γαλιλαῖος ἐν ταῖς ἡμέραις τῆς ἀπογραφῆς[1] καὶ ἀπέστησε λαὸν ὀπίσω αὐτοῦ.
11. εἰ Μωϋσέως καὶ τῶν προφητῶν οὐκ ἀκούουσιν, οὐδ᾽ ἐάν τις ἐκ νεκρῶν ἀναστῇ πεισθήσονται.
12. εἶπεν δὲ τῷ ἀνδρὶ τῷ ξηρὰν ἔχοντι τὴν χεῖρα· ἔγειρε καὶ στῆθι εἰς τὸ μέσον· καὶ ἀναστὰς ἔστη.

35.2(β) Translate the following sentences (part 2):

1. ἄνθρωπε, τίς με κατέστησεν κριτὴν ἢ μεριστὴν[2] ἐφ᾽ ὑμᾶς;
2. οὐδεὶς δύναται ἐλθεῖν πρός με ἐὰν μὴ ὁ πατὴρ ὁ πέμψας με ἑλκύσῃ αὐτόν, καὶ ἀναστήσω αὐτὸν ἐν τῇ ἐσχάτῃ ἡμέρᾳ.
3. ἡ μήτηρ καὶ οἱ ἀδελφοὶ αὐτοῦ εἱστήκεισαν ἔξω ζητοῦντες αὐτῷ λαλῆσαι.
4. οἱ ὑποκριταὶ φιλοῦσιν ἐν ταῖς συναγωγαῖς ἑστῶτες προσεύχεσθαι, ὅπως φανῶσιν τοῖς ἀνθρώποις.
5. δοὺς δὲ αὐτῇ χεῖρα ἀνέστησεν αὐτήν.
6. τὸ δὲ πνεῦμα ῥητῶς[3] λέγει ὅτι ἐν ὑστέροις καιροῖς ἀποστήσονταί τινες τῆς πίστεως.
7. πῶς ὁμοιώσωμεν τὴν βασιλείαν τοῦ θεοῦ, ἢ ἐν τίνι αὐτὴν παραβολῇ θῶμεν;
8. ὁ δὲ Ἰησοῦς ἐπιλαβόμενος παιδίον ἔστησεν αὐτὸ παρ᾽ ἑαυτῷ.
9. πορεύεσθε καὶ σταθέντες λαλεῖτε ἐν τῷ ἱερῷ τῷ λαῷ πάντα τὰ ῥήματα τῆς ζωῆς ταύτης.
10. καὶ καταβαινόντων αὐτῶν ἐκ τοῦ ὄρους ἐνετείλατο[4] αὐτοῖς ὁ Ἰησοῦς λέγων· μηδενὶ εἴπητε τὸ ὅραμα ἕως οὗ ὁ υἱὸς τοῦ ἀνθρώπου ἐκ νεκρῶν ἀναστῇ.

1 ἀπογραφῆς, "census"
2 μεριστὴν, "a divider"
3 ῥητῶς, "expressly"
4 ἐνετείλατο, third-person singular first aorist middle from ἐντέλλω

11. οἷς καὶ παρέστησεν ἑαυτὸν ζῶντα μετὰ τὸ παθεῖν αὐτὸν ἐν πολλοῖς τεκμηρίοις.
12. καὶ προσελθὼν ἥψατο τῆς σοροῦ,[1] οἱ δὲ βαστάζοντες ἔστησαν.
13. καὶ ἔστησαν μάρτυρας ψευδεῖς λέγοντας·
ὁ ἄνθρωπος οὗτος οὐ παύεται λαλῶν ῥήματα κατὰ τοῦ τόπου τοῦ ἁγίου.
14. ἀγάγοντες δὲ αὐτοὺς ἔστησαν ἐν τῷ συνεδρίῳ.

Composition Exercises

35.3 Translate the following sentences into Greek:

1. I will cause you to stand before Caesar for my name's sake.[2]
2. The righteous will stand in the kingdom of their Father.
3. Paul therefore stood before Festus.[3]
4. The priests caused the tax collector to stand in the middle of the marketplace.
5. But Peter stood up and preached the word to the multitude.
6. He is not here, for he has risen[4] from the dead.[5]
7. Who appointed you to be the ruler of this people?
8. Then we arose and departed from the city.
9. You all made the king to stand in the holy place.
10. In the last days many departed from the faith.
11. We stood outside,[6] wishing to see the prophet.
12. Stand on your feet and take up your bed.
13. We hope to stand before the Lord in that day.
14. Then the spirit of the Lord lifted me up and caused me to stand on the waters.

1 σοροῦ, "coffin"
2 Use ἕνεκα + genitive ("for the sake of").
3 "Festus," Φῆστος, -ου
4 Use second (athematic) aorist of ἀνίστημι ("has risen").
5 "from the dead," ἐκ νεκρῶν ("dead people" is implied)
6 "outside," ἔξω

15. After these things many robbers arose and led away many people after them.
16. If any man believes in me I will raise him up at the last day.
17. We commanded the soldiers to stand apart from the multitude.
18. How will we stand in the day of his wrath?[1]
19. And standing up he cried with a loud voice, "Stand apart from these men and make them to stand beside the king."
20. Those who heard these things stood still.

Scripture Translation Exercises

35.4 Translate the following verses from Scripture:

1. εἶπεν δέ τις αὐτῷ· ἰδοὺ ἡ μήτηρ σου καὶ οἱ ἀδελφοί σου ἔξω ἑστήκασιν ζητοῦντές σοι λαλῆσαι (Matt 12:47)
2. ἔφη αὐτῷ ὁ κύριος αὐτοῦ· εὖ, δοῦλε ἀγαθὲ καὶ πιστέ, ἐπὶ ὀλίγα ἦς πιστός, ἐπὶ πολλῶν σε καταστήσω· εἴσελθε εἰς τὴν χαρὰν τοῦ κυρίου σου (Matt 25:21)
3. καὶ λαβὼν παιδίον ἔστησεν αὐτὸ ἐν μέσῳ αὐτῶν (Mark 9:36)
4. ὁ δὲ ἀποκριθεὶς εἶπεν αὐτοῖς· τί ὑμῖν ἐνετείλατο Μωϋσῆς; (Mark 10:3)
5. ἀναστὰς δὲ ἀπὸ τῆς συναγωγῆς εἰσῆλθεν εἰς τὴν οἰκίαν Σίμωνος (Luke 4:38)
6. εἶπεν δὲ τῷ ἀνδρὶ τῷ ξηρὰν ἔχοντι τὴν χεῖρα· ἔγειρε καὶ στῆθι εἰς τὸ μέσον· καὶ ἀναστὰς ἔστη (Luke 6:8)

1 "wrath," ὀργή, -ῆς, ἡ

LESSON 36

Other Athematic Verbs and οἶδα

The verb ἵημι occurs in the New Testament only in compounds, the most common of which are:

ἀφίημι ("I send away, I let go, I forgive")

συνίημι ("I understand")

ἵημι IN COMPOUNDS

The verbal root of ἵημι is ἑ-. Its general meaning refers to sending. (The root, ἑ-, is very similar to the root of εἰμι, which is ἐς-.) In the first principal part (present and imperfect forms) the rough breathing passes to the reduplicating syllable, which is ι. Since the rough breathing is part of the root and not generated through the reduplication of a consonant, all principal parts for the verb incorporate the rough breathing. The rough breathing will affect prepositional prefixes (i.e., changing ἀπο- to ἀφ- throughout its principal parts).[1] Also note that the root vowel is lengthened before the ending -μι, as in τίθημι. Analogous to other athematic verbs, perfect forms lengthen differently and the root vowel does not lengthen at all in the sixth principal part (aorist passive).

PRINCIPAL PARTS OF ἵημι

1	2	3	4	5	6
ἵημι ἀφίημι	ἥσω ἀφήσω	ἧκα ἀφῆκα	— ἀφεῖκα	εἷμαι ἀφεῖμαι	ἕθην ἀφέθην
EXAMPLES:					
Luke 7:49 ἀφίησιν	Matt 6:14 ἀφήσει	Matt 6:12 ἀφήκαμεν	—	Heb 12:12 παρειμένας	Rom 4:7 ἀφέθησαν

1 See elision in Lesson 2.

PRESENT AND IMPERFECT FORMS OF ἀφίημι

The forms of ἀφίημι ("send away," "forgive," or "leave") given below are those that occur most frequently in the New Testament. Some persons within the conjugation (such as the second person singular and the first and third person plural of the present indicative) are formed as if coming from ἀφίω or ἀφέω; this is because, over time, athematic verbs have a tendency to adopt thematic stems and associated regular endings (using the regular pattern beginning with ω). It is only important that you be able to recognize either of these variations in context at this point; it is not necessary to memorize which personal endings prefer which root forms. In composition, a correctly spelled form from either root would have been understood at the time.

Prepositional Prefix Takes Augment

Note that in the imperfect, the preposition—not the stem—receives the augment. This is helpful since the augment would not be visible if it were merely represented by a long ι. The secondary endings mark past time. As with other athematic verbs, subjunctive forms use standard lengthened stems (like regular verbs) that replace the root vowel. Forms appearing in blue do not occur in the New Testament but are listed here for comparison with other ἵημι compounds.

Present & Imperfect Active Forms

	Present Indicative	Present Imperative	Present Subjunctive	Imperfect Indicative
1 sg.	ἀφίημι		ἀφιῶ	ἄφιον
2 sg.	ἀφεῖς[1]	ἀφίει	ἀφιῇς	ἄφιες
3 sg.	ἀφίησι(ν)	ἀφιέτω	ἀφιῇ	ἄφιε(ν)
1 pl.	ἀφίεμεν[2]		ἀφιῶμεν	ἀφίομεν
2 pl.	ἀφίετε	ἀφίετε	ἀφιῆτε	ἀφίετε
3 pl.	ἀφίουσι(ν)[3]	ἀφιέτωσαν	ἀφιῶσι(ν)	ἄφιον
	Present Infinitive	**Present Participle**		
	ἀφιέναι	Nom. ἀφιείς,[4] ἀφιεῖσα, ἀφιέν Acc. ἀφιέντα, ἀφιεῖσαν, ἀφιέν		

Present & Imperfect Middle/Passive Forms

	Present Indicative	Present Imperative	Present Subjunctive	Imperfect Indicative
1 sg.	ἀφίεμαι		ἀφιῶμια	ἀφιέμην
2 sg.	ἀφίεσαι	ἀφίεσο	ἀφιῇ	ἀφίεσο
3 sg.	ἀφίεται	ἀφιέσθω	ἀφιῆται	ἀφίετο
1 pl.	ἀφιέμεθα		ἀφιώμεθα	ἀφιέμεθα
2 pl.	ἀφίεσθε	ἀφίεσθε	ἀφιῆσθε	ἀφίεσθε
3 pl.	ἀφίενται	ἀφιέσθων	ἀφιῶνται	ἀφίεντο
	Present Infinitive	**Present Participle**		
	ἀφίεσθαι	Nom. ἀφιέμενος, ἀφιεμένη, ἀφιέμενον		

1 from ἀφίω
2 or ἀφίομεν; from ἀφίω
3 from ἀφίω

4 Note how the ε root follows the same pattern learned for the ε stem for aorist passive participles. Also note that Rom 3:11 has συνίων for a masculine singular participle, drawing from the later regular form of the verb συνίω.

AORIST ACTIVE FORMS OF ἀφίημι

Aorist forms for performative verbs, such as "sending," are far more common than present forms. Only aorist active forms are summarized below. Aorist middle forms simply don't occur in the New Testament. Aorist passive forms can be easily derived from knowledge of the sixth principal part.

The third principal part functions like a sigmatic aorist (except the σ is replaced with a κ). The augment is reflected in the lengthened root vowel. Prepositional prefixes occur prior to augments.

Like other athematic verbs, the nonindicative forms use athematic aorist forms. The only difference between these forms and the present nonindicative forms is the absence of reduplication (no ι prior to the root vowel). The aorist imperative and subjunctive for these verbs are not uncommon.

Aorist Active Forms

	Indicative	Imperative	Subjunctive
1 sg.	ἀφῆκα		ἀφῶ
2 sg.	ἀφῆκας[1]	ἄφες	ἀφῇς
3 sg.	ἀφῆκε(ν)	ἀφέτω	ἀφῇ
1 pl.	ἀφήκαμεν		ἀφῶμεν
2 pl.	ἀφήκατε	ἄφετε	ἀφῆτε
3 pl.	ἀφῆκαν	ἀφέτωσαν	ἀφῶσι(ν)

Aorist Infinitive	Aorist Participle
ἀφεῖναι	Nom. ἀφείς, ἀφεῖσα, ἀφέν
	Acc. ἀφέντα, ἀφεῖσαν, ἀφέν

1 Rev 2:4 has ἀφῆκες instead.

-νυμι VERBS

There is also another class of athematic verbs that adds νυ to the verbal root to create a present root spelling for the present and imperfect tenses. These will conjugate like τίθημι but have υ instead of ε. These verbs were also in the process of becoming regular thematic verbs, so you may find some of these roots with regular stems and endings.

Verbal Root	Present Active Indicative
δεικ-	δείκνυμι
ὀλ-	ὄλλυμι (ὄλνυμι)
ζω-	ζώννυμι

DEPONENT ATHEMATIC VERBS

There are a number of other common athematic verbs in Greek; most of these are deponent. This makes their spelling patterns easy to learn and intuit. The personal endings for the middle voice are the same for thematic and athematic verbs. They all begin with a consonant, so they follow the verb's root vowel without unexpected contractions.

The verbs δύναμαι ("I am able") and ἐπίσταμαι ("I know") are conjugated like the present passive of ἵστημι. Notice that the imperfect has a double augment (η instead of ε). The aorist passive ἠδυνήθην also generally has a double augment.

	Present & Imperfect Deponent (Middle) Forms	
	Present Indicative	Imperfect Indicative
1 sg.	δύναμαι	ἠδυνάμην
2 sg.	δύνασαι (δύνῃ)	ἠδύνασο
3 sg.	δύναται	ἠδύνατο
1 pl.	δυνάμεθα	ἠδυνάμεθα
2 pl.	δύνασθε	ἠδύνασθε
3 pl.	δύνανται	ἠδύναντο
	Present Infinitive	Present Participle
	δύνασθαι	δυνάμενος, -η, -ον

οἶδα The verb οἶδα is a perfect[1] derived from the present form, εἴδω, that had passed out of use by the New Testament period. The original perfect tense of this verb focused so strongly on the present result of having observed or recognized (which effectively means "knowing") that it is simply used as a present tense verb meaning "I know." The pluperfect form is used as a simple past, "I knew."

Here are the moods and tenses of οἶδα ("I know") that are found in the New Testament. Forms that don't occur in the New Testament are in blue.

	Perfect Active (Used as Present)			Pluperfect Active (Used as Past)
	Indicative	Imperative	Subjunctive	Indicative
1 sg.	οἶδα		εἰδῶ	ᾔδειν
2 sg.	οἶδας	ἴσθι[2]	εἰδῇς	ᾔδεις
3 sg.	οἶδε(ν)	ἴστω	εἰδῇ	ᾔδει
1 pl.	οἴδαμεν		εἰδῶμεν	ᾔδειμεν
2 pl.	οἴδατε	ἴστε[3]	εἰδῆτε	ᾔδειτε
3 pl.	οἴδασι(ν)[4]	ἴστωσαν	εἰδῶσι(ν)[5]	ᾔδεισαν

Infinitive	Participle	
εἰδέναι	Nom.	εἰδώς, εἰδυῖα, εἰδός
	Acc.	εἰδότα, εἰδυῖαν, εἰδός

1 It is not uncommon for perfect forms to change a root vowel to omicron (called o-grade). Cf. γέγονα, which is the perfect of γίνομαι.

2 Note that this is the same form as the second person singular of the present imperative of εἰμί.

3 Heb 12:17 is the only occurrence of this form in the New Testament, and the author uses it as an indicative.

4 Acts 26:4 has ἴσασι as an alternative to this indicative form.

5 Heb 8:11 uses this root to construct the only future indicative form of this verb in the New Testament: εἰδήσουσιν, "they will know."

EXERCISES

Memorization Exercises

36.1(α) Learn the parts of:

1. ἀφίημι, ἀφήσω, ἄφηκα, ἀφέωνται, ἀφεῖμαι, ἀφέθην
2. δύναμαι, δυνήσομαι, ἐδυνησάμην, —, δεδύνημαι, ἠδυνήθην
3. δείκνυμι, δείξω, ἔδειξα, δέδειχα, δέδειγμαι, ἐδείχθην
4. γράφω, γράψω, ἔγραψα, γέγραφα, γέγραμμαι, ἐγράφην

36.1(β) Learn Vocabulary List 30.

Translation Exercises

36.2 Translate the following sentences:

1. καὶ νῦν λέγω ὑμῖν· ἀπόστητε ἀπὸ τῶν ἀνθρώπων τούτων καὶ ἄφετε αὐτούς.
2. ὁ δὲ Ἰησοῦς εἶπεν αὐτῷ· ἄφες ἄρτι, οὕτω γὰρ πρέπον ἐστὶν ἡμῖν πληρῶσαι πᾶσαν δικαιοσύνην. τότε ἀφίησιν αὐτόν.
3. τότε συνῆκαν οἱ μαθηταὶ ὅτι περὶ Ἰωάννου τοῦ βαπτιστοῦ εἶπεν αὐτοῖς.
4. τίς δύναται ἀφιέναι ἁμαρτίας εἰ μὴ εἷς, ὁ θεός;
5. οἱ δὲ εὐθέως ἀφέντες τὰ δίκτυα ἠκολούθησαν αὐτῷ.
6. καὶ ἄφες ἡμῖν τὰ ὀφειλήματα ἡμῶν, ὡς καὶ ἡμεῖς ἀφήκαμεν τοῖς ὀφειλέταις ἡμῶν.
7. ἐὰν γὰρ ἀφῆτε τοῖς ἀνθρώποις τὰ παραπτώματα αὐτῶν, ἀφήσει καὶ ὑμῖν ὁ πατὴρ ὑμῶν ὁ οὐράνιος.
8. οἶδά σε τίς εἶ, ὁ ἅγιος τοῦ θεοῦ.
9. τότε δείκνυσιν αὐτῷ ὁ διάβολος πάσας τὰς βασιλείας τοῦ κόσμου.
10. πλανᾶσθε μὴ εἰδότες τὰς γραφὰς μηδὲ τὴν δύναμιν τοῦ θεοῦ.
11. ἐκείνοις δὲ τοῖς ἔξω ἐν παραβολαῖς τὰ πάντα γίγνεται, ἵνα ἀκούοντες ἀκούωσιν καὶ μὴ συνίωσιν.
12. θάρσει τέκνον, ἀφίενταί σοι αἱ ἁμαρτίαι.

13. τί ὅτι ἐζητεῖτέ με; οὐκ ᾔδειτε ὅτι ἐν τοῖς τοῦ πατρός μου δεῖ εἶναί με;
14. ᾔδει δὲ καὶ Ἰούδας ὁ παραδιδοὺς αὐτὸν τὸν τόπον.
15. πάτερ, εὐχαριστῶ σοι ὅτι ἠκούσας μου, ἐγὼ δὲ ᾔδειν ὅτι πάντοτέ μου ἀκούεις.
16. ταῦτα ἔγραψα ὑμῖν ἵνα εἴδητε ὅτι ζωὴν ἔχετε αἰώνιον.
17. θέλω δὲ ὑμᾶς εἴδεναι ὅτι παντὸς ἀνδρὸς ἡ κεφαλὴ ὁ Χριστός ἐστι.
18. καὶ οὐκ ἤφιεν τὰ δαιμόνια λαλεῖν ὅτι ᾔδεισαν αὐτόν.

Composition Exercises

36.3 Translate the following sentences into Greek:

1. Master, we know that you are true.
2. God will forgive all our sins if we believe on[1] his name.
3. Then the priests understood that he had spoken this parable against them.
4. But since they did not know this, they arose and went to Jerusalem.
5. Did you all understand all these things?
6. I forgave you all that debt.
7. I write this to you that you all may know that you all are saved.
8. Let these men alone that they may worship the God of their fathers.
9. How will I forgive you for this?
10. He did not allow the man who had been healed to follow him.
11. Know well that the Lord will not allow you to err.
12. I am not able to understand this unless[2] you teach me.

1 "on," εἰς

2 "unless," εἰ μή

13. Who is able to know all his faults?
14. They knew that their soldiers were of good courage.
15. Know that all your (pl.) faults will be forgiven.

36.4 Translate the following verses from Scripture (Matt 6:9–15):

Scripture Translation Exercises

9 Οὕτως οὖν προσεύχεσθε ὑμεῖς·
Πάτερ ἡμῶν ὁ ἐν τοῖς οὐρανοῖς·
ἁγιασθήτω τὸ ὄνομά σου·
10 ἐλθέτω ἡ βασιλεία σου·
γενηθήτω τὸ θέλημά σου,
ὡς ἐν οὐρανῷ καὶ ἐπὶ γῆς·
11 τὸν ἄρτον ἡμῶν τὸν ἐπιούσιον[1] δὸς ἡμῖν σήμερον·
12 καὶ ἄφες ἡμῖν τὰ ὀφειλήματα ἡμῶν,
ὡς καὶ ἡμεῖς ἀφήκαμεν τοῖς ὀφειλέταις ἡμῶν·
13 καὶ μὴ εἰσενέγκῃς ἡμᾶς εἰς πειρασμόν,
ἀλλὰ ῥῦσαι[2] ἡμᾶς ἀπὸ τοῦ πονηροῦ.
14 Ἐὰν γὰρ ἀφῆτε τοῖς ἀνθρώποις τὰ παραπτώματα
αὐτῶν, ἀφήσει καὶ ὑμῖν ὁ πατὴρ ὑμῶν ὁ οὐράνιος· 15 ἐὰν
δὲ μὴ ἀφῆτε τοῖς ἀνθρώποις, οὐδὲ ὁ πατὴρ ὑμῶν ἀφήσει
τὰ παραπτώματα ὑμῶν.

1 ἐπιούσιον, "daily"

2 ῥῦσαι, "deliver" (aorist middle imperative second person singular from ῥύομαι)

LESSON 37

Optative Mood and Periphrastic Constructions

THE OPTATIVE MOOD

The optative mood was fading out of use by the time of the New Testament. Only a few of its older uses were preserved during this time, and it rarely is used in the New Testament. Like the subjunctive mood, it only uses present and aorist stems. The only examples in the New Testament are limited to first person singular and third person plural forms.

Wishing

The optative mood generally expresses a wish in the New Testament. For example:

> ὦ παῖ, γένοιο πατρὸς εὐτυχέστερος.
> "O boy, may you become more fortunate than your father."

Used in Subordinate Clauses

Latin and English have a sequence of tenses (a subordinate verb must use a secondary tense if the governing verb is in a secondary tense). Ancient Greek had a sequence of moods. If the governing verb was a secondary tense and the dependent clause was indefinite, general, or otherwise would expect a subjunctive, the optative would be used instead. Luke occasionally uses the optative in this way within dependent questions, sometimes with the particle ἄν. For example:

1. καὶ αὐτοὶ ἤρξαντο συζητεῖν πρὸς ἑαυτοὺς τὸ τίς ἄρα εἴη ἐξ αὐτῶν ὁ τοῦτο μέλλων πράσσειν.
   "And they began to discuss among themselves which it should be of them who should do this." (Luke 22:23)

2. ὡς δὲ ἐν ἑαυτῷ διηπόρει ὁ Πέτρος τί ἂν εἴη τὸ ὅραμα ὃ εἶδεν, ἰδοὺ οἱ ἄνδρες οἱ ἀπεσταλμένοι ὑπὸ τοῦ Κορνηλίου ... ἐπέστησαν ἐπὶ τὸν πυλῶνα.
"And while Peter was doubting within himself what the vision should be that he had seen, behold, the men who had been sent by Cornelius ... stood before the door." (Acts 10:17)

The optative forms are provided in the table of verbs in the morphology summary at the end of this textbook. The optative of εἰμί is as follows:

Present Active Optative of εἰμί		
1 sg.	εἴην	may I be
2 sg.	εἴης	may you be
3 sg.	εἴη	may he/she/it be
1 pl.	εἴημεν	may we be
2 pl.	εἴητε	may you all be
3 pl.	εἴησαν	may they be

PERIPHRASTIC CONSTRUCTIONS

Like in English, biblical Greek tenses sometimes are formed with the verb "to be" and a participle. They are called "periphrastic constructions" because they are expressed in a roundabout way (περιφράζειν). Such constructions are another way to express an incomplete aspect: the subject exists in the state of doing x.

Periphrastic Imperfect

The periphrastic imperfect is formed of the imperfect of εἶναι and the present participle:

καὶ ἦν προάγων αὐτοὺς ὁ Ἰησοῦς.
"And Jesus was going before them." (Mark 10:32)

Periphrastic Perfect

The periphrastic perfect is formed of the present of εἶναι and the perfect participle:

> ὁ λαὸς καταλιθάσει ἡμᾶς, πεπεισμένος γάρ ἐστιν Ἰωάννην προφήτην εἶναι.
> "The people will stone us, for they are persuaded that John is a prophet." (Luke 20:6)

Periphrastic Pluperfect

The periphrastic pluperfect is formed of the imperfect of εἶναι and the perfect participle:

> καὶ ἦν ὁ Ἰωάννης ἐνδεδυμένος τρίχας καμήλου.
> "And John was clothed with camel's hair." (Mark 1:6)

Periphrastic Future

The periphrastic future is formed of the future of εἶναι and the present participle. This form of the tense has the force of a future continuous.

> ἀπὸ τοῦ νῦν ἀνθρώπους ἔσῃ ζωγρῶν.
> "From henceforth you will catch men." (Luke 5:10)

EXERCISES

Memorization Exercises

37.1 Learn Vocabulary List 31.

Translation Exercises

37.2 Translate the following sentences:

1. ἰδοὺ ἡ δούλη κυρίου· γένοιτό μοι κατὰ τὸ ῥῆμά σου.
2. καὶ πάντες διελογίζοντο ἐν ταῖς καρδίαις αὐτῶν περὶ τοῦ Ἰωάννου, μή ποτε αὐτὸς εἴη ὁ Χριστός.
3. τὸ ἀργύριόν σου σύν σοι εἴη εἰς ἀπώλειαν.
4. ἀκούσας δὲ ὄχλου διαπορευομένου[1] ἐπυνθάνετο τί ἂν εἴη τοῦτο.
5. ὁ δὲ θεὸς τῆς ὑπομονῆς δῴη[2] ὑμῖν τὸ αὐτὸ φρονεῖν ἐν ἀλλήλοις.
6. καὶ πᾶν τὸ πλῆθος ἦν τοῦ λαοῦ προσευχόμενον ἔξω τῇ ὥρᾳ τοῦ θυμιάματος.[3]
7. καὶ ἦν ὅλη ἡ πόλις ἐπισυνηγμένη πρὸς τὴν θύραν.
8. Ἰερουσαλὴμ ἔσται πατουμένη ὑπὸ τῶν ἐθνῶν.
9. ἐπηρώτων δὲ αὐτὸν οἱ μαθηταὶ αὐτοῦ τίς αὕτη εἴη ἡ παραβολή.
10. οὐ γάρ ἐστιν ἐν γωνίᾳ[4] πεπραγμένον τοῦτο.
11. καὶ ἦσαν οἱ μαθηταὶ Ἰωάννου νηστεύοντες.
12. εἶπεν δὲ ὁ Παῦλος· ἑστὼς ἐπὶ τοῦ βήματος[5] Καίσαρός εἰμι οὗ με δεῖ κρίνεσθαι.
13. ἦν γὰρ διδάσκων αὐτοὺς ὡς ἐξουσίαν ἔχων καὶ οὐχ ὡς οἱ γραμματεῖς αὐτῶν.
14. καὶ προσκαλεσάμενος ἕνα τῶν παίδων ἐπυνθάνετο τί ἂν εἴη ταῦτα.

1 διαπορευομένου, "passing by"
2 δῴη, from δίδωμι
3 θυμιάματος, "incense"
4 γωνίᾳ, "corner"
5 βήματος, "judgment seat"

Composition Exercises

37.3 Translate the following sentences into Greek, using the optative mood and periphrastic constructions where possible:

1. Then the blind man asked what this might be.
2. The disciples of Jesus were eating and drinking.
3. This thing has been done before many witnesses.
4. May it happen to us according to your will.
5. You will be walking the way of righteousness.
6. The disciples were disputing[1] who should be the greatest.
7. May all the workers of iniquity[2] perish.[3]
8. Then all the multitude was gathered together to the sea.
9. We desire to know what this saying may be.
10. May I become more like to you, O Lord.

Scripture Translation Exercises

37.4 Translate the following verses from Scripture (John 1:1–14):

1 Ἐν ἀρχῇ ἦν ὁ λόγος, καὶ ὁ λόγος ἦν πρὸς τὸν θεόν,
καὶ θεὸς ἦν ὁ λόγος. 2 οὗτος ἦν ἐν ἀρχῇ πρὸς τὸν θεόν.
3 πάντα δι᾽ αὐτοῦ ἐγένετο, καὶ χωρὶς αὐτοῦ ἐγένετο οὐδὲ
ἕν. ὃ γέγονεν 4 ἐν αὐτῷ ζωὴ ἦν, καὶ ἡ ζωὴ ἦν τὸ φῶς
τῶν ἀνθρώπων· 5 καὶ τὸ φῶς ἐν τῇ σκοτίᾳ[4] φαίνει, καὶ
ἡ σκοτία αὐτὸ οὐ κατέλαβεν.

6 Ἐγένετο ἄνθρωπος, ἀπεσταλμένος παρὰ θεοῦ,
ὄνομα αὐτῷ Ἰωάννης· 7 οὗτος ἦλθεν εἰς μαρτυρίαν ἵνα
μαρτυρήσῃ περὶ τοῦ φωτός, ἵνα πάντες πιστεύσωσιν

1 "disputing," συζητέω
2 "iniquity," ἀνομία , -ας, ἡ
3 "may … perish," ἀπόλλοιντο
4 σκοτίᾳ, "darkness"

δι᾽ αὐτοῦ. 8 οὐκ ἦν ἐκεῖνος τὸ φῶς, ἀλλ᾽ ἵνα μαρτυρήσῃ
περὶ τοῦ φωτός.

9 Ἦν τὸ φῶς τὸ ἀληθινόν,[1] ὃ φωτίζει[2] πάντα ἄνθρωπον,
ἐρχόμενον εἰς τὸν κόσμον. 10 ἐν τῷ κόσμῳ ἦν, καὶ
ὁ κόσμος δι᾽ αὐτοῦ ἐγένετο, καὶ ὁ κόσμος αὐτὸν οὐκ ἔγνω.
11 εἰς τὰ ἴδια ἦλθεν, καὶ οἱ ἴδιοι αὐτὸν οὐ παρέλαβον.
12 ὅσοι δὲ ἔλαβον αὐτόν, ἔδωκεν αὐτοῖς ἐξουσίαν τέκνα
θεοῦ γενέσθαι, τοῖς πιστεύουσιν εἰς τὸ ὄνομα αὐτοῦ,
13 οἳ οὐκ ἐξ αἱμάτων οὐδὲ ἐκ θελήματος σαρκὸς οὐδὲ ἐκ
θελήματος ἀνδρὸς ἀλλ᾽ ἐκ θεοῦ ἐγεννήθησαν.

14 Καὶ ὁ λόγος σὰρξ ἐγένετο καὶ ἐσκήνωσεν[3] ἐν ἡμῖν, καὶ
ἐθεασάμεθα τὴν δόξαν αὐτοῦ, δόξαν ὡς μονογενοῦς[4]
παρὰ πατρός, πλήρης χάριτος καὶ ἀληθείας.

1 ἀληθινόν, "genuine," "true"
2 φωτίζω, "illuminate," "give light to"
3 σκηνόω, "to tent," "to encamp"
4 μονογενοῦς, "one and only" (adjective)

APPENDIX 1

Vocabulary Lists

The verbs marked with * are compounded with prepositions. The same rules for elision apply when adding prepositions to verbs as apply to prepositions that are followed by separate words. See Lesson 2. Greek expands its vocabulary considerably by using prepositions in compounds. Learning to recognize the Greek root that follows the prepositional prefix will be an aid for learning additional vocabulary and for taking educated guesses about the meanings of unfamiliar words when reading Greek.

Principal parts in blue are not used in the New Testament. Dashes represent principal parts not used at all in Greek; words in gray indicate tenses that the student has not learned when the vocabulary list was first assigned in the memorization exercises. Greek words in parentheses are alternate spellings.

Parenthetical notes in the English column may include grammatical information or English derivatives. Bear in mind that derivatives don't necessarily reflect the meaning of the Greek vocabulary word.

VOCABULARY 1

ἀκούω	I hear (acoustics)
*ἀποθνῄσκω	I die ("thanatos" is a death instinct in psychology)
*ἀποστέλλω	I send (apostle)
βάλλω	I throw; put
βλέπω	I see; look at
γράφω	I write (graphic, telegraph)
ἐγείρω	I rouse; raise
ἐσθίω	I eat

εὑρίσκω	I find (heuristic)
ἔχω	I have
κρίνω	I judge (critic)
λαμβάνω	I take; receive (syllable)
λέγω	I say (Latin *lego* and words derived from it such as "lecture")
λύω	I release (analysis)
μένω	I remain; abide, dwell; continue
πιστεύω	I believe
σῴζω	I save (soteriology)

VOCABULARY 2

αἰτέω	I ask
ζητέω	I seek
θεωρέω	I behold (theory)
καλέω	I call
λαλέω	I speak
μαρτυρέω	I bear witness (martyr)
*παρακαλέω	I exhort; comfort (Paraclete)
ποιέω	I make; I do (poetry)
τηρέω	I keep safe; keep, observe
φιλέω	I love (philosophy)

VOCABULARY 3

In the following vocabulary lists, the second form -ου is the termination for the genitive case. It should be learned with the words thus—ἄγγελος, ἀγγέλου. It is useful to learn nouns in this way, because the genitive form identifies the noun stem (declension) and reveals an uncontracted root for some nouns. To identify the true gender for a noun, the vocabulary lists (and most lexicons and dictionaries) also provide the article (ὁ: masculine; ἡ: feminine; τό: neuter). When memorizing vocabulary, it is helpful to change the order and pronounce the article, the nominative form of the noun, and then the genitive (e.g., ὁ ἄγγελος, ἄγγέλου).

ἄγγελος, -ου, ὁ	angel, messenger
ἀδελφός, -οῦ, ὁ	brother (Philadelphia)
ἄνθρωπος, -ου, ὁ	man (anthropology)

ἀπόστολος, -ου, ὁ	apostle
ἄρτος, -ου, ὁ	bread; pl. "loaves"
δοῦλος, -ου, ὁ	slave, servant (doula)
θάνατος, -ου, ὁ	death (same root, θαν-, as ἀποθνῄσκω)
θεός, -οῦ, ὁ	God; god (theist, theology)
καί	and
κόσμος, -ου, ὁ	world (cosmic)
κύριος, -ου, ὁ	lord; Lord
λαός, -οῦ, ὁ	people (laity)
λόγος, -ου, ὁ	word, reason (the termination "-logy" in such words as "theology" comes from this word)
νόμος, -ου, ὁ	law (the termination "-nomy" in such words as "astronomy" comes from this word)
οἶκος, -ου, ὁ	house (economics)
ἔρημος, -ου, ἡ	desert
ὁδός, -οῦ, ἡ	way; road (Exodus)
παρθένος, -ου, ἡ	maiden, virgin (Parthenon)

VOCABULARY 4

All of the nouns in this list are neuter in spite of the fact that two of them mean "child."

ἀργύριον, -ου, τό	silver; money (periodic table symbol Ag)
βιβλίον, -ου, τό	book (Bible)
δαιμόνιον, -ου, τό	devil, demon
δένδρον, -ου, τό	tree (rhododendron)
εἰς	+ acc. into; to
ἐν	+ dat. in; on
ἔργον, -ου, τό	work (ergonomics)
εὐαγγέλιον, -ου, τό	gospel (evangelist)
ἱερόν, -οῦ, τό	temple (hierarchy)
ἱμάτιον, -ου, τό	garment
παιδίον, -ου, τό	young child (pedagogy)
πλοῖον, -ου, τό	boat; ship
πρόβατον, -ου, τό	sheep

πρόσωπον, -ου, τό	face
σάββατον, -ου, τό	Sabbath
σημεῖον, -ου, τό	sign, miracle (semiotics)
τέκνον, -ου, τό	child

VOCABULARY 5

ἀγάπη, -ης, ἡ	love
ἀλήθεια, -ας, ἡ	truth
ἁμαρτία, -ας, ἡ	sin (harmartiology)
ἀρχή, -ῆς, ἡ	beginning (archaic)
βασιλεία, -ας, ἡ	kingdom (basilica)
γῆ, γῆς, ἡ	earth, land (geology)
γραφή, -ῆς, ἡ	writing; in the pl. "the Scriptures"
δικαιοσύνη, -ης, ἡ	righteousness
εἰρήνη, -ης, ἡ	peace (Irene)
ἐκκλησία, -ας, ἡ	church, assembly (ecclesiastical)
ἐντολή, -ῆς, ἡ	commandment
ἐξουσία, -ας, ἡ	power
ἐπαγγελία, -ας, ἡ	promise
ζωή, -ῆς, ἡ	life (zoological)
ἡμέρα, -ας, ἡ	day (ephemeral)
καρδία, -ας, ἡ	heart (cardiac)
κεφαλή, -ῆς, ἡ	head (cephalopod)
παραβολή, -ῆς, ἡ	parable
σοφία, -ας, ἡ	wisdom (philosophy, i.e., the love of wisdom)
συναγωγή, -ῆς, ἡ	synagogue
φωνή, -ῆς, ἡ	voice; sound (telephone)
χαρά, -ᾶς, ἡ	joy
ψυχή, -ῆς, ἡ	soul (psychology)
ὥρα, -ας, ἡ	hour

VOCABULARY 6

ἀλλά	but
ἀπό	+ gen. from

βαπτιστής, -οῦ, ὁ	baptist
γάρ	for, because, since [postpositive word]
γλῶσσα, -ης, ἡ	tongue, language (glossary)
δέ	but; and [postpositive word]
δεσπότης, -ου, ὁ	master (despot)
δόξα, -ης, ἡ	glory (doxology)
ἐκ, ἐξ[1]	+ gen. out of
θάλασσα, -ης, ἡ	sea; lake
μαθητής, -οῦ, ὁ	disciple (mathematics)
νεανίας, -ου, ὁ	young man
οὐ, οὐκ, οὐχ[2]	not
οὖν	therefore, then [postpositive word]
πρό	+ gen. for; before
προφήτης, -ου, ὁ	prophet
σύν	+ dat. together with

VOCABULARY 7

ἀγαθός, -ή, -όν	good (Agatha)
ἀγαπητός, -ή, -όν	beloved
ἅγιος, -α, -ον	holy (hagiography)
αἰώνιος,[3] -ον	eternal (eon)
δίκαιος, -α, -ον	just, righteous
ἔσχατος, -η, -ον	last (eschatology)
ἕτερος, -α, -ον	different, another (heterodoxy)
ἴδιος, -α, -ον	one's own (idiosyncrasy, idiom) [κατ' ἰδίαν is a common idiom meaning "privately"]
κακός, -ή, -όν	bad (cacophony)
πιστός, -ή, -όν	faithful
πονηρός, -ά, -όν	wicked [ὁ πονηρός may refer to the Evil One]
πρῶτος, -η, -ον	first (protagonist)

1 The second form is used before a word beginning with a vowel

2 The last two forms are used before words that begin with a vowel—οὐκ prior to a smooth breathing mark, οὐχ prior to a rough breathing mark.

3 Note that αἰώνιος only uses o-stems (the second declension); the masc. ending is used with fem. as well as masc. nouns.

VOCABULARY 8

ἄγω	I drive, lead, bring
*ἀναγινώσκω	I read
*ἀποκτείνω	I kill
*ἀπολύω	I release
αὐτός, -ή, -ό[1]	he, she, it; himself, etc.; the same (automatic)
βαπτίζω	I baptize
διδάσκω	I teach (didactic)
δοξάζω	I glorify (doxology)
*ἐκβάλλω	I cast out
ἐκεῖνος, -η, -ο	that
Ἰησοῦς, -οῦ, ὁ	Jesus
Ἰουδαῖος, -αία, -αῖον	Jewish [often used substantively for a Jewish person]
Ἰωάννης, -ου, ὁ	John
κηρύσσω	I preach; proclaim
κράζω	I cry aloud, shout
οὗτος, αὕτη, τοῦτο	this
πείθω	I persuade
πέμπω	I send
*περιπατέω	I walk about
*συνάγω	I drive together, gather
υἱός, -οῦ, ὁ	son
*ὑπάγω	I depart
φέρω	I bear, carry (offer)
χαίρω	I rejoice

VOCABULARY 9

ἀπόστολος, -ου, ὁ	apostle
διά	+ gen. through (place or time), by means of + acc. on account of, because of
διδάσκαλος, -ου, ὁ	teacher

1 For the declension of adjectives ending on -o in the neut., see Lesson 12.

ἐργάτης, -ου, ὁ	workman, laborer
εὐθύς	immediately
θρόνος, -ου, ὁ	throne
Ἱεροσόλυμα, -ων, τα	Jerusalem [neut. pl.]
Ἰερουσαλήμ	Jerusalem [indeclinable fem. noun]
καρπός, -οῦ, ὁ	fruit
κριτής, -οῦ, ὁ	judge (critic)
λῃστής, -οῦ, ὁ	robber
λίθος, -ου, ὁ	stone (lithography)
μετά	+ gen. together with, in company with + acc. after
οἰκοδεσπότης, -ου, ὁ	head of household
οὐρανός, -οῦ, ὁ	heaven (Uranus)
ὀφθαλμός, -οῦ, ὁ	eye (ophthalmic)
ὄχλος, -ου, ὁ	crowd or multitude
πρεσβύτερος, -ου, ὁ	elder (presbyter)
πρός	+ acc. toward, to
τελώνης, -ου, ὁ	tax collector
τόπος, -ου, ὁ	place (topic)
ὑπό	+ gen. by + acc. under (hypodermic, hypothermia)
ὑποκριτής, -οῦ, ὁ	hypocrite
χρόνος, -ου, ὁ	time (chronology, chronic)

VOCABULARY 10

ἀγρός, -οῦ, ὁ	field (Latin *ager*, hence agriculture)
ἀδικία, -ας, ἡ	injustice, wickedness
ἁμαρτωλός, -οῦ, ὁ	sinner
*ἀπέρχομαι	I go away, depart
*ἀποκρίνομαι	I answer + dat. to whom
ἅπτομαι	I touch + gen. object
ἀρνέομαι	I deny
δέχομαι	I receive
*διέρχομαι	I go through, go about
ἐργάζομαι	I work

εὐαγγελίζομαι	I preach the gospel
ἔρχομαι	I come; go
Ἰσραήλ	Israel [indeclinable noun, masc.]
μή	not
οἰκοδομέω	I build
ὅς, ἥ, ὅ	who, which
πορεύομαι	I come; go; travel

VOCABULARY 11

ἄρχομαι	I begin
βούλομαι	I wish; want
γάμος, -ου, ὁ	wedding (monogamy)
δεῖ	it is necessary; it is right, fitting [impersonal verb]
δέομαι	I implore, plead, request + gen. [doesn't contract with omicron stem vowels]
διάβολος, -ου, ὁ	the devil
δύναμαι	I am able (dynamite) [present indicative δύναμαι, δύνασαι, δύναται, δυνάμεθα, δύνασθε, δύνανται; imperfect ἐδυνάμην, ἐδύνασο, ἐδύνατο, ἐδυνάμεθα, ἐδύνασθε, ἐδύναντο][1]
ἐγώ	I
ἐκεῖ	there
ἐλεύθερος, -α, -ον	free
*ἔξεστι	it is lawful [impersonal verb]
ἡμεῖς	we
θέλω	I am willing; wish; want
θεραπεύω	I heal (therapeutic)
Ἰορδάνης, -ου, ὁ	Jordan
καλός, -ή, -όν	good, beautiful
κελεύω	I command; order; urge

1 See Lesson 36 for morphological explanation.

μέν	[used to show contrasts between substantives, generally not translated]
οἰκία, -ας, ἡ	house
ὁμολογέω	I confess + dat. to whom
*παραγγέλλω	I command
Παῦλος, -ου, ὁ	Paul
πειράζω	I tempt; try (pirate)
πτωχός, -ή, -όν	poor
Σαμάρεια, -ας, ἡ	Samaria
σύ	you
τυφλός, -ή, -όν	blind
ὑμεῖς	you all
*ὑπακούω	I obey + dat. for person obeyed
ὧδε	here

VOCABULARY 12

ἀδικέω	I injure
*ἀνοίγω[1]	I open
ἄρχω	I rule + gen. [in the mid. voice "I begin"]
διακονέω	I serve + dat.
διάκονος, -ου, ὁ	servant, minister (deacon)
διώκω	I pursue
ἐλεέω	I have mercy on (eleemosynary)
ἐνδύω	I put on
εὐλογέω	I bless; praise (eulogy)
ἐχθρός, -ά, -όν	hated; as a noun "enemy"
*κατοικέω	I dwell in + ἐν or + dat.; settle, inhabit + acc.
ὅτι	because ; that [conj. for indirect statement]
*προφητεύω	I prophesy
σοφός, -ή, -όν	wise

1 When augmented, the prepositional prefix often receives the augment.

VOCABULARY 13

The two forms provided for verbs are first person present and future indicatives. These are the first two principal parts lexicons will provide for verbs. Dashes indicate principal part forms not used in ancient or biblical Greek. Principal parts in blue are forms that do not occur in the New Testament. * indicates that a preposition prefix is added to the verb root.

ἁγιάζω, —	I sanctify; consecrate; revere
ἀγοράζω, ἀγοράσω	I buy
*ἀπάγω, ἀπάξω	I drive away
*ἀποκαλύπτω, ἀποκαλύψω	I reveal (apocalypse)
βαστάζω, βαστάσω	I carry
ἐγγίζω, —	I draw near + dat. to whom or what
*ἐκκόπτω, ἐκκόψω	I cut off; cut out; remove
ἐλπίζω, ἐλπιῶ	I hope
ἑτοιμάζω, ἑτοιμάσω	I make ready; prepare
θαυμάζω, θαυμάσω	I wonder at + acc.
καθαρίζω, καθαριῶ	I cleanse (catharsis)
κρύπτω, κρύψω	I hide (crypt)
λεπρός, -οῦ, ὁ	leper
ποταμός, -οῦ, ὁ	river (Mesopotamia)
πράσσω, πράξω	I do (practice)
σκανδαλίζω, —	I cause to stumble; offend (scandalize)
τάσσω, τάξω	I set in order, arrange; appoint, designate (tactic)
ταχέως	quickly; soon
φυλάσσω, φυλάξω	I guard

VOCABULARY 14

Starting in this lesson, vocabulary lists will include the third principal part (aorist tense) for verbs. Principal parts in blue are forms that do not occur in the New Testament. Greek words in parentheses are alternate stem forms.

ἁμαρτάνω, ἁμαρτήσω, ἥμαρτον	I sin + dat. [or εἰς + acc.] for whom sinned against
ἀμνός, -οῦ, ὁ	lamb

βαίνω,[1] βήσομαι, ἔβην	I go
γινώσκω,[2] γνώσομαι, ἔγνων	I know
ὁράω, ὄψομαι, εἶδον	I see (panorama, optometry, video)
λέγω, ἐρῶ, εἶπον	I say, speak, tell
πάσχω, πείσομαι, ἔπαθον	I suffer (paschal, —, pathogen)
ἔχω, ἕξω,[3] ἔσχον	I have; hold
ἐσθίω, ἔδομαι, ἔφαγον	I eat
ἔρχομαι, ἐλεύσομαι, ἦλθον	I come; go
φέρω, οἴσω, ἤνεγκον	I carry; endure, bear
*καταλείπω, καταλείψω,[4] κατέλιπον	I leave behind
μανθάνω, μαθήσομαι, ἔμαθον	I learn
οἶνος, -ου, ὁ	wine
πίνω, πίομαι, ἔπιον	I drink
πίπτω, πεσοῦμαι, ἔπεσον	I fall
πολλά[5]	many things
τίκτω, τέξομαι, ἔτεκον	I beget, give birth to; produce, bring forth
φεύγω, φεύξομαι, ἔφυγον	I flee
ὦ	O!

VOCABULARY 15

ἀδύνατος, -η, -ον	impossible
Αἴγυπτος, -ου, ἡ	Egypt
αἴρω, ἀρῶ, ἦρα	I take up; take away, remove from service
*ἀπαγγέλλω, ἀπαγγελῶ, ἀπήγγειλα	I announce; report
Βηθλεέμ	Bethlehem [indeclinable]
δυνατός, -ή, -όν	possible
ἕως	while, until
Ἡρῴδης, -ου, ὁ	Herod
Ἰωσήφ	Joseph [indeclinable]
καιρός, -οῦ, ὁ	time, season

1 Occurs only with prepositional prefixes.
2 The older present form is γιγνώσκω.
3 Note the rough breathing for this principal part.
4 Exceptional present root in the future.
5 Nom./acc. pl. of the adjective πολύς, πολλή, πολύ (cf. Vocabulary List 18).

*κατακρίνω, κατακρινῶ, κατέκρινα	I condemn
κλίνη, -ης, ἡ	bed, couch (recliner)
Κορνήλιος, -ου, ὁ	Cornelius
κώμη, -ης, ἡ	village
Μαριάμ	Mary [indeclinable]
Μαρία, -ας, ἡ	Mary
μάχαιρα, -ας, ἡ	sword
ὀπίσω	after, behind + gen.
ὅτε	when
ὀφείλω (ὀφειλέω),[1] ὀφειλήσω, ὠφείλησα	I owe; I ought + inf.
πάντα[2]	all things
παρά	+ gen. from beside; from (of persons); + acc. to the side of; beside (of places); + dat. near; at the house of (of persons)
παραλυτικός, -οῦ, ὁ	paralytic
ποτήριον, -ου, ὁ	cup
σπείρω, σπερῶ, ἔσπειρα	I sow
σταυρός, -οῦ, ὁ	cross
στρατιώτης, -ου, ὁ	soldier
φαίνω, φανῶ, ἔφανα	I shine; pass. appear, be seen
Φαρισαῖος, -ου, ὁ	Pharisee
φθείρω, φθερῶ, ἔφθειρα	I destroy
φυλή, -ῆς, ἡ	tribe
χήρα, -ας, ἡ	widow
ὡς	when, as

VOCABULARY 16

αἰών, αἰῶνος, ὁ	age
ἀλέκτωρ, ἀλέκτορος, ὁ	rooster
ἀμπελών, ἀμπελῶνος, ὁ	vineyard
ἄρχων, ἄρχοντος, ὁ	ruler (monarchy)
ἀστήρ, ἀστέρος, ὁ	star (asteroid)

1 Alternate present tense spelling.
2 Nom./acc. pl of the adjective πᾶς, πᾶσα, πᾶν (cf. Vocabulary List 18).

εἰκών, εἰκόνος, ἡ	image (icon)
ἐλπίς, ἐλπίδος, ἡ	hope
ἡγεμών, ἡγεμόνος, ὁ	leader, governor (hegemony)
θύρα,-ας, ἡ	door
λαμπάς, λαμπάδος, ἡ	lamp
μήν, μηνός, ὁ	month
νυμφίος, -ου, ὁ	bridegroom, groom (nymph)
νύξ, νυκτός, ἡ	night
ὀδούς, ὀδόντος, ὁ	tooth (orthodontist)
παῖς, παιδός, ὁ or ἡ	child, boy or girl (pedagogue)
Πέτρος, -ου, ὁ	Peter
ποιμήν, ποιμένος, ὁ	shepherd
σάλπιγξ, σάλπιγγος, ἡ	trumpet
σάρξ, σαρκός, ἡ	flesh (sarcophagus)
σωτήρ, σωτῆρος, ὁ	savior (soteriology)
τρεῖς, τρία[1]	three
φύλαξ, φύλακος, ὁ	guard (phylactery)
φωνέω	I call; make a noise
χάρις, χάριτος, ἡ	grace, favor (charity)
χιτών, χιτῶνος, ὁ	garment, especially an undergarment or shirt

VOCABULARY 17

αἷμα, αἵματος, τό	blood (hemorrhage)
ἀνήρ, ἀνδρός, ὁ	man, husband (android)
ἄφεσις, ἀφέσεως, ἡ	remission, forgiveness [declines like πόλις]
βάπτισμα, βαπτίσματος, τό	baptism
βασιλεύς, βασιλέως, ὁ	king (basilica)
γένος, γένους, τό	race; nation; generation (genesis)
γόνυ, γόνατος, τό	knee
γράμμα, γράμματος, τό	letter of the alphabet; pl. document
γραμματεύς, γραμματέως, ὁ	scribe (grammarian)
γυνή, γυναικός, ἡ	woman; wife (misogynist) [exceptional nom.]

1 This number functions as an adjective. See p. 440 for its full paradigm.

ἐπιστολή, -ῆς, ἡ	letter (epistle)
ἔτος, ἔτους, τό	year [declines like γένος]
θέλημα, θελήματος, τό	will, desire
θρίξ, τριχός, ἡ	hair [guttural]
θυγάτηρ, θυγατρός, ἡ	daughter [irregular]
ἰχθύς, ἰχθύος, ὁ	fish (acc. sg. ἰχθύν)
κύων, κυνός, ὁ	dog (cynic, cynical) [nasal]
κωφός, -ή, -όν	deaf; mute; deaf and mute [adj.]
μετάνοια, ας, ἡ	repentance [first declension]
μήτηρ, μητρός, ἡ	mother (Latin *mater*) [irregular]
οὖς, ὠτός, τό	an ear [acc. pl. common ὦτα]
πατήρ, πατρός, ὁ	father (Latin *pater*)
πνεῦμα, πνεύματος, τό	spirit, wind (pneumatic)
πόλις, πόλεως, ἡ	city (politics)
ποῦς, ποδός, ὁ	foot (podiatrist, cephalopod)
πῦρ, πυρός, τό	fire (pyrotechnics)
τέρας, τέρατος, τό	wonder, miracle
ὕδωρ, ὕδατος, τό	water (hydraulic, hydroelectric)
φῶς, φωτός, τό	light (photon, phosphorus)
χείρ, χειρός, ἡ	hand (chiropractor)

VOCABULARY 18

ἀληθής, ἀληθές	true
ἀνάστασις, ἀναστάσεως, ἡ	resurrection (Anastasia)
ἀρχιερεύς, ἀρχιερέως, ὁ	high priest [ἀρχ- + ἱερόν]
ἀσθενής, -ές	weak; sick
ἄφρων, ἄφρον	foolish
γονεύς, γονέως, ὁ	progenitor, ancestor; in the pl. parents [related to γένος ("generation") with an o-grade root vowel, not γόνυ ("knee")]
Δαυίδ (Δαβίδ), ὁ	David [indeclinable]
ἔθνος, ἔθνους, τό	race; in the pl. the gentiles (ethnic) [looks masc. but is really neut.; cf. γένος in Lesson 22]

εἰ	if
εἷς, μία, ἕν	one (hendiadys)
ἤ	than
ἱερεύς, ἱερέως, ὁ	priest (hierarchy)
κρίμα, κρίματος, τό	judgment, sentence, condemnation
κρίσις, κρίσεως, ἡ	judgment (crisis)
μᾶλλον	more [adverb]
μέγας, μεγάλη, μέγα	great
μηδείς, μηδεμία, μηδέν	no one [with the impv., inf., etc.]
μηκέτι	no more
νεκρός, -ά, -όν	dead (necropolis)
ὄνομα, ὀνόματος, τό	name (synonym)
ὄρος, ὄρους, τό	hill; mountain [neut. following γένος; cf. Lesson 22]
οὐδείς, οὐδεμία, οὐδέν	no one [with the indic.]
πᾶς, πᾶσα, πᾶν	all; every (pandemic, pangea, panacea)
πίστις, πίστεως, ἡ	faith
πολύς, πολλή, πολύ	many; much (polygon)
ῥῆμα, ῥήματος, τό	word; saying
σκότος, σκότους, τό	darkness
σπέρμα, σπέρματος, τό	seed (sperm)
στόμα, στόματος, τό	mouth (stomach)
σῶμα, σώματος, τό	body (somatic)
ὑγιής, ὑγιές	whole, healthy (hygienic)

VOCABULARY 19

ἀκάθαρτος, -ον	unclean (catharsis)
*ἀμφιβάλλω, ἀμφιβαλλῶ,—	I throw around, throw on this side and that (especially used of net)
Ἀνανίας, -ου, ὁ	Ananias
Ἀνδρέας, -ου, ὁ	Andrew
Γαλιλαία, -ας, ἡ	Galilee
*διασπείρω, διασπερῶ, διέσπειρα	I scatter abroad, disperse

*εἰσέρχομαι, εἰσελεύσομαι, εἰσῆλθον	I go into, enter
*ἐξέρχομαι, ἐξελεύσομαι, ἐξῆλθον	I go out
Ἠλίας, -ου, ὁ	Elijah
μακάριος, -α, -ον	blessed
Μωϋσῆς, -έως, ὁ	Moses
*παραγίνομαι, —, παρεγενόμην, —, — παρεγενήθην[1]	I arrive, am present; draw near, come to, approach
*παράγω, —, παρήγαγον	I pass by [lit. I lead past]
πεντακισχίλιοι, -αι, -α	five thousand
πῶς	how
Σατανᾶς, gen. Σατανᾶ, ὁ	Satan [violates the α-pattern rule but has the persistent *alpha* in all forms; acc. Σατανᾶν; dat. Σατανᾷ]
Σίμων, Σίμωνος, ὁ	Simon
σπαράσσω, σπαράξω, ἐσπάραξα	I convulse, shake; rip apart
*συλλαλέω	I speak with [σύν + λαλέω]
τεσσεράκοντα	forty [indeclinable]
φοβέομαι, φοβηθήσομαι,[2] ἐφοβήθην[3]	I fear, am afraid
φόβος, -ου, ὁ	fear
χρῆμα, χρήματος, τό	money, nearly always used in the pl.

VOCABULARY 20

*ἀναχωρέω, —, ἀνεχώρησα	I depart
Ἄννας (gen. Ἄννα), ὁ	Annas
ἀπόκρισις, -εως, ἡ	answer
διδαχή, -ῆς, ἡ	teaching (didactic)
δίκτυον, -ου, τό	net
δύναμις, -εως, ἡ	power (dynamics)
δύο	two
ἐγγύς	near
*ἐκπλήσσομαι, —, —	I am astonished
*ἐπέρχομαι, ἐπελεύσομαι, ἐπῆλθον	I come upon

1 This is the sixth principle part form, the aor. pass.
2 This form is a future passive form that uses the sixth principal part (aorist passive) stem.
3 This is the sixth principle part form, the aor. pass.

ἐπί	+ acc. upon (placed on), up to, as far as; + gen. on, in the presence of, in the time of; + dat. on, at, on account of, in addition to
*ἐπιθυμέω, ἐπιθυμήσω, ἐπεθύμησα	I desire
ἐπιστάτης, -ου, ὁ	master
Ζαχαρίας, -ου, ὁ	Zacharias
Ἰόππη, -ης, ἡ	Joppa
Καιάφας (gen. Καιάφα), ὁ	Caiaphas
κατά	+ acc. down along; throughout; with regard to, according to; + gen. down from; down upon; against
κοπιάω, κοπιάσω, ἐκοπίασα	I toil; become weary
κρατέω, κρατήσω, ἐκράτησα	I seize; hold fast; attain
Λύδδα, -ας, ἡ	Lydda
μνημεῖον, -ου, τό	tomb
νεφέλη, -ης, ἡ	cloud
ὅλος, -η, -ον	whole
ὅσος, -η, -ον	as much as, how great, as many as, how much
ὅστις	whoever, but in the NT practically the same as ὅς, who
*παραλαμβάνω, παραλήμψομαι, παρέλαβον	I take with me
πέτρα, -ας, ἡ	rock
*προσέρχομαι, προσελεύσομαι, προσῆλθον	I go toward
*προσκαρτερέω, προσκαρτερήσω, προσεκαρτερήσα	I persist in; am devoted to + dat. of thing; I stick with + dat. with whom
στενός, -ή, -όν	narrow
συνέδριον, -ου, τό	council (Sanhedrin)
τίς, τί	who? which? what?
τις, τι	certain person, certain thing

VOCABULARY 21

Verbs in vocabulary lists now will include all principal parts for each verb. Words in parentheses are alternate forms for a principal part. A dash represents that the stem does not occur in ancient Greek. Principal parts in blue represent stems that do not occur in the New Testament. Principal parts in gray are stems that have not yet been introduced. * indicates that a verb has a prepositional prefix.

ἀληθῶς	truly
ἀπολούομαι, ἀπολούσομαι, ἀπελουσάμην, —, —, —	I wash away from myself
γίνομαι (γίγνομαι), γενήσομαι, ἐγενόμην, γέγονα, γεγένημαι, ἐγενήθην	I become [ἐγένετο "it happened, it came to pass" often + inf.]
*ἐκλέγομαι, ἐκλέξομαι, ἐξελεξάμην, —, ἐκλέλεγμαι, ἐξελέγην	I choose
*ἐπιβάλλω, ἐπιβαλῶ, ἐπέβαλον, ἐπιβέβληκα, —, ἐπεβλήθη	I cast upon; lay upon; put upon [aor. act. indic. third person pl. ἐπέβαλαν]
*ἐπικαλέω, ἐπικαλέσομαι, ἐπεκάλεσα, —, ἐπικέκλημαι, ἐπεκλήθην	I put a name on; mid. call upon, invoke
ἰδού	behold, look here
ἰσχυρός, -ά, -όν	strong
καταλαμβάνω, καταλήψομαι, κατέλαβον, κατείληφα, κατείλημμαι, κατελήμφθην	I overtake; take possession; mid. comprehend, perceive
λοιπός, -ή, -όν	the persons or things remaining [neut. pl. substantive "the rest"]
μέλλω, μελλήσω, —, —, —, —	I am about to; delay; tarry
μικρός, -ά, -όν	little
ναός, -οῦ, ὁ	the shrine of a temple, the holy place
νέος, -α, -ον	young, new
νῦν, νυνί	now, at this present time
ὁδοιπορέω, ὁδοιπορέω, —, ὡδοιπόρησα, ὡδοιπόρημαι, —, —	I travel; make my way [from ὁδός + πόρος "passage"]
οὐχί	an emphatic form of οὐ "not," especially used in questions that expect the answer "yes"
παλαιός, -ά, -όν	old

προσεύχομαι, προσεύξομαι, προσηυξάμην, —, —, —	I pray
ῥίπτω, ῥίψω, ἔ(ρ)ριψα, ἔρριφα, ἐ(ρ)ρίμμαι, ἐρρίφθην	I throw; cast
Σολομῶν, Σολομῶνος, ὁ	Solomon
συμβουλεύω, συμβουλεύσω, συνεβούλευσα, —, —,—	I advise; mid. consult; plot; consider
σχίσμα, -ατος, τό	rip, division (schism)
σωτηρία, -ας, ἡ	salvation
τί	why?
τρία	three [neut. of τρεῖς]
τροφή, -ῆς, ἡ	nourishment, meat, food
ὑπέρ	+ acc. above, beyond; + gen. on behalf of, for

VOCABULARY 22

ἀγαλλιάω, ἀγαλλιάσομαι,[1] ἠγαλλίασα, —, —, ἠγαλλιάθην	I rejoice greatly [typically mid., with same meaning]
ἀγαπάω, ἀγαπήσω, ἠγάπησα, ἠγάπηκα, ἠγάπημαι, ἠγαπήθην	I love
βοάω, βοήσω, ἐβόησα, βεβόηκα, βεβόημαι, ἐβώσθην	I cry out; shout; roar
γεννάω, γεννήσω, ἐγέννησα, γεγέννηκα, γεγέννημαι, ἐγεννήθην	I am born
δικαιόω, δικαιώσω, ἐδικαίωσα, —, δεδικαίωμαι ἐδικαιώθην	I justify
ἐάω, ἐάσω, εἴασα,[2] εἴακα, εἴαμαι, εἰάθην	I allow; permit
ἔξοδος, -ου, ἡ	departure (exodus)
ἐρωτάω, ἐρωτήσω, ἠρώτησα (ἠρόμην), ἠρώτηκα, ἠρώτημαι, ἠρωτήθην	I ask a question
ζάω, ζήσω, ἔζησα, ἔζωκα, —, —	I live
ἰάομαι, ἰάσομαι, ἰασάμην, —, ἴαμαι, ἰάθην	mid. dep. I heal; pass. I am healed

1 The contract α for this verb doesn't lengthen before consonant stems.
2 The augmented tenses begin with ει.

ὁράω, ὄψομαι, εἶδον, ἑώρακα or ἑόρακα, ὦμμαι, ὤφθην	I see
πληρόω, πληρώσω, ἐπλήρωσα, πεπλήρωκα, πεπλήρωμαι, ἐπληρώθην	I fill; fulfill
ποῦ	where?
* προσκυνέω, προσκυνήσω, προσεκύνησα, προσκεκύνηκα, —, προσεκυνήθην	I worship + dat.
πυνθάνομαι, πεύσομαι, ἐπυθόμην, —, πέπυσμαι, ἐπυθόμην	I inquire
σταυρόω, σταυρώσω, ἐσταύρωσα, —, ἐσταύρωμαι, ἐσταυρώθην	I crucify
ταπεινόω, ταπεινώσω, ἐταπείνωσα, —, τεταπείνωμαι, ἐταπεινώθην	I humble
ὑψόω, ὑψώσω, ὕψωσα, —, ὕψωμαι, ὑψώθην	I exalt (hyper)
φανερόω, φανερώσω, ἐφανέρωσα, πεφανέρωκα, πεφανέρωμαι, ἐφανερώθην	I make manifest

VOCABULARY 23

* εἰσάγω, εἰσάξω, εἰσήγαγον, εἰσαγήοχα, εἰσῆγμαι, εἰσήχθην	I lead in; bring in
Ἕλλην, Ἕλληνος, ὁ	Greek
* ἐπιγινώσκω, ἐπιγνώσομαι, ἐπέγνων, ἐπέγνωκα, —, ἐπεγνώσθην	I know
ἑπτά	seven (heptarchy)
καθώς	even as
κλέπτω, κλέψω, ἔκλεψα, κέκλοφα, κέκλεμμαι, ἐκλάπην	I steal (kleptomania)
κοιμάομαι, κοιμήσομαι, ἐκοιμησάμην, —, κεκοίμημαι, ἐκοιμήθην	I sleep
κοινόω, κοινώσω, ἐκοίνωσα, κεκοίνωκα, κεκοίνωμαι, ἐκοινώθην	I make common; defile; desecrate
Λάζαρος, -ου, ὁ	Lazarus
Μαγδαληνή, -ῆς, ἡ	Magdalene
πειρασμός, -οῦ, ὁ	temptation (pirate)

VOCABULARY 24

ἀθετέω, ἀθετήσω, ἠθέτησα, ἠθέτηκα, —, —	I set aside; disregard
ἀπολέσει	I will destroy, lose [fut. act. indic. 3 pl. from ἀπόλλυμι]
δέω, δήσω, ἔδησα, δέδεκα, δέδεμαι, ἐδέθην	I bind; fasten
εὖ	well; εὖ ποιεῖν means "to benefit"
παράδοσις, -εως, ἡ	tradition

VOCABULARY 25

ἅλας, ἅλατος, τό	salt
ἁλίζω, ἁλισθήσομαι, ἡλίσθην, —, ἥλισμαι, ἡλίσθην	I salt
αὔριον	adv. meaning "on the next day," ἡ αὔριον = tomorrow [with ἡμέρα implied]
γεύομαι, γεύσομαι, ἐγευσάμην, —, γέγευμαι, —	I taste + gen.
ἐνθάδε	here
*καταλύω, καταλύσω, κατέλυσα, καταλέλυκα, καταλέλυμαι, κατελύθην	I release thoroughly, destroy
μεριμνάω, μεριμνήσω, ἐμερίμνησα, —, μεμερίμνημαι, —	I am anxious for
μισθός, -οῦ, ὁ	reward, pay
νομίζω, νομιῶ, ἐνόμισα, νενόμικα, νενόμισμαι, ἐνομίσθην	I think
ὅραμα, ὁράματος, τό	vision
*περιβάλλω, περιβαλῶ, περιέβαλον, —, περιβέβλημαι, περιβλήθην	I cast around; (mid.) I dress myself
*περισσεύω, περισσεύσω, ἐπερίσσευσα, —, —, ἐπερισσεύθην	I surpass; have in abundance
σιωπάω, σιωπήσω, ἐσιώπησα, σεσιώπηκα, —, —	I am silent

VOCABULARY 26

ἀνομία, -ας, ἡ	lawlessness, wickedness
*ἀπαρνέομαι, ἀπαρνήσομαι, ἀπηρνησάμην, —, ἀπήρνημαι, ἀπηρνήθην	I deny
ἄργυρος, -ου, ὁ	silver
Ἀχελδαμάχ	Acheldama
γνωστός, -ή, -όν	known
δέσμιος, -ου, ὁ	prisoner
*ἐκπορεύομαι, ἐκπορεύσομαι, —, —, ἐκπεπόρευμαι, —	I go out
*ἐκφεύγω, ἐκφεύξομαι, ἐξέφυγον, ἐκπέφευγα, —, —	I escape
ἔξω	outside + gen.
θαμβέομαι, —, —, —, —, ἐθαμβήθην	I wonder; am astonished
θυσία, -ας, ἡ	sacrifice
Ἰάκωβος, -ου, ὁ	James
Καισαρεία, -ας, ἡ	Caesarea
καταλιθάζω, καταλιθάσω, —, —, —, —	I stone to death
λιθάζω, —, ἐλίθασα, —, —, ἐλιθάσθην	I stone
ὅμοιος, -α, -ον	like
περισσός, -ή, -όν	surpassing, great
πληθύνω, πληθυνῶ, ἐπλήθυνα, —, πεπλήθυμμαι, ἐπληθύνθην	I multiply
πλησίον	adv. meaning "near," hence ὁ πλησίον, "one's neighbor"
πρίν	before
*προσέχω, προσέξω, προσέσχον, προσέσχηκα, —, —	I am concerned for, care about, give heed to
*συζητέω, —, συνεζήτησα, —, —, —	I discuss; argue [from σύν + ζητέω]
*συνεσθίω, —, συνέφαγον, —, —, —	I eat with
σύρω, συρῶ, ἔσυρα, σέσυρκα, σέσυρμαι, ἐσύρην	I drag
τρίς	thrice, three times

Φῆστος, -ου, ὁ	Festus
Φίλιππος, -ου, ὁ	Philip
χρυσός, -οῦ, ὁ	gold

VOCABULARY 27

*ἀποδίδωμι, ἀποδώσω, ἀπέδωκα, —, ἀποδέδομαι, ἀπεδόθην	I give back; mid. I hand over for my own sake, hence "I sell"
δίδωμι, δώσω, ἔδωκα, δέδωκα, δέδομαι, ἐδόθην	I give
Καῖσαρ, Καίσαρος, ὁ	Caesar
μυστήριον, -ου, τό	mystery
*παραδίδωμι, παραδώσω, παρέδωκα, παραδέδωκα, παραδέδομαι, παρεδόθην	I give up; betray
ποῖος, -α, -ον	of what kind?
*προμεριμνάω, —, —, —, —, —	I am anxious beforehand
φυλακή, -ῆς, ἡ	watch, guard, prison
χωρίον, -ου, τό	a piece of land, a field

VOCABULARY 28

ἀγορά, -ᾶς, ἡ	marketplace
*ἀποσπάω, ἀποσπάσω, ἀπέσπασα, —, —, ἀπεσπάσθην	I draw out; pass. withdraw
ἀσθενέω, ἀσθενήσω, ἠσθένησα, ἠσθένικα, —, —	I am weak or sick
βολή, -ῆς, ἡ	toss, cast
δεξιός, -ά, -όν	right [side]
*εἰσπορεύομαι, εἰσπορεύσομαι, —, —, εἰσπεπόρευμαι, εἰσεπορεύθην	I go to
*εἰσφέρω, εἰσοίσω, εἰσήνεγκα (εἰσήνεγκον), —, εἰσενήνεγμαι, εἰσηνέχθην	I carry to
ἐνώπιον	before (of place) + gen.
καινός, -ή, -όν	new
καίω, καύσω, ἔκαυσα, —, κέκαυμαι, ἐκαύθην	I burn, I kindle
*κατευλογέω, —, —, —, —, —	I bless

κλάω, κλάσω, ἔκλασα, —, κέκλασμαι, ἐκλάσθην	I break
παραλυτικός, ή, όν	lame
*παρατίθημι, παραθήσω, παρέθηκα, —, —, παρεθέμην	I place beside, I set beside, I set before [of food]
τίθημι, θήσω, ἔθηκα, τέθεικα, τέθειμαι, ἐτέθην	I place, I lay down
τιμή, -ῆς, ἡ	honor

VOCABULARY 29

*ἀνίστημι, ἀναστήσω, ἀνέστην (ἀνέστησα), ἀνέστακα, —, ἀνεστάθην	transitive tenses "I cause to stand up," "I raise up"; intransitive "I stand up, rise, arise"
*ἀφίστημι, ἀποστήσω, ἀπέστην (ἀπέστησα), ἀφέστηκα, —, —	transitive tenses "I cause to stand away," "I remove, separate"; intransitive "I stand away from"
ἑλκύω, ἕλκυσω, εἵλκυσα, εἵλκυκα, εἵλκυσμαι, εἱλκύσθην	I drag
ἔμπροσθεν	+ gen. before
*ἐντέλλω, ἐντελοῦμαι, ἐνετειλάμην, —, ἐντέταλμαι, ἐντάλθην	I command
*ἐπαίρω, ἐπαρῶ, ἐπῆρα (ἔπαρον), ἐπῆρκα, ἔπηρμαι, ἐπήρθην	I raise up
*ἐπιλαμβάνομαι, ἐπιλήψομαι, ἐπελαβόμην, —, ἐπείλημμαι, —	I lay hold of + gen., I snatch, I take over
ἵστημι, στήσω, ἔστησα (ἔστην), ἕστηκα, ἕσταμαι, ἐστάθην	transitive tenses "I cause to stand"; intransitive "I stand"
*καθίστημι, καταστήσω, κατέστησα, καθέστακα, καθέσταμαι, καθεστάθην	I set up; establish; appoint
λύχνος, -ου, ὁ	lamp
μάρτυς, μάρτυρος, ὁ	witness (martyr)
μερίζω, μεριῶ, ἐμέρισα, μεμέρικα, μεμέρισμαι, ἐμερίσθην	I divide
μέσος, -η, -ον	middle

*μετανοέω, μετανοήσω, μετενόησα, —, —,—	I change my mind, repent
ξηρός, -ά, -όν	dry, withered
οἰκουμένη, -ης, ἡ	the inhabited land, the world
ὁμοιόω, ὁμοιώσω, ὡμοίωσα, —, ὡμοίωμαι, ὡμοιώθην	I make like; compare
πανταχοῦ	everywhere
*παρίστημι, παραστήσω, παρέστησα (παρέστην), παρέστηκα, —, παρεστάθην	transitive tenses "I cause to stand beside"; transitive "I present"
παύομαι, παύσομαι, ἐπαυσάμην, —, πέπαυμαι, ἐπαύθην	I cease
τεκμήριον, -ου, τό	certain proof
ὕστερος, -α, -ον	last
ψευδής, ές	false

VOCABULARY 30

ἀκολουθέω, ἀκολουθήσω, ἠκολούθησα, ἠκολούθηκα, —, —	I follow + dat.
*ἀφίημι, ἀφήσω, ἄφηκα, ἀφεῖκα, ἀφεῖμαι, ἀφέθην	I let go, I let alone, I allow, I forgive (ἀφέωνται, third person pl., is the only perf. pass. form that occurs in the NT)
δείκνυμι, δείξω, ἔδειξα, δέδειχα, δέδειγμαι, ἐδείχθην	I show
εὐθέως	immediately
εὐχαριστέω, —, ηὐχαρίστησα, —, —, ηὐχαριστήθην	I thank (Eucharist)
θαρσέω, —, ἐθάρσησα, —, —, —	I am brave; take courage
οἶδα, εἰδήσω, ᾔδειν, —, —, —[1]	I know
οὐράνιος, -α, -ον	heavenly
ὀφειλέτης, -ου, ὁ	debtor
ὀφείλημα, -ατος, τό	debt
πάντοτε	always
παράπτωμα, -ατος, τό	fault, transgression

1 The first and third principle parts for this verb are perfect and pluperfect in form but present and aorist in meaning.

πλανάω, πλανήσω, ἐπλάνησα, —, πεπλάνημαι, ἐπλανήθην	I err (planet)
πρέπει	it is fitting; proper; right (impersonal third person verb); inf. + dat. "It is fitting for [dat.] to perform [inf.]"; neut. periphrastic ptc. construction is also common (πρέπον ἐστίν, it is proper . . .)
*συνίημι, συνήσω, συνῆκα, συνεῖκα, —, —	I understand
τότε	then (at that time)

VOCABULARY 31

ἀλλήλων (gen. pl.)	one another (nom. not used)
ἀπώλεια, -ας, ἡ	destruction
*διαλογίζομαι, διαλογιοῦμαι, διελογισάμην, διαλελόγισμαι, —, —	I discuss
διαπορεύομαι, διαπορεύσομαι, —, —, —, διεπορεύθην	I make my way through
ἐπερωτάω, ἐπερωτήσω, ἐπηρώτησα, —, —, ἐπηρωτήθην	I ask
*ἐπισυνάγω, ἐπισυνάξω, ἐπισυνήγαγον (ἐπισυνῆξα), —, ἐπισυνῆγμαι, ἐπισυνήχθην	I gather together to
νηστεύω, νηστεύσω, ἐνήστευσα, νενήστευκα, —, —	I fast
πατέω, πατήσω, ἐπάτησα, —, —, ἐπατήθην	I trample on
*προσκαλέω, προσκάλεσω, προσεκάλεσα, —, προσκέκλημαι, προσεκλήθην	I call to; summon
*ὑπομονή, -ῆς, ἡ	patience
φρονέω, φρονήσω, ἐφρόνησα, πεφρόνηκα, —, —	I think

APPENDIX 2

Answer Key

Scripture translation exercises should be checked against an English Bible.

LESSON 1

Memorization Exercises

1.1 Alphabet memorization: See chart in lesson

1.2 Become familiar with transliteration: See chart in lesson

Grammar Exercises

1.3(α) Learn to recognize and pronounce digraphs:

1. ου
2. αι
3. ευ
4. υι
5. ει
6. ει
7. αυ
8. οι
9. ου
10. οι
11. υι
12. αυ
13. ευ
14. ου
15. αυ

1.3(β) Learn how to pronounce γ and χ:

Back Sounds	Forward Sounds
χα	γε
γου	χαι
γω	χε
γα	γυ
χου	χι
χω	γευ
	γη
	γι
	χοι

1.3(γ) Be able to distinguish δ and ϑ:

1. brother (δ)
2. theater (ϑ)
3. three (ϑ)
4. there (δ)
5. think (ϑ)
6. this (δ)
7. tithe (δ)
8. their (δ)
9. whether (δ)
10. thistle (ϑ)
11. thought (ϑ)
12. though (δ)
13. together (δ)
14. with (ϑ)
15. length (ϑ)

LESSON 2

Grammar Exercises

2.1(α) Accent mark exercises:

1. ἀδελφός (different accent location than English)
2. βιβλίον (different accent location than English)
3. γένεσις
4. δαυίδ (different accent location than English)
5. ἔξοδος
6. ζηλωτής (different accent location than English)
7. ἥλιος
8. θεός (different accent location than English)
9. Ἰησοῦς (different accent location than English)
10. προφήτης (may be different than English as in "prophecy" or the same as in "prophetic")

2.1(β) Elision exercises:

1. ἀπ᾽
2. ἐπ᾽
3. ὑπὸ
4. κατὰ
5. ἀπὸ
6. κατ᾽
7. διὰ
8. ὑπ᾽
9. καθ᾽
10. διὰ
11. παρ᾽
12. μεθ᾽
13. ἐπὶ
14. κατ᾽
15. ἀφ᾽
16. κατὰ
17. ἀφ᾽
18. παρὰ
19. ὑφ᾽
20. καθ᾽

2.1(γ) Square of stops exercises:

1. πτ
2. χθ
3. γβ
4. τκ
5. γδ
6. πτ
7. χφ
8. χθ
9. κτ
10. θθ
11. βδ
12. θφ
13. κτ
14. φθ
15. κπ

Transliteration Exercise

2.2 Greek transliteration exercise:

Ἐν ἀρχη ἠν ὁ λογος, και ὁ λογος ἠν προς τον θεον, και θεος ἠν ὁ λογος. οὑτος ἠν ἐν ἀρχῃ προς τον θεον. παντα δι' αὐτου ἐγενετο, και χωρις αὐτου ἐγενετο οὐδε ἑν. ὁ γεγονεν ἐν αὐτῳ ζωη ἠν, και ἡ ζωη ἠν το φως των ἀνθρωπων· και το φως ἐν τῃ σκοτιᾳ φαινει, και ἡ σκοτια αὐτο οὐ κατελαβεν. ἐγενετο ἀνθρωπος, ἀπεσταλμενος παρα θεου, ὀνομα αὐτῳ Ἰωαννης. οὑτος ἠλθεν εἰς μαρτυριαν ἱνα μαρτυρησῃ περι του φωτος, ἱνα παντες πιστευσωσιν δι' αὐτου. οὐκ ἠν ἐκεινος το φως, ἀλλ' ἱνα μαρτυρησῃ περι του φωτος. ἠν το φως το ἀληθινον, ὁ φωτιζει παντα ἀνθρωπον, ἐρχομενον εἰς τον κοσμον.

LESSON 3

Translation Exercises

3.2 Translation exercises:

1. he/she/it says
2. we say
3. they say
4. you all say
5. you say
6. we find
7. he/she/it writes
8. you all throw
9. he/she/it dies
10. you see
11. they lift
12. you all judge
13. we throw
14. I eat

15. they send
16. they hear
17. you all receive
18. we save
19. he/she/it remains
20. you throw

Composition Exercises

3.3 Composition exercises:

1. λύομεν
2. λύουσι
3. λύεις
4. λύετε
5. λύει
6. λύουσι
7. λύει
8. λύεις
9. ἀποθνῄσκουσι
10. ἀποθνῄσκει
11. βάλλω
12. ἐγείρει
13. κρίνομεν
14. μένεις
15. βάλλω
16. κρίνετε
17. ἀποστέλλει
18. γράφεις
19. ἐσθίεις
20. εὑρίσκει
21. λαμβάνομεν
22. βλέπουσι
23. ἀκούει
24. βάλλουσι
25. κρίνετε

LESSON 4

Translation Exercises

4.2 Translation exercises:

1. we speak
2. you ask
3. they keep
4. you all do
5. he/she/it exhorts
6. they bear witness
7. you all seek
8. I call
9. we behold
10. you keep

Composition Exercises

4.3 Composition exercises:

1. ζητοῦσι
2. αἰτεῖ
3. καλεῖς
4. μαρτυροῦμεν
5. λαλοῦσι
6. τηρεῖτε
7. παρακαλῶ
8. ποιεῖ
9. θεωρεῖς
10. φιλοῦμεν
11. καλοῦσι
12. αἰτεῖ
13. ζητοῦμεν
14. μαρτυροῦσι
15. θεωρεῖ

LESSON 5

Grammar Exercises

5.2(α) Case identification exercises:

1. κύριος, nom. sg.
2. ἁγιασμόν, acc. sg.
3. ἀγρούς, acc. pl.
4. ἄνθρωπον, acc. sg.
5. ἀποστόλῳ, dat. sg.
6. ἄρτου, gen. sg.
7. διδάσκαλοι, nom. pl.
8. δούλοις, dat. pl.
9. δούλων, gen. pl.
10. θεῷ, dat. sg.
11. κυρίου, gen. sg.
12. λόγοις, dat. pl.
13. ὁδούς, acc. pl.
14. οἴκους, acc. pl.
15. σταυρῷ, dat. sg.

5.2(β) Case composition exercises:

1. ἄγγελος, nom. sg. (nom. pl. = ἄγγελοι)
2. ἀδελφῶν, gen. pl. (gen. sg. = ἀδελφοῦ)
3. ἄνθρωπος, nom. sg. (nom. pl. = ἄνθρωποι)
4. ἀπόστολος, nom. sg. (nom. pl. = ἀπόστολοι)
5. ἀποστόλῳ, dat. sg. (dat. pl. = ἀποστόλοις)
6. ἄρτος, nom. sg. (nom. pl. = ἄρτοι)
7. διδάσκαλοι, nom. pl. (nom. sg. = διδάσκαλος)
8. ἐρήμου, gen. sg. (gen. pl. = ἐρήμων)
9. θανάτοις, dat. pl. (dat. sg. = θανάτῳ)
10. θεοί, nom. pl. (nom. sg. = θεός)

11. κυρίου, gen. sg. (gen. pl. = κυρίων)
12. λόγοις, dat. pl. (dat. sg. = λόγῳ)
13. ὁδούς, acc. pl. (acc. sg. = ὁδόν)
14. οἴκοις, dat. pl. (dat. sg. = οἴκῳ)
15. οἶκον, acc. sg. (acc. pl. = οἴκους)

5.3 Translation exercises:

Translation Exercises

1. A man has slaves.
2. An angel saves a people.
3. A lord writes words.
4. You are rousing a slave.
5. Men find a way.
6. A slave sees houses.
7. A man sends brothers.
8. You all receive a house.
9. A slave has a lord.
10. We are finding a way.
11. You all keep laws.
12. A man and a slave find brothers.

5.4 Composition exercises:

Composition Exercises

1. ἄνθρωπος ἀκούει ἄγγελον.
2. ἄγγελος ἐγείρει ἄνθρωπον.
3. δοῦλοι εὑρίσκουσιν ὁδόν.
4. ἀδελφὸς ἔχει οἶκον.
5. κύριοι ἀποστέλλουσι δούλους.
6. γράφουσι λόγους.
7. εὑρίσκετε ἄγγελον.
8. κύριος κρίνει ἀνθρώπους.
9. ἐγείρομεν δούλους.
10. τηρεῖς νόμους.
11. ἄνθρωπος καὶ ἄγγελος βλέπουσιν ὁδόν.
12. θεωρεῖς θάνατον.

LESSON 6

Grammar Exercises

6.2(α) Genitive and dative case identification exercises:

1. ἀποστόλῳ, dat. sg. — to/for an apostle
2. ἄρτοις, dat. pl. — to/for loaves
3. θεοῦ, gen. sg. — of God
4. ἀδελφῶν, gen. pl. — of brothers
5. ἀγγέλοις, dat. pl. — to/for angels
6. θανάτου, gen. sg. — of death
7. λόγων, gen. pl. — of words
8. νόμῳ, dat. sg. — to/for a law
9. ἐρήμοις, dat. pl. — to/for deserts
10. ὁδοῦ, gen. sg. — of a way

6.2(β) Case identification exercises:

1. οἶκον, acc. sg. — house (object)
2. νόμων, gen. pl. — of laws
3. κυρίους, acc. pl. — lords (object)
4. κόσμου, gen. sg. — of a lord
5. λαοῖς, dat. pl. — to/for peoples
6. οἶκος, nom. sg. — house (subject)
7. ὁδοί, nom. pl. — roads (subject)
8. ἀποστόλοις, dat. pl. — to/for apostles
9. ἀνθρώπων, gen. pl. — of men
10. ἄρτον, acc. sg. — bread (object)

6.2(γ) Accenting exercises:

1. λόγος (correct)
2. κόσμους
3. ἀποστόλῳ
4. ἀγγέλων (correct)
5. λαούς (correct)
6. ὁδοῖς
7. ἀγγέλου (correct)
8. ἄρτον
9. κυρίων
10. νόμους (correct)
11. θεοῦ
12. κόσμον (correct)
13. ἀδελφοῖς
14. οἶκοι
15. ἀπόστολος

6.2(δ) Case composition exercises:

1. ἄγγελον acc. sg. (acc. pl. = ἀγγέλους)
2. νόμοι nom. pl. (nom. sg. = νόμος)
3. κόσμοις dat. pl. (dat. sg. = κόσμῳ)
4. δούλους acc. pl. (acc. sg. = δοῦλον)
5. ἐρήμῳ dat. sg. (dat. pl. = ἐρήμοις)
6. κυρίου gen. sg. (gen. pl. = κυρίων)
7. ἀδελφῶν gen. pl. (gen. sg. = ἀδελφοῦ)
8. ἄρτος nom. sg. (nom. pl. = ἄρτοι)
9. ἄνθρωπον acc. sg. (acc. pl. = ἀνθρώπους)
10. οἴκων gen. pl. (gen. sg. = οἴκου)

6.2(ε) Identify the function of the prepositions in the following sentences:

1. **Attributive** — οἱ ἄνθρωποι οἵ ἐν τῷ οἴκῳ βλέπουσι τοὺς ἀγγέλους. The men are in the house.
2. **Adverbial** — οἱ ἄνθρωποι ζήτουσιν τοὺς ἀγγέλους ἐν ταῖς ὁδοῖς. The prepositional phrase describes where the angels are.
3. **Substantive** — τοὺς ἐν τῷ κόσμῳ λαμβάνουσιν τὸν νόμον.
4. **Adverbial** — λαμβάνομεν τὸν νόμον εἰς τὸν κόσμον. The prepositional phrase describes where the receiving occurs.

6.3 Translation exercises:

Translation Exercises

1. The slaves make a way for the Lord.
2. The men seek the angels on roads.
3. He writes the law of the Lord.
4. The slave's brother sees the house.
5. We write the laws for the people.
6. God loves the brethren.
7. You all seek the men's brother.
8. They keep the word of God.

9. The slaves find the way for the lords.
10. We receive the law into the world.
11. I speak the words to the people and the people believe.
12. You all send the bread to a people in a desert.

Composition Exercises

6.4 Composition exercises:

1. ὁ ἄγγελος εὑρίσκει ἀνθρώπους ἐν ἐρήμῳ.
2. γράφουσι τοὺς νόμους τῷ λαῷ.
3. ζητοῦμεν τοὺς ἀδελφοὺς τοῦ δούλου ἐν τῷ οἴκῳ.
4. οἱ δοῦλοι τοῦ κυρίου ποιοῦσιν ὁδόν.
5. ὁ δοῦλος μένει ἐν τῷ οἴκῳ.
6. θεωρεῖτε τὸν οἶκον τοῦ θεοῦ.
7. τηροῦμεν τὸν νόμον τοῦ κυρίου.
8. γράφουσι λόγους τοῖς δούλοις.
9. εὑρίσκομεν ὁδὸν εἰς ἔρημον τῷ λαῷ.
10. ὁ ἄνθρωπος σῴζει τὸν ἀδελφὸν τοῦ δούλου.
11. ὁ ἄνθρωπος καὶ ὁ δοῦλος ποιοῦσιν ἄρτον.
12. οἱ ἀδελφοὶ πιστεύουσι.
13. ὁ ἄγγελος γράφει νόμους τῷ κόσμῳ.
14. ἀποστέλλει ἄγγελον εἰς τὸν κόσμον.

LESSON 7

Grammar Exercises

7.2(α) Case identification exercises:

1. βιβλίον, neut. nom./acc. sg.
2. δένδρων, neut. gen. pl.
3. ἀργύρια, neut. nom./acc. pl.
4. ἀδελφοῖς, masc. dat. pl.
5. εὐαγγελίου, neut. gen. sg.
6. πλοίων, neut. gen. pl.
7. σαββάτῳ, neut. dat. sg.
8. τέκνα, neut. nom./acc. pl.
9. πρόσωπον, neut. nom./acc. sg.
10. σημεῖα, neut. nom./acc. pl.

7.2(β) Case form exercises:

1. πλοῖα, neut. nom./acc. pl.
   (πλοῖον = neut. nom./acc. sg.)
2. νόμοι, masc. nom. pl.
   (νόμος = masc. nom. sg.)
3. δαιμονίων, neut. gen. pl.
   (δαιμονίου = neut. gen. sg.)
4. δούλους, masc. acc. pl.
   (δοῦλον = masc. acc. sg.)
5. ἔργοις, neut. dat. pl.
   (ἔργῳ = neut. dat. sg.)

7.2(γ) Case form exercises:

1. πρόβατον, neut. nom./acc. sg.
   (πρόβατα = neut. nom./acc. pl.)
2. ἱματίου, neut. gen. sg.
   (ἱματίων = neut. gen. pl.)
3. δοῦλον, masc. acc. sg.
   (δούλους = masc. acc. pl.)
4. δένδρῳ, neut. dat. sg.
   (δένδροις = neut. dat. pl.)
5. ἔργον, neut. nom./acc. sg.
   (ἔργα = neut. nom./acc. pl.)

7.3 Translation exercises:

Translation Exercises

1. The slave looks at the men's trees, which are in a desert.
2. The Lord does the works for the world.
3. We find the temple of God.
4. The sheep behold the trees.
5. They hear the gospel.
6. You keep the books safe.
7. You have a demon.
8. You all receive the boats.
9. We behold the face of the Lord.

10. They send the slave's children into the world.
11. We keep the Sabbaths of the Lord.
12. You all save the children.
13. The children have the books.

Composition Exercises

7.4 Composition exercises:

1. λαμβάνουσι τὰ ἱμάτια τῶν ἀνθρώπων εἰς τὸ ἱερόν.
2. ἀποστέλλομεν τὰ παιδία τοῦ ἀδελφοῦ εἰς τὸν οἶκον τοῦ κυρίου.
3. ὁ ἄγγελος λαμβάνει τὰ βιβλία τῷ λαῷ.
4. τὰ παιδία ἔχει τὰ ἱμάτια.
5. θεωρεῖ τὸ πρόσωπον τοῦ θεοῦ.
6. ἔχεις τὰ πρόβατα.
7. εὑρίσκετε τὰ δένδρα ἐν ἐρήμῳ.
8. ὁ κύριος κρίνει τὰ ἔργα τῶν ἀνθρώπων.
9. ζητοῦμεν τὸ ἱερόν.
10. ὁ θεὸς ποιεῖ σημεῖα τῷ λαῷ.
11. ὁ ἄνθρωπος ζητεῖ τὸ παιδίον.
12. τὰ παιδία ἐσθίει τοὺς ἄρτους ἐν πλοίῳ.
13. τηρεῖς τὸ ἀργύριον.

LESSON 8

Grammar Exercises

8.2(α) Case identification exercises:

1. ἁμαρτιῶν, gen. pl.
2. ἀρχαί, nom. pl.
3. ἄρτους, acc. sg.
4. κεφαλήν, acc. sg.
5. ἀργύρια, nom./acc.pl.
6. γῇ, dat. sg.
7. εἰρήνην, acc. sg.
8. ἐντολῶν, gen. pl.
9. δικαιοσύνης, gen. sg.
10. ἡμέραις, dat. pl.
11. καρδίαι, nom. pl.
12. φωνῶν, gen. pl.
13. ψυχάς, acc. pl.
14. ὥρας, gen. sg. or acc. pl.
15. παραβολή, nom. sg.

8.2(β) Stem pattern exercises:

1. βασιλείας
2. ἀγάπην
3. γραφαῖς
4. κόσμος
5. δικαιοσύναι
6. ὥρα
7. ἱμάτιαν
8. σοφίαν
9. παραβολῆς
10. παραβολάς
11. πρόσωπον
12. ἐπαγγελίας
13. ἀρχῆς
14. εἰρήνην
15. ἐκκλησίας

8.2(γ) Supply the proper article:

1. **τὴν** εἰρήνην
2. **τὴν** ἐκκλησίαν
3. **ταῖς** ἐπαγγελίαις
4. **τῶν** κεφαλῶν
5. **ἡ** ἔρημος
6. **ταῖς** καρδίαις
7. **τῆς** ζωῆς
8. **τοῦ** κυρίου
9. **τὰς** γραφάς
10. **τὴν** ὁδόν
11. **τῇ** ἐντολῇ
12. **οἱ** δοῦλοι
13. **αἱ** παρθένοι
14. **τὴν** ἡμέραν
15. **τὸ** τέκνον

8.3 Translation exercises: **Translation Exercises**

1. Love remains.
2. We receive righteousness.
3. They encourage the church.
4. The Lord judges the souls of men.
5. You all see the synagogue of the brothers.
6. We seek the kingdom of God.
7. You have wisdom and joy.
8. You all keep the commandments of the angels.
9. The brothers send the Scriptures.

Composition Exercises

8.4 Composition exercises:

1. λαμβάνομεν τὰς ἐπαγγελίας τοῦ θεοῦ.
2. ἔχουσι τὰς τοῦ κυρίου ἐντολάς (or τὰς ἐντολάς τοῦ κυρίου).
3. αἱ ἁμαρτίαι τοῦ κόσμου μένουσι(ν).
4. ἀκούεις τὴν φωνὴν τοῦ κυρίου.
5. μαρτυροῦμεν τῇ ἀλήθεια.
6. παρακαλεῖτε τὴν ἐκκλησίαν.
7. ἔχει τὴν δικαιοσύνην καὶ τὴν εἰρήνην καὶ τὴν χαράν.

   In Greek, when three items are mentioned together as in a list, the conjunction καί often occurs between each item. English prefers adding the conjunction only between the final two items (e.g. "righteousness, peace, and joy") and separates preceding items with commas.

8. οἱ ἀδελφοὶ γράφουσι τὰς γραφάς.
9. ὁ κύριος τηρεῖ τὰς ψυχὰς τῶν ἀνθρώπων.
10. ζητεῖτε τὴν σοφίαν.

LESSON 9

Grammar Exercises

9.2 Case identification exercises:

1. **ὁ** βαπτιστής
2. **τῆς** γραφής
3. **τὴν** ἐξουσίαν
4. **τοῦ** νεανίου
5. **τῆς** θαλάσσης
6. **τὰς** γλώσσας
7. **τῇ** θαλάσσῃ
8. **τὸν** δεσπότην
9. **τοῖς** μαθηταῖς
10. **αἱ** δόξαι
11. **τοῦ** προφήτου
12. **ταῖς** φωναῖς
13. **τὴν** ἡμέραν
14. **αἱ** ὧραι
15. **τῇ** ἐξουσίᾳ

9.3 Translation exercises:

Translation Exercises

1. They do not call the prophets into the synagogue.
2. For the Lord writes the promises in the hearts of the brothers.
3. They encourage the prophets with the disciples.
4. And the boats do not remain in the sea.
5. In the beginning God sends the prophets.
6. They do not find the children on the way.
7. The disciples remain in the power of the master.
8. The young man takes the garment from the head of the child.
9. The maiden finds the books.

9.4 Composition exercises:

Composition Exercises

1. οὐ βλέπομεν τὰ πλοῖα ἐν τῇ θαλάσσῃ.
2. ὁ δεσπότης ἀποστέλλει τὰ παιδία σὺν τοῖς δούλοις ἀπὸ τῆς συναγωγῆς.
3. μένεις πρὸ τοῦ οἴκου τοῦ κυρίου.
4. οἱ προφῆται παρακαλοῦσι τοὺς ἀδελφοὺς καὶ τὸν λαόν.
5. ἡ οὖν ἁμαρτία τοῦ κοσμοῦ μένει.
6. θεωροῦσι τὴν δόξαν τοῦ κυρίου ἐν τῷ ἱερῷ.
7. ὁ βαπτιστὴς μένει ἐν τῇ συναγωγῇ σὺν τοῖς μαθηταῖς.
8. ἀποστέλλουσι τὸν προφήτην ἀπὸ τῆς θαλάσσης σὺν τῷ βαπτιστῇ.
9. ἀποστέλλετε τὰ παιδία ἐκ τοῦ οἴκου.
10. ἡ γὰρ ἐκκλησία οὐκ ἀκούει τὰς ἐντολὰς καὶ τὰς ἐπαγγελίας τοῦ προφήτου.
11. καλοῦσι τοὺς μαθητὰς εἰς τὴν ἐκκλησίαν.
12. ὁ γὰρ θεὸς γράφει τὰς ἐντολὰς ἐν ταῖς καρδίαις τῶν μαθητῶν.
13. οἱ νεανίαι ἀκούουσι τὰς παραβολὰς τῆς βασιλείας.

LESSON 10

Grammar Exercises

10.2 Matching adjectives and nouns:

1. πρῶτον σημεῖον
2. ἐσχάτοις προφηταῖς
3. ἀγαθῆς ζωῆς
4. ἰδίου νόμου
5. πονηροῖς νεανίαις
6. πρώτην θάλασσαν
7. πονηρῷ δεσπότῃ
8. ἀγαθοῦ μαθητοῦ
9. δικαίας ἔντολης
10. ἑτέραν φώνην

Translation Exercises

10.3 Translation exercises:

1. The church is faithful.
2. The men are prophets.
3. The kingdom is bad.
4. The commandment of the eternal God is just.
5. They take their own clothes.
6. Other men stay in the first boat.
7. We are beloved children of God.
8. The first is the last, and the last first.
9. The saints keep the holy Sabbaths of God.
10. The tongue is evil.
11. The faithful women remain in the temple.
12. You all are disciples of the Lord.
13. You are holy, Lord.
14. We call the other young men.

Composition Exercises

10.4 Composition exercises:

1. οἱ ἀδελφοὶ μαθηταί εἰσιν.
2. ἐσμὲν προφῆται.
3. ἀγαθὸς εἶ, ὦ δέσποτα.
4. αἱ γραφαὶ τῶν ἀποστόλων ἅγιαί εἰσιν.
5. ἕτερος ἄνθρωπος ἐν τῷ ἐσχάτῳ πλοίῳ ἐστίν.
6. μένομεν ἐν τῷ πονηρῷ κόσμῳ.
7. ποιεῖ τὰ ἴδια ἱμάτια.
8. ὁ ἄνθρωπος δίκαιος καὶ ἀγαθός ἐστιν.

9. ὁ οὖν βαπτιστὴς παρακαλεῖ τοὺς πονηρούς.
10. οἱ ἅγιοι μένουσιν πρὸ τοῦ οἴκου τοῦ θεοῦ.
11. ὁ θεὸς τηρεῖ τὰς ψυχὰς τῶν ἁγίων.
12. παρακαλεῖτε τοὺς μαθητάς.

LESSON 11

Grammar Exercises

11.2(α) Accent the following imperfect verbs:

1. ἐξέβαλλε
2. ἐφιλοῦμεν
3. ἐζήτουν
4. ἐδόξαζον
5. ἐκάλουν
6. ἐθεωρεῖτε
7. ἀπέθνῃσκες
8. ἤσθιον
9. ἔβλεπεν
10. ἐθεωροῦμεν
11. ἐλάλει
12. ἐμαρτύρουν
13. ἐλάμβανον
14. ἔμενε
15. ἀπέστελλες

11.2(β) Vocabulary identification:

1. ἦγε — ἄγω
2. ἔπειθον — πείθω
3. ἐκηρύσσομεν — κηρύσσω
4. ἐδόξαζον — δοξάζω
5. ἐζητεῖτε — ζητέω
6. παρεκάλουν — παρακαλέω
7. ἐθεώρει — θεωρέω
8. ἐλέγομεν — λέγω
9. εἶχεν — ἔχω
10. ἔμενον — μένω

11.2(γ) Augment identification:

1. ἀπεκτείνετε τοὺς προφήτας τοῦ κυρίου.
2. ὁ θεὸς ἔπεμπε τοὺς ἀγγέλους εἰς τὸν κόσμον.
3. ἦγε τοὺς μαθητὰς ἀπὸ τῆς θαλάσσης.
4. οἱ νεανίαι ἔχαιρον.

5. τὰ πρόβατα ὑπῆγον ἐκ τῆς ἐρήμου.
6. ὁ βαπτιστὴς βαπτίζει τὰς παρθένους.
7. ὁ ἄγγελος ἀπέλυε τὸν ἀπόστολον.
8. οἱ μαθηταὶ ἐδόξαζον τὸν κύριον.
9. ἔφερον οἱ ἀγαθοὶ δοῦλοι τὰ πρόβατα.
10. Ἰωάννης ὁ βαπτιστὴς ἔκραζε ἐν τῇ ἐρήμῳ.
11. ἐδίδασκες τὰ παιδία σὺν τοῖς δούλοις.
12. ἐκηρύσσομεν τὸ εὐαγγέλιον τῷ λαῷ.
13. ἔπειθον οὖν τοὺς ἀνθρώπους.
14. περιεπατοῦμεν ἐν τῷ ἱερῷ.
15. ἐξέβαλλες τὰ δαιμόνια.

Translation Exercises

11.3 Translation exercises:

1. You all were killing the prophets of the Lord.
2. God was sending the angels into the world.
3. He was leading the disciples from the sea.
4. The young men were rejoicing.
5. The sheep were going out of the wilderness/desert.
6. The baptist baptizes the maidens.
7. The angel was releasing the apostle.
8. The disciples were glorifying the Lord.
9. The good servants were carrying the sheep.
10. John the Baptist was shouting in the wilderness.
11. You were teaching the children with the servants.
12. We were preaching the gospel to the people.
13. Therefore, I was (or they were) persuading the men.
14. We were walking around in the temple.
15. You were casting out demons.

Composition Exercises

11.4 Composition exercises:

1. ἐκήρυσσον τὸ εὐαγγέλιον τοῖς μαθηταῖς.
2. αἱ παρθένοι ὑπῆγον ἐκ τοῦ οἴκου.
3. ἦγον τὸ τοῦ δούλου πλοῖον εἰς τὴν θάλασσαν.
4. οἱ προφῆται ἐδίδασκον τὰ τέκνα ἐν τοῖς οἴκοις.

5. ἐδοξάζετε τὸν κύριον, ὦ ἄγγελοι.
6. ἐδίδασκες τὸν λαόν.
7. συνῆγον τὰ πρόβατα εἰς τὰ δένδρα.
8. τὸ τέκνον ἀνεγίνωσκε τὰς γραφὰς ἐν τῷ ἱερῷ.
9. ὑπήγομεν ἀπὸ τῆς θαλάσσης.
10. Ἰωάννης ὁ βαπτιστὴς οὐκ ἐποίει σημεῖα.
11. ὁ κύριος περιεπάτει ἐν τῇ ἐρήμῳ.
12. ἔπειθες οὖν τὸν λαόν.
13. οἱ ἅγιοι ἐχαίρουν.
14. ἐξέβαλλε τὰ δαιμόνια.
15. ἐφέρομεν τὸ πλοῖον.
16. ἀπελύετε τοὺς δούλους.

LESSON 12

Translation Exercises

12.2 Translation exercises:

1. These men were dying in the wilderness.
2. We were looking at their houses.
3. Therefore, this man was a disciple of John the Baptist.
4. For we were slaves of sin.
5. But I/they cast those trees into the sea.
6. These women were staying in the boat.
7. For God saves them from the evil one.
8. Therefore you all were masters of the people.
9. For we do not judge these things.
10. His sons were bad.
11. For this was his commandment.
12. We were proclaiming these things in the church.
13. But those men were casting out demons.
14. In that day they were glorifying the wisdom of the Lord.
15. The maidens were driving their sheep together to the trees.
16. In that hour we were rejoicing.
17. Jesus himself didn't baptize, but his disciples.
18. The life remains in them.

Composition Exercises

12.3 Composition exercises:

1. ἐν ἀρχῇ ἦν ὁ λόγος.
2. αὕτη ἐστὶν ἡ ἀγάπη τοῦ θεοῦ.
3. ὁ γὰρ κύριος σῴζει τὰς ψυχὰς τῶν ἀνθρώπων ἀπὸ τοῦ πονηροῦ.
4. ἡ εἰρήνη καὶ ἡ ἀλήθεια ἐν τῇ βασιλείᾳ τοῦ θεοῦ εἰσιν.
5. ἐδόξαζον τὴν ἐξουσίαν καὶ τὴν σοφίαν αὐτοῦ.
6. ἐν γὰρ ἐκείνῃ τῇ ἡμέρᾳ ἐκηρύσσομεν τὸ εὐαγγέλιον τῆς βασιλείας ἐν τῇ συναγωγῇ, καὶ ἐξεβάλλομεν τὰ δαιμόνια.
7. ἐβλέπετε τοὺς υἱοὺς αὐτῆς ἐν τῷ οἴκῳ.
8. ἐλαμβάνομεν αὐτοὺς εἰς τὸ πλοῖον.
9. ἦτε ἐν τῷ ἱερῷ ἐν ἐκείναις ταῖς ἡμέραις.
10. αὕτη ἐστὶν ἡ ζωὴ αἰώνιος.
11. ἠκούομεν τὴν φωνὴν τοῦ ἀγγέλου ἀπὸ τῶν δένδρων.
12. ἦσαν ἅγιοι καὶ ἀγαπητοί.
13. τὰ τέκνα αὐτῶν ἦσαν ἐν τῇ ἐκκλησίᾳ.
14. ἀνεγίνωσκες τὰς γραφὰς αὐτοῖς ἐν τῇ συναγωγῇ.
15. οἱ Ἰουδαῖοι ἀπέκτεινον τοὺς προφήτας αὐτοῦ.
16. ὁ βαπτιστὴς αὐτὸς ἐβάπτιζε τοὺς μαθητὰς αὐτοῦ.

LESSON 13

Grammar Exercises

13.2 Convert verb voice forms:

1. λύει
2. τηρεῖ
3. ἐφίλουν
4. ἄγονται
5. πειθόμεθα
6. ἐφέρομεν
7. ἤγετε
8. συνάγεται
9. ἔπειθον
10. κηρύσσεται

13.3 Translation exercises:

Translation Exercises

1. You all were being sent by the teachers to the other crowd.
2. In this place we were beholding with our eyes the Lord of the heavens.

   The word "our," in this case, reflects the context. It's perfectly acceptable Greek idiom not to include the possessive here.

3. These words were being spoken by the apostles to the elders.
4. And immediately the sheep were being driven together with stones by the robbers.
5. We were being sent with the prophets through the crowd.
6. Because of this you were being persuaded by the words of the judges.
7. After these things the tax collectors were being taught with the young men by the elders.
8. The sons of the head of household were eating the loaves.
9. O you hypocrite, you are not walking in the ways of the Lord.
10. The throne was being made by the workmen for the house of the Lord in Jerusalem.
11. The laborers were sending the fruits of the earth to the householders.
12. O Jerusalem, you are not found faithful.
13. We were comforted by the words of the disciples at that time.
14. We were leading the children through the temple.
15. After those days the robbers departed into the wilderness.

Composition Exercises

13.4 Composition exercises:

1. ὁ λόγος τοῦ θεοῦ ἐκηρύσσετο ὑπὸ τῶν ἀποστόλων.
2. οὗτοι οἱ καρποὶ ἀπεστέλλοντο ὑπὸ τοῦ οἰκοδεσπότου πρὸς τοὺς πρεσβυτέρους.
3. διὰ τοῦτο οἱ κριταὶ ἐπείθοντο ὑπὸ τῶν πιστῶν διδασκάλων.
4. ἦγες τὸν λαὸν διὰ τῆς ἐρήμου εἰς Ἰερουσαλήμ.
5. μετὰ τοῦτο ἐζητοῦντο ὑπὸ τοῦ ὄχλου.
6. πονηροὶ ἦσαν ἐν τοῖς ὀφθαλμοῖς τοῦ κυρίου.
7. ὁ θρόνος ἐφέρετο ὑπὸ τῶν ἐργάτων εἰς ἕτερον τόπον διὰ τοῦ οἴκου.
8. εὐθὺς οἱ πρεσβύτεροι περιεπάτουν σὺν τοῖς προφήταις διὰ Ἰερουσαλήμ.
9. ὁ κόσμος ἐποιεῖτο διὰ τοῦ υἱοῦ τοῦ θεοῦ.
10. ὦ ὑποκριτά, οὐ τηρεῖς τὰς ἐντολὰς τοῦ κυρίου.
11. οἱ νεανίαι ἐδιδάσκοντο ὑπὸ τῶν ἰδίων διδασκάλων.
12. οὐκ ἀπεστέλλου ὑπὸ τῶν υἱῶν τῶν προφήτων.
13. εὐθὺς οὖν μετὰ ταῦτα ἐκηρύσσομεν τὸν λόγον τοῦ θεοῦ τοῖς μαθηταῖς.
14. ἠγείρεσθε τοῖς λόγοις τοῦ οἰκοδεσπότου.

LESSON 14

Grammar Exercises

14.2 Case identification:

	Antecedent	Pronoun
1.	men — acc.	whom — acc.
2.	those — acc.	who — nom.
3.	he — nom.	who — nom.
4.	no antecedent	whom — acc.
5.	son — nom.	in whom — dat.
6.	for those — dat.	who — nom.
7.	he — nom.	who — nom.

	Antecedent	Pronoun
8.	by those — gen.	who — nom.
9.	him — acc.	by whose — gen.
10.	men — acc.	whom — acc.
11.	no antecedent	that which — acc.
12.	he — nom.	whose — gen.

14.3 Translation exercises:

Translation Exercises

1. We were going to the sea with the disciples.
2. They were denying the Lord of glory who keeps them from the evil one.
3. You all received the fields which the people of Israel had.
4. Do not answer the master.
5. They departed to the wilderness in which John was baptizing.
6. I answered the messengers who used to come from the elders.
7. Do not work wickedness.
8. This man receives the sinners who come to him and eats with them.
9. Touch the heads of the children whom I send.
10. The slaves whom he received work in the fields.
11. Let them send the garments which they take to the house.
12. Let him/her/it receive the book which the apostle is writing.
13. Therefore we went through their fields with the tax collectors.
14. You all were bad and evil slaves.
15. Let them touch the stones of the temple which was built for the Lord.

Composition Exercises

14.4 Composition exercises:

1. μενέτω ἡ ἀγάπη τῶν ἀδελφῶν ἐν ταῖς καρδίαις αὐτῶν.
2. τηρεῖτε τὰς ἁγίας ἐντολὰς ἃς δέχεσθε ἀπὸ τῶν διδασκάλων.
3. μὴ ἀρνεῖσθε τὸν κύριον τῆς δόξης ὃς σῴζει ὑμᾶς ἀπὸ τοῦ πονηροῦ κόσμου.
4. δεχέσθωσαν τὸν νόμον τῷ λαῷ οἱ πρεσβύτεροι οὓς ἀποστέλλουσιν.
5. διηρχόμεθα τοὺς ἀγροὺς ἐν οἷς οἱ δοῦλοι ἠργάζοντο.
6. μετὰ ταῦτα ᾠκοδομοῦντο ἱερὸν τῷ θεῷ Ἰσραήλ.
7. μὴ περιπατεῖτε ἐν τῇ ὁδῷ τῶν ἁμαρτωλῶν.
8. δεχέσθω τοὺς ἀγγέλους οἳ κηρύσσουσιν τὴν βασιλείαν τῶν οὐρανῶν.
9. οἱ μαθηταὶ οὓς Ἰωάννης ἐβάπτιζεν ἔμενον ἐν τῇ ἐρήμῳ.
10. ἐργάσθωσαν τὰ ἔργα τοῦ κυρίου τῆς δόξης.
11. ὁ γὰρ προφήτης δέχεται τοὺς ἁμαρτωλοὺς οἳ ἀποστέλλονται πρὸς αὐτὸν καὶ ἐσθίει μετ᾽ αὐτῶν.
12. μὴ ἀποκρινου τῷ διδασκάλῳ.
13. μετὰ ἐκείνας τὰς ἡμέρας ἀπήρχοντο πρὸς τὸν τόπον ἐν ᾧ οἱ νεανίαι ἔμενον μετὰ τῶν προβάτων.
14. οὗτός ἐστιν ὁ πρεσβύτερος οὗ τὰ τέκνα ἀνεγίνωσκον τὰ βιβλία τοῦ νόμου ἃ ἔγραφεν ὁ προφήτης.

LESSON 15

Grammar Exercises

15.2 Pronoun exercises:

1. τοῖς διδάσκαλοις ἡμετέροις — to our teachers
2. τοῖς ὀφειλέταις ἡμῶν — to our debtors
3. τοὺς λίθους μου — my stones
4. αἱ ὑμέτεραι καρδίαι — your own hearts
5. ἡ χαρὰ ἡ ἐμή — my joy
6. ἡ ὥρα μου — my hour

7. ἐν τῷ νόμῳ δὲ τῷ ὑμετέρῳ — even in your own law
8. τὸ φῶς ὑμῶν — your light
9. τὸν οἶκόν σου — your house
10. ὁ λόγος ὁ σός — your very word

15.3 Translation exercises: **Translation Exercises**

1. They wished to hear the words which Jesus was speaking.
2. Master, it is good for us to be here.
3. Therefore they implored him to heal their sons.
4. This man begins to build, but is not able to do the work.
5. You all must answer the elders.
6. I order you to come out of the house.
7. It is permitted for us to preach the kingdom of the heavens.
8. He was sending his slaves to call the poor and the blind to the wedding.
9. He commanded them to fetch Paul.
10. For God sends his son to save the world.
11. The prophets exhorted them to remain in the truth.
12. For you all do not want to come to me.
13. Jesus therefore was being led into the wilderness to be tempted by the devil.
14. The disciples came to Jordan to confess their sins to John.
15. We commanded the messengers to be sent.
16. But he did not wish to walk in the ways of the Lord.
17. I order you to remain there, but you do not obey.
18. Some were slaves, and some were free.
19. We were exhorting the people to obey the prophets.

Composition Exercises

15.4 Composition exercises:

1. οὐ δεῖ ἡμᾶς ἀρνεῖσθαι τὸν κύριον τῆς δόξης.
2. οὐκ ἤθελον ὑπακούειν τοῖς πρεσβυτέροις.
3. ἔξεστιν αὐτοῖς δέχεσθαι τὸ ἀργύριον ἀπὸ τῶν τελωνῶν.
4. ἐγὼ μέν εἰμι ἄνθρωπος, ὑμεῖς δὲ τέκνα ἐστέ.
5. θέλομεν θεωρεῖν τὸ ἱερὸν τοῦ θεοῦ Ἰσραήλ.
6. πέμπομεν τοὺς δούλους καλεῖν τοὺς τυφλοὺς καὶ τοὺς πτωχοὺς εἰς τὸν γάμον.
7. κακόν ἐστιν αὐτοὺς εἶναι ἐκεῖ.
8. ἔδει τὸν Ἰησοῦν διέρχεσθαι διὰ τῆς Σαμαρείας κηρύσσειν τὸ εὐαγγέλιον τῷ λαῷ.
9. ἐκελεύομεν τὸν προφήτην ἄγεσθαι.
10. ἐδεόμην αὐτοῦ θεραπεύειν τὸ τέκνον μου, ὁ δὲ οὐκ ἤθελε.
11. ὁ Ἰησοῦς ἐκέλευσεν αὐτοὺς πέμπειν τὸν τυφλόν.
12. ου δύναμαι παρακαλεῖν αὐτοῦς μένειν ἐν Ἰερουσαλήμ.
13. ὡμολόγουν τὰς ἁμαρτίας αὐτῶν ἡμῖν.
14. οἱ μὲν ἤρχοντο εἰς τοὺς οἴκους αὐτῶν, οἱ δὲ εἰς τὸ ἱερόν.
15. ἡμεῖς μέν ἐσμεν ἐλεύθεροι, ὑμεῖς δὲ δοῦλοί ἐστε.
16. ὁ Ἰησοῦς ἄγεται εἰς τὴν ἔρημον πειράζεσθαι ὑπὸ τοῦ διαβόλου.
17. ἐπορευόμεθα πρὸς τὸν Ἰωάννην βαπτίζεσθαι ὑπ᾽ αὐτοῦ ἐν τῷ Ἰορδάνῃ.
18. οὐ δύνανται ποιεῖν τοῦτο.
19. ἔπεμπον τὸν ἄγγελον πρὸς ὑμᾶς, ὁ δὲ οὐκ ἤθελε ἀπέρχεσθαι.
20. δεῖ ὑμᾶς τὰ ἔργα αὐτοῦ ἐργάζεσθαι ὅς ἔπεμπε ὑμᾶς.
21. θέλουσι ἀναγινώσκειν τὰ βιβλία ἃ ἔχεις.

LESSON 16

16.2 Consonant combination exercises: **Grammar Exercises**

1. $\delta + \sigma = \sigma$
2. $\chi + \sigma = \xi$
3. $\beta + \sigma = \psi$
4. $\kappa + \sigma = \xi$
5. $\zeta + \sigma = \sigma$
6. $\tau + \sigma = \sigma$
7. $\varphi + \sigma = \psi$
8. $\pi + \sigma = \psi$
9. $\gamma + \sigma = \xi$
10. $\vartheta + \sigma = \sigma$

16.3 Translation exercises: **Translation Exercises**

1. They will not injure the children.
2. But they will put on the garments.
3. He will open the eyes of the blind who are gathered together in the synagogue.
4. We will persuade the workmen to work in the fields.
5. I will send to them wise men and prophets, but the sons of Israel will not hear them.
6. He will be holy to the Lord.
7. You all will rule over the Jews who inhabit that land.
8. You will prophesy to this people and they will obey you.
9. You all will serve your enemies because you were not willing to obey me, but I will have mercy upon you in that day.
10. We will inhabit the fields of our enemies whom we served because we did not hear the word of the Lord.
11. The ministers of the synagogue will not pursue the robbers on the Sabbath.
12. Let them praise the glory of the God of Israel.
13. We will send the young men to settle the land.
14. The elders will have the sheep which are saved from the enemies.
15. We will begin to praise the sons of the prophets.

Composition Exercises

16.4 Composition exercises:

1. ἀνοίξω τὰ βιβλία ἅ ἐστιν ἐν τῇ συναγωγῇ.
2. δίκαιοι καὶ πιστοὶ ἔσονται ἐν ἐκείνῃ τῇ ἡμέρᾳ, καὶ εὐλογήσω αὐτοὺς ὅτι ἀκούουσιν τὴν φωνήν μου.
3. θεωρήσομεν τὸ πρόσωπον τοῦ κυρίου ἐν τῷ ἱερῷ ὃ οἰκοδομεῖται ἐν Ἰερουσαλήμ.
4. ὁ κύριος ἐλεήσει αὐτοὺς ὅτι κατοικοῦσιν τὴν γῆν τῶν ἐχθρῶν αὐτῶν, καὶ ἄξει αὐτοὺς εἰς τὴν γῆν αὐτῶν.
5. ὁ Ἰησοῦς οὖν ἔπεμπε τοὺς ἀποστόλους κηρύσσειν τὸ εὐαγγέλιον τῷ οἴκῳ Ἰσραήλ.
6. πέμψομεν τοὺς δούλους διώκειν τοὺς λῃστάς.
7. ἡ εἰρήνη καὶ ἡ ἀλήθεια κατοικήσουσιν ἐν τῇ γῇ ἡμῶν ὅτι ὑπακούομεν ταῖς ἐντολαῖς τοῦ κυρίου.
8. λαλήσει ταῦτα τοῖς ὄχλοις ἐν παραβολαῖς.
9. ἐγὼ μὲν ἔσομαι πρῶτος, σὺ δὲ ἔσῃ ἔσχατος.
10. μὴ εὐλογεῖτε τοὺς πονηρούς, οἱ γὰρ πονηροὶ οὐ κατοικήσουσιν ἐν τῇ γῇ ἡμῶν.

LESSON 17

Grammar Exercises

17.2 Write the future active indicative first person singular using the following verbal roots:

1. (κραγ-) κράξω
2. (κρυπ-) ἀποκαλύψω
3. (φυλακ-) φυλάξω
4. (ἐκκοπ-) ἐκκόψω
5. (ταγ-) τάξω
6. (ἐλπιδ-) ἐλπιῶ
7. (κηρυκ-) κηρύξω
8. (διδαχ-) διδάξω
9. (ἀποκτεν-) ἀποκτενῶ

Translation Exercises

17.3 Translation exercises:

1. Will we hide the child in the house?
2. They will not revere my Sabbaths.
3. The same messengers will prepare themselves to go.
4. Cleanse yourselves, you hypocrites.

5. You will reveal to them the glory of wisdom.
6. You all have life in yourselves.
7. For you will do the same things.
8. Jesus himself was drawing near to the same disciples.
9. They will arrange the same men in the fields.
10. Will you all cause the saints to stumble?
11. He will touch the garment of the prophet.
12. Will I come to the same house?
13. Sanctify your hearts by the love of the truth.
14. They will drive the lepers from the temple.
15. You all will cut down the trees that are in that land.
16. He will wonder at the glory of the Lord.

Composition Exercises

17.4 Composition exercises:

1. τάξετε τὰ βιβλία ἐν τῇ συναγωγῇ.
2. ἐλπίσουσι θεωρεῖν τὰ σημεῖα τῶν ἀποστόλων.
3. ἐγγίσομεν ἀκούειν τὴν φωνὴν τοῦ διδασκάλου.
4. ὁ πονηρὸς ποιήσει τὰ πονηρά.
5. καθαρίσει ἑαυτὸν ἐν τῇ αὐτῇ θαλάσσῃ;
6. ἑτοιμάσει ἑαυτὴν ἔρχεσθαι.
7. κόψω τὰ δένδρα ἅ ἐστιν ἐν τῷ ἀγρῷ.
8. ἀγοράσομεν τὰ αὐτὰ βιβλία τοῖς τέκνοις ἡμῶν.
9. ὁ κύριος τηρήσει τὰς ψυχὰς τοῦ λαοῦ αὐτοῦ.
10. ἀρξόμεθα ἁγιάζειν τὰς καρδίας ἡμῶν.
11. ἡ παρθένος βαστάσει τοὺς ἄρτους τοῖς ἐργάταις.
12. κρύψουσιν ἑαυτοὺς ἐν τοῖς δένδροις.
13. ἄρξεσθε θαυμάζειν τὴν ἐξουσίαν τῶν πρεσβυτέρων.
14. οὐκ ἀποκαλύψομεν ἑαυτοὺς αὐτοῖς.
15. θέλεις θεωρεῖν εἰρήνην καὶ δικαιοσύνην[1] ἐν τῇ βασιλείᾳ τοῦ θεοῦ;
16. κελεύσομεν αὐτοὺς ἀναγινώσκειν τὰς γραφὰς τοῖς ἀδελφοῖς;

1 It is perfectly acceptable to have articles preceding these nouns, since abstract nouns are often used with articles.

LESSON 18

Grammar Exercises

18.2 Verbal root identification:

1. ἐκαλέσαμεν — καλε-
2. ᾔτησας — αἰτε-
3. ἀνοίξεις — ἀνα + οιγ-
4. βλέπειν — βλεπ-
5. κρυψάτωσαν — κρυπ
6. ἠλπίσατε — ἐλπιδ-
7. γράψαι — γραφ
8. κηρύξουσι — κηρυκ-
9. ἐλπιοῦμεν — ἐλπιδ-

Translation Exercises

18.3 Translation exercises:

1. They pursued the robbers who were driving away the sheep.
2. But the lepers believed the word of Jesus.
3. You sent the tax collectors to buy the garments.
4. Save the money from the robbers.
5. I am saving your people (i.e., keeping them safe) from the evil one.
6. Let them set the books in order in the temple.
7. After these things we persuaded them to hide the children.
8. We cleansed ourselves in the river.
9. The teacher himself wondered at the wisdom of the disciples.
10. He went through the land to cut down the trees.
11. On this account it is not right to cause the faithful to stumble.
12. Carry the boat from the sea.
13. Sanctify yourselves, for the day of the Lord draws near.
14. The prophet commanded the leper to cleanse himself in the river Jordan.
15. The voice of John cried in the wilderness, "You all prepare the way for the Lord."

16. We kept the commandments which we heard from the holy apostles.
17. It is good for us to practice righteousness.
18. They implored him not to do himself any harm.
19. After this therefore he opened the eyes of the blind man.
20. You are hoping to behold the glory of the angels.
21. Let peace inhabit your hearts.
22. For the angels wished to see these things.

18.4 Composition exercises:

Composition Exercises

1. ἐβάπτισαν τοὺς τελώνας ἐν τῷ ποταμῷ.
2. διήρχεσθε τὴν γῆν θεωρεῖν τοὺς οἴκους καὶ τὸν λαόν.
3. κρῦψον τοὺς λίθους ἐν τῷ ἀγρῷ.
4. μὴ σκανδαλίζετε τοὺς ἀδελφούς.
5. ταξάτωσαν τοὺς ἀνθρώπους.
6. ἀπεκαλύψατε τὰς ἐντολὰς καὶ τὰς ἐπαγγελίας τῇ ἐκκλησίᾳ.
7. ἀρξόμεθα ἀναγινώσκειν τὰ βιβλία;
8. καθαρίσατε τὰς καρδίας, ἁμαρτωλοί, καὶ ὁμολογεῖτε τὰς ἁμαρτίας ὑμῶν τῇ ἐκκλησίᾳ.
9. ἔξεστι θεραπεύειν ἐν τῷ σαββάτῳ;
10. σῶσον τὸν λαόν σου, κύριε, ἀπὸ τῆς ἀδικίας τοῦ κοσμοῦ τούτου.
11. ἑτοιμάσατε οὖν κρύψαι ἑαυτοὺς καὶ τὰ τέκνα ὑμῶν ἐν Ἰερουσαλήμ.
12. κατοικείτωσαν ἡ ἀγάπη καὶ ἡ δικαιοσύνη ἐν ταῖς καρδίαις ὑμῶν.
13. ἐκέλευσέ με γράφειν ταῦτα ἐν βιβλίῳ.
14. καλόν ἐστιν αὐτοὺς τα αὐτὰ ἀναγινώσκειν.
15. μετὰ τοῦτο ἀποκαλύψω τὴν ἐξουσίαν μου τοῖς υἱοῖς Ἰσραήλ.
16. ἤθελε καλεῖν τοὺς τελώνας εἰς τὸν γάμον.

LESSON 19

Grammar Exercises

19.2(α) Verbal root identification, part 1:

1. βα-
2. ἐλθ-
3. σεχ-
4. ἐπ-
5. ἰδ-

19.2(β) Verbal root identification, part 2:

1. ὁρα-, ἰδ-
2. πασχ-, παθ-
3. φερ-, ἐνεγκ-
4. ἐρχ-, ἐλθ-

Translation Exercises

19.3 Translation exercises:

1. After these things the poor man died.
2. We went to the temple in that hour.
3. You learned that the judge was coming.
4. O Lord, I have sinned against you.
5. We saw that the tax collector was carrying the money out of the house.
6. Behold the masters of the land.
7. We know that the Son of God came into the world to save sinners.
8. He said that they were drinking the wine and eating the bread.
9. We carried the stones from the sea.
10. The trees fell into the field.
11. The robbers were fleeing from the young men.
12. But the prophets fled into the wilderness.
13. In this we know the love of God because he sent his beloved Son into the world.
14. Go to the fields and take the fruit from the laborers.
15. I knew that the Lord had sent his angel to save me.
16. Let the children come to me.
17. We said that they must suffer many things.

18. They saw that we had led the crowd to the synagogue.
19. He had my brother's books.
20. We knew that the disciples had learned many things from the apostles.

Composition Exercises

19.4 Composition exercises:

1. ἐβάλομεν ἑαυτοὺς εἰς τὸν ποταμόν.
2. ἐλάβετε τὰ ἱμάτια ἃ οἱ πρεσβύτεροι ἔπεμψαν τοῖς πτωχοῖς.
3. ἔφυγον ἀπὸ τοῦ προσώπου τῶν κριτῶν.
4. μετὰ ταῦτα οἱ μαθηταὶ ἔγνων ὅτι ἥμαρτον.
5. οὗτός ἐστιν ὁ λίθος ὃς ἔπεσε ἐκ τοῦ οὐρανοῦ.
6. ἡ παρθένος ἔτεκεν υἱόν, καὶ ἐκάλεσαν αὐτὸν Ἰησοῦν.
7. ἀκολουθεῖτέ μοι οὐχ ὅτι εἴδετε σημεῖα ἀλλ᾽ ὅτι ἐφάγετε τοὺς ἄρτους.
8. δεῖ τὸν υἱὸν τοῦ ἀνθρώπου παθεῖν πολλά.
9. μετὰ ταύτας τὰς ἡμέρας ἤλθομεν εἰς τὴν Σαμάρειαν.
10. ἴδε τὸν ἀμνὸν τοῦ θεοῦ.
11. εἶπεν ὅτι πολλὰ ἔμαθεν ἀπὸ τοῦ προφήτου.
12. γινώσκομεν ὅτι δεῖ ἡμᾶς παθεῖν πολλά.
13. διὰ τοῦτο κατέλιπον τὰ πρόβατα ἐν τοῖς ἀγροῖς καὶ ἔφυγον.
14. ἐκέλευσε τὸν ὄχλον φαγεῖν τὸν ἄρτον καὶ πιεῖν τὸν οἶνον ὃν οἱ νεανίαι ἔφερον.
15. ὁ προφήτης ὃς ἔσχε τὸ βιβλίον ἀπέθανε ἐν τῇ ἐρήμῳ.
16. εἴδομεν ὅτι οἱ δοῦλοι φέρουσι τὸ πλοῖον εἰς τὴν θάλασσαν.
17. εἶπον ὅτι τὰ τέκνα ἔφαγον τὸν καρπόν.
18. ἔγνωσαν ὅτι αἱ παρθένοι εἰσιν ἐν τῷ οἴκῳ.
19. ἤκουσα ὅτι οἱ ἀπόστολοι ἔρχονται εἰς Ἰερουσαλήμ.

LESSON 20

Grammar Exercises

20.2 Verbal root identification:

1. σπείρουσι — ἔσπειραν
2. ἀπαγγελεῖς — ἀπήγγειλας
3. κατακρινεῖ — κατέκρινεν
4. αἴρομεν — ἤραμεν
5. σπερεῖτε — ἐσπείρατε
6. φθεροῦμεν — ἐφθείραμεν
7. μένεις — ἔμεινας
8. ἀποκτείνω — ἀπέκτεινα
9. ἐγείρουσι — ἤγειραν
10. ἀποστέλλει — ἀπέστειλε

Translation Exercises

20.3 Translation exercises:

1. But when the soldiers came to the house they announced that Cornelius had sent them.
2. They will condemn the widows and will kill their children with the sword.
3. You all will not remain in this place, but will die in the land of your enemies.
4. The apostles sowed the word in the hearts of the disciples.
5. He took up, therefore, the cross and came after Jesus.
6. At that time the judges judged the tribes of Israel.
7. We destroyed the villages which were beside the sea.
8. I remained there until he had read the book.
9. But when Herod slew the children in Bethlehem, Joseph fled to Egypt with Mary.
10. Are you all able to drink the cup which I must drink?
11. I will reveal my face to them and they will see my glory.
12. We remained in the temple while the workmen were building the throne.

13. But when they heard these things from the widow, they remained with her.
14. You used to owe money to the tax collectors.
15. But Jesus said to the paralytic, "Arise, take up your bed and go to your house," and when he heard these things he took up his bed, and departed.
16. We sent the messengers to make ready the way.
17. The prophet said that all things are possible with God.
18. Command them not to destroy the boats.
19. You didn't want to drive the sheep to the side of the trees.
20. With men it is impossible, but not with God, for all things are possible with God.
21. And this we heard from him, that we ought (lit. it is necessary) to love our brethren.
22. The Pharisees said that he was eating with a sinner.

Composition Exercises

20.4 Composition exercises:

1. πέμψον τοὺς νεανίας ἐγεῖραι τοὺς στρατιώτας.
2. ὁ Ἰωσὴφ ἔλαβε τὸ παιδίον καὶ τὴν Μαριάμ, καὶ ὑπῆγε εἰς τὴν Αἴγυπτον.
3. οὐκ ἀποθανοῦνται ἐν τῇ ἐρήμῳ, οἱ γὰρ στρατιῶται σώσουσιν αὐτούς.
4. φανοῦμαι ἐμαυτόν τοῖς δούλοις μοῦ ἐν ἐκείνῳ τῷ καιρῷ λέγει ὁ κύριος.
5. οἱ Φαρισαῖοι ἦλθον φαγεῖν ἄρτον παρὰ τῷ προφήτῃ.
6. τοῦτο ἀδύνατον μέν ἐστι παρὰ τοῖς ἀνθρώποις, δυνατὸν δὲ παρὰ τῷ θεῷ.
7. ὅτε Ἡρώδης ἤκουσεν τοὺς λόγους τούτους ἔπεμψεν τοὺς δούλους αὐτοῦ φθεῖραι τὰ τέκνα ἐν Βηθλεὲμ μαχαίρᾳ.
8. ἔμειναν ἐν τῇ οἰκίᾳ ἕως ὁ παραλυτικὸς ἦρεν τὴν κλίνην αὐτοῦ.
9. ἠγγείλαμεν ὅτι ὁ ἀπόστολος μένει παρὰ τῷ Κορνηλίῳ.
10. ἆρον τὸν σταυρόν σου, καὶ φέρε αὐτὸν ὀπίσω μου.

11. οὐ δεῖ σε κατακρῖναι τὰς χήρας ταύτας.
12. βαλῶ τὴν μάχαιραν εἰς τὴν θάλασσαν.
13. ὅτε οἱ μαθηταὶ ἦλθον εἰς τὴν κώμην ἔσπειραν τὸν λόγον ἐν ταῖς καρδίαις τοῦ λαοῦ.
14. δεῖ τὸν υἱὸν τοῦ ἀνθρώπου παθεῖν πολλά.
15. ἤκουσα τοῦτο παρὰ τοῦ προφήτου ὃς μένει παρὰ τῇ χήρᾳ ἐν Βηθλεέμ.
16. οὐκ ἀποκτενεῖς τοὺς πονηρούς, ὦ κύριε;
17. ἤθελον βαλεῖν τοὺς λίθους παρὰ τὸ ἱερόν.
18. οἱ Φαρισαῖοι εἶπον ὅτι οἱ μαθηταὶ τοῦ Ἰωάννου οὐκ ἐσθίουσιν παρὰ τελώναις καὶ ἁμαρτωλοῖς.

LESSON 21

Translation Exercises

21.2 Translation exercises:

1. You all are aroused by the sound of the trumpet.
2. Let the doors be guarded by the guards.
3. They sent the shepherds to drive together the sheep during the night.
4. The boys took up the image.
5. They will remain in their land forever.
6. But when Peter went out the cock crowed.
7. You received the fruit of the vineyard for the shepherds.
8. I made this coat for the boy.
9. But the maidens took the lamps and went out to see the bridegroom.
10. For we are saved by hope and by the grace of God.
11. Behold the stars in the heaven.
12. They called him the savior of the world.
13. Unless you all eat the flesh of the Son of Man you all do not have life in yourselves.
14. I am sent by the leaders to announce these things to you.
15. Hear us, savior of Israel.

16. They received this grace from the Lord.
17. But after three months the rulers entered into the temple during the night.

21.3 Composition exercises:

Composition Exercises

1. ἐφθείραμεν τὰς εἰκόνας ἃς εἴδομεν ἐν τῷ ἱερῷ.
2. ἐξῆλθεν ὁ Πέτρος ἐκ τῆς θύρας, καὶ εὐθὺς ὁ ἀλέκτωρ ἐφώνησεν.
3. ὁ δεσπότης ἔπεμψε τοὺς ἐργάτας εἰς τὸν ἀμπελῶνα αὐτοῦ.
4. μετὰ τρεῖς μῆνας εἴδομεν τὸν ἀστέρα ἐν τοῖς οὐρανοῖς.
5. ὅτε ὁ νυμφίος ἦλθε νυκτὸς ἔλαβον τὰς λαμπάδας αὐτῶν καὶ ἐξῆλθον ἰδεῖν αὐτόν.
6. ἠγείρεσθε τοῖς σάλπιγξι.
7. ἠγγείλαμεν ὑμῖν ὅτι ἐστὶν ὁ σωτὴρ τοῦ κόσμου.
8. δέχου τὴν χάριν τοῦ θεοῦ.
9. τὰ ἱμάτια ἐπέμπετο τοῖς παισὶ ὑπὸ τῶν χήρων.
10. οἱ ποιμένες ἐκάλουν τὰ ἴδια πρόβατα, τὰ δὲ ἦλθε μετ᾽ αὐτούς.
11. εἰ μὴ ἐσθίομεν τὴν σάρκα τοῦ υἱοῦ τοῦ ἀνθρώπου, οὐκ ἕξομεν ζωὴν ἐν ἑαυτοῖς.
12. ὧδε μενῶ εἰς τὸν αἰῶνα, λέγει ὁ κύριος.

LESSON 22

22.2 Morphology exercises:

Grammar Exercises

1. θέλημα, θελήματος, τό

nom. sg.	θέλημα	nom. pl.	θελήματα
acc. sg.	θέλημα	acc. pl.	θελήματα
gen. sg.	θελήματος	gen. pl.	θελημάτων
dat. sg.	θελήματι	dat. pl.	θελήμασι

2. αἶμα, αἵματος, τό

nom. sg.	αἶμα	nom. pl.	αἵματα
acc. sg.	αἶμα	acc. pl.	αἵματα
gen. sg.	αἵματος	gen. pl.	αἱμάτων
dat. sg.	αἵματι	dat. pl.	αἵμασι

3. φῶς, φωτός, τό

nom. sg.	φῶς	nom. pl.	φῶτα
acc. sg.	φῶς	acc. pl.	φῶτα
gen. sg.	φωτός	gen. pl.	φώτων
dat. sg.	φωτί	dat. pl.	φωσίν

4. πῦρ, πυρός, τό

nom. sg.	πῦρ	gen. sg.	πυρός
acc. sg.	πῦρ	dat. sg.	πυρί

5. τέρας, τέρατος, τό

nom. sg.	τέρας	nom. pl.	τέρατα
acc. sg.	τέρας	acc. pl.	τέρατα
gen. sg.	τέρατος	gen. pl.	τεράτων
dat. sg.	τέρατι	dat. pl.	τέρασι

6. οὖς, ὠτός, τό

nom. sg.	οὖς	nom. pl.	ὦτα
acc. sg.	οὖς	acc. pl.	ὦτα
gen. sg.	ὠτός	gen. pl.	ὤτων
dat. sg.	ὠτί	dat. pl.	ὠσίν

Translation Exercises

22.3 Translation exercises:

1. John came to the river Jordan and preached the baptism of repentance for the remission of sins.
2. See with how large letters I have written to you all with my own hand.
3. He said that he was not the light, but that he came to bear witness about the light.
4. The enemies destroyed our cities with fire.

5. You are sought by your mother and your brethren.
6. It is not proper to take the children's bread and cast it to dogs.
7. The men walked about the fields with their wives.
8. I commanded the men to make ready the way for the king.
9. I indeed baptize you with water, but he will baptize you with the Holy Spirit and with fire.
10. For we have the forgiveness of our sins through his blood.
11. He will work signs and wonders for this generation.
12. The boys took the fish out of the water.
13. He will open the ears of the deaf.
14. And after these things his disciples came and marvelled that he was speaking with a woman.
15. I wrote all this by the hand of my daughter.
16. For I came not to do my own will, but the will of the Father who sent me.
17. The scribes said that they had seen the king's daughter.

22.4 Composition exercises:

Composition Exercises

1. οὗτος ὁ ἄνθρωπος ἐποίησε σημεῖα καὶ τέρατα ἐν τῇ πόλει.
2. ἴδετε τὰς χεῖρας καὶ τοὺς πόδας μου.
3. ὑμεῖς ἐστε τὸ φῶς τοῦ κόσμου.
4. ἡ γυνὴ ἐξέμασσε τοὺς πόδας τοῦ Ἰησοῦ ταῖς θριξὶν αὐτῆς.
5. οἱ πατέρες ἡμῶν ἤσθιον τὸ μάννα ἐν τῇ ἐρήμῳ.
6. ἥψατο τοῦ ὠτὸς τοῦ κωφοῦ τῇ χειρὶ αὐτοῦ.
7. ὁ βασιλεύς ἔπεμψε τὴν γυναῖκα ταύτην ἄγειν τὸν πατέρα αὐτῆς ἀπὸ τῆς πόλεως.
8. ἐζήτει τὴν μητέρα καὶ τὴν θυγατέρα αὐτοῦ.
9. τὸ ἅγιον πνεῦμα μενεῖ μετ᾽ αὐτῶν εἰς τὸν αἰῶνα.
10. λέγεις ὅτι γινώσκεις τὸ θέλημα τοῦ θεοῦ.
11. οἱ κύνες ἤσθιον τὸν ἰχθὺν ὃν ἔλαβον ἐκ τοῦ ὕδατος.

12. ἐν ἐκείνῳ τῷ ἔτει ὁ πατήρ μου διῆλθε τὴν πόλιν ὑμῶν.
13. οἱ γραμματεῖς οὐκ ἤθελον δέχεσθαι τὸ βάπτισμα εἰς ἄφεσιν ἁμαρτιῶν.
14. ἀνέγνων τὰ γράμματα ἃ ἔγραψε τῇ χειρὶ τῆς γυναικὸς αὐτοῦ.
15. αἱ πόλεις ὑμῶν φθείρονται πυρί.
16. ἐκάμψαμεν τὰ γόνατα ὑμῶν τῷ βασιλεῖ.
17. ὦ γύναι, ὑπάγε ἐν εἰρήνῃ, ἐγὼ γὰρ θεραπεύσω τὴν θυγατέρά σου.

LESSON 23

Translation Exercises

23.2 Translation exercises:

1. Behold I have made you whole, sin no more.
2. The robbers fled to the hills.
3. No one wants to drink this wine.
4. My name will be great among all the gentiles.
5. The priests came by night and took up the body of the prophet.
6. If therefore the light is darkness in you, how great is the darkness.
7. O woman, great is your faith.
8. We know that these words are true, because the Lord spoke them by the mouth of David the prophet.
9. And this is the judgement, that light came into the world, and men loved the darkness rather than the light, for their deeds were evil.
10. Let one of the slaves be sent to sow the seed in my field.
11. And many came together out of the villages, and they brought to him the sick and cast them before his feet, and they implored him to heal them.

12. Let no one cause one of these children to stumble.
13. But his parents did not know that he was remaining in the city.
14. Did not the Scripture say that the Christ comes out of the seed of David and from Bethlehem the village where David was?
15. In that hour many of the high priests were gathered together unto him, who say that there will be no resurrection.

23.3 Composition exercises:

Composition Exercises

1. ἀνοίξεις τὸ στόμα μου, κύριε, καὶ ἡ γλῶσσά μου εὐλογήσει τὸ ὄνομα σου.
2. οὐκ ἔσπειρας καλὸν σπέρμα ἐν τῷ ἀγρῷ σου;
3. μὴ βαστάζετε μηδένα ἀσθενῆ εἰς τὴν συναγωγὴν ἐν τῷ σαββάτῳ.
4. εἰ θέλεις δύνασαι θεραπεύειν με.
5. ἦλθον εἰς τὸν κόσμον τοῦτον εἰς κρίσιν.
6. εἷς τῶν λεπρῶν ὅτε εἶδεν ὅτι θεραπεύεται ἔβαλεν ἑαυτὸν εἰς τοὺς πόδας αὐτοῦ.
7. οἱ ἀρχιερεῖς ἔγνων ὅτι τὸ ῥῆμα τοῦτο ἀληθὲς ἦν.
8. πάντες οἱ μαθηταὶ πληρεῖς πίστεως ἦσαν καὶ τοῦ ἁγίου πνεύματος, καὶ ἐθεράπευσαν τοὺς ἀσθενεῖς καὶ ἐξέβαλον πολλὰ δαιμόνια.
9. οὐδεὶς τῶν ἱερῶν πιστεύει ὅτι ἀνάστασίς ἐστι.
10. οἱ γονεῖς μου ᾠκοδόμησαν πολλοὺς οἴκους ἐν τῇ πόλει ταύτῃ.
11. μηδεὶς φιλείτω τὸ σκότος μᾶλλον ἢ τὸ φῶς.
12. ὅτε ἦλθον εἰς τὰς κώμας ἐκήρυξαν τὸ εὐαγγέλιον πᾶσι τοῖς ἔθνεσι οἵ κατῴκουν ἐκεῖ.
13. εἰ κρίνω ἐγὼ, ἡ κρίσις μου ἀληθής ἐστι.
14. ὅτε οἱ μαθηταὶ τοῦ Ἰωάννου ἤκουσαν ὅτι ἀπέθανε, ἦλθον καὶ ἦρον τὸ σῶμα.

LESSON 24

Translation Exercises

24.2 Translation exercises:

1. Jesus was led by the Spirit into the hills to be tempted by the devil.
2. The high priest was hidden in the hills many years.
3. My name will be proclaimed among all the gentiles.
4. For by grace we were saved through the will of God.
5. The dead will be raised in the day of judgement by the voice of the angel and the trumpet.
6. And when the demon was cast out, the people wondered, and many said "These wonders were not done in the days of our fathers."
7. After these things he was seen by all the apostles.
8. He commanded the man to be carried through the city.
9. In that day all the people will be called holy to the Lord.
10. The women were comforted by their husbands.
11. I will make my word to be heard by the king.
12. None of the messengers will be heard.
13. All the fish were cast into the water.
14. These things were spoken by the mouth of David.
15. Let one of the priests be sent to persuade the king.
16. When the good seed produced fruit, then the tares also appeared.
17. O king, You will be loved by all the nation.
18. The bodies of the saints were sown in dishonour, but they will be raised in glory.
19. You all were called foolish by the wise men of this age.

24.3 Composition exercises:

Composition Exercises

1. πᾶν τὸ γένος τοῦτο ἐκλήθη δίκαιον.
2. πολλὰ τῶν ῥημάτων τούτων ἐγράφησαν ἐν βιβλίῳ ὑπὸ τοῦ ἀρχιερέως.
3. οἱ ἰχθύες ἐλήφθησαν ὑπὸ τῶν παίδων τούτων.
4. ἐσπάρημεν ἐν ἀσθενείᾳ, ἐγερθησόμεθα ἐν ἐξουσίᾳ.
5. εἰ τὸ δαιμόνιον ἐκβληθήσεται ὁ ὄχλος θαυμάσει.
6. τὸ καλὸν σπέρμα εἰσηνέχθη εἰς τοὺς ἀγρούς.
7. ἐστάλην ὑπὸ τῶν διακόνων τοῦ βασιλέως ζητεῖν σε.
8. γινώσκομεν ὅτι τοῦτο τὸ εὐαγγέλιον κηρυχθήσεται πᾶσι τοῖς ἔθνεσι καὶ ὅτι πολλοὶ ἀκούσουσιν.
9. ἐν ἐκείνῃ ἡμέρᾳ πολλὰ σώματα τῶν ἁγίων ἐγέρθη, καὶ ἦλθον εἰς τὴν πόλιν, καὶ ἐφάνησαν πολλοῖς.
10. θέλομεν τὰ πρόβατα ταῦτα ἀχθῆναι εἰς τὰ ὄρη.
11. σωθήσῃ πίστει καὶ ἐλπίδι εἰ μενεῖς ἐν αὐταῖς.
12. ἐκελεύσατε τοὺς λίθους βληθῆναι εἰς τὸ ὕδωρ.
13. πάντα ταῦτα ποιηθήσεται ἐν τῷ σκότει.
14. ἠκούσατε ὅτι ἐρρήθη ὑπὸ τῶν πατέρων ἡμῶν ὅτι οὐ ποιήσεις εἰκόνα κυρίου τοῦ θεοῦ σου.
15. ἐκλήθημεν ἄφρονες ὑπὸ πολλῶν τῶν ἀρχόντων τῶν ἔθνων, γινώσκομεν δὲ ὅτι οἱ λόγοι οὓς λαλοῦμεν ἀληθεῖς εἰσιν.

LESSON 25

25.2 Translation exercises:

Translation Exercises

1. And passing by the sea of Galilee he saw Simon and Andrew the brother of Simon casting nets into the sea.
2. And he went preaching in their synagogues and casting out demons.
3. With what difficulty will they that have money enter into the kingdom of God.

4. And those that ate the loaves were five thousand men.
5. Therefore, the ones who had been scattered abroad went about preaching the word.
6. And coming to Jerusalem he was trying to join himself to the disciples, and they were all afraid of him, because they did not believe that he was a disciple.
7. And Ananias hearing these words fell down and expired, and great fear came upon all that heard.
8. And the unclean spirit having shook him and having cried with a loud voice, came out of him.
9. And he was in the wilderness forty days and forty nights being tempted by Satan.
10. Therefore (you all) hear the parable of the sower!
11. And there appeared to them Moses and Elias speaking with him.

Composition Exercises

25.3 Composition exercises:

1. οἱ κηρύξαντες τὸν λόγον διεσπάρησαν.
2. καὶ παράγοντες τὴν θάλασσαν τῆς Γαλιλαίας οἱ μαθηταὶ ἐδίδαξαν πολλούς.
3. μακάριοι οἱ ἀκούοντες καὶ οἱ πιστεύοντες τοῖς λόγοις τοῦ βιβλίου τούτου.
4. πολλοὶ οὖν τῶν τελώνων ἐβαπτίσθησαν ἐξομολογούμενοι τὰς ἁμαρτίας αὐτῶν.
5. ὁ δὲ ἀποκριθεὶς εἶπεν πῶς δυσχόλως εἰσελεύσεσθε εἰς τὴν βασιλείαν τῶν οὐρανῶν.
6. ὁ σπείρων σπείρει τὸν λόγον.
7. ἐξελθὼν δὲ εἶδεν μέγαν ὄχλον.
8. καὶ πάντες οἱ ἀκούσαντες ἐτήρησαν τοὺς λόγους τούτους ἐν ταῖς καρδίαις αὐτῶν.
9. ἐφοβούμεθα δὲ μὴ πιστεύοντες ὅτι οἱ λόγοι αὐτοῦ ἀληθεῖς εἰσιν.
10. οὗτός ἐστιν ὁ πεμφθεὶς ὑπὸ τοῦ βασιλέως.

11. διδάσκοντες δὲ τὸν λαὸν ἔμειναν ἐν τῷ ἱερῷ.
12. καὶ ἐξελθὼν ἐκ τῆς πόλεως ἀπῆλθε εἰς ἕτερον τόπον.
13. ὁ δὲ προφήτης ἔκραξε λέγων ἰδοὺ τὸν ἄνθρωπον τὸν ἐρχόμενον μετ᾽ ἐμέ, ἐκεῖνον ἀκούσετε.
14. ὁ οὖν ἄρχων ἀκούσας τοῦτο ἐφοβεῖτο καὶ πάντες οἱ μετ᾽ αὐτοῦ ὄντες.
15. καὶ ἀμφιβαλόντες ἐν τῇ θαλάσσῃ ἔλαβον πολλοὺς ἰχθύας.
16. καὶ πορευόμενοι εἰς Βηθλεὲμ ἐπείρασαν εἰσελθεῖν εἰς τὴν συναγωγήν, οἱ δὲ φυλάσσοντες ἐξέβαλον αὐτούς.
17. περιπατῶν δὲ διὰ τῶν ἀγρῶν εἶδον φῶς μέγα ἐκ τοῦ οὐρανοῦ, καὶ ἤκουσα φωνὴν λαλοῦσάν μοι.
18. ὁ προφήτης ἔμεινε ἐν τῷ ὄρει τεσσαράκοντα ἡμέρας καὶ τεσσαράκοντα νύκτας γραφῶν τὰ ῥήματα τοῦ νόμου τούτου.

LESSON 26

Translation Exercises

26.2(α) Translation exercises, part 1:

1. And while Peter was still speaking these words the Holy Spirit fell upon all that heard the word.
2. For the flesh desires against the spirit and the spirit against the flesh.
3. And since Lydda was near to Joppa, the disciples, after hearing that Peter was in it (that place), sent two men to him.
4. But he that was sown upon the rocky ground, this is he who hears the word and immediately receives it with joy.
5. But as they are departing, behold an angel of the Lord appears in a dream to Joseph saying, "Take the child and his mother, and flee into Egypt."
6. But the multitudes were astonished at his teaching.
7. But you all will receive power after the Holy Spirit comes upon you.

8. And daily they continued with one accord in the temple.
9. And they will see the Son of Man coming upon the clouds of heaven.
10. Which of the two did the will of his father?
11. Then there came to him a certain woman asking something of him, and he said to her, "What do you want?"

26.2(β) Translation exercises, part 2:

1. In the time of the high priesthood of Annas and Caiaphas the word of the Lord came to John the son of Zacharias in the wilderness.
2. On this rock I will build my church.
3. But the high priests and the whole council sought false witness against Jesus.
4. I was daily with you all in the temple and you all did not seize me.
5. Jesus saw the Spirit of God coming down like a dove coming upon him.
6. And they wondered at his answer and became silent.
7. He that is not with me is against me.
8. And he was moved with compassion for them and healed some of them.
9. You all judge according to the flesh, but I judge no man.
10. And he went away through the whole city proclaiming what things Jesus had done for him.
11. And the herd rushed down the cliff into the sea.
12. And certain of those with us went to the tomb.
13. Lord, if it is you, command me to come to you upon the water.
14. And he went into the synagogue as was his custom on the Sabbath day.

15. Master, after toiling all the night we have taken nothing, but at your word I will let down the nets.
16. And he said to them, "Strive to enter in through the narrow gate."

26.3 Composition exercises:

Composition Exercises

1. εἰσελθόντων δὲ τῶν μαθητῶν εἰς τὸ πλοῖον ἀπέστειλεν ὁ Ἰησοῦς τοὺς ὄχλους.
2. τότε ἄνθρωπός τις ἐλθὼν πρὸς αὐτὸν εἶπε· τί ποιεῖς σὺ ὧδε;
3. ἐλθόντος τοῦ ἁγίου πνεύματος ἐφ᾽ ἡμᾶς τίνα δύναμιν λημψόμεθα;
4. ἐγγίζει ἡ ἡμέρα ἐν ᾗ ὁ υἱὸς τοῦ ἀνθρώπου ἐλεύσεται ἐπὶ τῶν νεφέλων τοῦ οὐρανοῦ.
5. λάβετε καὶ κρίνατε τοὺς ἀνθρώπους τούτους κατὰ τὸν νόμον ὑμῶν.
6. ὁ δὲ Πέτρος ἦλθε πρὸς αὐτὸν περιπατῶν ἐπὶ τὸ ὕδωρ.
7. οἱ μαθηταὶ ἐκήρυσσον ἐπ᾽ ἀρχιερέως Καιάφα.
8. εἰσῆλθον εἰς τὴν ἐκκλησίαν κατὰ τὸ εἰωθὸς ἐν τῇ ἡμέρᾳ τοῦ κυρίου.
9. καθ᾽ ἡμέραν ἤμην πρὸς ὑμᾶς ἐν Ἰερουσαλήμ.
10. ὁ ἀρχιερεὺς οὖν εἶπεν πρὸς τοὺς μαθητάς· τίς ὑμῖν ἔδωκεν ἐξουσίαν ποιεῖν ταῦτα;
11. οἱ Φαρισαῖοι ἐροῦσιν πολλὰ κατὰ τοῦ υἱοῦ τοῦ ἀνθρώπου.
12. ἀναχωρησάντων δὲ τῶν ἀγγέλων τοῦ Ἡρώδου οἱ μαθηταὶ ἔλεγον αὐτῷ κατ᾽ ἰδίαν πάντα ὅσα ἐποίησαν.
13. πέμψαντος δὲ αὐτοῦ τὸν ἴδιον υἱὸν πρὸς αὐτούς, οὐκ ἤθελον δέχεσθαι αὐτόν.
14. ἐξεπλήσσεσθε ἐπὶ ταῖς ἐπαγγελίαις αὐτοῦ.
15. κοπιασάντων δὲ ἡμῶν δι᾽ ὅλης νυκτὸς Ἰησοῦς ἦλθε πρὸς ἡμᾶς περιπατῶν ἐπὶ τὴν θάλασσαν.
16. κρατοῦντος δὲ αὐτοῦ τὴν χεῖρά μου ἔλαβον ἐξουσίαν περιπατεῖν.

17. τίς δύναται προσκαρτερεῖν ταῦτα;
18. ἐγγιζόντων δὲ αὐτῶν τῇ πόλει ὁ πᾶς ὄχλος ἔχαιρε λέγων· εὐλογημένος ὁ ἐρχόμενος ἐν ὀνόματι κυρίου.
19. ἐπ' Ἡρώδου τοῦ βασιλέως ὁ Ἰωσὴφ κατέβη εἰς Αἴγυπτον παραλαβὼν τὸ παιδίον Ἰησοῦν καὶ Μαριὰμ τὴν μητέρα αὐτοῦ.

LESSON 27

Translation Exercises

27.2(α) Translation exercises, part 1:

1. And on the next day while they were going on their way and drawing nigh to the city, Peter went up upon the house top to pray.
2. Isn't the soul more than food?
3. And they took counsel together to kill Paul.
4. Let the greater among you all become as the younger.
5. They perceived that they were unlettered and ignorant men.
6. For now is our salvation nearer than when we believed.
7. Truly this man was a Son of God.
8. And having cast the money into the temple he departed, and went out and hanged himself.
9. But he that is least[1] in the kingdom of heaven is greater than he.
10. And now there remains[2] faith, hope, love, these three, but the greatest[3] of these is love.
11. He that is stronger than I comes after me.
12. You will see greater things than these.

1 Sometimes a comparative is used for a superlative in the NT.

2 Sometimes a verb doesn't end up agreeing in number to its subject.

3 This is another example of a comparative being used as a superlative.

13. And now why do you delay? Get yourself baptized and wash away your sins, having called on the name of the Lord.
14. All our fathers were baptized into Moses in the cloud and in the sea.

27.2(β) Translation exercises, part 2:

1. But they cried out the more saying, "Lord, have mercy upon us."
2. You O Lord, show the man whom you have chosen.
3. The queen of the south came from the furthest parts of the earth to hear the wisdom of Solomon, and behold one greater than Solomon is here.
4. No one puts a patch of undressed cloth on an old garment, for that which fills it up lifts it away from the garment and a worse tear is made.
5. Verily I say unto you, inasmuch as you all did it to one of the least of these my brethren, you did it unto me.
6. And the last state of that man becomes worse than the first.
7. For I am the least of the apostles.
8. If therefore you can't even do the smallest thing, why are you worried about the rest?
9. I say unto you, there is no one greater than John among the offspring of women, but he that is least in the kingdom of God is greater than he.
10. We must obey God rather than men.

27.3 Composition exercises:

Composition Exercises

1. προσευξάμενος δὲ ὁ Σολομῶν ἀπῆλθεν ἐκ τοῦ ἱεροῦ.
2. ὁ νεώτερος τῶν υἱῶν οὐκ ἤθελεν ἐργάζεσθαι ὑπὲρ τοῦ πατρὸς αὐτοῦ.

3. οἱ λῃσταὶ ἀπήγξαντο, οἱ γὰρ διώκοντες αὐτοὺς μείζονες αὐτῶν ἦσαν.
4. ἐπεκαλεσάμεθα τὸ ὄνομα τοῦ κυρίου, ἰσχυρότερος γάρ ἐστι πάντων τῶν βασιλέων τῆς γῆς.
5. ἐξελέξατο Σίμωνα ὃν ἐπεκάλεσε Πέτρον.
6. ἰδοὺ ἡ ἀγάπη μείζων ἐστὶ τῆς πίστεως.
7. τί οὖν μέλλετε ἐλθεῖν εἰς Ἰερουσαλήμ, ἰδοὺ γὰρ μείζων Σολομῶνος ἐκεῖ;
8. πειθαρχεῖν δεῖ τῷ βασιλεῖ μᾶλλον ἢ τῷ ἱερεῖ.
9. λέγουσι ὅτι αὗται αἱ ἡμέραι ἥσσονές εἰσιν ἢ αἱ ἡμέραι τῶν πατέρων ἡμῶν.
10. συνεβουλεύσατε ἀποκτείνειν τὸν σοφώτατον τῶν ἀνθρώπων.
11. ὁ μικρότερος γενήσεται ὁ μείζων.
12. ὁ δὲ ἔκραξε μᾶλλον· ἰδοὺ ὅσα πάσχω ταῖς χερσὶ τῶν ἐχθρῶν μου.
13. ἀληθῶς καταλαμβάνομαι ὅτι ἐστι σχίσμα ἐν αὐτοῖς.
14. οὐ δυνάμεθα τὸ ἐλάχιστον τούτων ποιεῖν.
15. ἐφ' ὅσον ἐποίησας τοῦτο, ἐποίησας ἧσσον πάντων τῶν ἀδελφῶν σου.
16. ὁ δὲ ἀπεκρίθη αὐτοῖς σοφώτερον τοῦ πατρός.

LESSON 28

Translation Exercises

28.2 Translation exercises:

1. He enquired from them where Christ was[1] to be born.
2. He is not a God of the dead, but of the living, for all live to him.
3. This word is not made manifest to us.
4. They were speaking of his departure which he was about to fulfil in Jerusalem.
5. Simon son of John, do you love me more than these?

1 The English sequence of tenses makes this past in translation.

6. The voice of one crying in the wilderness.
7. In the same hour the disciples were rejoicing.
8. For God humbles those that exalt themselves, and exalts those that humble themselves.
9. Then they crucified with him two robbers.
10. Why do you ask me about the good?
11. Jesus says to him, "Go on, your son lives."
12. But God suffered all the nations to walk in their own ways.
13. Aeneas, Jesus Christ heals you.
14. Jesus was not allowing the demons to speak.

28.3 Composition exercises:

Composition Exercises

1. οἱ μαθηταὶ ἐφανέρουν ταῦτα ἃ ἤκουσαν.
2. οὐκ εἰῶμεν αὐτοὺς σταυρῶσαι τὸν δοῦλον.
3. ὁ βασιλεὺς ἐταπείνωσε τοὺς ὑψωθέντας.
4. πυνθάνονται εἰ ὁ δοῦλος ἰᾶται.
5. τί ἐᾶτε αὐτοὺς ζῆν ἐν τῇ πόλει ἡμῶν;
6. θέλετε ἀγαπᾶν κύριον τὸν θεὸν ὑμῶν, ὦ υἱοὶ τῶν ἀνθρώπων;
7. ἡ φωνὴ εἶπε· βόα, καὶ ἀπεκρίθη· τί βοήσω;
8. νῦν πληροῦται ὁ λόγος τοῦ προφήτου.
9. ὅτε ὁ Ἰησοῦς ἐγεννήθη ἐν Βηθλεὲμ σοφοὶ ἦλθον προσκύνησαι αὐτῷ, πυνθανόμενοι ποῦ ὁ βασιλεὺς τῶν Ἰουδαίων δεῖ γεννᾶσθαι.
10. ὁ θεὸς δικαιοῖ τοὺς υἱοὺς τῶν ἀνθρώπων πίστει καὶ οὐκ ἔργοις.
11. καὶ πάντες ἠγαλλιῶντο ὅτι ὁ ἔχων τὸ δαιμόνιον ἰάθη.
12. ἀγαλλιῶ,[1] ὁ γὰρ υἱός σου ζῇ.
13. ταπεινοῦτε οὖν ἑαυτοὺς ὑπὸ τὴν κραταιὰν χεῖρα τοῦ θεοῦ, ὑψώσει γὰρ ὑμᾶς ἐν καιρῷ.
14. ἐφανέρωσα τὸ ὄνομά σου τούτῳ τῷ λαῷ, καὶ φανερώσω αὐτὸ τοῖς τέκνοις αὐτῶν.

1 Present middle imperative

LESSON 29

Translation Exercises

29.2 Translation exercises:

1. He brought Greeks into the temple and has desecrated the holy place.
2. And a certain poor man, Lazarus by name, had been cast at his door.
3. Little children, it is the last hour, and as you all heard that an antichrist comes even now many antichrists have come about.
4. Jesus says to him, “Because you have seen me have you believed? Blessed are they that have not seen, and yet have believed.”
5. But when (now) I have become a man I have put away childish things.
6. And going to her house she found the child cast upon the bed and the demon gone out.
7. The time is fulfilled and the kingdom of God is at hand.
8. There Mary who was called Magdalene, out of whom seven devils had departed, comes to him.
9. And many bodies of the saints that slept arose.
10. His disciples came by night and stole him while we slept.
11. I have done no wrong to the Jews as you very well know.
12. No temptation has taken you all except such as man can bear.
13. For God has spoken this by the mouth of all the prophets.
14. But we preach Christ crucified.

Composition Exercises

29.3 Composition exercises:

1. αἱ ἡμέραι τῆς βασιλείας τῶν οὐρανῶν πεπλήρωνται.
2. οὐκ ἠδίκηκέ σε ἢ τοὺς φίλους σου.

3. ἑωράκαμεν καὶ μεμαρτυρήκαμεν ὅτι οὗτός ἐστιν ὁ προφήτης ὁ λεγόμενος διὰ Μωυσέως.
4. τότε οἱ νεανίαι ἐξεπλήσσοντο, ὅτι φόβος μέγας εἰλήφει αὐτούς.
5. ὁ κύριος κακὸν εἴρηκεν περί σου.
6. κεκοινώκασι τὸν οἶκον τοῦ κυρίου νεκροῖς.
7. δεῖ σε κηρύσσειν ἃ ἑώρακας καὶ ἀκήκοας.
8. ὁ ἡγεμὼν ἐρωτᾷ τί οἱ δοῦλοι πεποιήκασι.
9. πεπόνθατε πολλὰ διὰ τῶν Ἰουδαίων.
10. τότε ὁ Πιλάτος ἀπεκρίθη λέγων· ὃ γέγραφα, γέγραφα.
11. ὅτε δὲ γέγονα βασιλεὺς περιεπάτησα ἐν ταῖς ὁδοῖς τῶν πατέρων μου.
12. οἱ πτωχοὶ καὶ οἱ τυφλοὶ βέβληνται πρὸς τοὺς πυλῶνας τῶν πλουσίων.
13. ὦ κύριε, ἐν σοὶ πεπιστεύκαμεν.
14. εὗρον τὰ δαιμόνια ἐξεληλύθοτα.
15. εἴρηκα ὑμῖν τοὺς λόγους τῆς βασιλείας, ὑμεῖς δὲ οὐ πεπιστεύκατέ μοι.
16. οἱ τετηρήκοτες τὴν πίστιν λήμψονται τὸν στέφανον τῆς ζωῆς ὃν ἐπήγγειλεν ὁ κύριος τοῖς ἠγαπηκόσι αὐτόν.
17. ἐθεώρουν τὸ ἱερὸν πεπληρωμένον τῇ δόξῃ τοῦ κυρίου.

LESSON 30

30.2 Translation exercises:

Translation Exercises

1. You all set aside the commandment of God well, so that you may keep your own tradition.
2. Let us go elsewhere into the next villages, in order that I may preach there also.
3. Whoever receives one of such children in my name receives me, and whoever receives me, doesn't receive me, but him that sent me.
4. Do not judge, so that you all may be not judged.
5. Whoever wants to save his soul will lose it.

6. And they closed their eyes so they would not see with their eyes.
7. Whatever you will bind on earth will be bound[1] in heaven.
8. Sirs, what must I do that I may be saved?[2]
9. You all will listen to him according to whatever he will say to you.
10. Will we say then, "Let us do evil that good may come"?
11. For you all have the poor always with you, and whenever you want you can do them good.
12. Flee to Egypt and be there until I tell you.

Composition Exercises

30.3 Composition exercises:

1. οἱ Φαρισαῖοι ἠθέτουν τὴν ἐντολὴν τοῦ θεοῦ ἵνα τὴν παράδοσιν αὐτῶν τηρήσωσι.
2. ὃ ἂν λέγω ὑμῖν κατ᾽ ἰδίαν τοῦτο κηρύσσετε παντὶ τῷ λαῷ.
3. τί οὖν ποιήσωμεν; μένωμεν ἐν ἁμαρτίᾳ ἵνα περισσεύῃ ἡ χάρις;
4. ὅταν ἴδητε τὰ ἔθνη ἐν τῷ ἁγίῳ τόπῳ, γνῶτε ὅτι τὸ τέλος τοῦ αἰῶνος ἐγγίζει.
5. ὅπου ἂν τὸ εὐαγγέλιον κηρύξηται οἱ πιστεύοντες σωθήσονται.
6. ἀπόστειλον τὰ τέκνα εἰς τὴν ἔρημον ἵνα μὴ ἀποκτείνωσιν αὐτὰ οἱ λῃσταί.
7. ὁ θεὸς πολλοὺς προφήτας ἀπέστειλεν ἵνα διδάσκωσιν τὸν λαὸν τοῦτον.
8. φάγωμεν καὶ πίωμεν, δεῖ γὰρ ἡμᾶς ταχέως ὑπάγειν.
9. ἄγωμεν ἀλλαχοῦ ἵνα τοὺς ὄχλους παρακαλῶμεν.
10. ὅταν θέλωμεν δυνάμεθα εὖ ποιεῖν τοῖς πτωχοῖς.
11. μεῖνον ἐν τῇ οἰκίᾳ ἕως ἂν καλέσω σε.

1 Notice the resultant meaning from the perfect participle.

2 Notice how an English infinitive "to be saved" would also communicate purpose here.

12. ἐκόψαμεν πάντα τὰ δένδρα ἵνα μὴ οἱ ἐχθροὶ φάγωσι τὸν καρπόν.
13. οὐ πίομαι οἶνον ἵνα μὴ σκανδαλίσω τὸν ἀδελφόν μου.
14. δέομαί σου φυλάσσειν τὰ πρόβατά μου ἕως ἂν εὕρω τὸ ἀπολλύμενον.
15. ὃς ἂν θέλῃ μείζων[1] ἐν ὑμῖν εἶναι ταπεινωσάτω ἑαυτὸν ὡς παιδίον.
16. ὦ κύριε, φανέρωσον τὴν δύναμίν σου ἡμῖν ἵνα δοξασθῇ τὸ ὄνομά σου.
17. φέρε τὰ ἱμάτια πρός με ἵνα εἰσενέχθῃ πρὸς τὰς χήρας.

LESSON 31

Translation Exercises

31.2 Translation exercises:

1. Lord, if you desire, you can cleanse me.
2. But Paul cried out with a loud voice saying, "Don't do harm to yourself, for we are all here."
3. Unless your righteousness increases more than the righteousness of the Scribes and Pharisees, you all will in no way enter into the kingdom of heaven.
4. Therefore do not be anxious for tomorrow.
5. Whoever does not receive the kingdom of God as a little child will in no way enter into it.
6. For I say to you that I will certainly not eat it until it is fulfilled in the kingdom of God.
7. If any one desires to do his will, he will know about the teaching whether it is of God.
8. You all are the salt of the earth: but, if the salt has become tasteless, with what will it be salted?
9. But the Lord said to Paul, "Be not afraid, but speak, and do not be silent."
10. If you all love me, you will keep my commandments.

1 Comparative adjectives are often used with a superlative sense in the New Testament.

11. Verily I say to you that there are some of those that are here who will certainly not taste of death until they see the Son of Man coming in his kingdom.
12. For if you all love those that love you, what reward do you have?
13. And he appointed twelve that they might be with him, and that he might send them to preach and to have power to cast out demons.
14. Don't say then, "What will we eat?" or "What will we drink?" or "What will we put on?"

Composition Exercises

31.3 Composition exercises:

1. ἐὰν γὰρ εὖ ποιῆτε τοῖς εὖ ποιοῦσιν ὑμῖν, τίνα μισθὸν ἔχετε;
2. μὴ εἰσαγάγῃς τὰ ἔθνη εἰς τὸ ἱερόν.
3. μὴ ζητῶμεν τὰ τοῦ αἰῶνος τούτου ἀλλὰ τὰ τοῦ ἐρχομένου.
4. ἐὰν ποιῆτε ταῦτα ἀγαπηθήσεσθε ὑπὸ τοῦ πατρός μου.
5. μὴ δέχεσθε τοὺς ἐχθροὺς τοῦ εὐαγγελίου.
6. οὐ μὴ ἐάσω σε φαγεῖν ἄρτον ἐν τῷ τόπῳ τούτῳ.
7. ἐὰν ὁμολογήσωμεν τὰς ἁμαρτίας ἡμῶν ἐλεήσει ἡμᾶς.
8. ἦλθον πρὸς τὸν ἱερέα, ἵνα ἐρωτῶσιν αὐτὸν περὶ τοῦ ὁράματος.
9. καὶ πᾶς ὁ λαὸς ἐσίγα ἵνα ἀκούσῃ τοὺς ἀγγέλους Καίσαρος.
10. ἐὰν ἀγαπῶμεν αὐτὸν τηρήσομεν τὰς ἐντολὰς αὐτοῦ.
11. οἱ δοῦλοι ἤνεγκόν μοι ἄρτον καὶ ἰχθύν, ἵνα γεύσωμαι αὐτῶν.
12. μηκέτι ἁμάρτανε, μὴ ἧσσόν σοι ἐπέλθῃ.
13. ἐὰν οὗτοι πονηροὶ ὦσιν, ὁ κύριος φθερεῖ αὐτοὺς καὶ τὴν πόλιν αὐτῶν.
14. οὐ μὴ φανερώσω ἐμαυτὸν τῷ γένει τούτῳ.
15. μὴ εἰσενέγκῃς οἶνον τοῖς δούλοις.
16. ἐὰν ὁ ἔχθρος ἐγγίσῃ, τάξω τοὺς στρατιώτας.

17. πῶς ἀγοράσωμεν ἄρτον, ἵνα οὗτοι φάγωσι;
18. ἀγαπῶμεν τοὺς γονεῖς ἡμῶν, ἵνα ὑπ' αὐτῶν ἀγαπώμεθα.

LESSON 32

Translation Exercises

32.2 Translation exercises:

1. To love God out of one's whole heart and to love one's neighbour as oneself is better than all whole burnt offerings and sacrifices.
2. But the multitudes gave heed to the things spoken by Philip while (*or* as) they heard them and were seeing the signs which he was doing.
3. For, before certain ones came from James, Peter was eating with the gentiles.
4. And because wickedness will abound, the love of many will grow cold.
5. And after they became silent, James answered.
6. Whom do men say that the Son of Man is?
7. We ought not to think that the divinity is like gold or silver or stone.
8. And after they stoned Paul they were dragging him out of the city, supposing that he was dead.
9. But if we will say, "from men," the whole people will stone us, for it (the people) believes that John is a prophet.
10. Festus therefore answered that Paul be kept in Caesarea, and that he himself was about to depart shortly.
11. And they all were so astounded that they argued saying, "What is this?"
12. And it became so known to all the inhabitants of Jerusalem, that that place was called Acheldama.
13. Lord, come down before my child dies.
14. He was about to kill himself, thinking that the prisoners had fled.

Composition Exercises

32.3 Composition exercises:

1. τὸ γὰρ ἀγαπᾶν τὸν κύριον καὶ τὸ περιπατεῖν ἐν ταῖς ὁδοῖς αὐτοῦ ἀγαθόν ἐστι τοῖς υἱοῖς τῶν ἀνθρώπων.
2. ἐν δὲ τῷ προσέρχεσθαι τοὺς πρεσβυτέρους ἐμείναμεν ἐν τοῖς ἀγροῖς.
3. οἱ δὲ νεανίαι οὐκ εἰσῆλθον εἰς τὸ ἱερὸν διὰ τὸ ἀποθανεῖν τὸν ἱερέα.
4. μετὰ δὲ τὸ λαλῆσαι τὸν Παῦλον ἀπεκρίθη αὐτῷ ὁ Φῆστος.
5. πρὶν δὲ ἰδεῖν τὴν πόλιν ὁ βασιλεὺς τρεῖς ἀγγέλους πρὸς τοὺς ἄρχοντας ἔπεμψε.
6. πάντες δὲ ἐφοβήθημεν ὥστε κρύψαι ἑαυτοὺς ἐν τοῖς δένδροις.
7. πᾶς ὁ λαὸς πιστεύει Μωϋσῆν γράψαι ταῦτα.
8. ἀπέλθε ἀπὸ τῆς οἰκίας πρὶν ἐλθεῖν τὸν τελώνην.
9. μετὰ δὲ τὸ προσέχειν τὸν ὄχλον τοῖς ἀποστόλοις ἐποίησαν πολλὰ σημεῖα ἐν αὐτοῖς.
10. νομίζομεν αὐτὸν εὖ ποιῆσαι τῷ λαῷ τούτῳ ἐν τῷ διδάσκειν αὐτοὺς ὑπακούειν τῷ βασιλεῖ.
11. καὶ ἐθεράπευσεν τὸν τυφλόν ὥστε πάντας θαυμάζειν.
12. ὁ νεανίας ἀπέθανε πρὶν ἐλθεῖν τὸν προφήτην.
13. πιστεύομεν τὸν Πέτρον εἶναι ἀπόστολον.
14. ἐλίθασαν τὸν Παῦλον διὰ τὸ κηρύσσειν τὸ εὐαγγέλιον αὐτοῖς.
15. τὸ ἀγαπᾶν τὸν κύριον κρεῖσσόν ἐστι ἢ χρυσὸς καὶ ἄργυρος.
16. ἐν δὲ τῷ καταβαίνειν ἐκ τοῦ ὄρους ἐκέλευσεν τοὺς μαθητὰς μηδενὶ εἰπεῖν τὸ ὅραμα πρὶν ἐλθεῖν εἰς Ἱερουσαλήμ.
17. καὶ νῦν εἴρηκα ὑμῖν πάντα ταῦτα πρὶν γένεσθαι.
18. πάντες οἱ Ἰουδαῖοι ἔκραξαν μὴ δεῖν τὸν Παῦλον ζῆν μηκέτι.
19. κατελαβόμην δὲ αὐτὸν σοφὸν καὶ ἀγαθὸν εἶναι.
20. ὁ λαὸς προσεῖχε τῷ Ἰωάννῃ διὰ τὸ πιστεύειν αὐτὸν προφήτην εἶναι.

LESSON 33

Translation Exercises

33.2 Translation exercises:

1. But Jesus gave the bread to the disciples that they might give it to the crowds.
2. For God gives the Holy Spirit to them that ask him.
3. Tell us by what authority you do these things, or who it is that gave you this authority.
4. Forgive and you all will be forgiven, give and it will be given to you.
5. And why did you not give my money to the bank?
6. To you it is given to know the mysteries of the kingdom.
7. Pay me what you owe.
8. And he was unwilling, but went away and cast him into prison until he should pay the debt.
9. Is it lawful for us to give tribute to Caesar? Should we give, or should we not give?
10. All power in heaven and on earth was given to me.
11. The Father loves the Son and has given all things into his hand.
12. It is more blessed to give than to receive.
13. What is the wisdom that is given to this man?
14. Tell me if you sold the land for so much?
15. All these things will I give you, if you will fall down and worship me.
16. And whenever they lead you all away and give you up, do not be anxious beforehand what you should say, but say that which will be given you in that hour.
17. And now I have told you before it takes place, so that when it does take place you may believe.

Composition Exercises

33.3 Composition exercises:

1. δίδωμι ὑμῖν ἐξουσίαν πνευμάτων ἀκαθάρτων ὥστε ἐκβάλλειν αὐτά.
2. οὗτος ὁ κύων ἐδόθη μοι ὑπὸ τοῦ πατρός μου.
3. θέλομεν δοῦναι τὸν χρυσὸν τοῖς ἀρχιερεῦσι.
4. μὴ δίδου ἀγαθὰ τοῖς πονηροῖς.
5. τὸ χωρίον ἀπεδίδοτο ὑπὸ τῶν τελώνων τοῖς στρατιώταις.
6. περιεπάτουν διδόντες ἱμάτια τοῖς λεπροῖς.
7. οὐ μὴ δώσω τὸ σὸν τῷ κυρίῳ.
8. ἔδωκάς μοι ὕδωρ διψῶντι.
9. τηρήσωμεν τὰς ἐντολὰς τὰς ὑμῖν διδομένας.
10. ὁ διδοὺς ἄρτον τοῖς πεινῶσιν οὐ μὴ ἀπολέσῃ τὸν μισθὸν αὐτοῦ.
11. ἐδίδομεν τὸ ἀργύριον τοῖς διακόνοις ἵνα διδῶσιν αὐτὸ ταῖς χήραις.
12. ὁ βασιλεὺς ἡμῖν δέδωκεν ταύτην τὴν πόλιν ἵνα κατοικῶμεν αὐτήν· μὴ αὐτὴν παραδῶμεν τοῖς ἐχθροῖς αὐτοῦ.
13. ἀποδοῦ πάντα ἃ ἔχεις καὶ δὸς τοῖς πτωχοῖς.
14. ἐὰν αἰτήσητε ἄρτον, δώσει ὑμῖν ὁ πατὴρ ὑμῶν λίθον;
15. ὅτι ἂν αἰτήσωμεν δοθήσεται ἡμῖν.
16. δίδοτε καὶ δοθήσεται ὑμῖν.
17. τοῦτο τὸ ἀργύριον ἐδόθη σοι ἵνα τὸ χωρίον ἀποδίδῳ.
18. δὸς ἡμῖν, ὦ κύριε, τὴν χάριν σου ἵνα προσκυνῶμέν σοι ἐν πνεύματι καὶ ἐν ἀληθείᾳ.
19. τίς ἐστιν ἡ σοφία ἡ δοθεῖσα τούτῳ;

LESSON 34

Translation Exercises

34.2 Translation exercises:

1. They do not light a lamp and put it under a measuring pot, but on a lamp stand.
2. And Joseph took the body and placed it in his own new tomb.

3. The lamp doesn't come so that it may be put under the measure pot, does it?
4. And wherever he entered they laid the sick in the marketplaces.
5. And hugging the children he laid his hands upon them and blessed them.
6. The good shepherd lays down his life for the sheep.
7. They have taken away the Lord out of the tomb, and we do not know where they have laid him.
8. It is not yours to know times and seasons which the Father has set in his own power.
9. And he broke the loaves and gave them to the disciples so that they might set them before them.
10. And into whatever city you all enter and they receive you, eat those things that are placed before you.
11. And behold men carrying on a bed a man that was lame, and they were seeking to bring him in and to lay him before him.
12. And he withdrew from them about a stone's throw, and he fell on his knees and prayed.
13. Lord, why can't I follow you now? I will lay down my life for your sake.
14. They brought the price of the fields and laid it at the apostles' feet.
15. Sit down on my right until I place your enemies as a footstool for your feet.

34.3 Composition exercises:

Composition Exercises

1. παρέθεμεν αὐτοῖς οἶνον καὶ ὕδωρ ἐν ποτήριοις.
2. ἠθελήσαμεν θεῖναι τοὺς ἀσθενεῖς ἐν ταῖς ἀγοραῖς.
3. καὶ θεὶς τὰ γόνατα προσηύχετο τῷ θεῷ τοῦ οὐρανοῦ.
4. πῶς θῶμεν τὸν παραλυτικὸν παρὰ τοὺς πόδας αὐτοῦ;
5. ἐτίθουν τὰ βιβλία ἐν τῇ συναγωγῇ.
6. θήσομεν τὸν λύχνον ὑπὸ τὸν μόδιον.

7. ἔθηκάς με ἐν ἀγαθῇ γῇ.
8. ἰδοὺ οὗτοι πάντες ἔθεσαν τὰς ψυχὰς αὐτῶν ὑπὲρ τῶν ἀδελφῶν.
9. μὴ θῇς ταύτην τὴν γραφὴν ἐπὶ τῷ σταυρῷ.
10. οὗτός ἐστιν ὁ θρόνος ὁ τεθεὶς ἐν τῷ ἱερῷ.
11. θέτε τὸ σῶμα τοῦ προφήτου ἐν τῷ μνημείῳ τῶν πατέρων.
12. ἡ μάχαιρα τίθεται ἐν τῇ χειρὶ τοῦ βασιλέως.
13. οἱ ἀπόστολοι κατευλόγησαν ἡμᾶς τιθέντες τὰς χεῖρας ἐφ᾽ ἡμᾶς.
14. καταβήσομαι ἵνα θῶ τὰς χεῖρας ἐπ᾽ αὐτὴν καὶ ζήσει.
15. οἱ λύχνοι τεθήσονται ἐν τῷ οἴκῳ τοῦ πρεσβυτέρου.
16. τὰ δίκτυα ἐτέθη παρὰ τὸ πλοῖον.
17. ὁ ἀσθενὴς εἰσηνέχθη ἐπὶ κλίνης καὶ ἐτέθη ἐνώπιον αὐτοῦ.
18. ἐγώ εἰμι ὁ θεὶς τὰς χεῖρας ἐπὶ τὴν σὴν κεφαλὴν ὅτε παῖς ἦς.
19. οὐ μὴ φάγητε τὰ παρατιθέμενα ὑμῖν.
20. ὁ ἄρτος ἐκλάσθη καὶ παρετέθη αὐτοῖς.

LESSON 35

Translation Exercises

35.2(α) Translation exercises, part 1:

1. Then the devil takes him to the holy city and set him on the pinnacle of the temple.
2. And while they were saying these things he himself stood in the middle of them.
3. They saw the man who had been healed standing with them.
4. But if Satan casts out Satan, he is divided against himself; how then will his kingdom stand?
5. Now God commands men that all everywhere repent, because he has fixed a day in which he is about to judge the world in righteousness.

6. The Pharisee having taken his stand prayed these things by himself.
7. But the tax collector standing afar off was not willing even to lift up his eyes to heaven.
8. But Jesus was caused to stand before the governor.
9. And having kneeled down he cried with a loud voice, "Lord, lay not this sin to their charge."
10. After these things, Judas the Galilean rose up in the days of the census and led away the people after him.
11. If they do not hear Moses and the prophets, neither will they be persuaded if one rose from the dead.
12. And he said to the man that had the withered hand, "Rise and stand in the middle." And he arose and stood.

35.2(β) Translation exercises, part 2:

1. Man, who made me a judge or a divider over you all?
2. No man is able to come to me unless the Father who sent me draw him, and I will raise him up at the last day.
3. His mother and his brethren stood outside desiring to speak to him.
4. The hypocrites love to pray standing in the synagogues, that they may make themselves seen with respect to men.
5. And giving her his hand he raised her up.
6. But the Spirit says expressly that in later times certain men will depart from the faith.
7. How will we liken the kingdom of God or in what comparison will we place it?
8. But Jesus taking a child placed it by himself.
9. Go and take your stand in the temple and speak to the people all the words of this life.

10. And as they were coming down from the mountain Jesus charged them saying, “Tell the vision to no man until the Son of Man is raised from the dead.”
11. To whom also he showed himself to be living after his suffering in many proofs.
12. And coming up he touched the coffin, and they that were carring it stood still.
13. And they brought false witnesses, which said, “This man does not stop speaking words against the holy place.”
14. And leading them they placed them in the council.

Composition Exercises

35.3 Composition exercises:

1. παραστήσω σε τῷ καίσαρι ἕνεκα τοῦ ἀνόματός μου.
2. οἱ δίκαιοι σταθήσονται ἐν τῇ βασιλείᾳ τοῦ πατρὸς αὐτῶν.
3. ὁ Παῦλος οὖν παρέστη τῷ Φήστῳ.
4. οἱ ἱερεῖς ἔστησαν τὸν τελώνην ἐν μέσῳ τῆς ἀγορᾶς.
5. ὁ δὲ Πέτρος ἀναστὰς ἐκήρυξε τὸν λόγον τῷ ὄχλῳ.
6. οὐκ ἔστιν ὧδε, ἀνέστη γὰρ ἐκ νεκρῶν.
7. τίς σε κατέστησε ἄρχοντα τοῦ λαοῦ τούτου εἶναι;
8. τότε ἀναστάντες ἀπήλθομεν ἐκ τῆς πόλεως.
9. ἐστήσετε τὸν βασιλέα ἐν τῷ ἁγίῳ τόπῳ.
10. ἐν ταῖς ἐσχάταις ἡμέραις πολλοὶ ἀπέστησαν ἀπὸ τῆς πίστεως.
11. ἕστημεν ἔξω θέλοντες ἰδεῖν τὸν προφήτην.
12. ἀναστὰς ἐν τοῖς ποσὶν αἶρε τὴν κλίνην σου.
13. ἐλπίζομεν παραστῆναι τῷ κυρίῳ ἐν ἐκείνῃ τῇ ἡμέρᾳ.
14. τότε τὸ πνεῦμα τοῦ κυρίου ἄραν με κατέστησέ με ἐπὶ τὰ ὕδατα.
15. μετὰ ταῦτα πολλοὶ λῃσταὶ ἀνέστησαν καὶ ἀπέστησαν πολλοὺς ὀπίσω αὐτῶν.
16. εἴ τις πιστεύει ἐν ἐμοὶ ἀναστήσω αὐτὸν ἐν τῇ ἐσχάτῃ ἡμέρᾳ.

17. ἐκελεύσαμεν τοὺς στρατιώτας ἀποστῆναι τοῦ ὄχλου.
18. πῶς στῶμεν ἐν τῇ ἡμέρᾳ τῆς ὀργῆς αὐτοῦ;
19. καὶ ἀναστὰς ἔκραξε φωνῇ μεγάλῃ· ἀποστῆτε τῶν ἀνθρώπων τούτων καὶ παρίστατε αὐτοὺς τῷ βασιλεῖ.
20. οἱ ἀκούοντες ταῦτα ἔστησαν.

LESSON 36

36.2 Translation exercises: **Translation Exercises**

1. And now I say to you, "Stand apart from these men and let them go."
2. But Jesus said to him, "Tolerate it for now, for thus it is fitting for us to fulfil all righteousness." Then he leaves him alone.
3. Then the disciples understood that he spoke to them of John the Baptist.
4. Who can forgive sins but one, that is God?
5. And they immediately left their nets and followed him.
6. And forgive us our debts as we too have forgiven our debtors.
7. For if you all forgive men their trespasses, your heavenly father will also forgive you.
8. I know you, who you are, the holy one of God.
9. Then the devil shows him all the kingdoms of the world.
10. You all do err not knowing the Scriptures nor the power of God.
11. But to those that are outside, all comes in parables, that hearing they may hear and not understand.
12. Son, be of good cheer, your sins are forgiven.
13. Why is it that you sought me? Didn't you all know that I must be about my father's business?
14. And also Judas that betrayed him knew the place.
15. Father, I thank you that you heard me, and I knew that you always hear me.

16. These things I wrote to you all that you may know that you have eternal life.
17. But I want you to know that Christ is the head of every man.
18. And he didn't allow the demons to speak because they knew him.

Composition Exercises

36.3 Composition exercises:

1. ἐπίστατα, οἴδαμεν ὅτι ἀληθὴς εἶ.
2. ὁ θεὸς ἀφήσει πάσας τὰς ἁμαρτίας ἡμῶν εἰ πιστεύομεν εἰς τὸ ὄνομα αὐτοῦ.
3. τότε οἱ ἱερεῖς συνῆκαν ὅτι εἶπεν ταύτην τὴν παραβολὴν κατ᾽ αὐτῶν.
4. οἱ δέ, μὴ εἰδότες τοῦτο, ἀναστάντες ἀπῆλθον εἰς Ἰερουσαλήμ.
5. συνήκετε ταῦτα;
6. ἀφῆκά σοι πᾶν τὸ ὀφείλημα ἐκεῖνο.
7. γράφω ὑμῖν τοῦτο ἵνα εἴδητε ὅτι σῴζεσθε.
8. ἄφετε τούτους ἵνα προσκυνῶσι τῷ θεῷ τῶν πατέρων.
9. πῶς ἀφήσω σοι τοῦτο;
10. οὐκ ἀφῆκε τῷ τεθεραπευμένῳ ἀκολουθεῖν αὐτῷ.
11. εὖ ἴστε ὅτι ὁ κύριος οὐκ ἐάσει σε πλανᾶσθαι.
12. οὐ δύναμαι συνιέναι τοῦτο εἰ μὴ διδάξεις με.
13. τίς δύναται εἰδέναι πάντα τὰ παραπτώματα αὐτοῦ;
14. ᾔδεισαν ὅτι οἱ στρατιῶται αὐτῶν ἐθάρρουν.
15. ἴστε ὅτι πάντα τὰ παραπτώματα ὑμῶν ἀφεθήσονται.

LESSON 37

Translation Exercises

37.2 Translation exercises:

1. Behold the maidsevant of the Lord: may it happen to me according to your word.

2. And all reasoned in their hearts about John, whether he wasn't perhaps the Christ.
3. Your money perish with you!
4. And hearing a crowd passing by he asked what it might be.
5. But the God of patience grant you to have the same mind one to another.
6. And all the multitude of the people was praying outside at the hour of incense.
7. And the whole city was gathered together at the door.
8. Jerusalem will be trodden down by the gentiles.
9. And his disciples asked him what this parable might be.
10. For this thing was not done in a corner.
11. And the disciples of John were fasting.
12. And Paul said, "I am standing at the judgment seat of Caesar where I ought to be judged."
13. For he was teaching them as one having authority, and not as their scribes.
14. And calling one of the servants he asked what these things might be.

37.3 Composition exercises:

Composition Exercises

1. τότε ὁ τυφλὸς ἠρώτησε τί ἂν εἴη τοῦτο.
2. οἱ μαθηταὶ τοῦ Ἰησοῦ ἦσαν ἐσθίοντες καὶ πίνοντες.
3. τοῦτο πεπραγμένον ἐστὶ ἐνώπιον πολλῶν μαρτύρων.
4. γένοιτο ἡμῖν κατὰ τὸ θέλημά σου.
5. ἔσῃ περιπατῶν ἐν τῇ ὁδῷ τῆς δικαιοσύνης.
6. οἱ μαθηταὶ συνεζήτουν τίς εἴη ὁ μείζων.
7. ἀπόλλοιντο πάντες οἱ ἐργάζοντες τὴν ἀνομίαν.
8. τότε πᾶς ὁ ὄχλος ἦν ἐπισυνηγμένη πρὸς τὴν θάλασσαν.
9. θέλομεν εἰδέναι τί ἂν εἴη τὸ ῥῆμα τοῦτο.
10. γενοίμην ὁμοιότερός σοι, ὦ κύριε.

APPENDIX 3

Accentuation

SYLLABLE- AND STRESS-TIMED LANGUAGES

Greek was originally a syllable-timed language rather than a stress-timed language. In every language some syllables are pronounced for a longer duration than others, and a system governs the timing that produces various rhythms of languages. "Syllable-timed" and "stress-timed" are two such systems. Poets and rhetoricians either intentionally or unintentionally use a language's system to greater or lesser effect; such knowledge and skill with one's own language can help explain why some speech patterns sound better than others.

In a syllable-timed language, specific vowels and syllables have a particular length ascribed to them. Greek was originally this type of language: the ω (mega "o") was pronounced for a longer duration than ο (the micro "o"). Both letters had the same sound. Any reference to vowel "length" originally referred to this difference in sound duration in Greek. All classical poetic works depended on this system to produce various poetic meters (rhythms).

Early Syllable-timed Tonal System

In this early period, Greek was also a tonal language with a system that affected the pitch of a particular syllable within each word. Greek had three tonal options: a rising or high tone, a falling or low tone, and a combination tone. Later, these three tones were recorded with an accent marking system with three accent marks: the acute (´), the grave (`), and the circumflex (῀). Each of these tones was conditioned and governed by a system of rules involving vowel length. For example, the combination tone (later represented by circumflex) could only be used with a long syllable (probably due to the time it takes to produce that type of tone).

Transition to Stress-timed System

As a result of the conquests of Alexander the Great, Greek became a world language, with many new learners and speakers. The tonal system was not easily learned, and often a syllable with the intonation (especially with a higher tone) would be pronounced more loudly and for a longer duration (stressed). Eventually the change in pitch was replaced by a change in volume and duration of vocalization (length). This occurred without respect to the original vowel length for particular letters. Thus the ο in πρόσωπον came to be pronounced longer than the ω in the same word. In the classical period the meter of πρόσωπον would be classified as an amphibrach (short-long-short), but in the New Testament period it would be a dactyl (long-short-short). Thus a classical poem performed with the meter that made the poem work would have an affected "stage" sound within the New Testament period.

BASIC ACCENTUATION RULES

Even though the stress-timed system of Greek in the New Testament period is far simpler than the classical tonal system, one must still learn the rules affecting the position of each of the three accents to properly pronounce the language.

Names of the Syllables

Greek words may be accented only on their final three syllables. The final syllable is called the "ultima,"[1] the second to last syllable of a word is called the "penult,"[2] and the third to last syllable is called the "antepenult."[3]

Acute Accent Rules

For the sake of brevity, it is helpful to have a shorthand way to refer to particular syllables accented with a particular accent. In contrast to the names for each syllable (ultima, penult, and antepenult), which are Latin, the terms for the combination of an accent and syllable are Greek. The acute may be used only over the final three syllables of a word. A word with its ultima accented with an acute is an "oxytone"

1 Latin for "last."

2 Since "pene" means "almost" in Latin, "penult" is used to refer to the syllable that is almost last.

3 "Ante" is the Latin prefix meaning "prior to." So "antepenult" refers to what is prior to that which is almost last.

(or sharp-toned).[1] If the acute is on the penult, the word is a "paroxytone."[2] A word with its antepenult accented is a "proparoxytone."[3]

Circumflex Accent Rules

The circumflex is more restricted than the acute: it may only be placed over the final two syllables of a word (one less than the acute), and it may only be placed over long vowels. There is only one situation where the circumflex excludes the possibility for an acute to be used on a syllable: when the penult is long and must be accented. In that situation, the circumflex is the only option.

A word with a circumflex accent on its ultima is classified as "perispomenon."[4] If this accent is on the penult, the word is classified as "properispomenon."

Grave Accent Rules

The grave is the most limited of all three accents; it may only stand on the ultima. A word with a grave accent is classified as "barytone" or flat-toned. It is actually a modification of an acute in this position. Oxytone words will become barytone if the word is followed by another word. A punctuation mark separating the word from others will cause the oxytone to remain with its acute.

How the Ultima Governs Accenting

If the ultima is long, both the acute and circumflex lose one possible position for accenting. In this situation the acute may only be placed over the final two syllables of the word, and the circumflex is restricted to the ultima.

For purposes of accentuation, the two digraphs, οι and αι, are considered short vowels when they are the final letters of a word (e.g., οι is still long in λόγοις).[5]

1 From the Greek ὀξύτονος, meaning sharp-toned. It is a linguistic irony (perhaps the first of too many) that the name for this word isn't accented on its ultima.

2 The Greek prepositional prefix παρα is analogous to the Latin "pen," but in this case it would mean "near or alongside the oxytone."

3 The Greek prepositional prefix προ simply means "before," referring to the antepenult position.

4 From the Greek neuter participle form of περισπάω, which referred to the circumflex accent and the way it represented a tonal diversion.

5 The οι in the optative mood is an exception to this (contrast the nouns ἄνθρωποι and νῆσοι with the optative ποιήσοι).

ACCENTUATION OF NOUNS AND ADJECTIVES

The general principle for accenting nonverbs is retention. Nonverbs will strive to keep the accent placed over the same syllable[1] as occurs in the nominative form. Thus the placement of the accent on the nominative singular must be memorized along with learning a word's spelling and meaning. A change from a short to a long ultima will affect words accented with the earliest position of acute and circumflex (proparoxytone and properispomenon).[2] A long ultima will not allow acute on the antepenult, so a proparoxytone reduces to a paroxytone (ἄνθρωπος to ἀνθρώπου). A properispomonen (circumflex on the penult) can keep the same syllable accent by changing the accent type. So a properispomenon will also become paroxytone with a long ultima (δοῦλος to δούλου).

Exceptions to Principle of Retention

Of course, there are exceptions:

1. The genitive plural of all nouns of the first declension is circumflexed.

2. The genitive and dative of oxytone nouns of the first and second declensions are circumflexed. Examples:

1 The term "same syllable" refers to a syllable relative to the root. For most nouns and adjectives, the accented position will be the same relative to the verb root and relative to the ultima. However, to apply the principal of retention most comprehensively one must understand this distinction. Retention relative to the root is seen in liquid stem nouns such as the nominative forms of the same word, ποιμήν and ποιμένες. (Note how commitment for placement is the final syllable of the root rather than a commitment to a penultimate position which would have rendered ποίμην or the ultima which would have rendered ποιμενές.) A paroxytone word doesn't necessarily want to remain paroxytone if an additional syllable is added to the word. Some words will become proparoxytone to keep the same syllable accented relative to the root. (e.g., φιλόφρων becomes proparoxytone with multisyllabic endings like we find in the masc. acc. sg. φιλόφρονα. It isn't that this word simply always wants to proparoxytone and is limited by a lack of syllables in the masc. nom. sg. form, since the neut. nom. sg., φιλόφρον, retains stress over the same root syllable even when the ending would have allowed for an earlier placement.) The necessary exception to retaining position of the accent relative to root syllables is when the accented root syllable drops out, as in syncopated roots. In such cases the accent is placed over the preceding root vowel. For example, ἀστήρ loses the accented root syllable in the dative plural and yields ἄστρασι. Since the principle of retention refers to a position relative to the root, it may be necessary to find a form that allows for that accentuation of any root syllable. Only the neut. nom. and acc. sg. provide this opportunity. It is the only form that allows us to see that εὐσχήμων prefers to be accented on the second to last syllable of the root, εὔσχημον. However, the occasions where the preferred accented root position are different than what is presented in the nominative are so rare (e.g. πολλαπλασίων and ἀσχήμων) that one can generally infer accent placement from a noun's or adjective's lexical form.

2 A helpful mnemonic is to call this the "pro" position.

	Oxytone First Declension		Oxytone Second Declension	
	Singular	Plural	Singular	Plural
Nom.	ἀρχή	ἀρχαί	θεός	θεοί
Acc.	ἀρχήν	ἀρχάς	θεόν	θεούς
Gen.	ἀρχῆς	ἀρχῶν	θεοῦ	θεῶν
Dat.	ἀρχῇ	ἀρχαῖς	θεῷ	θεοῖς

3. The tendency of the genitive and dative to be accented differently (having their ultima accented) also occurs in single-syllable roots of the third declension. Examples:

	Monosyllabic Third Declension Roots			
	Singular	Plural	Singular	Plural
Nom.	ἅλς	ἅλες	νύξ	νύκτες
Acc.	ἅλα	ἅλας	νύκτα	νύκτας
Gen.	ἁλός	ἁλῶν	νυκτός	νυκτῶν
Dat.	ἁλί	ἁλσί(ν)	νυκτί	νυξί(ν)

ACCENTUATION OF VERBS

The general principle for accenting verbs is recession. Verbs throw back their accent as far as the length of the last syllable will permit. For example: δουλεύω, δουλεύουσι, δούλευε, ἐδούλευον.

The accent of a verb compounded with a preposition can never precede the augment. For example: παρεῖχον, not πάρειχον.

For the accentuation of contract verbs, see Lesson 4.

Accenting Participles and Infinitives

The accentuation of participles and infinitives may seem to violate the principle of recession for verbs. However, participles and infinitives operate according to the principles for nonverbs, since they aren't verbs—participles are verbal adjectives, and infinitives are verbal nouns.

1. Participles are accented as proparoxytone adjectives. (Perfect passive participles, which do not have a thematic

vowel, are accented on their penult.) For example: βουλεύων, neuter βουλεῦον, not βούλευον.

2. Participles that use third declension endings (other than first aorist participles) are accented on the first syllable of the stem. These are the second aorist active participle, aorist passive participle, and perfect active participle. Examples from various verbs: λιπών, λυθείς, λελυκώς.

Thematic Aorist Active Participle

	Singular			Plural		
	Masc.	Fem.	Neut.	Masc.	Fem.	Neut.
Nom.	λιπών	λιποῦσα	λιπόν	λιπόντες	λιποῦσαι	λιπόντα
Acc.	λιπόντα	λιποῦσαν	λιπόν	λιπόντας	λιπούσας	λιπόντα
Gen.	λιπόντος	λιπούσης	λιπόντος	λιπόντων	λιπουσῶν	λιπόντων
Dat.	λιπόντι	λιπούσῃ	λιπόντι	λιποῦσι(ν)	λιπούσαις	λιποῦσι(ν)

3. Many infinitives are accented on their penult (the first aorist active infinitive, the second aorist middle infinitive, the perfect passive infinitive and participles, and all infinitives ending in -ναι). Examples: βουλεῦσαι, γενέσθαι, λελύσθαι, λελυμένος, ἱστάναι, διδόναι, λελυκέναι.

4. The second (thematic) aorist active infinitive, ending in -ειν, and the second person singular second aorist middle imperative, ending in -ου, have the circumflex accent on the last syllable. Examples: εἰπεῖν, γενοῦ.

ENCLITICS

An enclitic is a word that typically loses its own accent and is pronounced as part of the preceding word. The enclitics that principally occur in the New Testament are:

1. The oblique cases of the personal pronouns of the first and second person singular: με, μου, μοι, σε, σου, σοι
2. The indefinite pronouns τις, τι; the indefinite adverbs ποτε, που, πως (etc.); and the conjunction τε
3. The present indicative of εἰμί ("I am"), except the second person singular[1]

Since an enclitic is considered part of the preceding word for pronunciation purposes, the word before an enclitic does not change a final acute accent to a grave accent.

If the last syllable of the preceding word is accented, there is no need to modify the accenting of the preceding word or add an accent to the enclitic. Examples: σοφός τις, καλόν ἐστι.

If the preceding word has an acute accent on the antepenult, or a circumflex accent on the penult, it receives a secondary accent (an acute accent on the ultima). Examples: ἄνθρωπός τις, οὗτός ἐστι.

If the preceding word has an acute accent on the penult, it receives no second accent. A monosyllabic enclitic here remains unaccented; a disyllabic enclitic is accented. Examples: λόγος τις, λόγοι τινές.

PROCLITICS

A proclitic is a word that has no accent but leans on the pronunciation of the following word; if a proclitic precedes an enclitic, it receives the accent from the following enclitic: εἴ τις. The most common proclitics are the articles ὁ, ἡ, οἱ, αἱ; the prepositions εἰς, ἐκ ἐξ, ἐν; and the words εἰ, ὡς, οὐ.

1 Another exception for accenting εἰμί is when the present active third person form (ἐστι) follows οὐκ. In this situation it is accented as a regular verb (as early as possible). For example: οὐκ ἔστιν οὗτος ἀγαθὸς ἄνθρωπος.

WORDS DIFFERING IN ACCENT OR BREATHING

There are many words in Greek that only differ in spelling in their use of breathing or accent marks. Often context helps to distinguish such words, but this list shows it is a good practice to learn proper breathing and accenting when learning vocabulary.

1.	ἀλλά	"but"
	ἄλλα	"other things"
2.	αὐτή	feminine nominative singular of αὐτός
	αὕτη	feminine nominative singular of οὗτος
	αὑτή	another form of ἑαυτή
3.	αὐταί	feminine nominative plural of αὐτός
	αὗται	feminine nominative plural of οὗτος
4.	εἶ	"you are"
	εἰ	"if"
5.	εἷς	"one" (masculine)
	εἰς	"to"
6.	ἕν	"one" (neuter)
	ἐν	"in"
7.	ἡ	feminine nominative singular of the definite article
	ἥ[1]	feminine nominative singular of the relative pronoun
	ἤ	"than," "or"
	ᾗ	feminine dative singular of the relative pronoun
	ᾖ	subjunctive third person singular from εἶναι

1 This form may also be the result of a feminine nominative singular definite article being followed by an enclitic.

8.	ἦν	imperfect first person singular from εἶναι
	ἤν	another form of ἐάν
	ἥν	feminine accusative singular of the relative pronoun
9.	ὁ	masculine nominative singular of the definite article
	ὅ[1]	neuter nominative and accusative singular of the relative pronoun
10.	ὄν	present active participle neuter nominative and accusative singular of εἰμί
	ὅν	masculine accusative singular of the relative pronoun
11.	ταῦτα	neuter nominative and accusative plural of οὗτος
	ταὐτά	contracted for τὰ αὐτά.
12.	τίς, τί, etc.	"who?" "what?"
	τις, τι, etc.	"a certain man," "a certain thing"
13.	ὦ, ὤ	"O," "Oh"
	ὦ	subjunctive first person singular from εἶναι
	ᾧ	masculine and neuter dative singular of the relative pronoun
14.	ὤν	present active participle masculine nominative singular of εἰμί
	ὧν	genitive plural of the relative pronoun

1 This form may also occur as a masculine nominative singular definite article followed by an enclitic.

APPENDIX 4

Prepositions

Parts of speech are the basic building blocks of language. There aren't very many. When working between languages, it is crucial to understand how each of these parts functions so you can understand translation and interpretive options.

PREPOSITIONS DESIGNATE RELATIONSHIPS BETWEEN WORDS

Prepositions are a part of speech often overlooked in English or taken for granted without much reflection. This is ironic, since the relationships between words—which prepositions designate—are just as important as the words being related. Prepositions are words that join a substantive (noun or pronoun) to another noun, phrase, or clause. They typically precede the noun—thus the label "prepositions."

PREPOSITIONAL PHRASE FUNCTIONS

By definition a preposition must have an object. These two elements considered together are called a "prepositional phrase." A prepositional phrase may be used attributively (like an adjective) to provide more information about a substantive or adverbially (like an adverb) to provide more information about a clause's verb. Like an adjective, a prepositional phrase may be preceded by an article. Thus a prepositional phrase can function as a substantive, adjective, or adverb.

		Function		
		Substantive	Attributive	Adverbial
Part of Speech	Noun or Pronoun	Noun with various case endings		
	Preposition	article + preposition + object	preposition + object	anarthrous preposition + object
	Adjective & Adverb	article + adjective (in place of noun)	adjective	adverb

Substantive Function

"The (things) *unto* death" is an example of a substantive use of a prepositional phrase. "Unto" is the preposition. The phrase could be translated with an adjective ("deathly things," or "deadly things"). One can also convey the same idea with a noun in Greek where we can translate the meaning of this phrase with the genitive case of θάνατος (θανάτου, "of death"). Some contexts in English even may allow the possessive case of a noun to communicate an overlapping meaning (e.g., "death's door").

Attributive Function

For an attributive example consider "the mountain *of* holiness." "Of" is the preposition, and with the noun "mountain" it forms a phrase equivalent to an adjective. Compare it to this expression using an adjective: "the holy mountain."

Adverbial Function

Consider the following adverbial examples—"he walked *for* six hours" and "they sat *by* the sea." The prepositional phrases "for six hours" and "by the sea" are equivalent to adverbs; they qualify the verbs "walked" and "sat." It shouldn't be surprising that prepositional phrases can function adverbially, since prepositions are often added to the front of a verb stem (e.g., "intervene," "invoke," "excise"). Since prepositions may take objects in various cases in Greek (not just the accusative case, as in English), often these prepositional prefixes make the verb take a direct object in a case to match the function of the preposition.

PROPER CASES FOR PREPOSITIONS

In English all prepositions are followed by their object (a noun or pronoun) in the accusative case. Greek uses a total of three cases to help communicate or reinforce the specific relationship the preposition is referencing.[1] Some of the basic relationships that generated the case system in Greek are:

- Extension, or motion toward (termed "accusative")
- Separation, or motion from (termed "ablative")
- Place where, or rest at (termed "locative")
- Means by which an action was accomplished, or necessary for the action, association (termed "instrumental")

The three oblique cases that were generated in Greek incorporated these relationships.

- The accusative case expresses extension and motion toward.
- The genitive case is used to express ablative meaning (separation, or motion from) as well as its own meaning (membership and possession).
- The dative case expresses the locative and instrumental meanings.

ORIGIN OF PREPOSITIONS

These general case meanings then used adverbs to make their meaning more precise, and, when these adverbs had become fixed in this use by custom, they were treated as a separate part of speech, called prepositions. Although prepositions originally served to clarify case meanings, the language developed to the point where the meaning of the preposition superseded the case meaning.

As the horse in the fable called in the man to help him against the stag, and allowed him to get on his back, and then found that

1 These three cases, genitive, dative, and accusative, are called the "oblique cases" since they were seen as falling away (declining) from the nominative case. This is also where we get the term "declension" and why we say that we "decline" nouns.

he himself had lost his liberty, so the cases called in the help of the prepositions, and then found themselves weakened and lost their independent meaning in these situations.

In English, French, Italian, and to some extent in Modern Greek, the cases have disappeared, wholly or in part, and the prepositions do the work that they once did. For example, we say "of a man" where the Greeks said ἀνθρώπου, and "to a man" where the Greeks said ἀνθρώπῳ.

We can see this process happening in the New Testament. Prepositions are used with the case of a noun where the case alone sufficed in Classical Greek. Another example is the simple dative, which was used in Classical Greek to express the instrument, but in New Testament Greek, ἐν with the dative often expresses the instrument. For example:

κύριε, εἰ πατάξομεν ἐν μαχαίρᾳ;
"Lord, will we strike with the sword?" (Luke 22:49)

In estimating the meaning of a prepositional phrase (i.e., a preposition followed by a noun) the proper course is first to consider the lexical meaning of the preposition and then check to see if the force of the case of the noun adjusts it. The combination of the two ideas will generally explain the meaning of the phrase.

If the force of the case is kept in view, it can explain how the same preposition can have such wholly different meanings with different cases. We may see the joint influence of the case of the noun and the root meaning of the preposition best by considering some prepositions that are used with all three cases.

For example, παρά means "beside." When it is used with the accusative, it denotes motion to beside or motion alongside of. When it is used with the genitive, it denotes motion from beside. When it is used with the dative, it denotes rest beside and is translated "near" or "with." Examples:

Accusative:

1. περιπατῶν δὲ παρὰ τὴν θάλασσαν τῆς Γαλιλαίας εἶδεν δύο ἀδελφούς
   "And walking along the side of the Sea of Galilee he saw two brethren" (Matt 4:18)

2. καὶ ἔρριψαν αὐτοὺς παρὰ τοὺς πόδας αὐτοῦ
   "And they cast them at his feet" (Matt 15:30)

Genitive:

1. ἐγένετο ἄνθρωπος ἀπεσταλμένος παρὰ θεοῦ
   "There came into being a man sent from God" (John 1:6)

2. δόξαν παρὰ ἀνθρώπων οὐ λαμβάνω
   "I receive not glory from men" (John 5:41)

Dative:

1. ἐπιλαβόμενος παιδίον ἔστησεν αὐτὸ παρ᾽ ἑαυτῷ
   "Taking a child he placed him near him" (Luke 9:47)

2. καὶ παρ᾽ αὐτῷ ἔμειναν τὴν ἡμέραν ἐκείνην
   "And they remained with him that day" (John 1:39)

PREPOSITIONS CONNECTED WITH ONE CASE ONLY

The uses of the prepositions given in the following lists are those that occur most frequently in the New Testament. Their use in Classical Greek is somewhat different.

The translation after each preposition may be regarded as indicating the meaning of the preposition; it also generally indicates the meaning of the preposition when it is compounded with a verb or some other word. Master these meanings thoroughly, and pick up the derived meanings in the course of reading.

Prepositions with the Accusative Only	ἀνά[1]	+ acc. =	up (frequent in composition with verbs, but rare before a noun)
	εἰς	+ acc. =	into indicating motion into a location, or unto a state, intention, or result
Prepositions with the Genitive Only	ἀντί[2]	+ gen. =	over against, instead of, in return for
	ἀπό	+ gen. =	away from (from the exterior)
	ἐκ	+ gen. =	out of (from the interior)
	πρό	+ gen. =	in front of, before (of time or place)
Prepositions with the Dative Only	ἐν	+ dat. =	in (of time or place)
	σύν[3]	+ dat. =	together with
PREPOSITIONS WITH TWO CASES (GENITIVE AND ACCUSATIVE)	διά	+ acc. =	on account of, owing to
		+ gen. =	through, throughout, by means of
	κατά	+ acc. =	down along, during, with regard to, according to
		+ gen. =	down from, down upon, against
	μετά	+ acc. =	after
		+ gen. =	with, among
	περί	+ acc. =	about, around (of place or time)
		+ gen. =	about, concerning, on account of
	ὑπέρ	+ acc. =	above, beyond
		+ gen. =	on behalf of, for the sake of, concerning
	ὑπό	+ acc. =	under
		+ gen. =	under the influence of, hence "by" as the agent after passive verbs

1 ἀνά occurs in the English word "analysis" (ἀνάλυσις), a thorough releasing or loosening up.

2 The likenesses between the prepositions ἀντί, ἀπό, ἐκ, πρό, ἐν and the Latin prepositions "ante," "ab," "ex," "pro," and "in" are obvious. They occur in such English words as "antipathy," a feeling against a person or thing; "abstraction," a taking away; "expulsion," a driving out; "propulsion," a driving forward; and "intrusion," a thrusting in.

3 σύν is found in many English words, such as "sympathy" and "symphony" (συμπάθεια, συμφωνία). The dental nasal, ν, changes to a labial nasal, μ, prior to a labial (in both English and Greek).

Notes on the above prepositions

- διά is found in words such as "dialect," a language spoken through a district, and "diagram."
- κατά is found in "catastrophe," which means a turning upside down.
- μετά is found in the word "metaphysics"—science that is above or beyond the science of physics. However, the Greek preposition does not mean "above" or "beyond." *Metaphysics* was the title of the book that Plato wrote after a book titled *Physics*. So originally, the literal meaning of the title was simply "After Physics." The content of the book dealt with what is beyond the physical realm.

  It is also found in the words "metaphor" and "metamorphosis," but there it has the sense of change, of transference from one state to another, which it commonly has when compounded with a verb or other word in Greek. This idea of change is part of the sequential concept behind the idea of "after." "Metaphor" means the transference of a word properly referring to one set of objects to another set of objects. "Metamorphosis" means a change of form from an original state.
- περί is found in such words as "perimeter," the length of a thing all around, and "peripatetic," a man who walks about.
- ὑπέρ is the same word as the Latin "super." It occurs in such English words as "hypercritical," meaning overcritical.

PREPOSITIONS WITH THREE CASES (ACCUSATIVE, GENITIVE, AND DATIVE)

ἐπί	+ acc. =	upon (placed on), up to, as far as
	+ gen. =	on, in the presence of, in the time of
	+ dat. =	on, at, on account of, in addition to
παρά	+ acc. =	to the side of, beside, beyond, contrary
	+ gen. =	from beside, from (of persons)
	+ dat. =	near (generally of persons)
πρός	+ acc. =	toward, up to, in reference to, with regard to
	+ gen. =	from (very rare in the New Testament)
	+ dat. =	at, close to

Notes on the above prepositions

- ἐπί is found in the words "epitaph," an inscription on a tomb, and "epigram," a writing on a given subject.
- παρά is found in the word "parable" (παραβολή, -ῆς, ἡ, from παρά + βάλλω), the placing of one thing beside another for comparison.

PREPOSITIONS COMPOUNDED WITH VERBS

In English certain words that are generally classified as prepositions are joined with verbs and nouns to form compound words—for example, "undertake," "overtake," "outbid," "overcoat," and "outrigger." But very frequently these "prepositions" are written after the word with which they go and separately from it. In this case it is plain that these so-called prepositions are really adverbs. For example:

They went away.

We took over the business.

This coat is quite worn out.

In Greek, prepositions generally join to the words that they qualify and form compound words. Examples:

ἀποστέλλω ("I send away")

συνάγω ("I drive together/gather together")

συναγωγή ("A synagogue [a gathering together]")

ἐκκλησία ("An assembly [a body of people called out]")

ἐκλεκτός ("Chosen out")

Sometimes two prepositions may be joined to one word:

ἀντιπαρέρχομαι ("I pass by opposite to")

Consider the force of the prepositions in the following compound words:

1. ἀνέρχομαι "I go up"
2. ἀπέρχομαι "I go away"
3. διέρχομαι "I go through"
4. εἰσέρχομαι "I go into"
5. ἐξέρχομαι "I go out of"
6. ἐπέρχομαι "I come upon"
7. παρέρχομαι "I go by the side of"
8. προσέρχομαι "I go toward" (especially of going toward people)
9. συνέρχομαι "I go with"
10. ἐμβαίνω "I go in"
11. καταβαίνω "I go down"
12. προβαίνω "I go before"
13. ἀντιλέγω "I speak against," "I contradict"
14. ὑπερέχω "I have over," "I excel"
15. ὑπομένω "I remain under," "I endure"
16. ἀποκαλύπτω "I cover away from," "I uncover," "I reveal"
17. ἐπιστρέφω "I turn towards," "I turn again," "I return," "I repent"
18. ἐπικαλέομαι "I call upon," "I name"
19. προσκαλέομαι "I call to myself," "I summon"
20. προσκυνέω "I kiss my hand to," "I worship"
21. προσεύχομαι "I pray to"

In all these examples of compound words, the prepositions have the same meanings that they have when they are used before the case of a noun or pronoun. Some of them, however, have a somewhat extended or different meaning when they are used to form compound words. For example, in composition ἀνά means not only "up" but also "over again," "anew" (the Latin "re") and also "back" and "to and fro."

1. ἀναβλέπω	"I look up," but also "I look anew" or "I receive my sight"
2. ἀναπίπτω	"I fall back" or "I recline"
3. μεταβαίνω[1]	"I pass from one place to another," "I remove," "I depart"
4. μετανοέω	"I change my mind," "I repent"
5. μετάνοια	"repentance"
6. παρέρχομαι[2]	"I pass by the side of," "I pass from the side of," "I pass away"
7. παραβαίνω	"I go by the side of," "I violate," "I transgress"
8. παραιτέομαι	"I avert by entreaty," "I beg off," "I refuse," "I excuse myself"
9. παρακούω	"I hear amiss," "I disobey"
10. ὑπό	a sense of subjection or inferiority (from its meaning, "under")
11. ὑπακούω	"I listen to," "I obey," "I submit to"
12. ὑπακοή	"obedience"
13. ὑποτάσσομαι	"I order myself under," "I submit to"

1 μετά in composition generally has the sense of change or alteration.

2 παρά, from its meaning of "beside" or "along," has a further sense of passing on one side and so of averting, neglecting, transgressing.

Certain prepositions—such as ἀπό, διά, κατά, and σύν—sometimes practically lose their local meaning in composition and denote that the action of the verb with which they are connected is to be regarded as fully accomplished.

Examples of compound words:

1. ἀποκτείνω "I kill"
2. ἀπόλλυμι "I destroy"
3. ἀπολαμβάνω "I receive to the full"
4. διαμένω "I remain"
5. κατεργάζομαι "I perform"
6. κατεσθίω "I eat up"
7. καταλείπω "I abandon"
8. κατοικέω "I inhabit"
9. συντηρέω "I keep safe"

The following compound verbs differ greatly in meaning from the simple verbs from which they are formed; learn them carefully.

1. ἀναγινώσκω "I read"
2. ἀποκρίνομαι "I answer (I give a decision from myself)"
3. ἐπαγγέλλομαι "I promise (I announce concerning myself)"
4. παραγγέλλω "I command (I pass a message along a line)"
5. παρακαλέω "I call to my side," "I summon," "I admonish," "I exhort," "I entreat," "I comfort," "I encourage"
6. ὑπάγω "I withdraw myself," "I depart (I drive or draw under)"
7. ὑπάρχει "He is (he begins below, he commences)"

Notice also the derived nouns ἐπαγγελία ("a promise"), παραγγελία ("a command"), and ὁ παράκλητος ("the advocate" or "the comforter").

APPENDIX 5

Morphology Reference Tables

NOUNS

First Declension (A-stems): Feminine

	ἡ ἡμέρα α-Stem		ἡ ἀρχή η-Stem		ἡ δόξα Mixed Stem	
	Singular	Plural	Singular	Plural	Singular	Plural
Nom.	ἡμέρα	ἡμέραι	ἀρχή	ἀρχαί	δόξα	δόξαι
Acc.	ἡμέραν	ἡμέρας	ἀρχήν	ἀρχάς	δόξαν	δόξας
Gen.	ἡμέρας	ἡμερῶν	ἀρχῆς	ἀρχῶν	δόξης	δοξῶν
Dat.	ἡμέρᾳ	ἡμέραις	ἀρχῇ	ἀρχαῖς	δόξῃ	δόξαις

First Declension (A-stems): Masculine

	ὁ νεανίας α-Stem		ὁ προφήτης η-Stem	
	Singular	Plural	Singular	Plural
Nom.	νεανίας[1]	νεανίαι	προφήτης[2]	προφῆται
Acc.	νεανίαν	νεανίας	προφήτην	προφήτας
Gen.	νεανίου	νεανιῶν	προφήτου	προφητῶν
Dat.	νεανίᾳ	νεανίαις	προφήτῃ	προφήταις

1 The vocative, νεανία, differs from the nominative singular.
2 The vocative, προφῆτα, differs from the nominative singular.

Second Declension (O-stems)

	Masculine ὁ λόγος		Feminine ἡ παρθένος		Neuter τὸ ἔργον	
	Singular	Plural	Singular	Plural	Singular	Plural
Nom.	λόγος	λόγοι	παρθένος	παρθένοι	ἔργον	ἔργα
Acc.	λόγον	λόγους	παρθένον	παρθένους	ἔργον	ἔργα
Gen.	λόγου	λόγων	παρθένου	παρθένων	ἔργου	ἔργων
Dat.	λόγῳ	λόγοις	παρθένῳ	παρθένοις	ἔργῳ	ἔργοις

Third Declension: Dental Stems

	ἡ ἐλπίς **Dental Stem**		τὸ γράμμα **Dental Stem (neuter)**		ὁ or ἡ παῖς **Monosyllabic Dental Stem**	
	Singular	Plural	Singular	Plural	Singular	Plural
Nom.	ἐλπίς	ἐλπίδες	γράμμα	γράμματα	παῖς[1]	παῖδες
Acc.	ἐλπίδα	ἐλπίδας	γράμμα	γράμματα	παῖδα	παῖδας
Gen.	ἐλπίδος	ἐλπίδων	γράμματος	γραμμάτων	παιδός	παίδων
Dat.	ἐλπίδι	ἐλπίσι(ν)	γράμματι	γράμμασι(ν)	παιδί	παισί(ν)

1 The vocative, παῖ, differs from the nominative singular.

Third Declension: Guttural Stems

	ὁ φύλαξ **Guttural Stem**		ἡ νύξ **Monosyllabic Guttural Stem**	
	Singular	Plural	Singular	Plural
Nom.	φύλαξ	φύλακες	νύξ	νύκτες
Acc.	φύλακα	φύλακας	νύκτα	νύκτας
Gen.	φύλακος	φυλάκων	νυκτός	νυκτῶν
Dat.	φύλαξι	φύλαξι(ν)	νυκτί	νυξί(ν)

Third Declension: Liquid Stems

	ὁ ἡγεμών **Nasal Stem**		ὁ ἄρχων -ντ **Liquid Stem**		ἡ χείρ **Monosyllabic Liquid Stem**	
	Singular	Plural	Singular	Plural	Singular	Plural
Nom.	ἡγεμών	ἡγεμόνες	ἄρχων	ἄρχοντες	χείρ	χεῖρες
Acc.	ἡγεμόνα	ἡγεμόνας	ἄρχοντα	ἄρχοντας	χεῖρα	χεῖρας
Gen.	ἡγεμόνος	ἡγεμόνων	ἄρχοντος	ἀρχόντων	χειρός	χειρῶν
Dat.	ἡγεμόνι	ἡγεμόσι(ν)	ἄρχοντι	ἄρχουσι(ν)	χειρί	χερσί(ν)

Third Declension: Labial Stem

	ὁ Ἄραψ	
	Singular	Plural
Nom.	Ἄραψ	Ἄραβες
Acc.	Ἄραβα	Ἄραβας
Gen.	Ἄραβος	Ἀράβων
Dat.	Ἄραβι	Ἄραψι(ν)

Third Declension: Sibilant Stem

	τὸ γένος -εσ Stem	
	Singular	Plural
Nom.	γένος	γένη
Acc.	γένος	γένη
Gen.	γένους	γενέων (γενῶν)
Dat.	γένει	γένεσι(ν)

Third Declension: Syncopated Stems

	ὁ πατήρ		ἡ μήτηρ		ὁ ἀνήρ	
	Singular	Plural	Singular	Plural	Singular	Plural
Nom.	πατήρ[1]	πατέρες	μήτηρ[2]	μητέρες	ἀνήρ[3]	ἄνδρες
Acc.	πατέρα	πατέρας	μητέρα	μητέρας	ἄνδρα	ἄνδρας
Gen.	πατρός	πατέρων	μητρός	μητέρων	ἀνδρός	ἀνδρῶν
Dat.	πατρί	πατράσι(ν)	μητρί	μητράσι(ν)	ἀνδρί	ἀνδράσι(ν)

1 The vocative, πατέρ, differs from the nominative singular.
2 The vocative, μήτερ, differs from the nominative singular.
3 The vocative, ἄνερ, differs from the nominative singular.

Third Declension: Semivowel Stems

	ἡ πόλις **Semivowel ι-Stem**		ὁ ἰχθύς **Semivowel υ-Stem**		ὁ βασιλεύς **Semivowel ευ-Stem**	
	Singular	Plural	Singular	Plural	Singular	Plural
Nom.	πόλις[4]	πόλεις	ἰχθύς[5]	ἰχθύες	βασιλεύς[6]	βασιλεῖς
Acc.	πόλιν	πόλεις	ἰχθύν	ἰχθύας (ἰχθῦς)	βασιλέα	βασιλεῖς (βασιλέας)
Gen.	πόλεως	πόλεων	ἰχθύος	ἰχθύων	βασιλέως	βασιλέων
Dat.	πόλει	πόλεσι(ν)	ἰχθύϊ	ἰχθύσι(ν)	βασιλεῖ	βασιλεῦσι(ν)

4 The vocative, πόλι, differs from the nominative singular.
5 The vocative, ἰχθύ, differs from the nominative singular.
6 The vocative, βασιλεῦ, differs from the nominative singular.

ARTICLE AND PRONOUNS

Definite Article

ὁ, ἡ, τό ("the")

	Singular Masc.	Singular Fem.	Singular Neut.	Plural Masc.	Plural Fem.	Plural Neut.
Nom.	ὁ	ἡ	τό	οἱ	αἱ	τά
Acc.	τόν	τήν	τό	τούς	τάς	τά
Gen.	τοῦ	τῆς	τοῦ	τῶν	τῶν	τῶν
Dat.	τῷ	τῇ	τῷ	τοῖς	ταῖς	τοῖς

Relative Pronoun

ὅς, ἥ, ὅ ("who," "what," "which")

	Singular Masc.	Singular Fem.	Singular Neut.	Plural Masc.	Plural Fem.	Plural Neut.
Nom.	ὅς[1]	ἥ	ὅ	οἵ[2]	αἵ	ἅ
Acc.	ὅν	ἥν	ὅ	οὕς	ἅς	ἅ
Gen.	οὗ[3]	ἧς	οὗ	ὧν	ὧν	ὧν
Dat.	ᾧ	ᾗ	ᾧ	οἷς	αἷς	οἷς

1 Alternate nominative singular forms are ὅστις, ἥτις, and ὅτι.
2 Alternate nominative plural forms are οἵτινες, αἵτινες, and ἅτινα.
3 The form ὅτου occurs in five places in the New Testament (Matt 5:25, Luke 12:50, Luke 13:8, Luke 22:16, John 9:18)—always in the expression ἕως ὅτου ("until").

Near Demonstrative Pronouns

οὗτος, αὕτη, τοῦτο ("this," "these")

	Singular Masc.	Singular Fem.	Singular Neut.	Plural Masc.	Plural Fem.	Plural Neut.
Nom.	οὗτος	αὕτη	τοῦτο	οὗτοι	αὗται	ταῦτα
Acc.	τοῦτον	ταύτην	τοῦτο	τούτους	ταύτας	ταῦτα
Gen.	τούτου	ταύτης	τούτου	τούτων	τούτων	τούτων
Dat.	τούτῳ	ταύτῃ	τούτῳ	τούτοις	ταύταις	τούτοις

Far Demonstrative Pronouns

ἐκεῖνος, ἐκείνη, ἐκεῖνο ("that," "those")

	Singular Masc.	Singular Fem.	Singular Neut.	Plural Masc.	Plural Fem.	Plural Neut.
Nom.	ἐκεῖνος	ἐκείνη	ἐκεῖνο	ἐκεῖνοι	ἐκεῖναι	ἐκεῖνα
Acc.	ἐκεῖνον	ἐκείνην	ἐκεῖνο	ἐκείνους	ἐκείνας	ἐκεῖνα
Gen.	ἐκείνου	ἐκείνης	ἐκείνου	ἐκείνων	ἐκείνων	ἐκείνων
Dat.	ἐκείνῳ	ἐκείνῃ	ἐκείνῳ	ἐκείνοις	ἐκείναις	ἐκείνοις

Personal Pronouns

	First Person ("I," "we")		Second Person ("you," "you all")		Third Person ("he," "she," "it," "they")					
	Singular	Plural	Singular	Plural	Singular			Plural		
					Masc.	Fem.	Neut.	Masc.	Fem.	Neut.
Nom.	ἐγώ	ἡμεῖς	σύ	ὑμεῖς	αὐτός	αὐτή	αὐτό	αὐτοί	αὐταί	αὐτά
Acc.	με (ἐμέ)	ἡμᾶς	σε (σέ)	ὑμᾶς	αὐτόν	αὐτήν	αὐτό	αὐτούς	αὐτάς	αὐτά
Gen.	μου (ἐμοῦ)	ἡμῶν	σου (σοῦ)	ὑμῶν	αὐτοῦ	αὐτῆς	αὐτοῦ	αὐτῶν	αὐτῶν	αὐτῶν
Dat.	μοι (ἐμοί)	ἡμῖν	σοι (σοί)	ὑμῖν	αὐτῷ	αὐτῇ	αὐτῷ	αὐτοῖς	αὐταῖς	αὐτοῖς

Reflexive Personal Pronouns

	First Person ("myself")		Second Person ("yourself")		Third Person ("himself," "herself," "itself," "themselves")					
	Singular	Plural	Singular	Plural	Singular			Plural		
					Masc.	Fem.	Neut.	Masc.	Fem.	Neut.
Nom.	–	–	–	–	–	–	–	–	–	–
Acc.	ἐμαυτόν	ἑαυτούς[1]	σεαυτόν	ἑαυτούς[2]	ἑαυτόν	ἑαυτήν	ἑαυτό	ἑαυτούς	ἑαυτάς	ἑαυτά
Gen.	ἐμαυτοῦ	ἑαυτῶν	σεαυτοῦ	ἑαυτῶν	ἑαυτοῦ	ἑαυτῆς	ἑαυτοῦ	ἑαυτῶν	ἑαυτῶν	ἑαυτῶν
Dat.	ἐμαυτῷ	ἑαυτοῖς	σεαυτῷ	ἑαυτοῖς	ἑαυτῷ	ἑαυτῇ	ἑαυτῷ	ἑαυτοῖς	ἑαυταῖς	ἑαυτοῖς

1 The reflexive pronoun forms for the first person plural are identical to reflexive third person forms.
2 The reflexive pronoun forms for the second person plural are identical to reflexive third person forms.

Indefinite Pronouns

	τις, τι ("anyone," "a certain one")			
	Singular		Plural	
	Masc./Fem.	Neut.	Masc./Fem.	Neut.
Nom.	τις	τι	τινές	τινά
Acc.	τινά	τι	τινάς	τινά
Gen.	τινός	τινός	τινῶν	τινῶν
Dat.	τινί	τινί	τισί(ν)	τισί(ν)

Interrogative Pronouns

	τίς, τί ("Who?" "What?")			
	Singular		Plural	
	Masc./Fem.	Neut.	Masc./Fem.	Neut.
Nom.	τίς	τί	τίνες	τίνα
Acc.	τίνα	τί	τίνας	τίνα
Gen.	τίνος	τίνος	τίνων	τίνων
Dat.	τίνι	τίνι	τίσι(ν)	τίσι(ν)

ADJECTIVES

2-1-2 Pattern

η-stem feminine form pattern: ἀγαθός ("good")

	Singular Masc.	Singular Fem.	Singular Neut.	Plural Masc.	Plural Fem.	Plural Neut.
Nom.	ἀγαθός[1]	ἀγαθή	ἀγαθόν	ἀγαθοί	ἀγαθαί	ἀγαθά
Acc.	ἀγαθόν	ἀγαθήν	ἀγαθόν	ἀγαθούς	ἀγαθάς	ἀγαθά
Gen.	ἀγαθοῦ	ἀγαθῆς	ἀγαθοῦ	ἀγαθῶν	ἀγαθῶν	ἀγαθῶν
Dat.	ἀγαθός	ἀγαθή	ἀγαθόν	ἀγαθοῖς	ἀγαθαῖς	ἀγαθοῖς

1 The vocative, ἀγαθέ, differs from the nominative singular.

α-stem feminine form pattern: ἅγιος ("holy")

	Singular Masc.	Singular Fem.	Singular Neut.	Plural Masc.	Plural Fem.	Plural Neut.
Nom.	ἅγιος[2]	ἁγία	ἅγιον	ἅγιοι	ἅγιαι	ἅγια
Acc.	ἅγιον	ἁγίαν	ἅγιον	ἁγίους	ἁγίας	ἅγια
Gen.	ἁγίου	ἁγίας	ἁγίου	ἁγίων	ἁγίων	ἁγίων
Dat.	ἁγίῳ	ἁγίᾳ	ἁγίῳ	ἁγίοις	ἁγίαις	ἁγίοις

2 The vocative, ἅγιε, differs from the nominative singular.

Irregular 2-1-2 Pattern

μέγας ("great")

	Singular Masc.	Singular Fem.	Singular Neut.	Plural Masc.	Plural Fem.	Plural Neut.
Nom.	μέγας[3]	μεγάλη	μέγα	μεγάλοι	μεγάλαι	μεγάλα
Acc.	μέγαν	μεγάλην	μέγα	μεγάλους	μεγάλας	μεγάλα
Gen.	μεγάλου	μεγάλης	μεγάλου	μεγάλων	μεγάλων	μεγάλων
Dat.	μεγάλῳ	μεγάλῃ	μεγάλῳ	μεγάλοις	μεγάλαις	μεγάλοις

3 The vocative, μεγάλε, differs from the nominative singular.

πολύς ("much," "many")

	Singular Masc.	Singular Fem.	Singular Neut.	Plural Masc.	Plural Fem.	Plural Neut.
Nom.	πολύς	πολλή	πολύ	πολλοί	πολλαί	πολλά
Acc.	πολύν	πολλήν	πολύ	πολλούς	πολλάς	πολλά
Gen.	πολλοῦ	πολλῆς	πολλοῦ	πολλῶν	πολλῶν	πολλῶν
Dat.	πολλῷ	πολλῇ	πολλῷ	πολλοῖς	πολλαῖς	πολλοῖς

3-1-3 Pattern

πᾶς, πᾶσα, πᾶν ("all")
Stem: παντ- πασ- παντ-

	Singular Masc.	Singular Fem.	Singular Neut.	Plural Masc.	Plural Fem.	Plural Neut.
Nom.	πᾶς	πᾶσα	πᾶν	πάντες	πᾶσαι	πάντα
Acc.	πάντα	πᾶσαν	πᾶν	πάντας	πάσας	πάντα
Gen.	παντός	πάσης	παντός	πάντων	πασῶν	πάντων
Dat.	παντί	πάσῃ	παντί	πᾶσι(ν)	πάσαις	πᾶσι(ν)

3-3-3 Pattern: Sibilant Stem

ἀληθής ("true")
Stem: ἀληθεσ-

	Singular Masc./Fem.	Singular Neut.	Plural Masc./Fem.	Plural Neut.
Nom.	ἀληθής	ἀληθές	ἀληθεῖς	ἀληθῆ
Acc.	ἀληθῆ	ἀληθές	ἀληθεῖς	ἀληθῆ
Gen.	ἀληθοῦς	ἀληθοῦς	ἀληθῶν	ἀληθῶν
Dat.	ἀληθεῖ	ἀληθεῖ	ἀληθέσι	ἀληθέσι

3-3-3 Pattern: Liquid Stem

ἀφρονής ("foolish")
Stem: ἀφρον-

	Singular Masc./Fem.	Singular Neut.	Plural Masc./Fem.	Plural Neut.
Nom.	ἄφρων	ἄφρον	ἄφρονες	ἄφρονα
Acc.	ἄφρονα	ἄφρον	ἄφρονας	ἄφρονα
Gen.	ἄφρονος	ἄφρονος	ἀφρόνων	ἀφρόνων
Dat.	ἄφρονι	ἄφρονι	ἄφροσι(ν)	ἄφροσι(ν)

NUMBERS

Declinable Numbers

	εἷς, μία, ἕν ("one") **Stem: ἑν-, μια-, ἑν-**			**τρεῖς, τρία ("three")** **Stem: τρι-**		**τέσσαρες, τέσσαρα ("four")** **Stem: τεσσαρ-**	
	Singular Only			Plural Only		Plural Only	
	Masc.	Fem.	Neut.	Masc./Fem.	Neut.	Masc./Fem.	Neut.
Nom.	εἷς	μία	ἕν	τρεῖς	τρία	τέσσαρες	τέσσαρα
Acc.	ἕνα	μίαν	ἕν	τρία	τρία	τέσσαρας	τέσσαρα
Gen.	ἑνός	μιᾶς	ἑνός	τριῶν	τριῶν	τεσσάρων	τεσσάρων
Dat.	ἑνί	μιᾷ	ἑνί	τρισί(ν)	τρισί(ν)	τέσσαρσι(ν)	τέσσαρσι(ν)

Cardinal Numbers

1	εἷς, μία, ἕν	11	ἕνδεκα
2	δύο	12	δώδεκα
3	τρεῖς, τρία	13	τρεῖς (τρία) καὶ δέκα or τρεισκαίδεκα
4	τέσσαρες, τέσσαρα	14	τέσσαρες (τέσσαρα) καὶ δέκα
5	πέντε	15	δεκαπέντε
6	ἕξ	16	δεκαέξ
7	ἑπτά	17	δεκαεπτά
8	ὀκτώ	18	δεκαοκτώ
9	ἐννέα	19	δεκαεννέα
10	δέκα	20	εἴκοσι(ν)

VERBS

Charts on pages 442–454

Each verb root has at most six tense stems. These various stems are called principal parts. Sometimes multiple tenses or voices are produced by one tense stem. The charts on pages 442–43 show the forms that may be produced from the six principal parts for λύω.

Following the summary for a regular verb, other stem patterns are provided on pages 444–52. These include thematic and athematic aorist forms as well as an example of an athematic present. This section concludes with forms for irregular verbs, such as εἰμί and οἶδα (pages 453–54).

REGULAR VERBS (λύω)

Principal Parts for λύω

1	2	3	4	5	6
Present (all voices) Imperfect (all voices)	Future Active and Middle	Aorist Active and Middle	Perfect Active and Middle	Perfect Passive	Aorist Passive and Future Passive
λύω	λύσω	ἔλυσα	λέλυκα	λέλυμαι	ἐλύθην

Forms Derived from the 1st Principal Part

	Present Indicative		Present Imperative		Present Subjunctive		Imperfect Indicative	
	Active	Mid./Pass.	Active	Mid./Pass.	Active	Mid./Pass.	Active	Mid./Pass.
1 sg.	λύω	λύομαι			λύω	λύωμαι	ἔλυον	ἐλυόμην
2 sg.	λύεις	λύῃ	λύε	λύου	λύῃς	λύῃ	ἔλυες	ἐλύου
3 sg.	λύει	λύεται	λυέτω	λυέσθω	λύῃ	λύηται	ἔλυε(ν)	ἐλύετο
1 pl.	λύομεν	λυόμεθα			λύωμεν	λυώμεθα	ἐλύομεν	ἐλυόμεθα
2 pl.	λύετε	λυέσθε	λύετε	λύεσθε	λύητε	λύησθε	ἐλύετε	ἐλύεσθε
3 pl.	λύουσι(ν)	λύονται	λυέτωσαν	λυέσθωταν	λύωσι(ν)	λύωνται	ἔλυον	ἐλύοντο

Present Infinitive	
Active	Mid./Pass.
λύειν	λύεσθαι

	Present Participle					
	Active (singular)			Middle/Passive (singular)		
	Masc.	Fem.	Neut.	Masc.	Fem.	Neut.
Nom.	λύων	λύουσα	λῦον	λυόμενος	λυομένη	λυόμενον
Acc.	λύοντα	λύουσαν	λῦον	λυόμενον	λυομένην	λυόμενον

Forms Derived from the 2nd Principal Part

	Future Indicative	
	Active	Mid./Pass.
1 sg.	λύσω	λύσομαι
2 sg.	λύσεις	λύσῃ
3 sg.	λύσει	λύσεται
1 pl.	λύσομεν	λυσόμεθα
2 pl.	λύσετε	λυσέσθε
3 pl.	λύσουσι(ν)	λύσονται

Future Infinitive	
Active	Middle
λύσειν	λύσεσθαι

	Future Participle					
	Active (singular)			Middle/Passive (singular)		
	Masc.	Fem.	Neut.	Masc.	Fem.	Neut.
Nom.	λύσων	λύσουσα	λῦσον	λυσόμενος	λυσομένη	λυσόμενον
Acc.	λύσοντα	λύσουσαν	λῦσον	λυσόμενον	λυσομένην	λυσόμενον

Forms Derived from the 3rd Principal Part (Sigmatic Aorist Forms)

	Aorist Indicative		Aorist Imperative		Aorist Subjunctive	
	Active	Mid./Pass.	Active	Mid./Pass.	Active	Mid./Pass.
1 sg.	ἔλυσα	ἐλυσάμην			λύσω	λύσωμαι
2 sg.	ἔλυσας	ἐλύσω	λῦσον	λῦσαι	λύσῃς	λύσῃ
3 sg.	ἔλυσε(ν)	ἐλύσατο	λυσάτω	λυσάσθω	λύσῃ	λύσηται
1 pl.	ἐλύσαμεν	ἐλυσάμεθα			λύσωμεν	λυσώμεθα
2 pl.	ἐλύσατε	ἐλύσασθε	λύσατε	λύσασθε	λύσητε	λύσησθε
3 pl.	ἔλυσαν	ἐλύσαντο	λυσάτωσαν	λυσάσθωσαν	λύσωσι(ν)	λύσωνται

Aorist Infinitive	
Active	Middle
λῦσαι	λύσασθαι

	Aorist Participle					
	Active (singular)			Middle (singular)		
	Masc.	Fem.	Neut.	Masc.	Fem.	Neut.
Nom.	λύσας	λύσασα	λῦσαν	λυσάμενος	λυσαμένη	λυσάμενον
Acc.	λύσαντα	λύσασαν	λῦσαν	λυσάμενον	λυσαμένην	λυσάμενον

Forms Derived from the 4th (Active) and 5th (Passive) Principal Parts

	Perfect Indicative	
	Active	Passive
1 sg.	λέλυκα	λέλυμαι
2 sg.	λέλυκας	λέλυσαι
3 sg.	λέλυκε(ν)	λέλυται
1 pl.	λελύκαμεν	λελύμεθα
2 pl.	λελύκατε	λέλυσθε
3 pl.	λελύκασι(ν)	λέλυνται

Perfect Infinitive	
Active	Passive
λελυκέναι	λελύσθαι

	Perfect Participle					
	Active (singular)			Passive (singular)		
	Masc.	Fem.	Neut.	Masc.	Fem.	Neut.
Nom.	λελυκώς	λελυκυῖα	λελυκός	λελυμένος	λελυμένη	λελυμένον
Acc.	λελυκότα	λελυκυῖαν	λελυκός	λελυμένον	λελυμένην	λελυμένον

Forms Derived from the 6th Principal Part

	Aorist Indicative	Aorist Imperative	Aorist Subjunctive	Aorist Infinitive	Future Indicative
	Passive	Passive	Passive	Passive	Passive
1 sg.	ἐλύθην		λυθῶ	λυθῆναι	λυθήσομαι
2 sg.	ἐλύθης	λύθητι	λυθῇς		λυθήσῃ
3 sg.	ἐλύθη	λυθήτω	λυθῇ		λυθήσεται
1 pl.	ἐλύθημεν		λυθῶμεν		λυθησόμεθα
2 pl.	ἐλύθητε	λύθητε	λυθῆτε		λυθήσεσθε
3 pl.	ἐλύθησαν	λυθήτωσαν	λυθῶσι(ν)		λυθήσονται

	Aorist Participle		
	Passive (singular)		
	Masc.	Fem.	Neut.
Nom.	λυθείς	λυθεῖσα	λυθέν
Acc.	λυθέντα	λυθεῖσαν	λυθέν

VERBS WITH THEMATIC AORIST FORMS (Second Aorist Forms)

Some verbs don't have sigmatic stems for their aorist forms. They use the verbal root for their aorist forms and present root for their imperfect forms. These charts provide a comparison for present, imperfect, and aorist tenses.

Principal Parts for βάλλω

1	2	3	4	5	6
βάλλω	βαλῶ	ἔβαλον	βέβληκα	βέβλημαι	ἐβλήθην

Forms Derived from the 1st Principal Part

	Present Indicative		Present Imperative		Present Subjunctive		Imperfect Indicative	
	Active	Mid./Pass.	Active	Mid./Pass.	Active	Mid./Pass.	Active	Mid./Pass.
1 sg.	βάλλω	βάλλομαι			βάλλω	βάλλωμαι	ἔβαλλον	ἐβαλλόμην
2 sg.	βάλλεις	βάλλῃ	βάλλε	βάλλου	βάλλῃς	βάλλῃ	ἔβαλλες	ἐβάλλου
3 sg.	βάλλει	βάλλεται	βαλλέτω	βαλλέσθω	βάλλῃ	βάλληται	ἔβαλλε(ν)	ἐβάλλετο
1 pl.	βάλλομεν	βαλλόμεθα			βάλλωμεν	βαλλώμεθα	ἐβάλλομεν	ἐβαλλόμεθα
2 pl.	βάλλετε	βάλλεσθε	βάλλετε	βάλλεσθε	βάλλητε	βάλλησθε	ἐβάλλετε	ἐβάλλεσθε
3 pl.	βάλλουσι(ν)	βάλλονται	βαλλέτωσαν	βαλλέσθωσαν	βάλλωσι(ν)	βάλλωνται	ἔβαλλον	ἐβάλλοντο

Present Infinitive	
Active	Mid./Pass.
βάλλειν	βάλλεσθαι

	Present Participle					
	Active (singular)			Middle / Passive (singular)		
	Masc.	Fem.	Neut.	Masc.	Fem.	Neut.
Nom.	βάλλων	βάλλουσα	βάλλον	βαλλόμενος	βαλλομένη	βαλλόμενον
Acc.	βάλλοντα	βάλλουσαν	βάλλον	βαλλόμενον	βαλλομένην	βαλλόμενον

Forms Derived from the 3rd Principal Part (Thematic Aorist Forms)

	Aorist Indicative		Aorist Imperative		Aorist Subjunctive	
	Active	Middle	Active	Middle	Active	Middle
1 sg.	ἔβαλον	ἐβαλόμην			βάλω	βάλωμαι
2 sg.	ἔβαλες	ἐβάλου	βάλε	βάλου	βάλῃς	βάλῃ
3 sg.	ἔβαλε(ν)	ἐβάλετο	βαλέτω	βαλέσθω	βάλῃ	βάληται
1 pl.	ἐβάλομεν	ἐβαλόμεθα			βάλωμεν	βαλώμεθα
2 pl.	ἐβάλετε	ἐβάλεσθε	βάλετε	βάλεσθε	βάλητε	βάλησθε
3 pl.	ἔβαλον	ἐβάλοντο	βαλέτωσαν	βαλέσθωσαν	βάλωσι(ν)	βάλωνται

Aorist Infinitive	
Active	Middle
βαλεῖν	βαλέσθαι

	Aorist Participle					
	Active (singular)			Middle (singular)		
	Masc.	Fem.	Neut.	Masc.	Fem.	Neut.
Nom.	βαλών	βαλλοῦσα	βαλόν	βαλόμενος	βαλομένη	βαλόμενον
Acc.	βαλόντα	βαλλοῦσαν	βαλόν	βαλόμενον	βαλομένην	βαλόμενον

VERBS WITH ATHEMATIC AORIST FORMS

These common verbs have no stem (no theme) in their aorist forms. The vowel preceding endings is the verbal root vowel (long except in base participle forms.)

Principal Parts for γινώσκω

1	2	3	4	5	6
γινώσκω	γνώσομαι	ἔγνων	ἔγνωκα	ἔγνωσμαι	ἐγνώσθην

Forms Derived from the 3rd Principal Part

	Aorist Indicative	Aorist Imperative	Aorist Subjunctive
	Active	Active	Active
1 sg.	ἔγνων		γνῶ
2 sg.	ἔγνως	γνῶθι	γνῷς
3 sg.	ἔγνω	γνώτω	γνῷ
1 pl.	ἔγνωμεν		γνῶμεν
2 pl.	ἔγνωτε	γνῶτε	γνῶτε
3 pl.	ἔγνωσαν	γνώτωσαν	γνῶσι(ν)

Aorist Infinitive
Active
γνῶναι

Aorist Participle			
	Active (singular)		
	Masc.	Fem.	Neut.
Nom.	γνούς	γνοῦσα	γνόν
Acc.	γνόντα	γνοῦσαν	γνόν

Principal Parts for βαίνω[1]

1	2	3	4	5	6
βαίνω	βήσομαι	ἔβην	βέβηκα	–	–

Forms Derived from the 3rd Principal Part

	Aorist Indicative	Aorist Imperative	Aorist Subjunctive
	Active	Active	Active
1 sg.	ἔβην		βῶ
2 sg.	ἔβης	βῆθι (βά)	βῇς
3 sg.	ἔβη	βήτω (βάτω)	βῇ
1 pl.	ἔβημεν		βῶμεν
2 pl.	ἔβητε	βῆτε (βᾶτε)	βῆτε
3 pl.	ἔβησαν	βήτωσαν (βάτωσαν)	βῶσι(ν)

Aorist Infinitive
Active
βῆναι

Aorist Participle			
	Active (singular)		
	Masc.	Fem.	Neut.
Nom.	βάς	βᾶσα	βάν
Acc.	βάντα	βᾶσαν	βάν

1 This word is only used in compounds in the New Testament.

CONTRACT VERBS

Contract verbs only have vowel contractions in first principal part forms (present and imperfect tenses.) The tables below show those differences. Refer to the standard forms of λύω for other tense and principal part forms.

Principal Parts for φιλέω (Epsilon Contract Verb)

1	2	3	4	5	6
φιλέω	φιλήσω	ἐφίλησα	πεφίληκα	πεφίλημαι	ἐφιλήθην

Forms Derived from the 1st Principal Part

	Present Indicative		Present Imperative		Present Subjunctive		Imperfect Indicative	
	Active	Mid./Pass.	Active	Mid./Pass.	Active	Mid./Pass.	Active	Mid./Pass.
1 sg.	φιλῶ	φιλοῦμαι			φιλῶ	φιλῶμαι	ἐφίλουν	ἐφιλούμην
2 sg.	φιλεῖς	φιλῇ	φίλει	φιλοῦ	φιλῇς	φιλῇ	ἐφίλεις	ἐφιλοῦ
3 sg.	φιλεῖ	φιλεῖται	φιλείτω	φιλείσθω	φιλῇ	φιλῆται	ἐφίλει	ἐφιλεῖτο
1 pl.	φιλοῦμεν	φιλούμεθα			φιλῶμεν	φιλώμεθα	ἐφιλοῦμεν	ἐφιλούμεθα
2 pl.	φιλεῖτε	φιλεῖσθε	φιλεῖτε	φιλεῖσθε	φιλῆτε	φιλῆσθε	ἐφιλεῖτε	ἐφιλεῖσθε
3 pl.	φιλοῦσι(ν)	φιλοῦνται	φιλείτωσαν	φιλείσθωσαν	φιλῶσι(ν)	φιλῶνται	ἐφίλουν	ἐφιλοῦντο

Present Infinitive	
Active	Mid./Pass.
φιλεῖν	φιλεῖσθαι

	Present Participle					
	Active (singular)			Middle / Passive (singular)		
	Masc.	Fem.	Neut.	Masc.	Fem.	Neut.
Nom.	φιλῶν	φιλοῦσα	φιλοῦν	φιλούμενος	φιλουμένη	φιλούμενον
Acc.	φιλοῦντα	φιλοῦσαν	φιλοῦν	φιλούμενον	φιλουμένην	φιλούμενον

Principal Parts for τιμάω (Alpha Contract Verb)

1	2	3	4	5	6
τιμάω	τιμήσω	ἐτίμησα	τετιμήκα	τετίμημαι	ἐτιμήθην

Forms Derived from the 1st Principal Part

	Present Indicative		Present Imperative		Present Subjunctive		Imperfect Indicative	
	Active	Mid./Pass.	Active	Mid./Pass.	Active	Mid./Pass.	Active	Mid./Pass.
1 sg.	τιμῶ	τιμῶμαι			τιμῶ	τιμῶμαι	ἐτίμων	ἐτιμώμην
2 sg.	τιμᾷς	τιμᾷ	τίμα	τιμῶ	τιμῇς	τιμῇ	ἐτίμας	ἐτιμῶ
3 sg.	τιμᾷ	τιμᾶται	τιμάτω	τιμάσθω	τιμῇ	τιμῆται	ἐτίμα	ἐτιμᾶτο
1 pl.	τιμῶμεν	τιμώμεθα			τιμῶμεν	τιμώμεθα	ἐτιμῶμεν	ἐτιμώμεθα
2 pl.	τιμᾶτε	τιμᾶσθε	τιμᾶτε	τιμᾶσθε	τιμῆτε	τιμῆσθε	ἐτιμᾶτε	ἐτιμᾶσθε
3 pl.	τιμῶσι(ν)	τιμῶνται	τιμάτωσαν	τιμάσθωσαν	τιμῶσι(ν)	τιμῶνται	ἐτίμων	ἐτιμῶντο

Present Infinitive	
Active	Mid./Pass.
τιμᾶν	τιμᾶσθαι

	Present Participle					
	Active (singular)			Middle/Passive (singular)		
	Masc.	Fem.	Neut.	Masc.	Fem.	Neut.
Nom.	τιμῶν	τιμῶσα	τιμῶν	τιμώμενος	τιμωμένη	τιμώμενον
Acc.	τιμῶντα	τιμῶσαν	τιμῶν	τιμώμενον	τιμωμένην	τιμώμενον

Principal Parts for πληρόω (Omicron Contract Verb)

1	2	3	4	5	6
πληρόω	πληρώσω	ἐπλήρωσα	πεπλήρωκα	πεπλήρωμαι	ἐπληρώθην

Forms Derived from the 1st Principal Part

	Present Indicative		Present Imperative		Present Subjunctive		Imperfect Indicative	
	Active	Mid./Pass.	Active	Mid./Pass.	Active	Mid./Pass.	Active	Mid./Pass.
1 sg.	πληρῶ	πληροῦμαι			πληρῶ	πληρῶμαι	ἐπλήρουν	ἐπληρούμην
2 sg.	πληροῖς	πληροῖ	πλήρου	πληροῦ	πληρῇς	πληρῇ	ἐπλήρους	ἐπληροῦ
3 sg.	πληροῖ	πληροῦται	πληρούτω	πληρούσθω	πληρῇ	πληρῆται	ἐπλήρου	ἐπληρούτω
1 pl.	πληροῦμεν	πληρούμεθα			πληρῶμεν	πληρώμεθα	ἐπληροῦμεν	ἐπληρούμεθα
2 pl.	πληροῦτε	πληροῦσθε	πληροῦτε	πληροῦσθε	πληρῆτε	πληρῆσθε	ἐπληροῦτε	ἐπληροῦσθε
3 pl.	πληροῦσι(ν)	πληροῦνται	πληρούτωσαν	πληρούσθωσαν	πληρῶσι(ν)	πληρῶνται	ἐπλήρουν	ἐπληροῦντο

Present Infinitive	
Active	Mid./Pass.
πληροῦν	πληροῦσθαι

	Present Participle					
	Active (singular)			Middle/Passive (singular)		
	Masc.	Fem.	Neut.	Masc.	Fem.	Neut.
Nom.	πληρῶν	πληροῦσα	πληροῦν	πληρούμενος	πληρουμένη	πληρούμενον
Acc.	πληροῦντα	πληροῦσαν	πληροῦν	πληρούμενον	πληρουμένην	πληρούμενον

ATHEMATIC VERBS (μι verbs)

Principal Parts for δίδωμι

1	2	3	4	5	6
δίδωμι	δώσω	ἔδωκα	δέδωκα	δέδομαι	ἐδόθην

Forms Derived from the 1st Principal Part

	Present Indicative		Present Imperative		Present Subjunctive		Imperfect Indicative	
	Active	Mid./Pass.	Active	Mid./Pass.	Active	Mid./Pass.	Active	Mid./Pass.
1 sg.	δίδωμι	δίδομαι			διδῶ	διδῶμαι	ἐδίδουν	ἐδιδόμην
2 sg.	δίδως	δίδοσαι	δίδου	δίδοσο	διδῷς	διδῷ	ἐδίδους	ἐδίδοσο
3 sg.	δίδωσι(ν)	δίδοται	διδότω	διδόσθω	διδῷ	διδῶται	ἐδίδου	ἐδίδοτο
1 pl.	δίδομεν	διδόμεθα			διδῶμεν	διδώμεθα	ἐδίδομεν	ἐδιδόμεθα
2 pl.	δίδοτε	δίδοσθε	δίδοτε	δίδοσθε	διδῶτε	διδῶσθε	ἐδίδοτε	ἐδίδοσθε
3 pl.	διδόασι(ν)	δίδονται	διδότωσαν	διδόσθωσαν	διδῶσι(ν)	διδῶνται	ἐδίδουν (ἐδίδοσαν)	ἐδίδοντο

Present Infinitive	
Active	Mid./Pass.
διδόναι	δίδοσθαι

	Present Participle					
	Active (singular)			Middle / Passive (singular)		
	Masc.	Fem.	Neut.	Masc.	Fem.	Neut.
Nom.	διδούς	διδοῦσα	διδόν	διδόμενος	διδομένη	διδόμενον
Acc.	διδόντα	διδοῦσαν	διδόν	διδόμενον	διδομένην	διδόμενον

Forms Derived from the 3rd Principal Part

	Aorist Indicative		Aorist Imperative		Aorist Subjunctive	
	Active	Middle	Active	Middle	Active	Middle
1 sg.	ἔδωκα	ἐδόμην			δῶ	δῶμαι
2 sg.	ἔδωκας	ἔδου	δός	δοῦ	δῷς	δῷ
3 sg.	ἔδωκε(ν)	ἔδοτο	δότω	δόσθω	δῷ	δῶται
1 pl.	ἐδώκαμεν	ἐδόμεθα			δῶμεν	δώμεθα
2 pl.	ἐδώκατε	ἔδοσθε	δότε	δόσθε	δῶτε	δῶσθε
3 pl.	ἔδωκαν	ἔδοντο	δότωσαν	δόσθωσαν	δῶσι(ν)	δῶνται

Aorist Infinitive	
Active	Middle
δοῦναι	δόσθαι

	Aorist Participle					
	Active (singular)			Middle (singular)		
	Masc.	Fem.	Neut.	Masc.	Fem.	Neut.
Nom.	δούς	δοῦσα	δόν	δόμενος	δομένη	δόμενον
Acc.	δόντα	δοῦσαν	δόν	δόμενον	δομένην	δόμενον

Principal Parts for τίθημι

1	2	3	4	5	6
τίθημι	θήσω	ἔθηκα	τέθεικα	τέθειμαι	ἐτέθην

Forms Derived from the 1st Principal Part

	Present Indicative		Present Imperative		Present Subjunctive		Imperfect Indicative	
	Active	Mid./Pass.	Active	Mid./Pass.	Active	Mid./Pass.	Active	Mid./Pass.
1 sg.	τίθημι	τίθεμαι			τιθῶ	τιθῶμαι	ἐτίθην	ἐτιθέμην
2 sg.	τίθης	τίθεσαι	τίθει	τίθεσο	τιθῇς	τιθῇ	ἐτίθεις	ἐτίθεσο
3 sg.	τίθησι(ν)	τίθεται	τιθέτω	τιθέσθω	τιθῇ	τιθῆται	ἐτίθει	ἐτίθετο
1 pl.	τίθεμεν	τιθέμεθα			τιθῶμεν	τιθώμεθα	ἐτίθεμεν	ἐτιθέμεθα
2 pl.	τίθετε	τίθεσθε	τίθετε	τίθεσθε	τιθῆτε	τιθῆσθε	ἐτίθετε	ἐτίθεσθε
3 pl.	τιθέασι(ν)	τίθενται	τιθέτωσαν	τιθέσθωσαν	τιθῶσι(ν)	τιθῶνται	ἐτίθεσαν	ἐτίθεντο

Present Infinitive	
Active	Mid./Pass.
τιθέναι	τίθεσθαι

	Present Participle					
	Active (singular)			Middle/Passive (singular)		
	Masc.	Fem.	Neut.	Masc.	Fem.	Neut.
Nom.	τιθείς	τιθεῖσα	τιθέν	τιθέμενος	τιθεμένη	τιθέμενον
Acc.	τιθέντα	τιθεῖσαν	τιθέν	τιθέμενον	τιθεμένην	τιθέμενον

Forms Derived from the 3rd Principal Part

	Aorist Indicative		Aorist Imperative		Aorist Subjunctive	
	Active	Middle	Active	Middle	Active	Middle
1 sg.	ἔθηκα	ἐθέμην			θῶ	θῶμαι
2 sg.	ἔθηκας	ἔθου	θές	θοῦ	θῇς	θῇ
3 sg.	ἔθηκε(ν)	ἔθετο	θέτω	θέσθω	θῇ	θῆται
1 pl.	ἐθήκαμεν	ἐθέμεθα			θῶμεν	θώμεθα
2 pl.	ἐθήκατε	ἔθεσθε	θέτε	θέσθε	θῆτε	θῆσθε
3 pl.	ἔθηκαν	ἔθεντο	θέτωσαν	θέσθωσαν	θῶσι(ν)	θῶνται

Aorist Infinitive	
Active	Middle
θέναι	θέσθαι

	Aorist Participle					
	Active (singular)			Middle (singular)		
	Masc.	Fem.	Neut.	Masc.	Fem.	Neut.
Nom.	θείς	θεῖσα	θέν	θέμενος	θεμένη	θέμενον
Acc.	θέντα	θεῖσαν	θέν	θέμενον	θεμένην	θέμενον

Principal Parts for ἵστημι

1	2	3	4	5	6
ἵστημι	στήσω	ἔστησα[1] (ἔστην[2])	ἕστηκα	ἕσταμαι	ἐστάθην

1 Transitive form, "cause to stand," "place something"
2 Intransitive form, "stand"

Forms Derived from the 1st Principal Part

	Present Indicative		Present Imperative		Present Subjunctive		Imperfect Indicative	
	Active	Mid./Pass.	Active	Mid./Pass.	Active	Mid./Pass.	Active	Mid./Pass.
1 sg.	ἵστημι	ἵσταμαι			ἱστῶ	ἱστῶμαι	ἵστην	ἱστάμην
2 sg.	ἵστης	ἵστασαι	ἵστη	ἵστασο	ἱστῇς	ἱστῇ	ἵστης	ἵστασο
3 sg.	ἵστησι(ν)	ἵσταται	ἱστάτω	ἱστάσθω	ἱστῇ	ἱστῆται	ἵστη	ἵστατο
1 pl.	ἵσταμεν	ἱστάμεθα			ἱστῶμεν	ἱστώμεθα	ἵσταμεν	ἱστάμεθα
2 pl.	ἵστατε	ἵστασθε	ἵστατε	ἵστασθε	ἱστῆτε	ἱστῆσθε	ἵστατε	ἵστασθε
3 pl.	ἵστασι(ν)	ἵστανται	ἱστάτωσαν	ἱστάσθωσαν	ἱστῶσι(ν)	ἱστῶνται	ἵστασαν	ἵσταντο

Present Infinitive	
Active	Mid./Pass.
ἱστάναι	ἵστασθαι

Present Participle	Active (singular)			Middle/Passive (singular)		
	Masc.	Fem.	Neut.	Masc.	Fem.	Neut.
Nom.	ἱστάς	ἱστᾶσα	ἱστάν	ἱστάμενος	ἱσταμένη	ἱστάμενον
Acc.	ἱστάντα	ἱστᾶσαν	ἱστάν	ἱστάμενον	ἱσταμένην	ἱστάμενον

Athematic Active[1] Forms Derived from the 3rd Principal Part

	Aorist Indicative	Aorist Imperative	Aorist Subjunctive
	Active	Active	Active
1 sg.	ἔστην		στῶ
2 sg.	ἔστης	στῆθι	στῇς
3 sg.	ἔστη	στήτω	στῇ
1 pl.	ἔστημεν		στῶμεν
2 pl.	ἔστητε	στῆτε	στῆτε
3 pl.	ἔστησαν	στήτωσαν	στῶσι(ν)

Aorist Infinitive
Active
στῆναι

Aorist Participle	Active (singular)		
	Masc.	Fem.	Neut.
Nom.	στάς	στᾶσα	στάν
Acc.	στάντα	στᾶσαν	στάν

1 Since the athematic forms of this verb communicate the intransitive meaning ("stand"), they only use the active voice.

Principal Parts for εἰμί

1	2	3	4	5	6
εἰμί	ἔσομαι	–	–	–	–

Forms Derived from the 1st Principal Part

	Present Indicative	Present Imperative	Present Subjunctive	Imperfect Indicative
	Active	Active	Active	Active[1]
1 sg.	εἰμί		ὦ	ἤμην
2 sg.	εἶ	ἴσθι	ᾖς	ἦς (ἦσθα)
3 sg.	ἐστί(ν)	ἔστω	ᾖ[2]	ἦν
1 pl.	ἐσμέν		ὦμεν	ἦμεν (ἤμεθα)
2 pl.	ἐστέ	ἔστε	ἦτε	ἦτε
3 pl.	εἰσί(ν)	ἔστωσαν	ὦσι(ν)	ἦσαν

Present Infinitive
Active
εἶναι

	Present Participle		
	Active (singular)		
	Masc.	Fem.	Neut.
Nom.	ὤν	οὖσα	ὄν
Acc.	ὄντα	οὖσαν	ὄν

Forms Derived from the 2nd Principal Part

	Future Indicative
	Middle
1 sg.	ἔσομαι
2 sg.	ἔσῃ
3 sg.	ἔσται
1 pl.	ἐσόμεθα
2 pl.	ἔσεσθε
3 pl.	ἔσονται

Future Infinitive
Middle
ἔσεσθαι

1 The following imperfect forms are middle: 1 sg. ἤμην, 2 sg. ἦσθα, 1 pl. ἤμεθα.
2 There is one optative form of this verb used 12 times in the New Testament, the present active optative third person singular, εἴη.

VERB WITH PRESENT TENSE USING PERFECT FORMS: οἶδα

The original principal parts for this verb would be —, ἐιδήσω, —, οἶδα, —, —. But since this verb lost its perfect meaning using the perfect forms for present and aorist meanings, its first and third principal parts are exceptional. The old reduplication in verbs like διδάσκω and τιθήμι are examples of this trend (perfect stems becoming present and migrating to the first principal part). Forms in blue do not occur within the New Testament.

Principal Parts for οἶδα

1	2	3	4	5	6
οἶδα[1]	εἰδήσω	ᾔδειν[2]	–	–	–

1 Perfect forms having primary endings used for present tense.
2 Pluperfect forms having secondary endings used for aorist tense.

Forms Derived from its 1st Principal Part / Forms Derived from its 2nd Principal Part / Forms Derived from its 3rd Principal Part

	Perfect Indicative	Perfect Imperative	Perfect Subjunctive	Future Indicative	Pluperfect Indicative
	Active	Active	Active	Active	Active
1 sg.	οἶδα		εἰδῶ	εἰδήσω	ᾔδειν[3]
2 sg.	οἶδας	ἴσθι	εἰδῇς	εἰδήσεις	ᾔδεις
3 sg.	οἶδε(ν)	ἴστω	εἰδῇ	εἰδήσει	ᾔδει
1 pl.	οἴδαμεν		εἰδῶμεν	εἰδήσομεν	ᾔδειμεν
2 pl.	οἴδατε	ἴστε	εἰδῆτε	εἰδήσετε	ᾔδειτε
3 pl.	οἴδασι(ν)	ἴστωσαν	εἰδῶσι(ν)	εἰδήσουσι(ν)	ᾔδεισαν

Perfect Infinitive		Perfect Participle		
		Active (singular)		
Active		Masc.	Fem.	Neut.
εἰδέναι	Nom.	εἰδώς	εἰδυῖα	εἰδός
	Acc.	εἰδόντα	εἰδυῖαν	εἰδός

3 The pluperfect uses an augment and secondary endings on the perfect stem (without the o-grade root vowel for this verb).

APPENDIX 6

English-Greek Glossary

The numbers refer to the vocabulary lists where the Greek word was presented.

I abide, μένω 1
I am able, δύναμαι 11
I am about to, μέλλω 21
above, ὑπέρ + acc. 21
according to, κατά + acc. 20
Acheldama, Ἀχελδαμάχ 26
I am afraid, φοβέομαι 19
after, μετά + acc. 9; ὀπίσω (adv. or + gen.) 15
age, αἰών 16
all, πᾶς 18
all things, πάντα 15
I allow, ἐάω 22; ἀφίημι 30
always, πάντοτε 30
Ananias, Ἀνανίας 19
and, καί 3; δέ 6
Andrew, Ἀνδρέας 19
angel, ἄγγελος 3
Annas, Ἄννας 20
I announce, ἀπαγγέλλω 15
another, ἕτερος 7
I answer, ἀποκρίνομαι 10
answer, ἀπόκρισις 20
I am anxious, μεριμνάω 25
I am anxious beforehand, προμεριμνάω 27
Apostle, ἀπόστολος 3, 9
I appoint, καθίστημι 29
I approach, παραγίνομαι 19
I argue, συζητέω 26
I arise, ἀνίσταμαι 29
as, καθώς 23
as much as, ὅσος 20
I ask, αἰτέω 2
I ask a question, ἐρωτάω 22; ἐπερωτάω 31
assembly, ἐκκλησία 5
I am astonished, ἐκπλήσσομαι 20; θαμβέομαι 26
I ate, ἔφαγον 14
bad, κακός 7
baptism, βάπτισμα 17
baptist, βαπτιστής 6
I baptize, βαπτίζω 8
I bear, φέρω 8
I bear witness, μαρτυρέω 2
beautiful, καλός 11
I become, γίνομαι 21
bed, κλίνη 15
before (preposition), πρό + gen. 6; ἐνώπιον + gen. 28; ἔμπροσθεν 29; πρίν + gen. 26
I beg, δέομαι 11
I begin, ἄρχομαι 11
beginning, ἀρχή 5
on behalf of, ὑπέρ + gen. 21
I behold, θεωρέω 2
behold! ἰδού 21
I believe, πιστεύω 1
beloved, ἀγαπητός 7
I benefit, εὖ ποιέω 24
beside, παρά 15

daughter, θυγάτηρ 17
David, Δαυίδ, or Δαβίδ 18
day, ἡμέρα 5
dead, νεκρός 18
deaf, κωφός 17
death, θάνατος 3
a debt, ὀφείλημα 30
debtor, ὀφειλέτης 30
I defile, κοινόω 23
I delay, μέλλω 21
demon, δαιμόνιον 4
I deny, ἀρνέομαι 10
I depart, ὑπάγω 8; ἀπέρχομαι 10; ἀναχωρέω 20
departure, ἔξοδος 22
desert, ἔρημος 3
I desire, ἐπιθυμέω 20
I destroy, φθείρω 15; ἀπολλύω 24; καταλύω 25
destruction, ἀπώλεια 31
devil, δαιμόνιον 4; διάβολος 11
I die, ἀποθνῄσκω 1
different, ἕτερος 7
disciple, μαθητής 6
I discuss, συζητέω 26; διαλογίζομαι 31
I disperse, διασπείρω 19
I disregard, ἀθετέω 24
I divide, μερίζω 29
division, σχίσμα 21
I do, ποιέω 2; πράσσω 13
dog, κύων 17
door, θύρα 16
down, κατά, + gen. 20
I drag, σύρω 26; ἑλκύω 29
I draw away, ἀποσπάω 28
I draw near, ἐγγίζω 13
I drink, πίνω 14
I drive, ἄγω 8
I drive away, ἀπάγω 13
I drive together, συνάγω 8
dry, ξηρός 29
I dwell in, κατοικέω 12; μένω 1
ear, οὖς 17
earth, γῆ 5
I eat, ἐσθίω 1
I eat with, συνεσθίω 26
Egypt, Αἴγυπτος 15
elder, πρεσβύτερος 9
Elijah, Ἠλίας 19
I endure, προσκαρτερέω 20; φέρω 8
enemy, ἐχθρός 12
I enter, εἰσέρχομαι 19
I err, πλανάομαι 30
I escape, ἐκφεύγω 26
I establish, καθίστημι 29
eternal, αἰώνιος 7
even as, καθώς 23
every, πᾶς 18
everywhere, πανταχοῦ 29
the Evil One, ὁ πονηρός 7
I exalt, ὑψόω 22
I exhort, παρακαλέω 2
eye, ὀφθαλμός 9
face, πρόσωπον 4
faith, πίστις 18
faithful, πιστός 7
I fall, πίπτω 14
false, ψευδής 29
I fast, νηστεύω 31
father, πατήρ 17
fault, παράπτωμα 30
favor, χάρις 16

field, ἀγρός 10; χωρίον 27
I fill, πληρόω 22
I find, εὑρίσκω 1
fire, πῦρ 17
first, πρῶτος 7
fish, ἰχθύς 17
fitting, πρέπον 30
five thousand, πεντακισχίλιοι 19
I flee, φεύγω 14
flesh, σάρξ 16
I follow, ἀκολουθέω 30
food, τροφή 21
foolish, ἄφρων 18
foot, ποῦς 17
for (conj.), γάρ 6
for (prep.), πρό + gen. 6
I forgive, ἀφίημι 30
forgiveness, ἄφεσις 17
forty, τεσσαράκοντα 19
free, ἐλεύθερος 11
from, ἀπό + gen. 6
fruit, καρπός 9
I fulfill, πληρόω 22
Galilee, Γαλιλαία 19
garment, ἱμάτιον 4; χιτών 16
I gather together, ἐπισυνάγω 31
generation, γένος 17
gentiles, τὰ ἔθνη 18
I give, δίδωμι 27
I give back, ἀποδίδωμι 27
I give up, παραδίδωμι 27
I glorify, δοξάζω 8
glory, δόξα 6
I go, ἔρχομαι, πορεύομαι 10; βαίνω 14
I go about, διέρχομαι 10
I go away, ἀπέρχομαι 10
I go into, εἰσέρχομαι 19; εἰσπορεύομαι 28
I go out, ἐξέρχομαι 19; ἐκπορεύομαι 26
I go through, διέρχομαι 10
I go toward, προσέρχομαι 20
God, θεός 3
gold, χρυσός 26
good, ἀγαθός 7; καλός 11
gospel, εὐαγγέλιον 4
gospel, I preach the, εὐαγγελίζομαι 10
governor, ἡγεμών 16
grace, χάρις 16
great, μέγας 18
a Greek, Ἕλλην 23
I guard, φυλάσσω 13
guard, φύλαξ 16
I had, ἔσχον 14
hair, θρίξ 17
hand, χείρ 17
hated, ἐχθρός 12
I have, ἔχω 1
I have mercy on, ἐλεέω 12
he, she, it, αὐτός, αὐτή, αὐτό 8
head, κεφαλή 5
I heal, θεραπεύω 11; ἰάομαι 22
healthy, ὑγιής 18
I hear, ἀκούω 1
heart, καρδία 5
heaven, οὐρανός 9
heavenly, οὐράνιος 30
I give heed to, προσέχω 26
I held, ἔσχον 14
here, ὧδε 11; ἐνθάδε 25
Herod, Ἡρῴδης 15
I hide, κρύπτω 13

high priest, ἀρχιερεύς 18
hill, ὄρος 18
himself, etc., αὐτός 8
I hold, κρατέω 20
holy, ἅγιος 7
honor, τιμή 28
I hope, ἐλπίζω 13
hope, ἐλπίς 16
hour, ὥρα 5
house, οἶκος 3; οἰκία 11
householder, head of the house, οἰκοδεσπότης 9
how, πῶς 19
I humble, ταπεινόω 22
husband, ἀνήρ 17
hypocrite, ὑποκριτής 9
I, ἐγώ 11
if, εἰ 18
image, εἰκών 16
immediately, εὐθύς 9; εὐθέως 30
I implore, δέομαι 11
impossible, ἀδύνατος 15
in, ἐν + dat. 4
inhabit, κατοικέω 12
I injure, ἀδικέω 12
injustice, ἀδικία 10
I inquire, πυνθάνομαι 22
into, εἰς + acc. 4
I invoke, ἐπικαλέομαι 21
Israel, Ἰσραήλ 10
James, Ἰάκωβος 26
Jerusalem, Ἱεροσόλυμα, Ἰερουσαλήμ 9
Jesus, Ἰησοῦς 8
Jew, Ἰουδαῖος 8
John, Ἰωάννης 8
Joppa, Ἰόππη 20
Jordan, Ἰορδάνης 11
Joseph, Ἰωσήφ 15
I journey, πορεύομαι 10
joy, χαρά 5
I judge, κρίνω 1
judge, κριτής 9
judgment, κρίμα 18; κρίσις 18
just, δίκαιος 7
I justify, δικαιόω 22
I keep safe, τηρέω 2
I kill, ἀποκτείνω 8
I kindle, καίω 28
king, βασιλεύς 17
kingdom, βασιλεία 5
knee, γόνυ 17
I know, γινώσκω 14; ἐπιγινώσκω 23; οἶδα 30
known, γνωστός 26
I labor, κοπιάζω 20
laborer, ἐργάτης 9
lake, θάλασσα 6
lamb, ἀμνός 14
lamp, λαμπάς 16; λύχνος 29
land, γῆ 5
language, γλῶσσα 6
last, ἔσχατος 7; ὕστερος 29
law, νόμος 3
it is lawful, ἔξεστι 11
lawlessness, ἀνομία 26
I lay down, τίθημι 28
I lay hold of, καταλαμβάνω 21; ἐπιλαμβάνω 29
I lay upon, ἐπιβάλλω 21
Lazarus, Λάζαρος 23
I lead, ἄγω 8
I lead in, εἰσάγω 23

leader, ἡγεμών 16
I learn, μανθάνω 14
learner, μαθητής 6
I leave, καταλείπω 14
leper, λεπρός 13
I let alone, ἀφίημι 30
I let go, ἀφίημι 30
letter, γράμμα 17; ἐπιστολή 17
light, φῶς 17
life, ζωή 5
like, ὅμοιος 26
I make like, ὁμοιόω 29
little, μικρός 21
I live, ζάω 22
loaves, ἄρτοι 3
I look at, βλέπω 1
I release, λύω 1
lord, κύριος 3
I love, φιλέω 2; ἀγαπάω 22
love, ἀγαπή 5
Lydda, Λύδδα 20
Magdalene, Μαγδαληνή 23
maiden, παρθένος 3
I make, ποιέω 2
I make manifest, φανερόω 22
I make ready, ἑτοιμάζω 13
man, ἄνθρωπος 3; ἀνήρ 17
young man, νεανίας 6
I manifest, φαίνω 15; φανερόω 22
many, πολύς 18
many things, πολλά 14
marketplace, ἀγορά 28
Mary, Μαριάμ, Μαρία 15
master, δεσπότης 6; ἐπιστάτης 20
meat, τροφή 21
mercy, I have, ἐλεέω 12
messenger, ἄγγελος 3
middle, μέσος 29
minister, διάκονος 12
miracle, σημεῖον 4; τέρας 17
money, ἀργύριον 4; τὰ χρήματα 19
month, μήν 16
more, μᾶλλον 18
Moses, Μωϋσῆς 19
mother, μήτηρ 17
mountain, ὄρος 18
mouth, στόμα 18
much, πολύς 18
I multiply, πληθύνω 26
multitude, ὄχλος 9
I must, *see* necessary
mute, κωφός 17
mystery, μυστήριον 27
name, ὄνομα 18
I name, ἐπικαλέω 21
narrow, στενός 20
nation, γένος 17
near, ἐγγύς 20
necessary, it is, δεῖ 11
neighbor, ὁ πλησίον 26
net, δίκτυον 20
new, νέος 21; καινός 28
night, νύξ 16
no more, μηκέτι 18
no one, μηδείς, οὐδείς 18
not, οὐ 6; μή 10
nourishment, τροφή 21
now, νῦν 21
O, ὦ 14
I obey, ὑπακούω 11

I observe (adhere to), τηρέω 2
I offend, σκανδαλίζω 13
old, παλαιός 21
on, ἐπί + dat. 20
on account of, διά + acc. 9
on (resting), ἐπί + dat. 20
on (placed), ἐπί + acc. 20
one, εἷς, μία, ἕν 18
one another, ἀλλήλους 31
one's own, ἴδιος 7
I open, ἀνοίγω 12
other, ἕτερος 7
I ought, ὀφείλω 15
out of, ἐκ, ἐξ + gen. 6
outside, ἔξω 26
I owe, ὀφείλω 15
parable, παραβολή 5
paralytic, παραλυτικός 15; παραλελυμένος 28
parents, οἱ γονεῖς 18
I pass by, παράγω 19
patience, ὑπομονή 31
Paul, Παῦλος 11
pay, wages, μισθός 25
peace, εἰρήνη 5
people, λαός 3
I perceive, καταλαμβάνομαι 21
I permit, ἐάω 22
I persuade, πείθω 8
Peter, Πέτρος 16
Pharisee, Φαρισαῖος 15
Philip, Φίλιππος 26
I place, τίθημι 28
I place beside, παρατίθημι 28
place, τόπος 9
poor, πτωχός 11
possible, δυνατός 15
power, ἐξουσία 5; δύναμις 20
I praise, εὐλογέω 12
I pray, προσεύχομαι 21
I preach, κηρύσσω 8
I preach the gospel, εὐαγγελίζομαι 10
I present, παρίστημι 29
I am present, παραγίνομαι 19
priest, ἱερεύς 18
prison, φυλακή 27
prisoner, δέσμιος 26
I proclaim, κηρύσσω 8
promise, ἐπαγγελία 5
proof, τεκμήριον 29
I prophesy, προφητεύω 12
prophet, προφήτης 6
publican, tax collector, τελώνης 9
I pursue, διώκω 12
I put on, ἐνδύω 12
I put upon, ἐπιβάλλω 21
quickly, ταχέως 13
race, γένος 17; ἔθνος 18
I raise, ἐγέρω 1; ἀνίστημι 29; ἐπαίρω 29
I read, ἀναγινώσκω 8
I make ready, ἑτοιμάζω 13
reason, λόγος 3
I receive, λαμβάνω 1; δέχομαι 10
I rejoice, χαίρω 8; ἀγαλλιάω 22
I release, ἀπολύω 8
I remain, μένω 1; προσκαρτερέω 20
remission, ἄφεσις 17
I remove, ἀφίστημι 29
rent, rip, division, σχίσμα 21
I repent, μετανοέω 29
repentance, μετάνοια 17

the rest, οἱ λοιποί 21
resurrection, ἀνάστασις 18
I reveal, ἀποκαλύπτω 13
reward, μισθός 25
on the right hand, δεξιός 28
righteous, δίκαιος 7
righteousness, δικαιοσύνη 5
I rise, ἀνίσταμαι 29
river, ποταμός 13
robber, λῃστής 9
I roar, βοάω 22
rock, πέτρα 20
rooster ἀλέκτωρ 16
I rouse, ἐγείρω 1
I rule, ἄρχω 12
ruler, ἄρχων 16
Sabbath, σάββατον 4
sacrifice, θυσία 26
I keep safe, τηρέω 2
I said, εἶπον 14
saint, ἅγιος 7, see Lesson 10
I salt, ἁλίζω 25
salt, ἅλας 25
Samaria, Σαμάρεια 11
I sanctify, ἁγιάζω 13
Satan, Σατανᾶς 19
I save, σῴζω 1
savior, σωτήρ 16
I saw, εἶδον 14
I say, λέγω 1
saying, ῥῆμα 18
I scatter abroad, διασπείρω 19
scribe, γραμματεύς 17
scriptures, γραφαί 5
sea, θάλασσα 6
season, καιρός 15
I see, βλέπω 1; ὁράω 22
seed, σπέρμα 18
I seek, ζητέω 2
I sell, ἀποδίδομαι 27
I send, ἀποστέλλω 1; πέμπω 8
sentence, κρίμα 18
I separate, ἀφίστημι 29
servant, δοῦλος 3; διάκονος 12
I serve, διακονέω 12
I set aside, ἀθετέω 24
I set before, παρατίθημι 28
I set in order, τάσσω 13
I set up, καθίστημι 29
seven, ἑπτά 23
sheep, πρόβατον 4
shepherd, ποιμήν 16
ship, πλοῖον 4
I shout, βοάω 22; κράζω 8
I show, φαίνω 15; δείκνυμι 30
shrine, ναός 21
sick, ἀσθενής 18
I am sick, ἀσθενέω 28
sign, σημεῖον 4
I am silent, σιωπάω 25
silver, ἀργύριον 4; ἄργυρος 26
Simon, Σίμων 19
I sin, ἁμαρτάνω 14
sin, ἁμαρτία 5
sinner, ἁμαρτωλός 10
slave, δοῦλος 3
I sleep, κοιμάω 23
soldier, στρατιώτης 15
Solomon, Σολομῶν 21
son, υἱός 8

soon, ταχέως 13
soul, ψυχή 5
sound, φωνή 5
I sow, σπείρω 15
I speak, λαλέω 2
I speak with, συλλαλέω 19
spirit, πνεῦμα 17
I spoke, εἶπον 14
I cause to stand, ἵστημι 29
I cause to stand away, ἀφίστημι 29
I stand away, ἀφίστημι 29
I cause to stand up, ἀνίστημι 29
I stand up, ἀνίσταμαι 29
star, ἀστήρ 16
I steal, κλέπτω 23
I stone, λιθάζω; καταλιθάζω 26
stone, λίθος 9
strong, ἰσχυρός 21
stumble, I cause to, σκανδαλίζω 13
I suffer, πάσχω 14
I suffered, ἔπαθον 14
I summon, προσκαλέω 31
I surpass, περισσεύω 25
surpassing, περισσός 26
sword, μάχαιρα 15
synagogue, συναγωγή 5
I take, λαμβάνω 1
I take counsel with, συμβουλεύομαι 21
I take hold of, κρατέω 20
I take up, or away, αἴρω 15
I take with, παραλαμβάνω 20
I tarry, μέλλω 21
I taste, γεύομαι 25
tax-gatherer, τελώνης 9
I teach, διδάσκω 8
teacher, διδάσκαλος 9
teaching, διδαχή 20
I tear, σπαράσσω 19
temple, ἱερόν 4
I tempt, πειράζω 11
temptation, πειρασμός 23
than, ἤ 18
I thank, εὐχαριστέω 30
that, ἐκεῖνος 8
then, τότε 30
there, ἐκεῖ 11
therefore, οὖν 6
I think, νομίζω 25; φρονέω 31
this, οὗτος 8
three, τρεῖς 16; τρία 21
thrice, three times τρίς 26
throne, θρόνος 9
through, διά + gen. 9
I throw, βάλλω 1; ῥίπτω 21
I throw around (of a net), ἀμφιβάλλω 19
time, χρόνος 9; καιρός 15
to (motion to), εἰς + acc. 6; πρός + acc. 9
I toil, κοπιάζω 20
I told, εἶπον 14
tomb, μνημεῖον 20
tomorrow, ἡ αὔριον 25
tongue, γλῶσσα 6
tooth, ὀδούς 16
I touch, ἅπτομαι 10
toward, πρός + acc. 9
tradition, παράδοσις 24
trample on, πατέω 31
transgression, παράπτωμα 30
I travel, ὁδοιπορέω 21
tree, δένδρον 4

tribe, φυλή 15
true, ἀληθής 18
truly, ἀληθῶς 21
trumpet, σάλπιγξ 16
truth, ἀλήθεια 5
I try, πειράζω 11
two, δύο 20
unclean, ἀκάθαρτος 19
I understand, συνίημι 30
until, ἕως 15
I urge, κελεύω 11
village, κώμη 15
vineyard, ἀμπελών 16
virgin, παρθένος 3
vision, ὅραμα 25
voice, φωνή 5
I walk about, περιπατέω 8
I wash away, ἀπολούω 21
watch, φυλακή 27
water, ὕδωρ 17
way, ὁδός 3
we, ἡμεῖς 11
weak, ἀσθενής 18
I am weak, ἀσθενέω 28
wedding, γάμος 11
well, εὖ 24
I went, ἦλθον 14
what kind? ποῖος 27
when, ὅτε 15
where? ποῦ 22
while, ἕως 15
who, which, ὅς, ἥ, ὅ, 10; ὅστις 20
who? what? τίς, τί 20
whole (sound), ὑγιής 18
whole (complete), ὅλος 20
wicked, πονηρός 7
wickedness, ἀδικία 10; ἀνομία 26
widow, χήρα 15
wife, γυνή 17
wilderness, ἔρημος 3
will, θέλημα 17
I am willing, θέλω 11
wind, πνεῦμα 17
wine, οἶνος 14
wisdom, σοφία 5
wise, σοφός 12
I wish, βούλομαι, θέλω 11
with (together with), σύν + dat. 6; μετά + gen. 9
withered, ξηρός 29
witness, μάρτυς 29
I bear witness, μαρτυρέω 2
woman, γυνή 17
I wonder at, θαυμάζω 13; θαμβέομαι 26
wonder, τέρας 17
word, λόγος 3; ῥῆμα 18
I work, ἐργάζομαι 10
work, ἔργον 4
workman, ἐργάτης 9
world, κόσμος 3; οἰκουμένη 29
I worship, προσκυνέω 22
I write, γράφω 1
writing, γραφή 5
year, ἔτος 17
you, σύ 11
you all (you pl.), ὑμεῖς 11
young, νέος 21
young child, παιδίον 4
young man, νεανίας 6
Zacharias, Ζαχαρίας 20

APPENDIX 7

Greek-English Glossary

This glossary is designed to be a quick reference for someone who knows the basic elements of Greek. Nouns are presented in the typical lexical order of nominative case, genitive case (often abbreviated to genitive ending), and the definite article. Adjectives are presented with the singular nominative forms for all three genders. Adverbs only have one form. All six principal parts are provided for verbs. Words in parentheses are alternate forms; principal parts in blue occur outside of the New Testament; and a dash represents parts that do not occur anywhere. It is helpful to see forms used outside of the New Testament to get a feel for how various verb roots consistently interact with tense stems. Simple English glosses are provided rather than full definitions. The part of speech should be clear by the types of Greek forms provided.

ἀγαθός, -ή, -όν	good
ἀγαλλιάω, ἀγαλλιάσομαι,[1] ἠγαλλίασα, —, —, ἠγαλλιάθην	rejoice greatly
ἀγαπάω, ἀγαπήσω, ἠγάπησα, ἠγάπηκα, ἠγάπημαι, ἠγαπήθην	love
ἀγάπη, -ης, ἡ	love
ἀγαπητός, -ή, -όν	beloved
ἄγγελος, -ου, ὁ	angel, messenger
ἀγγέλλω, ἀγγελῶ, ἤγγειλα, ἤγγελκα, ἤγγελμαι, ἠγγέλθην	announce + dat. to someone (ἀπαγγέλλω more common)
ἁγιάζω, —, ἡγίασα, ἡγίακα, ἡγίασμαι, ἡγιάσθην	consecrate, sanctify; revere
ἅγιος, -α, -ον	holy
ἀγορά, -ᾶς, ἡ	marketplace

1 The contract α for this verb doesn't lengthen before consonant stems.

ἀγοράζω, ἀγοράσω, ἠγόρασα, ἠγόρακα, ἠγόρασμαι, ἠγοράσθην	buy
ἀγρός, -οῦ, ὁ	field
ἄγω, ἄξω, ἤγαγον, ἀγήοχα, ἦγμαι, ἤχθην	drive, lead, bring
ἀδελφός, -οῦ, ὁ	brother
ἀδικέω, ἀδικήσω, ἠδίκησα, ἠδίκηκα, ἠδίκημαι, ἠδικήθην	injure; do wrong
ἀδικία, -ας, ἡ	injustice, wickedness
ἀδύνατος, -η, -ον	impossible
ἀθετέω, ἀθετήσω, ἠθέτησα, ἠθέτηκα, —, —	set aside, disregard
Αἴγυπτος, -ου, ἡ	Egypt
αἷμα, αἵματος, τό	blood
αἱρέω, αἱρήσομαι, εἷλον (εἷλαν), ᾕρηκα, ᾕρημαι, ᾑρέθην	take; mid. (NT only) choose
αἴρω, ἀρῶ, ἦρα, ἦρκα, ἦρμαι, ἤρθην	take away; take up
αἰτέω, αἰτήσω, ᾔτησα, ᾔτηκα, ᾔτημαι, —	ask
αἰών, αἰῶνος, ὁ	age
αἰώνιος, -ον	eternal
ἀκάθαρτος, -ον	unclean
ἀκολουθέω, ἀκολουθήσω, ἠκολούθησα, ἠκολούθηκα, —, —	follow
ἀκούω, ἀκούσομαι, ἤκουσα, ἀκήκοα, ἤκουσμαι, ἠκούσθην	hear
ἅλας, ἅλατος, τό	salt
ἀλέκτωρ, ἀλέκτορος, ὁ	rooster
ἀλήθεια, -ας, ἡ	truth
ἀληθής, ἀληθές	true
ἀληθῶς	truly
ἁλίζω, ἁλισθήσομαι, ἡλίσθην, —, ἥλισμαι, ἡλίσθην	salt
ἀλλά	but
ἀλλαχοῦ	elsewhere
ἀλλήλων (gen. pl.)	one another (nom. not used)
ἁμαρτάνω, ἁμαρτήσω, ἥμαρτον (ἡμάρτησα), ἡμάρτηκα, ἡμάρτημαι, ἡμαρτήθην	sin

ἁμαρτία, -ας, ἡ	sin
ἁμαρτωλός, -οῦ, ὁ	sinner
ἀμνός, -οῦ, ὁ	lamb
ἀμπελών, ἀμπελῶνος, ὁ	vineyard
ἀμφιβάλλω, ἀμφιβαλλῶ, —, —, —, —	throw around, throw on this side and that, especially used of a net
ἀνά	+ acc. up
ἀναγινώσκω, ἀναγνώσομαι, ἀνέγνων, ἀνέγνωκα, ἀνέγνωσμαι, ἀνεγνώσθην	read
Ἁνανίας, -ου, ὁ	Ananias
ἀνάστσις, ἀναστάσεως, ἡ	resurrection
ἀναχωρέω, —, ἀνεχώρησα, ἀνακεχώρηκα, —, —	depart
Ἀνδρέας, -ου, ὁ	Andrew
ἀνήρ, ἀνδρός, ὁ	man; husband
ἄνθρωπος, -ου, ὁ	man
ἀνίστημι, ἀναστήσω, ἀνέστην[1] (ἀνέστησα[2]), ἀνέστακα, —, ἀνεστάθην	cause to stand, raise up; mid. and pass. stand up, rise, arise
Ἄννας (gen. Ἄννα), ὁ	Annas
ἀνοίγω, ἀνοίξω, ἤνοιξα[3] (ἀνέῳξα), ἀνέῳγα, ἠνέῳγμαι (ἀνέῳγμαι), ἠνεῴχθην (ἀνεῴχθην)	open
ἀνομία, -ας, ἡ	lawlessness, wickedness
ἀντί	+ gen. over against; instead of; in return for
ἀπαγγέλλω, ἀπαγγελῶ, ἀπήγγειλα, ἀπήγγελκα, ἀπήγγελμαι, ἀπηγγέλην	report; announce + dat. to someone
ἀπάγω, ἀπάξω, ἀπήγαγον, —, ἀπῆγμαι, ἀπήχθην	drive away
ἀπαρνέομαι, ἀπαρνήσομαι, ἀπηρνησάμην, —, ἀπήρνημαι, ἀπηρνήθην	deny
ἀπέρχομαι, ἀπελεύσομαι, ἀπῆλθον, ἀπελήλυθα, —, —	go away, depart

1 Intransitive form, "stand up," "raise up"

2 Transitive form, "cause to stand up," "cause to raise up"

3 The prepositional prefix typically receives the augment and reduplication.

ἀπό	+ gen. from (from exterior)
ἀποδίδωμι, ἀποδώσω, ἀπέδωκα, —, ἀποδέδομαι, ἀπεδόθην	give back; mid. hand over for one's own sake (hence: sell)
ἀποθνῄσκω, ἀποθανοῦμαι, ἀπέθανον, ἀποτέθνηκα, —, —	die
ἀποκαλύπτω, ἀποκαλύψω, ἀπεκάλυψα, —, ἀποκεκάλυμμαι, ἀπεκαλύφθην	reveal
ἀποκρίνομαι, ἀποκρινοῦμαι, ἀπεκρινάμην, —, ἀποκέκριμαι, ἀπεκρίθην	answer + dat.
ἀπόκρισις, -εως, ἡ	answer
ἀποκτείνω (ἀποκτέννω), ἀποκτενῶ, ἀπέκτεινα, ἀπέκτονα, ἀπέκταμμαι, ἀπεκτάνθην	kill
ἀπόλλυμι, ἀπολέσω (ἀπολῶ), ἀπώλεσα (mid. ἀπωλόμην), ἀπόλωλα (ἀπολώλεκα), —, —	destroy
ἀπολούομαι, ἀπολούσομαι, ἀπελουσάμην, —, —, —	wash away from myself
ἀπολύω, ἀπολύσω, ἀπέλυσα, ἀπολέλυκα, ἀπολέλυμαι, ἀπελύθην	release
ἀποστέλλω, ἀποστελῶ, ἀπέστειλα, ἀπέσταλκα, ἀπέσταλμαι, ἀπεστάλην	send out
ἀπόστολος, -ου, ὁ	apostle
ἀποσπάω, ἀποσπάσω, ἀπέσπασα, —, —, ἀπεσπάσθην	draw out; pass. withdraw
ἅπτω, ἅψομαι, ἧψα (ἡψάμην), ἧμμαι, ἥφθην	kindle; mid. touch + gen.
ἀπώλεια, -ας, ἡ	destruction
ἀργύριον, -ου, τό	silver; money
ἄργυρος, -ου, ὁ	silver
ἀρέσκω, ἀρέσω, ἤρεσα, ἀρήρεκα, —, ἠρέσθην	please
ἀρνέομαι, ἀρνήσομαι, ἠρνησάμην, —, ἤρνημαι, ἀρνηθῆναι	deny
ἄρτος, -ου, ὁ	bread; pl. "loaves"
ἀρχή, -ῆς, ἡ	beginning
ἀρχιερεύς, ἀρχιερέως, ὁ	high priest

ἄρχω, ἄρξω, ἦρξα, ἦρχα, ἦργμαι, ἤρχθην	rule over + gen.; mid. begin
ἄρχων, ἄρχοντος, ὁ	ruler
ἀσθενέω, ἀσθενήσω, ἠσθένησα, ἠσθένηκα, —, —	be weak or sick
ἀσθενής, -ές	weak; sick
ἀστήρ, ἀστέρος, ὁ	star
αὐξάνω, αὐξήσω, ηὔξησα, ηὔξηκα, αὐξάνομαι, ηὐξήθην	increase
αὔριον	on the next day (ἡ[1] αὔριον means tomorrow)
αὐτός, -ή, -ό	he, she, it; himself, herself, itself; the same
ἄφεσις, ἀφέσεως, ἡ	remission, forgiveness
ἀφίημι, ἀφήσω, ἄφηκα, ἀφεῖκα, ἀφεῖμαι,[2] ἀφέθην	cancel, forgive (+ dat. person); tolerate, allow; leave behind; leave alone
ἀφίστημι, ἀποστήσω, ἀπέστην[3] (ἀπέστησα[4]), ἀφέστηκα, —, —	remove, separate; mid. and pass. stand away from
ἄφρων, ἄφρον	foolish
Ἀχελδαμάχ	Acheldama
βαίνω,[5] βήσομαι, ἔβην, βέβηκα, —, —	go
βάλλω, βαλῶ, ἔβαλον, βέβληκα, βέβλημαι, ἐβλήθην	throw; put
βαπτίζω, βαπτίσω, ἐβάπτισα, —, βεβάπτισμαι, ἐβαπτίσθην	baptize
βάπτισμα, βαπτίσματος, τό	baptism
βαπτιστής, -οῦ, ὁ	baptist
βασιλεία, -ας, ἡ	kingdom
βασιλεύς, βασιλέως, ὁ	king
βαστάζω, βαστάσω, ἐβάστασα, —, βεβάσταγμαι, ἐβαστάχθην	carry
βέλτιον	better (adv.)
Βηθλεέμ,[6] ἡ	Bethlehem
βιβλίον, -ου, τό	book

1 This article refers to ἡμέρα (implied).
2 ἀφέωνται (third person plural) is the only perfect passive form that occurs in the NT.
3 Intransitive form, "stand away from"
4 Transitive form, "remove," "separate"
5 This word is only used in compounds in the NT.
6 Indeclinable feminine noun

βλέπω, βλέψω, ἔβλεψα, βέβλεφα, βέβλεμμαι, ἐβλέφθην	see; look at
βοάω, βοήσω, ἐβόησα, βεβόηκα, βεβόημαι, ἐβώσθην	cry out, shout; roar
βολή, -ῆς, ἡ	toss, cast
βούλομαι, βουλήσομαι, —, —, βεβούλημαι, ἐβουλήθην	want; wish
Γαλιλαία, -ας, ἡ	Galilee
γάμος, -ου, ὁ	wedding
γάρ	for, because, since (postpositive)
γεννάω, γεννήσω, ἐγέννησα, γεγέννηκα, γεγέννημαι, ἐγεννήθην	be born
γένος, γένους, τό	race; nation; generation
γεύομαι, γεύσομαι, ἐγευσάμην, —, γέγευμαι, —	taste + gen.
γῆ, γῆς, ἡ	earth, land
γίνομαι (γίγνομαι), γενήσομαι, ἐγενόμην, γέγονα, γεγένημαι, ἐγενήθην	become (ἐγένετο "it came to pass, it happened" often + inf.)
γινώσκω (γιγνώσκω), γνώσομαι, ἔγνων, ἔγνωκα, ἔγνωσμαι, ἐγνώσθην	know
γλῶσσα, -ης, ἡ	tongue, language
γνωστός, -ή, -όν	known
γονεύς, γονέως, ὁ	progenitor, ancestor; pl. parents
γόνυ, γόνατος, τό	knee
γράμμα, γράμματος, τό	sg. letter of the alphabet; pl. document
γραμματεύς, γραμματέως, ὁ	scribe
γραφή, -ῆς, ἡ	writing; pl. the Scriptures
γράφω, γράψω, ἔγραψα, γέγραφα, γέγραμμαι, ἐγράφην	write
γυνή, γυναικός, ἡ	woman; wife
δαιμόνιον, -ου, τό	devil, demon
Δαυίδ[1] (Δαβίδ), ὁ	David
δέ[2]	but; and (postpositive)

1 Indeclinable masculine noun

2 Postpositive

δεῖ	it is necessary; right; fitting (impersonal verb from δέω)
δείκνυμι, δείξω, ἔδειξα, δέδειχα, δέδειγμαι, ἐδείχθην	show
δέομαι	implore, plead, request + gen. (no contraction with omicron stems)
δένδρον, -ου, τό	tree
δεξιός, -ά, -όν	right (side)
δέσμιος, -ου, ὁ	prisoner
δεσπότης, -ου, ὁ	master
δέχομαι, δέξομαι, ἐδεξάμην, —, δέδεγμαι, ἐδέχθην	receive
δέω, δήσω, ἔδησα, δέδεκα, δέδεμαι, ἐδέθην	bind; fasten
διά	+ acc. on account of, because of; + gen. through (place or time); by means of
διάβολος, -ου, ὁ	the devil
διακονέω, διακονήσω, διηκόνησα, δεδιακόνηκα, δεδιακόνημαι, διηκονήθην	serve + dat.
διάκονος, -ου, ὁ	servant, minister
διαλογίζομαι, διαλογιοῦμαι, διελογισάμην, διαλελόγισμαι, —, —	discuss
διαπορεύομαι, διαπορεύσομαι, —, —, —, διεπορεύθην	make my way through
διασπείρω, διασπερῶ, διέσπειρα, —, διέσπαρμαι, διεσπάρην	scatter abroad, disperse
διδάσκαλος, -ου, ὁ	teacher
διδάσκω, διδάξω, ἐδίδαξαν, δεδίδαχα, δεδίδαγμαι, ἐδιδάχθην	teach
διδαχή, -ῆς, ἡ	teaching
δίδωμι, δώσω, ἔδωκα, δέδωκα, δέδομαι, ἐδόθην	give
διέρχομαι, διελεύσομαι, διῆλθον, —, διελήλυθα, —	go through; go about
δίκαιος, -α, -ον	just, righteous
δικαιοσύνη, -ης, ἡ	righteousness

δικαιόω, δικαιώσω, ἐδικαίωσα, —, δεδικαίωμαι ἐδικαιώθην	justify
δίκτυον, -ου, τό	net
διώκω, διώξω, ἐδίωξα, δεδίωχα, δεδίωγμαι, ἐδιώχθην	pursue
δοκέω, —, ἔδοξα, —, —, —	seem
δόξα, -ης, ἡ	glory
δοξάζω, δοξάσω, ἐδόξασα, δεδόξακα, δεδόξασμαι, ἐδοξάσθην	glorify
δοῦλος, -ου, ὁ	slave, servant
δύναμαι (impf. ἐδυνάμην or ἠδυνάμην), δυνήσομαι, ἐδυνησάμην, —, δεδύνημαι, ἠδυνήθην	be able
δύναμις, -εως, ἡ	power
δυνατός, -ή, -όν	possible
δύο	two
ἐάω, ἐάσω, εἴασα,[1] εἴακα, εἴαμαι, εἰάθην	allow, permit
ἐγγίζω, ἐγγιῶ, ἤγγισα, ἤγγικα, —, —	draw near + dat.
ἔγγιστα	nearest (adv.)
ἐγγύς	near (adv.)
ἐγγύτερον	nearer (adv.)
ἐγείρω, ἐγερῶ, ἤγειρα, ἐγήγερκα, ἐγήγερμαι, ἠγέρθην	raise; rouse
ἐγώ	I
ἔθνος, ἔθνους, τό	race; pl. gentiles
εἰ	if
εἶδον (third principal part of ὁράω)	saw
εἰκών, εἰκόνος, ἡ	image
εἰμί (impf. ἦν), ἔσομαι, —, —, —, —	be
εἶπον (third principal part of λέγω)	said
εἰρήνη, -ης, ἡ	peace
εἰς	+ acc. into; to
εἷς, μία, ἕν	one

1 The augmented tenses begin with ει.

εἰσάγω, εἰσάξω, εἰσήγαγον, εἰσαγήοχα, εἰσῆγμαι, εἰσήχθην	lead in, bring in
εἰσέρχομαι, εἰσελεύσομαι, εἰσῆλθον, εἰσελήλυθα, —, —	go into, enter
εἰσπορεύομαι, εἰσπορεύσομαι, —, —, εἰσπεπόρευμαι, εἰσεπορεύθην	go to
εἰσφέρω, εἰσοίσω, εἰσήνεγκα (εἰσήνεγκον), —, εἰσενήνεγμαι, εἰσηνέχθην	carry to
ἐκ (ἐξ)	+ gen. from, out of (from the interior)
ἐκβάλλω, ἐκβαλῶ, ἐξέβαλον, ἐκβέβληκα, ἐκβέβλημαι, ἐξεβλήθην	cast out, expel
ἐκεῖ	there
ἐκεῖνος, -η, -ο	that
ἐκκλησία, -ας, ἡ	church, assembly
ἐκκόπτω, ἐκκόψω, ἐξέκοψα, —, ἐκκέκομμαι, ἐξεκόπην	cut off; cut out, remove
ἐκλέγομαι, ἐκλέξομαι, ἐξελεξάμην, —, ἐκλέλεγμαι, ἐξελέγην	choose
ἐκπλήσσομαι, —, —, —, ἐκπέπληγμαι, ἐξεπλάγην	be astonished
ἐκπορεύομαι, ἐκπορεύσομαι, —, —, ἐκπεπόρευμαι, —	go out
ἐκφεύγω, ἐκφεύξομαι, ἐξέφυγον, ἐκπέφευγα, —, —	escape
ἐλάττων, ἔλαττον	less
ἐλάχιστος, -η, -ον	least
ἐλεέω, ἐλεήσω, ἠλέησα, —, ἠλέημαι, ἠλεήθην	have mercy on
ἐλεύθερος, -α, -ον	free
ἑλκύω, ἕλκυσω, εἵλκυσα,[1] εἵλκυκα, εἵλκυσμαι, εἱλκύσθην	drag
Ἕλλην, Ἕλληνος, ὁ	Greek (person)

1 ει augment and reduplication

ἐλπίζω, ἐλπιῶ, ἤλπισα, ἤλπικα, ἤλπισμαι, ἠλπίσθην	hope
ἐλπίς, ἐλπίδος, ἡ	hope
ἔμπροσθεν	+ gen. before (location)
ἐν	+ dat. in; on
ἐνδύω, ἐνδύσω, ἐνέδυσα, ἐνδέδυκα, ἐνδέδυμαι, —	put on
ἐνθάδε	here
ἐντέλλω, ἐντελοῦμαι, ἐνετειλάμην, —, ἐντέταλμαι, ἐντάλθην	command
ἐντολή, -ῆς, ἡ	commandment
ἐνώπιον	+ gen. before (of place)
ἐξέρχομαι, ἐξελεύσομαι, ἐξῆλθον, ἐξελήλυθα, —, —	go out, exit
ἔξεστι[1]	it is lawful
ἔξοδος, -ου, ἡ	departure
ἐξουσία, -ας, ἡ	power
ἔξω	+ gen. outside
ἐπαγγελία, -ας, ἡ	promise
ἐπαίρω, ἐπαρῶ, ἐπῆρα (ἔπαρον), ἐπῆρκα, ἔπηρμαι, ἐπήρθην	raise up
ἐπέρχομαι, ἐπελεύσομαι, ἐπῆλθον, ἐπελήλυθα, —, —	come upon
ἐπερωτάω, ἐπερωτήσω, ἐπηρώτησα, —, —, ἐπηρωτήθην	ask
ἐπί	+ acc. on (placed on); up to, as far as; + gen. on; in the presence of; in the time of; + dat. on; at; in addition to
ἐπιβάλλω, ἐπιβαλῶ, ἐπέβαλον,[2] ἐπιβέβληκα, —, ἐπεβλήθη	cast upon, lay upon, put upon
ἐπιγινώσκω, ἐπιγνώσομαι, ἐπέγνων, ἐπέγνωκα, —, ἐπεγνώσθην	know
ἐπιθυμέω, ἐπιθυμήσω, ἐπεθύμησα, —, —, —	desire

1 Impersonal verb

2 Third person plural ἐπέβαλαν

ἐπικαλέω, ἐπικαλέσομαι, ἐπεκάλεσα, —, ἐπικέκλημαι, ἐπεκλήθην	put a name on; mid. call upon, invoke
ἐπιλαμβάνομαι, ἐπιλήψομαι, ἐπελαβόμην, —, ἐπείλημμαι, —	lay hold of, snatch; take over + gen.
ἐπιστάτης, -ου, ὁ	master
ἐπιστολή, -ῆς, ἡ	letter
ἐπισυνάγω, ἐπισυνάξω, ἐπισυνήγαγον (ἐπισυνῆξα), —, ἐπισυνῆγμαι, ἐπισυνήχθην	gather together to
ἑπτά	seven
ἐργάζομαι, ἐργῶμαι,[1] εἰργασάμην, —, εἴργασμαι, ἠργάσθην	work
ἐργάτης, -ου, ὁ	workman, laborer
ἔργον, -ου, τό	work
ἔρημος, -ου, ἡ	desert
ἔρχομαι, ἐλεύσομαι, ἦλθον (ἦλθα), ἐλήλυθα, —, —	come or go
ἐρωτάω, ἐρωτήσω, ἠρώτησα (ἠρόμην), ἠρώτηκα, ἠρώτημαι, ἠρωτήθην	ask a question
ἐσθίω, φάγομαι (ἔδομαι), ἔφαγον, ἐδήδοκα, ἐδήδεμαι, —	eat
ἔσχατος, -η, -ον	last
ἕτερος, -α, -ον	different, another
ἑτοιμάζω, ἑτοιμάσω, ἡτοίμασα, ἡτοίμακα, ἡτοίμασμαι, ἡτοιμάσθην	make ready, prepare
ἔτος, ἔτους, τό	year
εὖ	well (idiom: εὖ ποιεῖν means "to benefit")
εὐαγγελίζομαι, εὐαγγελιοῦμαι, εὐηγγελισάμην, —, εὐηγγέλισμαι, εὐηγγελίσθην	preach the gospel
εὐαγγέλιον, -ου, τό	gospel
εὐθέως	immediately
εὐθύς	immediately

1 α-contract in future forms

εὐλογέω, εὐλογήσω, εὐλόγησα, εὐλόγηκα, εὐλόγημαι, εὐλογήθην	bless; praise
εὑρίσκω,[1] εὑρήσω, εὗρον, εὕρηκα, εὑρέθην	find
εὐχαριστέω, —, ηὐχαρίστησα, —, —, ηὐχαριστήθην	thank
ἔφαγον (third principal part of ἐσθίω)	
ἐχθρός, -ά, -όν	hated (substantive meaning: enemy)
ἔχω (impf. εἶχον), ἕξω, ἔσχον, ἔσχηκα, —, —	have
ἕως	while, until
Ζαχαρίας, -ου, ὁ	Zacharias
ζάω, ζήσω, ἔζησα, ἔζωκα, —, —	live (pres. indic. ζῶ, ζῇς, ζῇ, inf. ζῆν)
ζητέω, ζητήσω, ἐζήτησα, ἐζήτηκα, —, ἐζητήθην	seek
ζωή, -ῆς, ἡ	life
ἤ	than; or
ἡγεμών, ἡγεμόνος, ὁ	leader, governor
Ἠλίας, -ου, ὁ	Elijah
ἦλθον (third principal part of ἔρχομαι)	
ἡμεῖς	we
ἡμέρα, -ας, ἡ	day
ἤνεγκον (third principal part of φέρω)	
Ἡρῴδης, -ου, ὁ	Herod
ἧσσον (ἧττον)	worse (adv.)
ἥσσων, ἧσσον (ἥττων, ἧττον)	worse (adj.)
θάλασσα, -ης, ἡ	sea; lake
θαμβέομαι, —, —, —, —, ἐθαμβήθην	wonder, be astonished
θάνατος, -ου, ὁ	death
θαρσέω, —, ἐθάρσησα, —, —, —	be brave, take courage
θαυμάζω, θαυμάσω, ἐθαύμασα, τεθαύμακα, τεθαύμασμαι, ἐθαυμάσθην	wonder at + acc.
θέλημα, θελήματος, τό	will, desire
θέλω (impf. ἤθελον), θελήσω, ἠθέλησα, τεθέληκα, —, ἐθελήθην	want, be willing

1 Imperfect may have a double augment, ηὕρισκον.

θεός, -ου, ὁ	God, or a god
θεραπεύω, θεραπεύσω, ἐθεράπευσα, —, τεθεράπευμαι, ἐθεραπεύθην	heal
θεωρέω, θεωρήσω, ἐθεώρησα, τεθεώρηκα, τεθεώρημαι, ἐθεωρήθην	see, behold
θρίξ, τριχός, ἡ	hair
θρόνος, -ου, ὁ	throne
θυγάτηρ, θυγατρός, ἡ	daughter
θύρα,-ας, ἡ	door
θυσία, -ας, ἡ	sacrifice
Ἰάκωβος, -ου, ὁ	James
ἰάομαι, ἰάσομαι, ἰασάμην, —, ἴαμαι, ἰάθην	mid. (dep.) heal; pass. be healed
ἴδιος, -α, -ον	one's own (κατ' ἰδίαν, common idiom meaning "privately")
ἰδού	behold, look here
ἱερεύς, ἱερέως, ὁ	priest
ἱερόν, -οῦ, τό	temple
Ἱεροσόλυμα,[1] -ων, τα	Jerusalem
Ἰερουσαλήμ, ἡ[2]	Jerusalem
Ἰησοῦς, -οῦ, ὁ	Jesus
ἱμάτιον, -ου, τό	garment
Ἰόππη, -ης, ἡ	Joppa
Ἰορδάνης, -ου, ὁ	Jordan
Ἰουδαῖος, -αία, -αῖον	Jewish (substantive meaning: Jewish person)
Ἰσραήλ,[3] ὁ	Israel
ἵστημι, στήσω, ἔστησα[4] (ἔστην[5]), ἕστηκα, ἕσταμαι, ἐστάθην	cause to stand; mid. and pass. stand
ἰσχυρός, -ά, -όν	strong
ἰχθύς, ἰχθύος, ὁ	fish
Ἰωάννης, -ου, ὁ	John

1 Neuter plural
2 Indeclinable feminine noun
3 Indeclinable masculine noun
4 Transitive form, "cause to stand," "place something"
5 Intransitive form, "stand"

Ἰωσήφ,[1] ὁ	Joseph
καθαρίζω, καθαριῶ, ἐκαθάρισα, —, κεκαθάρισμαι, ἐκαθαρίσθην	cleanse
καθίστημι, καταστήσω, κατέστησα, καθέστακα, καθέσταμαι, καθεστάθην	set up; establish; appoint
καθώς	even as
καί	and, also
Καιάφας, Καιάφα, ὁ	Caiaphas
καινός, -ή, -όν	new
καιρός, -οῦ, ὁ	time, season
Καῖσαρ, Καίσαρος, ὁ	Caesar
Καισαρεία, -ας, ἡ	Caesarea
καίω, καύσω, ἔκαυσα, —, κέκαυμαι, ἐκαύθην	burn, kindle
κακός, -ή, -όν	bad
καλέω, καλέσω, ἐκάλεσα, κέκληκα, κέκλημαι, ἐκλήθην	call
κάλλιστος, -η, -ον	most beautiful
κάλλιον	better; more beautifully (adv.)
καλλίων, κάλλιον	more beautiful
καλός, -ή, -όν	good, beautiful
καρδία, -ας, ἡ	heart
καρπός, -οῦ, ὁ	fruit
κατά	+ acc. down along, throughout; with regard to, according to; + gen. down from; against
κατακρίνω, κατακρινῶ, κατέκρινα, —, κατακέκριμαι, κατεκρίθην	condemn
καταλαμβάνω, καταλήψομαι, κατέλαβον, κατείληφα, κατειλημμαι, κατελήμφθην	grasp; take possession, take control; mid. perceive; comprehend
καταλείπω, καταλείψω,[2] κατέλιπον (κατέλειψα), καταλέλοιπα, καταλέλειμμαι, κατελείφθην	leave behind
καταλιθάζω, καταλιθάσω, —, —, —, —	stone to death

1 Indeclinable masculine noun

2 Exceptional present root for the future tense

καταλύω, καταλύσω, κατέλυσα, καταλέλυκα, καταλέλυμαι, κατελύθην	release (thoroughly), destroy
κατευλογέω, —, —, —, —, —	bless
κατοικέω, κατοικήσω, κατῴκησα, κατῴκηκα, —, κατῳκήθην	dwell in, inhabit + acc.
κελεύω, κελεύσω, ἐκέλευσα, κεκέλευκα, κεκέλευσμαι, ἐκελεύσθην	command, order; urge
κερδαίνω, κερδήσω (κερδανῶ), ἐκέρδησα (ἐκέρδανα), κεκέρδαγκα, κεκέρδημαι, ἐκερδήθην	gain, acquire
κεφαλή, -ῆς, ἡ	head
κηρύσσω, κηρύξω, ἐκήρυξα, κεκήρυχα, κεκήρυγμαι, ἐκηρύχθην	proclaim
κλάω, κλάσω, ἔκλασα, —, κέκλασμαι, ἐκλάσθην	break
κλέπτω, κλέψω, ἔκλεψα, κέκλοφα, κέκλεμμαι, ἐκλάπην (ἐκλέφθην)	steal
κλίνη, -ης, ἡ	bed; couch
κοιμάομαι, κοιμήσομαι, ἐκοιμήσαμην, —, κεκοίμημαι, ἐκοιμήθην	sleep
κοινόω, κοινώσω, ἐκοίνωσα, κεκοίνωκα, κεκοίνωμαι, ἐκοινώθην	make common, defile, desecrate
κοπιάω, κοπιάσω, ἐκοπίασα, κεκοπίακα, —, ἐκοπιάθην	toil; grow weary
Κορνήλιος, -ου, ὁ	Cornelius
κόσμος, -ου, ὁ	world
κράζω, κράξω, ἔκραξα, κέκραγα,[1] —, —	shout
κρατέω, κρατήσω, ἐκράτησα, κεκράτηκα, κεκράτημαι, ἐκρατήθην	seize; hold fast; attain
κράτιστος, -η, -ον	best
κρεῖσσον	better (adv.)
κρείσσων, κρεῖσσον	better (adj.)

1 Perf. was used with present sense with additional conjugated forms (e.g. fut. κεκράξομαι) in ancient Greek.

κρίνω, κρινῶ, ἔκρινα, κέκρικα, κέκριμαι, ἐκρίθην	judge
κρίμα, κρίματος, τό	judgment; sentence; condemnation
κρίσις, κρίσεως, ἡ	judgment
κριτής, -οῦ, ὁ	judge
κρύπτω, κρύψω, ἔκρυψα, κέκρυφα, κέκρυμμαι, ἐκρύβην (ἐκρύφθην)	hide
κύριος, -ου, ὁ	lord
κύων, κυνός, ὁ	dog
κώμη, -ης, ἡ	village
κωφός, -ή, -όν	deaf; mute; deaf and mute
Λάζαρος, -ου, ὁ	Lazarus
λαλέω, λαλήσω, ἐλάλησα, λελάληκα, λελάλημαι, ἐλαλήθην	say, speak
λαμβάνω, λήψομαι, ἔλαβον, εἴληφα,[1] εἴλημμαι, ἐλήφθην	take; receive
λαμπάς, λαμπάδος, ἡ	lamp
λαός, -οῦ, ὁ	people
λέγω, ἐρῶ (λέξω), εἶπον (ἔλεξα), εἴρηκα, εἴρημαι (λέλεγμαι), ἐρρέθην (ἐλέχθην)	say; speak; tell
λεπρός, -οῦ, ὁ	leper
λῃστής, -οῦ, ὁ	robber
λιθάζω, —, ἐλίθασα, —, —, ἐλιθάσθην	stone
λίθος, -ου, ὁ	stone
λόγος, -ου, ὁ	word, reason
λοιπός, -ή, -όν	the persons or things remaining (neut. pl. substantive "the rest")[2]
Λύδδα, -ας, ἡ	Lydda
λύχνος, -ου, ὁ	lamp
λύω, λύσω, ἔλυσα, λέλυκα, λέλυμαι, ἐλύθην	release
Μαγδαληνή, -ῆς, ἡ	Magdalene
μαθητής, -οῦ, ὁ	disciple

1 λαβ root takes a double augment instead of reduplication in the perfect.

2 κτλ. (καὶ τὰ λοιπά) is the Greek equivalent for etc. You will see this abbreviation in reference works.

μακάριος, -α, -ον	blessed
μάλιστα	most (adv.)
μᾶλλον	more (adv.)
μανθάνω, μαθήσομαι, ἔμαθον, μεμάθηκα, —, —	learn
Μαρία, -ας, ἡ	Mary
Μαριάμ,[1] ἡ	Mary
μαρτυρέω, μαρτυρήσω, ἐμαρτύρησα, μεμαρτύρηκα, μεμαρτύρημαι, ἐμαρτυρήθην	bear witness
μάρτυς, μάρτυρος, ὁ	witness
μάχαιρα, -ας, ἡ	sword
μέγας, μεγάλη, μέγα	great
μέγιστος, -η, -ον	greatest
μείζων, μεῖζον	greater
μέλλω, μελλήσω, ἐμέλλησα, —, —, —	am about to; delay, tarry
μέν	used to contrast a person, or thing, or a class of persons or things, with some person, thing, or class
μένω, μενῶ, ἔμεινα, μεμένηκα, —, —	remain; dwell; continue
μερίζω, μεριῶ, ἐμέρισα, μεμέρικα, μεμέρισμαι, ἐμερίσθην	divide; apportion
μεριμνάω, μεριμνήσω, ἐμερίμνησα, —, μεμερίμνημαι, —	be anxious for
μέσος, -η, -ον	middle
μετά	+ acc. after; + gen. together with, in company with
μετανοέω, μετανοήσω, μετενόησα, —, —, —	change my mind; repent
μετάνοια, ας, ἡ	repentance
μή	not
μηδείς, μηδεμία, μηδέν	no one[2]
μηκέτι	no more, no longer[3]

1 Indeclinable feminine noun
2 Used with nonindicative verbs
3 Used with nonindicative verbs

μήν, μηνός, ὁ	month
μήτηρ, μητρός, ἡ	mother
μικρός, -ά, -όν	little; small; short
μισθός, -οῦ, ὁ	reward, pay
μνημεῖον, -ου, τό	tomb
μυστήριον, -ου, τό	mystery
Μωϋσῆς, -έως, ὁ	Moses
ναός, -οῦ, ὁ	the shrine of a temple, the holy place
νεανίας, -ου, ὁ	young man
νεκρός, -ά, -όν	dead
νέος, -α, -ον	young, new
νεφέλη, -ης, ἡ	cloud
νηστεύω, νηστεύσω, ἐνήστευσα, νενήστευκα, —, —	be fasting
νομίζω, νομιῶ, ἐνόμισα, νενόμικα, νενόμισμαι, ἐνομίσθην	think
νόμος, -ου, ὁ	law
νυμφίος, -ου, ὁ	bridegroom, groom
νῦν, νυνί	now, at this present time
νύξ, νυκτός, ἡ	night
ξηρός, -ά, -όν	dry, withered
ὁδοιπορέω, —, ὡδοιπόρησα, ὡδοιπόρημαι, —, —	travel, make one's way [from ὁδός + πόρος "passage"]
ὁδός, -οῦ, ἡ	way or road
ὀδούς, ὀδόντος, ὁ	tooth
οἶδα,[1] εἰδήσω, ᾔδειν,[2] —, —, —	know
οἰκία, -ας, ἡ	house
οἰκοδεσπότης, -ου, ὁ	head of household
οἰκοδομέω, οἰκοδομήσω, ᾠκοδόμησα, ᾠκοδόμηκα, ᾠκοδόμημαι, ᾠκοδομήθην	build
οἶκος, -ου, ὁ	house
οἰκουμένη, -ης, ἡ	the inhabited land; the world

1 Perfect forms having primary endings used for present tense

2 Pluperfect forms having secondary endings used for aorist tense

οἶνος, -ου, ὁ	wine
ὀλίγος, -η, -ον	few
ὀλίγιστος, -η, -ον	fewest
ὅλος, -η, -ον	whole
ὅμοιος, -α, -ον	like
ὁμοιόω, ὁμοιώσω, ὡμοίωσα, —, ὡμοίωμαι, ὡμοιώθην	make like, compare
ὁμολογέω, ὁμολογήσω, ὡμολόγησα, ὡμολόγηκα, ὡμολόγημαι, ὡμολογήθη	confess + dat. to whom
ὄνομα, ὀνόματος, τό	name
ὀπίσω	+ gen. after, behind
ὅραμα, ὁράματος, τό	vision; prophetic dream
ὁράω, ὄψομαι, εἶδον, ἑώρακα (ἑόρακα), ὦμμαι, ὤφθην	see
ὄρος, ὄρους, τό	hill; mountain
ὅς, ἥ, ὅ	who, which
ὅσος, -η, -ον	as much as, how great, as many as, how much
ὅστις	whoever, but in the NT practically the same as ὅς, who
ὅτε	when
ὅτι	because; that (conj. for indirect statement)
οὐ μή	in no way, certainly not
οὐ, οὐκ, οὐχ	not
οὐδείς, οὐδεμία, οὐδέν	no one
οὖν	therefore, then (postpositive)
οὐράνιος, -α, -ον	heavenly
οὐρανός, -οῦ, ὁ	heaven
οὖς, ὠτός, τό	ear
οὗτος, αὕτη, τοῦτο	this
οὐχί	no, not (an emphatic form of οὐ, especially used in questions that expect the answer "yes")

ὀφειλέτης, -ου, ὁ	debtor
ὀφείλημα, -ατος, τό	debt
ὀφείλω, ὀφειλήσω,[1] ὠφείλησα, ὠφείληκα, —, ὠφειλήθην	owe; ought + inf.
ὀφθαλμός, -οῦ, ὁ	eye
ὄχλος, -ου, ὁ	crowd or multitude
παιδίον, -ου, τό	young child
παῖς, παιδός, ὁ or ἡ	child, boy or girl
παλαιός, -ά, -όν	old
πάντα	all things (neut. pl. of πᾶς)
πανταχοῦ	everywhere
πάντοτε	always
παρά	+ acc. to the side of, beside; contrary; + gen. from beside; from (of persons); + dat. near; at the house of (of persons)
παραβολή, -ῆς, ἡ	parable
παραγγέλλω, παραγγελῶ, παρήγγειλα, —, παρήγγελμαι, παρηγγέλθην	command
παραγίνομαι, —, παρεγενόμην, παραγέγονα, —, παρεγενήθην	be present; arrive; draw near, come to, approach
παράγω, —, παρήγαγον, παραγέωχα, —, παρήχθη	pass by
παραδίδωμι, παραδώσω, παρέδωκα, παραδέδωκα, παραδέδομαι, παρεδόθην	give up, betray
παράδοσις, -εως, ἡ	tradition
παρακαλέω, παρακαλέσω, παρεκάλεσαν, —, παρακέκλημαι, παρεκλήθην	exhort; comfort
παραλαμβάνω, παραλήμψομαι, παρέλαβον, παρείληφα, παρείλημμαι, παρελήμφθην	take with me
παραλυτικός, -ή, -όν	lame (substantive meaning: paralytic)
παράπτωμα, -ατος, τό	fault, transgression

1 Liquid verbal root lengthens the inserted ε to η and intervocalic σ (and stem consonants for other principal parts) remain.

παρατίθημι, παραθήσω, παρέθηκα, —, —, παρεθέμην	place beside, set beside; set before (of food)
παρθένος, -ου, ἡ	maiden, virgin
παρίστημι, παραστήσω, παρέστησα[1] (παρέστην[2]), παρέστηκα, —, παρεστάθην	cause to stand beside; present; mid. and pass. stand
πᾶς, πᾶσα, πᾶν	all; every
πάσχω, πείσομαι, ἔπαθον, πέπονθα, —, —	suffer
πατέω, πατήσω, ἐπάτησα, —, —, ἐπατήθην	trample on
πατήρ, πατρός, ὁ	father
Παῦλος, -ου, ὁ	Paul
παύομαι, παύσομαι, ἐπαυσάμην, —, πέπαυμαι, ἐπαύθην	cease, stop
πείθω, πείσω, ἔπεισα, πέποιθα, πέπεισμαι, ἐπείσθην	persuade, convince
πειράζω, πειράσω, ἐπείρασα, —, πεπείρασμαι, ἐπειράσθην	tempt, try
πειρασμός, -οῦ, ὁ	temptation
πέμπω, πέμψω, ἔπεμψα, πέπομφα, πέπεμμαι, ἐπέμφθην	send
πεντακισχίλιοι, -αι, -α	five thousand
περί	+ acc. about, around, of place or time; + gen. about, concerning; on account of
περιβάλλω, περιβαλῶ, περιέβαλον, —, περιβέβλημαι, περιβλήθην	cast around; mid. dress oneself
περιπατέω, περιπατήσω, περιεπάτησα (ἐπεριπάτησα), περι(ε)πεπάτηκα, —, —	walk about
περισσεύω, περισσεύσω, ἐπερίσσευσα,[3] —, —, ἐπερισσεύθην	surpass, have in abundance
περισσός, -ή, -όν	surpassing, great
πέτρα, -ας, ἡ	rock
Πέτρος, -ου, ὁ	Peter

1 Transitive form, "cause to stand beside," "present"
2 Intransitive form, "stand"
3 Augment prior to prepositional prefix for all augmented forms.

πίνω, πίομαι, ἔπιον, πέπωκα, —, ἐπόθην	drink
πίπτω, πεσοῦμαι, ἔπεσον, πέπτωκα, —, —	fall
πιστεύω, πιστεύσω, ἐπίστευσα, πεπίστευκα, πεπίστευμαι, ἐπιστεύθην	believe
πίστις, πίστεως, ἡ	faith
πιστός, -ή, -όν	faithful
πλανάω, πλανήσω, ἐπλάνησα, —, πεπλάνημαι, ἐπλανήθην	err
πλεῖον, πλέον	more (adv.)
πλείων, πλεῖον (πλέων, πλεόν)	more (adj.)
πλεῖστος, -η, -ον	most
πληθύνω, πληθυνῶ, ἐπλήθυνα, —, πεπλήθυμμαι, ἐπληθύνθην	multiply
πληρόω, πληρώσω, ἐπλήρωσα, πεπλήρωκα, πεπλήρωμαι, ἐπληρώθην	complete; fill; fulfill
πλησίον	near (ὁ πλησίον, one's neighbor)
πλοῖον, -ου, τό	boat; ship
πνεῦμα, πνεύματος, τό	spirit; wind
ποιέω, ποιήσω, ἐποίησα, πεποίηκα, πεποίημαι, ἐποιήθην	make; do
ποιμήν, ποιμένος, ὁ	shepherd
ποῖος, -α, -ον	of what kind?
πόλις, πόλεως, ἡ	city
πολλά	many things (neut. pl. of πολύς)
πολύ	much (adv.)
πολύς, πολλή, πολύ	many; much
πονηρός, -ά, -όν	wicked
πορεύομαι	go, come
ποταμός, -οῦ, ὁ	river
ποτήριον, -ου, ὁ	cup
ποῦ	where?
πούς, ποδός, ὁ	foot
πράσσω, πράξω, ἔπραξα, πέπραχα, πέπραγμαι, ἐπράχθην	behave, do, accomplish

πρέπω, πρέψω, ἔπρεψα, —, —, —	fitting, proper (impersonal + dat. person —πρέπει it is fitting for someone[1])
πρεσβύτερος, -ου, ὁ	elder
πρίν	adv. or + gen. before, formerly
πρό	+ gen. for, in front of, before (of time or place)
πρόβατον, -ου, τό	sheep
προμεριμνάω, —, —, —, —, —	be anxious beforehand
πρός	+ acc. toward, to, in the presence (with "to be" verb); + gen. from (rare); + dat. at, close to
προσέρχομαι, προσελεύσομαι, προσῆλθον, προσελήλυθα, —, —	go toward
προσέχω, προσέξω, προσέσχον, προσέσχηκα, —, —	be concerned for, care about; give heed to
προσεύχομαι, προσεύξομαι, προσηυξάμην, —, —, —	pray
προσκαλέω,[2] προσκάλεσω, προσεκάλεσα, —, προσκέκλημαι, προσεκλήθην	call to; summon
προσκαρτερέω, προσκαρτερήσω, προσεκαρτερήσα, —, —, —	stick with; continue in; be devoted to + dat.
προσκυνέω, προσκυνήσω, προσεκύνησα, προσκεκύνηκα, —, προσεκυνήθην	worship + dat.
πρόσωπον, -ου, τό	face
προφητεύω, προφητεύσω, ἐπροφήτευσα, —, πεπροφήτευμαι, προεφητεύθην	prophesy
προφήτης, -ου, ὁ	prophet
πρῶτος, -η, -ον	first
πτωχός, -ή, -όν	poor
πυνθάνομαι, πεύσομαι, ἐπυθόμην, —, πέπυσμαι, —	inquire

1 A neuter periphrastic participle construction is also common (πρέπον ἐστίν, "it is proper").

2 Only mid. and pass. in the NT.

πῦρ, πυρός, τό	fire
πῶς	how
ῥῆμα, ῥήματος, τό	word; saying
ῥίπτω, ῥίψω, ἔ(ρ)ριψα, ἔρριφα, ἐ(ρ)ρίμμαι, ἐρρίφθην	throw, cast
σάββατον, -ου, τό	Sabbath
σάλπιγξ, σάλπιγγος, ἡ	trumpet
Σαμάρεια, -ας, ἡ	Samaria
σάρξ, σαρκός, ἡ	flesh
Σατανᾶς, Σατανᾶ, ὁ	Satan
σημεῖον, -ου, τό	sign, miracle
Σίμων, Σίμωνος, ὁ	Simon
σιωπάω, σιωπήσω, ἐσιώπησα, σεσιώπηκα, —, —	be silent
σκανδαλίζω, —, ἐσκανδάλισα, —, ἐσκανδάλισμαι, ἐσκανδαλίσθην	cause to stumble; offend
σκότος, σκότους, τό	darkness
Σολομῶν, Σολομῶνος, ὁ	Solomon
σοφία, -ας, ἡ	wisdom
σοφός, -ή, -όν	wise
σπαράσσω, σπαράξω, ἐσπάραξα, —, ἐσπάραγμαι, ἐσπαράχθην	convulse, shake; rip apart
σπείρω, σπερῶ, ἔσπειρα, ἔσπαρκα, ἔσπαρμαι, ἐσπάρην	sow
σπέρμα, σπέρματος, τό	seed
σταυρός, -οῦ, ὁ	cross
σταυρόω, σταυρώσω, ἐσταύρωσα, —, ἐσταύρωμαι, ἐσταυρώθην	crucify
στέλλω, στελῶ, ἔστειλα, ἔσταλκα, ἔσταλμαι, ἐστάλην	send
στενός, -ή, -όν	narrow
στόμα, στόματος, τό	mouth
στρατιώτης, -ου, ὁ	soldier
σύ	you
συζητέω, —, συνεζήτησα, —, —, —	join in seeking; discuss, I argue

συμβουλεύω, συμβουλεύσω, συνεβούλευσα, —, —, —	give advice + dat. to whom; mid. consult; plot; consider
σύν	+ dat. together with
συνάγω, συνάξω, συνήγαγον (συνῆξα), συνῆχα, συνῆγμαι, συνήχθην	gather, drive together
συναγωγή, -ῆς, ἡ	synagogue
συνέδριον, -ου, τό	council
συνεσθίω, —, συνέφαγον, —, —, —	eat with
συνίημι, συνήσω, συνῆκα, συνεῖκα, —, —	understand
σύρω, συρῶ, ἔσυρα, σέσυρκα, σέσυρμαι, ἐσύρην	drag
σχίσμα, -ατος, τό	rip, division
σῴζω, σώσω, ἔσωσα, σέσωκα, σέσωσμαι, ἐσώθην	save
σῶμα, σώματος, τό	body
σωτήρ, σωτῆρος, ὁ	savior
σωτηρία, -ας, ἡ	salvation
ταπεινόω, ταπεινώσω, ἐταπείνωσα, —, τεταπείνωμαι, ἐταπεινώθην	humble
τάσσω, τάξω, ἔταξα, τέταχα, τέταγμαι, ἐτάχθην	arrange; appoint, designate
ταχέως	quickly; soon (adv.)
τάχιον	quicker (adv.)
τάχιστα	most quickly (adv.)
ταχύ	quickly; soon (adv.)
τεκμήριον, -ου, τό	certain proof
τέκνον, -ου, τό	child
τελώνης, -ου, ὁ	tax collector
τέρας, τέρατος, τό	wonder, miracle
τεσσεράκοντα[1]	forty
τηρέω, τηρήσω, ἐτήρησα, τετήρηκα, τετήρημαι, ἐτηρήθην	keep safe; keep, observe
τί	why?

1 Indeclinable adjective

τίθημι, θήσω, ἔθηκα, τέθεικα, τέθειμαι, ἐτέθην	put, set, place
τίκτω, τέξομαι, ἔτεκον, τέτοκα, τέτεγμαι, ἐτέχθην	beget, give birth; produce, bring forth
τιμή, -ῆς, ἡ	honor
τιμάω, τιμήσω, ἐτίμησα, τετιμήκα, τετίμημαι, ἐτιμήθην	honor; set a price for
τίς, τί	who? which? what?
τις, τι	certain person, certain thing
τόπος, -ου, ὁ	place
τότε	then, at that time
τρεῖς, τρία	three
τρίς	thrice, three times
τροφή, -ῆς, ἡ	nourishment, food; meat
τυγχάνω, τεύξομαι, ἔτυχον, τέτυχα, τέτευγμαι, ἐτεύχθην	happen; happen upon; attain
τυφλός, -ή, -όν	blind
ὑγιής, ὑγιές	whole; healthy
ὕδωρ, ὕδατος, τό	water
υἱός, -οῦ, ὁ	son
ὑμεῖς	you all
ὑπάγω[1]	depart
ὑπακούω, ὑπακούσομαι, ὑπήκουσα, —, —, —	obey + dat. person obeyed
ὑπέρ	+ acc. above, beyond; + gen. on behalf or, for sake of
ὑπό	+ acc. under; + gen. by (agency)
ὑποκριτής, -οῦ, ὁ	hypocrite
ὑπομονή, -ῆς, ἡ	patience
ὕστερος, -α, -ον	last
ὑψόω, ὑψώσω, ὕψωσα, —, ὕψωμαι, ὑψώθην	exalt
φαίνω, φανοῦμαι, ἔφανα, πέφηνα, πέφασμαι, ἐφάνην	shine; pass. appear; be seen

1 Only present and imperfect forms in the NT.

φανερόω, φανερώσω, ἐφανέρωσα, πεφανέρωκα, πεφανέρωμαι, ἐφανερώθην	make manifest
Φαρισαῖος, -ου, ὁ	Pharisee
φέρω, οἴσω, ἤνεγκον (ἤνεγκα), ἐνήνοχα, ἐνήνεγμαι, ἠνέχθην	carry; bear, endure
φεύγω, φεύξομαι, ἔφυγον, πέφευγα, πέφυγμαι, —	flee
φημί (impf. ἔφην), φήσω, ἔφησα, —, —, ἐφάθην	say
Φῆστος, -ου, ὁ	Festus
φθείρω, φθερῶ, ἔφθειρα, ἔφθαρκα, ἔφθαρμαι, ἐφθάρην	destroy
φιλέω, φιλήσω, ἐφίλησα, πεφίληκα, πεφίλημαι, ἐφιλήθην	love; like; kiss
Φίλιππος, -ου, ὁ	Philip
φοβέομαι, φοβηθήσομαι, ἐφοβήθην, —, —, —	fear; be afraid
φόβος, -ου, ὁ	fear
φρονέω, φρονήσω, ἐφρόνησα, πεφρόνηκα, —, —	think
φυλακή, -ῆς, ἡ	guard watch; prison; guard
φύλαξ, φύλακος, ὁ	guard
φυλάσσω, φυλάξω, ἐφύλαξα, πεφύλαχα, πεφύλαγμαι, ἐφυλάχθην	guard
φυλή, -ῆς, ἡ	tribe
φωνέω, φωνήσω, ἐφώνησα, —, —, ἐφωνήθην	call, make a noise
φωνή, -ῆς, ἡ	voice; sound
φῶς, φωτός, τό	light
χαίρω, χαρήσομαι, ἐχαίρησα, κεχάρηκα, κεχάρημαι, ἐχάρην	rejoice
χαρά, -ᾶς, ἡ	joy
χάρις, χάριτος, ἡ	grace, favor
χείρ, χειρός, ἡ	hand
χείριστος, -η, -ον	worst
χείρων, χεῖρον	worse

χήρα, -ας, ἡ	widow
χιτών, χιτῶνος, ὁ	garment, especially an undergarment or shirt
χρῆμα, χρήματος, τό	money (nearly always used in the pl.)
χρόνος, -ου, ὁ	time
χρυσός, -οῦ, ὁ	gold
χωρίον, -ου, τό	piece of land, field
ψευδής, ψευδές	false
ψυχή, -ῆς, ἡ	soul
ὦ	O!
ὧδε	here
ὥρα, -ας, ἡ	hour
ὡς	when; as

Index